A Practitioner's Guide to the Duo Coaching Framework

A Practitioner's Guide to the Duo Coaching Framework is the definitive implementation manual for therapists seeking to move beyond the constraints of traditional couple therapy.

This comprehensive guide details the practical application of the Duo Coaching Framework: extended sessions, co-therapist collaboration, and transdisciplinary intervention. From first contact to final session, readers will find step-by-step protocols, assessment instruments, intervention tools, and professional development frameworks—everything needed to bring this innovative approach into practice.

Building on the theoretical foundations established in *Reinventing Relationship Therapy Through the Duo Coaching Framework*, this book answers the essential practitioner questions: How do co-therapists communicate during sessions? How are longer sessions structured? Which techniques work best at which moments? How do you build and sustain this kind of practice? Essential reading for relationship therapists, counsellors, coaches, and clinical educators ready to expand their therapeutic repertoire.

Neil Wilkie is a relationship therapist, author, and visiting fellow at Middlesex University, where he completed his PhD in the Phenomenology of Relationships. He is the founder of Duo Coaching and creator of the Relationship Paradigm framework. After a first career in business leadership, Neil retrained as a psychotherapist and has spent 15 years working with couples, developing and refining the extended-session co-therapy model detailed in this book. His previous work includes *Reinventing Relationship Therapy Through the Duo Coaching Framework* (Routledge).

A Practitioner's Guide to the Duo Coaching Framework

Reframe

Neil Wilkie

Routledge
Taylor & Francis Group
LONDON AND NEW YORK

Designed cover image: Getty Images

First published 2027
by Routledge
4 Park Square, Milton Park, Abingdon, Oxon OX14 4RN

and by Routledge
605 Third Avenue, New York, NY 10158

Routledge is an imprint of the Taylor & Francis Group, an informa business

British Library Cataloguing-in-Publication Data
A catalogue record for this book is available from the British Library

Library of Congress Cataloging-in-Publication Data
A catalogue record has been requested for this book

ISBN: 9781041202141 (hbk)
ISBN: 9781041201854 (pbk)
ISBN: 9781003715627 (ebk)

DOI: 10.4324/9781003715627

Typeset in Times New Roman
by codeMantra

Contents

About the Author

Neil Wilkie didn't start his career in a therapy room—he started it in a boardroom. As a chartered accountant who rose to lead large businesses and advise organisations as a strategy consultant, Neil understood systems, transformation, and the gap between what looks successful on paper and what actually works in practice. But in his late 40s, despite conventional measures of achievement, he recognised something essential was missing. The spreadsheets and strategic plans couldn't answer the question that kept surfacing: What genuinely matters?

That question led him away from boardrooms and towards the work that would become his calling—training as a psychotherapist and helping couples navigate the complex terrain of intimate relationship. But he didn't arrive as a detached expert. Now 70, Neil brings the kind of wisdom that only emerges from living relationships in their full complexity: marriage, divorce, remarriage, widowhood, and the courage to remain open to love despite knowing its costs. This lived experience, combined with his Doctorate in the Phenomenology of Relationships, means he understands both the theory and the tender, difficult reality of what couples face.

Over 15 years of intensive practice, Neil developed Duo Coaching—an approach that pairs two therapists in extended sessions to achieve breakthroughs traditional therapy often cannot reach. The Relationship Paradigm framework emerged from this work, offering practitioners a practical, integrative roadmap that honours multiple therapeutic traditions while remaining focused on what couples actually need: transformation, not just insight.

As Visiting Fellow at Middlesex University and creator of the Duo Coaching Academy, Neil bridges the worlds of rigorous academic inquiry and deeply human practice. His business background surfaces in unexpected ways—the strategic thinking that once optimised organisations now helps couples redesign their relational systems; the systems understanding that once served corporations now illuminates couple dynamics.

Perhaps his most important credential for teaching practitioners is his commitment to remaining a student himself. Some of his most profound insights have arrived in unexpected places—watching penguins navigate partnership on South Georgian beaches, or adjusting course aboard Moon River, the sailing yacht he shares with his wife Gwen. Ten days each month, they leave emails and appointments behind to practise what Neil teaches about protecting time for connection. They've created a family that honours both complexity and authentic joy.

At an age when many consider retirement, Neil describes himself as getting his "second wind." After witnessing hundreds of couples transform their relationships, he remains convinced that connection is humanity's greatest untapped resource—and that practitioners need approaches that match the complexity of what couples bring them.

This book represents 15 years of development, insights from hundreds of couples, wisdom from dozens of practitioners, and an invitation to join what Neil calls the "relationship revolution"—not through grand gestures, but through daily commitment to showing up with both competence and humanity.

Prologue

They sat at opposite ends of the sofa, close enough to touch, yet worlds apart.

"I don't even know who he is anymore."

Sarah's voice cracked on the last word. Across from her, Michael stared at the floor, his jaw tight, hands clasped between his knees like a man bracing for impact. They had been married for 19 years. They had built a life together—raised children, weathered redundancies, buried parents, celebrated promotions. And now they sat in our consulting room, two strangers who happened to share a surname.

Maria caught my eye. In that brief glance passed years of working together—an unspoken language we had developed, holding space for couples on the precipice. She leaned forward slightly, and I knew she had seen what I had seen: beneath Michael's rigid posture, something was breaking open.

This is what makes Duo Coaching different. Two therapists, fully present, each bringing their own way of seeing. Where I might notice the words left unsaid, Maria often senses the body's quieter truths. Where she might lean into emotion, I might hold the frame. Together, we create something neither of us could offer alone.

In that moment, I could have offered techniques. I could have explained communication patterns, introduced conflict resolution frameworks, assigned homework. Instead, something deeper emerged—a question shaped not by my training, but by years of sitting with couples on the edge of goodbye: "When did you stop being curious about each other?"

The silence that followed was not empty. It was filled with 19 years of conversations that never happened, needs that were never spoken, longings that calcified into resentment.

Then Michael looked up. And for the first time in what Sarah later told us was years, she saw tears in his eyes.

"I stopped," he said quietly, "because I was terrified of what I might find."

Maria's voice came soft but clear: "And Sarah—what do you feel, hearing that?"

Sarah's hand moved almost imperceptibly towards her husband. "I thought he'd stopped caring. I never imagined he was afraid."

This is the territory this book explores: the liminal space between two hearts that have forgotten how to reach for each other. Not the clinical landscape of dysfunction and diagnosis—though these have their place—but the sacred ground where love, once buried under years of disappointment and defence, can be excavated, examined, and brought back to life. And it explores why two therapists, working in concert, can hold this space in ways that transform what is possible.

What you hold in your hands is not merely a manual for relationship therapy. It is an invitation to a radically different approach—one where the therapeutic relationship itself models the partnership we hope to restore. Duo Coaching brings two practitioners into the room, creating a container strong enough to hold the intensity of extended sessions, the complexity of two individual stories, and the fragile hope of reconciliation.

Because here is the truth I have learned across 15 years of intensive couple work, hundreds of relationships in crisis, and thousands of hours holding space for hearts breaking open: The most powerful thing you will ever offer is not your expertise. It is your willingness to believe in love when the couple themselves have stopped believing. And when two therapists hold that belief together, something alchemical becomes possible.

When Michael spoke those words—"I was terrified of what I might find"—something shifted in the room. Sarah's posture softened. For 19 years, she had interpreted his distance as indifference. In that moment, she glimpsed the fear underneath. And in that glimpse, the first thread of connection rewove itself.

They came back the following week. And the month after. In our third session—two and a half hours of deep, uninterrupted work that only the Duo Coaching format allows—they finally spoke about the miscarriage they had never properly grieved. Maria held Sarah as she wept. I sat with Michael as he admitted, for the first time, that he had blamed himself. By the session's end, they were holding each other.

Three months later, they sat on that same sofa—but differently. Closer. Their hands found each other without conscious thought. "I'd forgotten," Sarah said, "that underneath everything, we actually like each other."

This is the alchemy we will explore together: how to create spaces where couples remember what drew them together in the first place. How two therapists can hold the tension between individual pain and shared history with a grace that neither could sustain alone. How to trust that healing is not something we impose upon relationships, but something we help couples discover was possible all along.

The journey will ask everything of you. It will require that you sit with despair without rushing towards hope. It will demand that you find a partner whose presence complements your own and learn the delicate dance of co-facilitation. It will challenge you to remain present when everything in you wants to fix, advise, or rescue.

But here is what I promise: If you are willing to learn this approach, you will discover that relationship transformation is not something you engineer. It is something you midwife. And in that sacred act of presence—two therapists holding space for two partners—you will witness ordinary couples discover extraordinary reserves of love they had forgotten they possessed.

Some will save their marriages. Others will find the courage to end them with dignity and grace. All of them will leave changed—not because of your clever interventions, but because you and your co-therapist created the conditions for them to truly see each other, perhaps for the first time in years.

The couples you will meet in these pages were drowning when they walked through our door. Affairs discovered. Trust shattered. Years of silence crystallised into walls of ice. And yet, again and again, Maria and I have watched love find its way back. Not easily. Not painlessly. But genuinely, deeply, transformatively.

The question is not whether your clients' relationships can heal. The question is whether you are willing to believe in that possibility—and find a partner to believe it with you—long enough for them to believe it too.

Acknowledgements

Writing an implementation guide for relationship therapy is an act of vulnerability—admitting that what we've learned came not from academic brilliance but from countless moments of not knowing, from mistakes courageously corrected, and from couples who taught us more than we taught them. This book exists because of the remarkable people who have shaped both my understanding and my practice.

First, I want to acknowledge the hundreds of clients who have allowed Maria and me into the inner sanctums of their lives. Their bravery, openness, and willingness to do the difficult work of transformation have been extraordinary. Every protocol in this book, every technique, every insight emerged from real sessions with real couples facing genuine challenges. They didn't just receive therapy—they actively co-created the approaches that now form this framework. Their trust has been both humbling and inspiring, teaching me as much as I hope I've been able to offer them.

To the amazing Transdisciplinary team at Middlesex University and my doctoral cohort, who challenged and inspired me to look at relationships through fresh eyes. They encouraged me not only to examine the dynamics between couples but also to look deep within myself, to explore my own experiences and learn from every facet of my journey. This reflexive practice became foundational to how I teach other practitioners.

I owe profound gratitude to Cathy, without whose partnership and collaboration Duo Coaching might never have come to fruition. Her insights and shared vision laid the foundation for everything that followed. Together we dared to break the mould of traditional relationship counselling, discovering what becomes possible when we design approaches for effectiveness rather than convention.

I'm particularly grateful to Maria, my co-therapist for nine years, whose calmness, energy, and profound insights continue to support both me and our clients. Her presence has been invaluable in refining and expanding our work. What we can achieve together far exceeds what either of us could accomplish alone—a living demonstration of the collaborative approach we teach. Maria's contribution to this book goes beyond her authored chapter; her wisdom and partnership inform every page.

To the practitioners who have trained with me, attended workshops, asked challenging questions, and shared their own innovations—you've pushed this work to evolve in ways I couldn't have imagined alone. Your willingness to take risks in your practice, to try new approaches, and to share both your successes and struggles has enriched this guide immeasurably.

I must acknowledge the relationships throughout my life—some joyful, others challenging—that taught me what this work truly means. These experiences, both triumphs and struggles, have been essential to understanding relationship dynamics from the inside. They've given me the humility to sit with couples in their pain and the conviction to believe transformation is always possible.

To my readers—fellow practitioners committed to serving couples with excellence—thank you for engaging with these ideas. Your willingness to question conventional approaches, to develop new competencies, and to join this relationship revolution gives this work life beyond these pages. The couples walking through your doors tomorrow will benefit from your courage to learn and grow.

Finally, and most importantly, I want to thank my wonderful wife, Gwen. It took 63 years before I found you, and it was worth every minute of that journey because only now do I fully understand what true love really feels like. You've created the relationship that allows me to do this work authentically—practising what I preach about connection, commitment, and fun. None of this—the books, the insights, the person I've become—would have been possible without you. Mo Anam Cara.

Thank you all.

Introduction

Image 1 Man on clouds with telescope.
"Seeing What Lies Ahead: The Vision That Drives This Work"

About This Book

This book is the second in a three-book collection that comprehensively presents the Duo Coaching approach to intensive relationship therapy:

Book 1: *Reinventing Relationship Therapy: The Duo Coaching Framework* ("Reinventing") explores **WHY** we need a radically different approach to couple therapy. It examines the limitations of traditional weekly therapy, presents the theoretical foundations of Duo Coaching, explains the paradigm shift required, and makes the case for intensive relationship work. If you're asking "Why should I change my approach?" start here.

Book 2: *A Practitioner's Guide to the Duo Coaching Framework ('Practitioner's Guide')* (this book) teaches **HOW** to practise Duo Coaching and **WHAT** to do in each session. It provides comprehensive, step-by-step implementation guidance from assessment through completion, with detailed protocols, exercises, and templates. This is your practical manual for actually doing the work.

DOI: 10.4324/9781003715627-1

Book 3: *Demystifying Relationship Therapy — A View from the Therapist's Chair'* brings the approach to life by showing **WHO**—the actual couples who have walked this journey. Through vivid case narratives, you'll witness Duo Coaching in action with diverse couples facing varied challenges, seeing how theory and technique translate into real transformation. When you wonder "What does this look like with an actual couple?" turn to Book 3.

Together, these three books form a complete professional education:

The WHY provides the rationale and conviction.

The HOW/WHAT builds the competence and skill.

The WHO deepens the understanding and wisdom through lived experience.

You can read them in order for systematic learning, or jump to whichever book matches your current needs.

Why This Book Exists

In *Reinventing Relationship Therapy*, we explored why traditional couple therapy often falls short—not because therapists lack skill or couples lack commitment, but because 50 minutes once a week simply cannot create the sustained focus and intensive work that relationship transformation requires. We made the case for a fundamentally different approach.

Now It's Time to Learn How to Do It

This book presents the implementation guide to Duo Coaching—the practical, step-by-step manual for conducting intensive relationship therapy that creates lasting change. Over 15 years of development and refinement with hundreds of couples, these protocols have proven that when you give couples the time, structure, and guidance they need, profound transformation becomes possible.

Where the first book answered "Why change?", this book answers "How do I do it?" Where theory meets practice. Where vision becomes reality.

What Is Duo Coaching?

Duo Coaching is an intensive, structured approach to relationship therapy consisting of six sessions:

Session 1: 3.5 hours of assessment and foundation-building.

Sessions 2–6: 2.5 hours each of skill-building and transformation.

The approach is built on a fundamental insight: relationships struggle not because couples lack love, but because they lack a healthy relationship paradigm—a framework for understanding communication, conflict, difference, emotions, needs, partnership, and growth.

Rather than simply teaching skills or processing feelings, Duo Coaching helps couples shift the fundamental paradigms that shape their relationship experience. When couples learn to see communication as understanding rather than winning, conflict as opportunity rather than threat, and differences as enrichment rather than problems, everything changes.

The intensive format allows couples to:

- Sustain focus without the interruption of daily life
- Work through difficult emotions without running out of time
- Practice new skills until they feel natural
- Experience immediate progress that builds hope and motivation
- Create momentum that carries forward between sessions

Co-therapy adds another powerful dimension—modelling healthy collaboration, providing multiple perspectives, and ensuring both partners feel heard and supported.

Who Should Read This Book

This book is written for the experienced practitioner—the therapist who already knows how to create rapport, listen deeply, ask the questions that matter, and respond with precision to what emerges in the room. If you're reading this, you've already developed the foundational skills of therapeutic engagement: you can track multiple streams of information simultaneously, hold complexity without rushing to resolution, and sense when to lean in and when to step back. This practitioner's guide is not about teaching you how to be a therapist; it's an invitation to expand what's possible in your work with couples.

The Duo Coaching Framework offers experienced practitioners both an extension of their therapeutic repertoire and a fundamentally different way of structuring couples' work. Within these pages, you'll encounter modalities you may not have applied to relationship therapy, approaches to session design that challenge conventional formats, and ways of working that may initially feel unfamiliar. We present these ideas as possibilities to explore, test, and adapt to your own practice—not as rigid protocols to follow.

This guide provides the conceptual framework, the underlying principles, and the practical considerations that inform Duo Coaching methodology. It offers ideas and invitations rather than exhaustive instruction. The deeper technical training—the detailed protocols, supervised practice, and nuanced application of specific interventions—lives within the Duo Coaching Academy's accreditation programme. Think of this book as opening the door to a new way of working; the Academy provides the comprehensive training to walk through it with confidence and competence.

You'll benefit most if you:

Have some couple therapy experience (not absolutely required, but helpful)
Can offer intensive sessions (2.5–3.5 hours) in your practice
Are committed to integrative, evidence-informed practice

You don't need to abandon your current theoretical orientation. Duo Coaching is integrative by design—it enhances rather than replaces your existing expertise.

What Makes This Book Different

This isn't just another couple's therapy manual. What sets it apart:

1 **Implementation Guide**—Session-by-session protocols with timing.
2 **Evidence-Informed Practice**—Integrates research from multiple couple therapy approaches, neuroscience, attachment theory, and practice-based evidence from hundreds of couples.
3 **Real-World Focus**—Addresses actual clinical challenges: couples in crisis, affairs and betrayals, safety concerns, diverse populations, ethical dilemmas, and practitioner self-care.
4 **Professional Development**—Beyond clinical skills, guides you in building a sustainable practice, marketing ethically, training others, and contributing to the field.
5 **Bridge to Cases**—While this book teaches techniques, Book 3 shows them in action. Together, they create a complete learning experience—theory, practice, and application.

How to Use This Book

This book follows a Competency Ladder progression:

Part I (Chapters 1–4)—Establishes why intensive work matters and the theoretical foundation.

Part II (Chapters 5–8)—Builds core clinical skills and framework fundamentals.

Part III (Chapters 9–11)—Develops integrative therapeutic mastery: working skilfully with what comes into the room and establishing your practice on solid foundations.

Part IV (Chapters 12–17)—Addresses professional development and advanced competencies.

Part V (Chapters 18–21)—Expert-level professional leadership: supervision, ethics, research, and bringing the work to completion.

Part VI (Chapters 22–24)—Explores prevention, research, and the field's future.

The Duo Coaching Competency Ladder

A Progressive Framework for Mastering Relationship Therapy Innovation

Excellence is never an accident. It is always the result of high intention, sincere effort, and intelligent execution; it represents the wise choice of many alternatives.—Aristotle

You can read sequentially for systematic learning or jump to chapters matching your immediate needs.

What This Book Assumes—And Does Not Cover

This book assumes master's-level mental health training, professional licensure (or working towards it), foundational counselling skills, and ethical commitment.

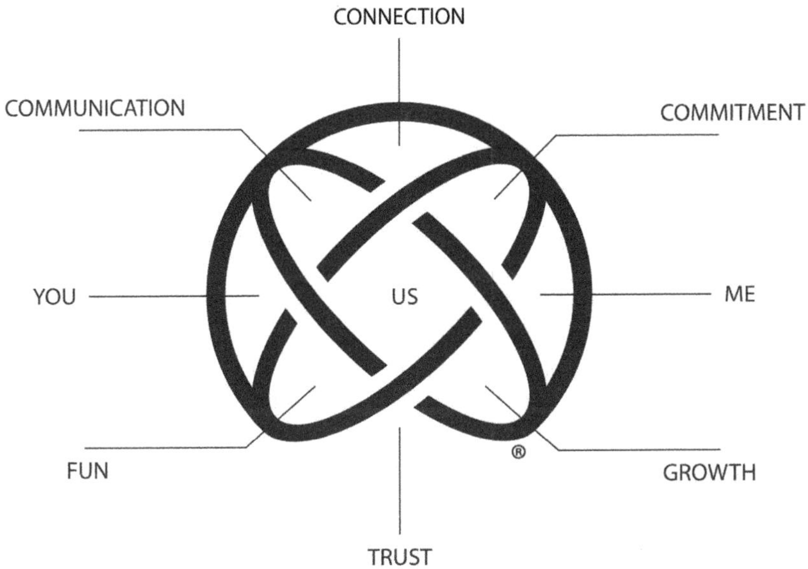

Infographic 1 The competency ladder: From building the vessel to leaving a legacy.

Some couple therapy experience helps but isn't required—seek robust supervision as you develop competency. The approach integrates multiple orientations (Gottman, Emotionally Focused Therapy (EFT), Cognitive Behavioural Therapy (CBT), systems theory, attachment, solution-focused), so openness to integration enhances effectiveness. This guide focuses on practitioner development for relationship therapy; it is not self-help for couples, does not address individual therapy, and cannot substitute for experienced supervision.

A Note on Language and Inclusivity

Throughout this book, "couples" is used inclusively for any two people in a committed relationship, regardless of gender, sexual orientation, marital status, or relationship structure. "Partner" replaces gendered terms unless specifically relevant. Case examples are composites designed to protect confidentiality while illustrating clinical points.

Navigating the Relational Landscape: Epistemological Humility and Presence in Therapeutic Practice

Before we explore the specific elements and practices of the Duo Coaching Framework, we must first establish a foundational stance—a way of being with couples that shapes everything that follows. This stance concerns not what we do, but how we attend to the couples who come to us seeking help.

Every therapeutic encounter is, in essence, an act of navigation. The couple arrives knowing where they are—in difficulty, in pain, often lost. They may have some sense of where they want to be—reconnected, understood, at peace. But the journey between here and there remains uncertain, shaped by forces neither we nor they can fully predict or control. Our work is to navigate this relational landscape together, staying responsive to what emerges in the room while maintaining direction towards healing and growth.

Like all navigation, therapy demands a particular relationship with certainty and knowledge. And like all navigators in the modern age, we face a seductive temptation: to mistake our theoretical maps for the territory itself, to trust our frameworks more than we trust what we observe, to assume that this couple matches patterns we've seen before.

This section explores two interrelated dangers that can compromise our effectiveness as therapists: the loss of epistemological humility and the trap of confirmation bias. Understanding these pitfalls—and actively working to avoid them—is essential to practising the Duo Coaching Framework with integrity and effectiveness.

The GPS of Therapeutic Theory

Our training provides us with invaluable tools: attachment theory, systems theory, emotion-focused approaches, the Duo Coaching Framework itself. These theoretical models help us make sense of complex relational dynamics. They offer patterns, principles, and pathways that have proven helpful with countless couples.

But here lies the danger: these frameworks can begin to function like GPS in the hands of an inattentive navigator. We start to believe that the model tells us exactly where we are and exactly where we need to go. We trust the theory more than we trust our observations. We assume that because this couple's presentation resembles other couples we've worked with, they must be experiencing the same underlying dynamics.

The screen—our theoretical framework—presents itself as omniscient. We've seen this pattern before. We know what this means. We understand what needs to happen next. The voice of theory speaks with the authority of expertise: "This is clearly an attachment issue. This couple needs to work on emotional regulation. This pattern indicates unresolved trauma."

We move from a relationship of dialogue with the couple before us to one of instruction from our theoretical model. And in doing so, we risk missing what is actually happening in the room.

Epistemological Humility: Knowing What We Don't Know

Epistemological humility is the recognition that all knowledge is provisional, incomplete, and context-dependent. In therapeutic practice, it means acknowledging several fundamental truths:

Every couple is unique. No matter how many couples we've worked with, no matter how familiar the presenting issues seem, this couple before us has never existed before. Their particular combination of histories, personalities, contexts, wounds, and strengths creates something entirely new. The moment we assume "I've seen this before," we stop truly seeing *them*.

Our perception is always partial. We see the couple through the lens of our own experiences, wounds, training, and biases. We notice what our attention is trained to notice. We inevitably miss things. What seems obvious to us may be tangential to their actual experience. What seems peripheral to us may be central to them.

The map is not the territory. Our theoretical frameworks are models—useful approximations, not perfect representations. The Duo Coaching Framework itself, valuable as it is, describes patterns and principles, not absolute truths. Real couples in real moments will always exceed and surprise our models.

We cannot know what we cannot see. Much of what shapes a couple's relationship remains invisible to us—their private moments, their internal experiences, the subtle dynamics that only they can feel. We work with what they choose to show us, what they're able to articulate, what emerges in the particular context of the therapy room.

Epistemological humility doesn't mean abandoning our expertise or doubting our frameworks. Rather, it means holding our knowledge lightly, treating our theories as provisional hypotheses rather than established facts, and remaining always open to correction, surprise, and revision.

The Danger of Confirmation Bias

Confirmation bias is the tendency to interpret ambiguous information in ways that confirm our existing beliefs. In therapeutic practice, this manifests in several problematic ways:

Seeking data that fits our hypothesis. Within the first few minutes of meeting a couple, we often form an initial impression: "This is about control." "This is an anxious-avoidant dynamic." "This is unresolved grief." Having formed this hypothesis, we unconsciously begin seeking information that confirms it. We notice the evidence that fits. We ask questions that elicit responses supporting our theory. We interpret ambiguous statements in ways that align with our initial assessment.

Dismissing contradictory information. When the couple presents information that doesn't fit our developing narrative, we rationalise it away. "That's just their defence mechanism." "They're not aware of the real issue." "That's a surface complaint, not the underlying dynamic." We trust our theoretical framework more than we trust their lived experience.

Imposing familiar patterns. Because we've seen certain dynamics before—pursuer-distancer, conflict-avoiding, emotionally volatile—we assume we're seeing them again. We fit this unique couple into familiar categories rather than allowing them to reveal their particular complexity. The screen of theory tells us what we're seeing, even when direct observation might suggest something different.

Over-relying on our models. Like the navigator who stops reading the water because GPS seems more reliable, we stop truly attending to what's happening in the room because our framework seems more authoritative. We miss the subtle shifts in energy, the unspoken communication, the moment when something new wants to emerge—because we're following the predetermined route our theory suggests.

The consequences can be significant. Couples feel unseen, misunderstood, reduced to categories. We miss opportunities for genuine insight and transformation. We impose interventions that don't fit, address issues that aren't central, and overlook what's actually needed. We become, in effect, therapists who have stopped truly paying attention.

Warm Data and Therapeutic Presence

The antidote to both epistemological overconfidence and confirmation bias is a return to presence—to warm data, to direct observation, to the evidence of our senses and intuition in the moment.

Warm data is a term from systems thinker Nora Bateson, referring to information about relationships, contexts, and living systems that can only be understood through direct participation and observation. Unlike "cold data"—the measurable, quantifiable, categorisable information our theories traffic in—warm data emerges from being present to the quality, texture, and aliveness of what's actually happening.

In therapeutic practice, warm data includes:

- The felt sense of energy in the room
- The subtle shifts in body language and tone
- The things said and unsaid, the pauses and hesitations
- The quality of connection or disconnection between partners
- Your own somatic and emotional responses to the couple
- The moments of resonance, resistance, or surprise
- The unique flavour and texture of *this* couple's way of being together

Attending to warm data requires epistemological humility—the recognition that what matters most may not fit our theoretical categories. It requires setting aside confirmation bias—being willing to be surprised, to have our initial hypotheses disproven, to discover that this couple is not who we thought they were in the first 15 minutes.

Practices for Maintaining Presence and Humility

How do we cultivate this stance of humble, present attention while still using our expertise and frameworks effectively?

Begin with not-knowing. Approach each couple, each session, with genuine curiosity rather than expert certainty. "I wonder what's happening here?" rather than "I know what's happening here." This doesn't mean feigning ignorance—it means holding space for discovery.

Cross-reference multiple sources. Just as traditional navigation used stars, sun, wind, and water rather than a single source, use multiple ways of knowing: theoretical frameworks, direct observation, the couple's own descriptions, your somatic responses, your co-therapist's perspective (in the Duo Coaching model), the patterns that emerge over time. When these sources conflict, pause and inquire rather than defaulting to theory.

Stay attuned to surprise. When something doesn't fit your developing understanding, pay attention. These moments of surprise or confusion often signal that you're imposing a familiar pattern rather than perceiving what's actually present. Let yourself be corrected by the data in the room.

Name your hypotheses as hypotheses. When sharing your understanding with couples, frame it provisionally: "I'm wondering if…" "It seems like…" "One possibility might be…" This invites dialogue rather than imposing interpretation. It keeps you open to correction.

Cultivate somatic awareness. Your body often knows things before your mind does. Notice your own felt sense: when you feel resonance, discomfort, confusion, energy, or flatness. These somatic responses are data about what's happening in the relational field.

Return to the present moment. When you notice yourself operating from theory rather than presence, gently return your attention to what's actually happening: the couple before you, the words being spoken, the energy in the room, the quality of connection or disconnection you can sense.

Embrace uncertainty. Some of the most powerful therapeutic moments come when we're willing to say "I don't know" or "I'm not sure what's happening here." This honest uncertainty often creates more space for insight than expert interpretation.

Use frameworks as lenses, not laws. The Duo Coaching Framework—with its six elements of Communication, Connection, Commitment, Fun, Growth, and Trust—offers invaluable lenses for understanding relationships. But they're lenses, not prescriptions. This couple may need something the framework doesn't explicitly name. They may experience these elements differently than theory predicts. Stay flexible.

The Unique Couple Before You

Perhaps the most important implication of epistemological humility is this: every couple is genuinely, irreducibly unique. Not unique in the sense of "special" or "different from all patterns," but unique in the sense that their particular configuration of histories, wounds, strengths, contexts, and aspirations has never existed before and will never exist again.

This couple's Communication challenges are not generic communication challenges—they're the specific ways *these two people* struggle to reach each other. Their loss of Connection isn't a textbook case—it's the particular texture of *their* disconnection, shaped by *their* histories and *their* present circumstances. The work of rebuilding Trust between them won't follow a predetermined formula—it will unfold according to *their* pace, *their* needs, *their* capacity.

When we treat each couple as unique, several things become possible:

- We remain genuinely curious rather than assuming we already understand
- We let the couple teach us about their relationship rather than teaching them about relationships
- We follow their process rather than imposing our agenda
- We discover possibilities and pathways that theory alone wouldn't reveal
- We honour the lived reality of their experience rather than reducing it to categories

This doesn't mean abandoning patterns or principles. The Duo Coaching Framework identifies genuine dynamics that show up across many couples. But it means holding those patterns lightly, using them to inform rather than determine our understanding, and remaining always attentive to how *this* couple embodies, adapts, or transcends the general principles.

Navigation, Not Destination

Returning to our navigation metaphor: the therapist's work is not to arrive at a destination on behalf of the couple, but to help them navigate their own journey. We don't have a GPS coordinate for where they should end up—we have principles, patterns, and practices that may help them find their way.

Our frameworks are like charts—useful representations that help orient us, but never perfect mirrors of the territory. Our expertise is like navigational skill—valuable competence that becomes problematic only when it replaces direct attention to conditions in the moment.

The wind, the water, the currents, the visibility—these are beyond our control. What remains within our control is how we respond: with presence, with humility, with willingness to be corrected by reality, with attention to warm data as well as cold theory.

The couples who come to us are not problems to be solved using predetermined solutions. They are living systems navigating uncertain relational territory, seeking help finding their way. Our work is to navigate alongside them with skill and humility, attending to what's actually happening rather than what we expect to happen, trusting the process of discovery more than the certainty of our theories.

Conclusion: The Foundational Stance

Before learning the specific practices and principles of the Duo Coaching Framework, this foundational stance must be established. Everything that follows—the assessment process, the six elements, the extended sessions, the dual-therapist model—works only if grounded in epistemological humility and freedom from confirmation bias.

This stance shapes how we listen, what we notice, how we intervene, what we trust. It determines whether we use the framework wisely (as a set of useful lenses and practices) or problematically (as a predetermined map we impose regardless of terrain).

As you learn and apply the Duo Coaching Framework throughout this guide, return regularly to these questions:

- Am I seeing this couple, or am I seeing my theory of couples?
- Am I present to what's happening in the room, or am I following a predetermined script?
- Am I holding my hypotheses lightly, open to correction?
- Am I attending to warm data—the felt sense, the quality, the aliveness—or only to what fits my categories?
- Am I treating this couple as genuinely unique, or as another instance of familiar patterns?

The framework that follows is powerful and proven. But it serves couples well only when wielded by therapists who maintain this foundational stance of humble, present, responsive attention to what's actually happening in the room.

Let us proceed, then, with both confidence in our tools and humility about our knowledge—skilled navigators attending to the unique relational landscape of each couple who comes seeking help.

The Journey Ahead

Learning Duo Coaching is a journey, not a destination. Be patient with yourself—this is complex work. Start small, build gradually, seek support. Stay curious—every couple teaches something new. Practice deliberately, connect with community, and remember why you're doing this work.

You hold more than a clinical manual. This book represents 15 years of development, insights from hundreds of couples, wisdom from dozens of practitioners, and a vision for relationship therapy's future. It contains everything you need to begin implementing the Duo Coaching Framework effectively.

As you practice, you'll want to see these techniques with real couples. That's when Book 3 becomes your companion—showing what these protocols look like in the messy, beautiful complexity of actual relationships.

The couples waiting for your help need what you're about to learn. They need more than 50 minutes once a week. They need intensive, structured, paradigm-shifting work that creates real transformation.

Meet Your Guides

Throughout this book, you'll follow two intertwined journeys through illustrative vignettes based on composite cases from my clinical practice. While fictionalised to protect confidentiality, they represent typical transformation patterns I've witnessed over years of Duo Coaching work, bringing the methodology to life without revealing proprietary training content reserved for Academy certification.

The Couple: Susan and David

Together 19 years. Married 17. Two children. On the brink of divorce.

David built a successful property development company—work became his refuge from a home where he felt he could never get it right. Susan gave up teaching when their youngest had health complications. Twelve years later, she's still "temporarily" at home, brilliantly managing household logistics but increasingly invisible, including to herself.

They perfected the choreography of life—school runs, schedules, logistics—but lost the music of them. When their son got caught with cannabis at school, Susan realised: I don't even want David here. That night, she said it: "I think we should separate."

David's response? "Can we talk Sunday? I've got the Birmingham meeting tomorrow."

But something in her face made him pause. One last thing.

This is the couple walking into Maya and James's practice room.

The Therapists: Maya Kapadia and James Crawford

Maya (42) came through integrative counselling—Person-Centred, Gestalt, psychodynamic. Warm, intuitive, brilliant at holding emotional space. Divorced three years ago, she questioned: What actually helps couples? She works phenomenologically, trusts emergence, sometimes gets absorbed in emotion, and loses structure.

James (38) has organisational psychology background—years consulting on team communication and systemic change. Excellent at seeing patterns, naming dynamics, holding structure. More cognitive in orientation, sometimes intellectualises as defence.

They met at Duo Coaching Academy training. Initially wary—Maya found James "too corporate," James found Maya "overly focused on feelings." But during demonstration, something clicked. Their different styles created stereo effect, offering multiple access points. After coffee, they decided to try working together.

Susan and David are their first couple.

As you read, you'll see Susan and David's transformation across six intensive sessions—the pebbles constellation revealing hidden patterns, drawings showing divergent visions, moments of breakdown and breakthrough. You'll see Maya and James learning alongside you—their nervousness, the rupture requiring their own pebbles work, their growth from uncertain beginners to, four years later, seasoned therapists supervising others.

These aren't just stories. They're windows into the lived experience of this work.

Why These Stories Matter

As you read this book, you'll see Susan and David's transformation unfold across six intensive sessions. You'll witness what happens in the room—the pebbles constellation that reveals their hidden patterns, the drawings that show their divergent visions, the moments of breakdown and breakthrough.

You'll also see Maya and James learning this work alongside you. Their nervousness before that first session. The rupture in their partnership around session three, and the pebbles work they had to do themselves. The gradual deepening of their collaboration. Their growth from uncertain beginners to skilled practitioners.

Four years later, you'll see them as seasoned Duo Coaching therapists, supervising other new pairs, reflecting on their journey with gratitude.

These aren't just stories. They're windows into the lived experience of this work—both as practitioner and as the couples you'll serve.

Setting Sail

Every sailor remembers their first time at the helm in open water.

You've studied the charts. You understand the theory of navigation—how wind and current interact, how to read the weather, the principles of trim and balance. You've watched experienced sailors make it look effortless, their vessels responding to the slightest adjustment as if reading their minds.

But theory dissolves the moment you're responsible for an actual boat in actual water with actual weather. Suddenly, there are a thousand variables you didn't account for. The wind shifts. The current pulls stronger than expected. What looked simple from the dock feels overwhelming from the helm.

Image 2 Two sailboats, line drawing — Competency Ladder header.

"Two Vessels, One Direction: The Art of Sailing in Formation"

And if you're learning to sail with a crew partner? That adds another dimension entirely. You must learn not just the vessel and the sea, but each other—how you each read conditions, when one sees danger the other misses, how to coordinate in real time without losing responsiveness to what's emerging moment by moment.

This Book Is Your Chart for That Journey

In *Reinventing Relationship Therapy*, we explored *why* new approaches are needed—the limitations of traditional models, the complexity of modern relationships, the theoretical foundation for intensive work. That was understanding the sea itself—its nature, its patterns, its demands.

This book is different. This is about **learning to sail**—the practical skills, the partnership coordination, the moment-by-moment navigation of actual couples through actual transformation.

You'll learn the fundamentals: how to set course, how to read conditions, how to make the thousand micro-adjustments that keep you moving towards destination rather than drifting off course.

You'll learn advanced techniques: how to navigate storms, how to find safe harbour when needed, how to read subtle shifts in wind and current that signal what's coming.

And crucially, you'll learn partnership sailing—how to work with a co-therapist so fluidly that you become a single crew, each knowing instinctively what the other is doing, complementing rather than competing, creating something together neither could achieve alone.

The couples you serve are not passengers. They're learning to sail their own vessel—their relationship. Your job isn't to captain their boat for them, but to sail alongside, teaching through modelling, holding space for their learning, keeping them safe enough to take risks but challenged enough to grow.

You'll make mistakes. You'll misjudge conditions. You'll have days when the coordination with your co-therapist feels clumsy rather than graceful. This is all part of learning.

Virginia Satir, the pioneering family therapist, once described co-therapy using a sailing metaphor:

> A stream in which two people can be is very powerful. And there are times that one person will be going in the direction of the wind, and the other will be going counter to the wind. And that's what you need—somebody to go counter to the wind, and somebody to go with the wind.

She understood: partnership sailing requires both sailors to be fully present, fully competent, yet willing to take different positions as conditions demand.

This Book Will Teach You to Sail in Partnership

Not perfectly—no one sails perfectly. But confidently. Responsively. With the kind of earned competence that comes from practice, from doing your own work, from learning through both success and struggle.

The couples walking into your practice room are setting sail on the most important voyage of their lives—the journey from disconnection to connection, from resignation to hope, from patterns that no longer serve to new possibilities.

They need skilled navigators. They need you.

Let's Begin

"The master has failed more times than the beginner has ever tried. But the master has also transformed more relationships than the beginner can yet imagine."

Part I: Theoretical Foundation (Chapters 1–4)

Before we can transform how we work, we must understand why transformation is needed. These opening chapters examine the limitations built into conventional approaches and introduce the theoretical framework that makes intensive co-therapy effective. This isn't abstract theory for its own sake—it's the foundation that will make everything that follows make sense.

Coming Next: Chapter 1—The Implementation Imperative

You've bridged the gap between vision and practice, understanding how theory transforms into action. Now you're ready to confront the urgent reality driving this transformation: the implementation imperative that makes intensive relationship work essential for modern couples.

Chapter 1 reveals the crisis couples face today—42% divorce rates, unprecedented complexity from digital disconnection to mental health challenges, and the stark inadequacy of traditional weekly therapy. You'll discover why couples arrive at your door having "tried everything" yet finding nothing that works, and why practitioners report feeling trapped in formats they know are ineffective.

More than documenting the problem, Chapter 1 establishes the urgency for change. The innovation-implementation gap keeps practitioners using inadequate approaches while couples desperately need transformation. Understanding this imperative prepares you for the alternative you're about to discover. Your journey into Duo Coaching begins here.

Part I

Foundation Level Competencies

Building the Vessel—Essential Skills for Duo Coaching

Chapter 1

The Implementation Imperative

Current Relationship Challenges and What Practitioners Actually Need

> If you have already committed through difficulty and emerged on the other side, remember what you learned. That you are capable of more than you thought. That the relationship can survive more than you feared. That choosing to stay, when staying is hard, is its own form of love.
>
> Neil Wilkie, *Relationship Inspirations*

The Couples Walking through Your Door

Sarah and Mark sit across from you in your office, their body language telling the story before they speak a word. She leans forward, hands clasped tightly, desperation in her eyes. He sits back, arms crossed, alternating between checking his phone and staring at the wall. They've been together eight years, married for five, and this is their "last attempt" before divorce.

"We've tried everything," Sarah begins, her voice cracking.

> We did online courses, read books, even tried that app that's supposed to improve communication. We've been to two other therapists. The first one just

Image 3 Hands Raised with Hearts.

"Reaching Upward: When Every Hand Carries a Heart"

DOI: 10.4324/9781003715627-3

listened and nodded for six months. The second one gave us homework assignments that felt like relationship chores. Nothing worked.

Mark finally looks up. "I'm here because she threatened to leave if I didn't come. But honestly? I don't think anyone can help us. We're just too different. Too much has happened."

Sound familiar? If you're reading this book, you've sat across from countless couples just like Sarah and Mark. They arrive not as hopeful newlyweds seeking enhancement, but as exhausted warriors from a battlefield they never intended to create. This is the reality of relationship therapy in 2027.

The Relationship Crisis We're Facing

The landscape of relationships today presents sobering realities that every practitioner encounters:

- 42% of marriages end in divorce in both the UK and US, with marriages lasting an average of 12–13 years before divorce
- Marriage rates declined significantly: married/civil partnered adults dropped from 58.4% in 1991 to 46.9% in 2021, while never-married adults rose from 26.3% to 37.9%
- Cohabiting couples increased by 144% from 1.5 million in 1996 to 3.6 million in 2021
- The majority of children now grow up in fractured families, with 1 million children having lost meaningful contact with their fathers

Despite decades of therapeutic development, relationship distress remains pervasive. This persistence suggests that current approaches, while well-intentioned, may be missing something crucial about what couples actually need.

The Complexity Explosion

Today's couples navigate unprecedented complexity that previous generations never encountered:

Digital Age Disconnection: Social media creates unrealistic relationship expectations while constant connectivity prevents quality couple time. Online affairs and emotional infidelity through social platforms add new layers of betrayal.

Economic Pressure: Dual incomes are now essential for survival, not choice. Partners become economic units with added stress of conflicting career demands, financial anxiety, and the loss of traditional homemaking roles.

Cultural Transitions: Traditional relationship scripts no longer exist. Couples must navigate changing gender roles, diverse family structures, and multicultural challenges without agreed-upon norms.

Mental Health Crisis: Anxiety, depression, and trauma function as silent third partners in relationships. Individual mental health challenges create relationship dynamics that traditional approaches struggle to address.

Extended Adolescence: Partners enter relationships with less emotional maturity, delayed life transitions, underdeveloped relationship skills, and increased dependency on parents.

Work-Life Integration Failure: The boundary between work and home has collapsed. Remote work brings job stress into intimate spaces while career demands create permanent relationship strain.

What Couples Tell Us They Need

When couples describe their experience with traditional therapy, certain themes emerge consistently:

"It felt like we were just managing pain, not actually healing." They want transformation, not symptom management. Weekly sessions that simply help them "cope better" feel inadequate when their relationship is collapsing.

"By the time we got back to therapy, we'd forgotten what we talked about last week." The fragmentation of weekly sessions prevents sustained momentum. Real breakthroughs need continuous attention, not interrupted progress.

"We needed to go deep, but we always ran out of time." Complex patterns and deep-rooted issues require extended exploration. Fifty-minute sessions create artificial constraints that prevent accessing underlying dynamics.

"We wanted tools we could actually use, not just talk about our feelings." Couples seek practical frameworks for understanding and changing their patterns. They need both insight and implementation.

These aren't complaints about individual therapists—they're reflections of structural limitations built into traditional therapeutic formats.

The Practitioner's Dilemma

Therapists report a different but equally frustrating reality. Research and practitioner surveys consistently reveal:

Couples work is the most challenging: Managing complex dynamics between two people, navigating high-conflict situations, and addressing deeply entrenched patterns within time constraints creates extraordinary demands.

Traditional formats feel inadequate: Practitioners know couples need more than weekly 50-minute sessions can provide, yet continue using this format because alternatives seem impractical or impossible.

The innovation-implementation gap: Despite knowing about intensive approaches, weekend workshops, and multi-hour sessions, most practitioners feel unprepared to implement them. Training programmes focus on weekly therapy models, leaving practitioners without practical frameworks for alternative delivery.

This creates a painful paradox: practitioners want to offer more effective help while feeling trapped by traditional formats, and couples desperately need deeper work while receiving only surface-level interventions.

Why This Matters Now

The convergence of increasing relationship complexity and inadequate therapeutic responses creates an urgent imperative for change. Every year that passes with ineffective approaches means:

- Thousands more couples divorcing unnecessarily
- Hundreds of thousands more children experiencing family fracture
- Millions more people losing faith in relationship therapy
- Practitioners continuing to feel frustrated and ineffective

We cannot afford to wait another generation for therapeutic approaches to catch up with couples' actual needs. The time for intensive relationship work is now.

The Bridge Forward

This book exists to bridge the gap between what couples need and what practitioners can actually deliver. You'll discover:

- Why traditional weekly therapy formats fundamentally limit relationship transformation (Chapter 2)
- The Duo Coaching Framework: a systematic approach for intensive relationship work (Chapter 3)
- Practical tools for assessment, session structure, and intervention (Chapters 13 and 14)
- Advanced techniques for complex dynamics and challenging cases (Chapters 12 and 16)
- Implementation strategies for building your practice (Chapter 11)

Sarah and Mark deserve better than ineffective approaches. You deserve better than feeling trapped in inadequate formats. The couples walking through your door today need what this book teaches. Let's begin.

Coming Next: Chapter 2—The Limitations of Current Approaches

You've seen the crisis couples face and the complexity overwhelming traditional approaches. But why exactly do weekly 50-minute sessions fall short? Chapter 2 reveals four structural limitations built into conventional therapy—constraints that have nothing to do with your skill and everything to do with format.

Discover why the 50-minute hour originated from Freud's bathroom breaks (not therapeutic research), how the triangulation trap sabotages even your best efforts, why weekly fragmentation prevents the sustained momentum couples desperately need, and how open-ended drift leaves everyone confused about progress.

More importantly, you'll learn why practitioners continue using approaches they know are inadequate—and how to bridge the innovation-implementation gap that keeps you trapped in traditional formats. Chapter 2 clears the path for the alternative you're about to discover.

Chapter 2

The Limitations of Current Approaches

Why Traditional Methods Fall Short with Complex Cases

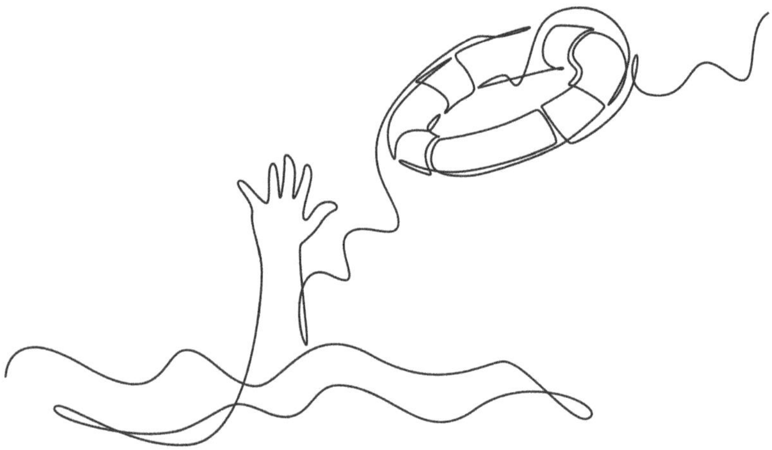

Image 4 Person Drowning, Reaching for Life-ring.

"The Moment Before the Rescue: Why Couples Need More Than a Lifeline"

Why Traditional Methods Fall Short

Understanding why traditional approaches struggle with complex couples isn't about criticising practitioners or invalidating established methods. Rather, it's about recognising how structural constraints built into conventional therapy formats inadvertently limit effectiveness. Four fundamental limitations shape outcomes more powerfully than therapeutic skill or couples' motivation.

The Four Structural Limitations

The 50-Minute Constraint

The standard 50-minute session originated from Freud's bathroom breaks between appointments, not from therapeutic research. Yet this arbitrary timeframe has become gospel in relationship therapy, creating profound limitations:

DOI: 10.4324/9781003715627-4

Surface Engagement Only: Couples spend 15 minutes settling in, 20 minutes discussing surface issues, and 15 minutes wrapping up—never reaching the underlying patterns driving their distress. The moment therapeutic tension builds towards breakthrough, time expires.

Interrupted Momentum: Just as couples begin accessing vulnerable emotions or recognising core patterns, the session ends. This interruption prevents the sustained work required for genuine transformation.

Incomplete Processing: Deep emotional work needs completion within a session. When couples leave mid-process, they return home carrying activated emotions without resolution, often triggering the very patterns that brought them to therapy.

Artificial Constraints on Intervention: Powerful interventions require time for processing. The 50-minute format forces practitioners to choose interventions based on available time rather than therapeutic necessity.

The Triangulation Trap

Individual therapy with one partner while the other remains uninvolved creates a structural problem masked as a therapeutic relationship:

Alliance Complications: When one partner develops a strong therapeutic alliance while the other feels excluded, the therapy itself becomes part of the couple's problem. The involved partner references "my therapist says…" while the excluded partner grows resentful.

Partial Information: Single-therapist couples work operates with fundamental information asymmetry. Each partner's internal experience, attachment patterns, and relational strategies remain partially visible, leading to interventions based on incomplete understanding.

System Blindness: Relationship patterns emerge between partners through unconscious complementarity. A single therapist inevitably develops blind spots about these dynamics, particularly when they mirror the therapist's own relational patterns.

Weekly Fragmentation

The standard weekly session schedule creates therapeutic fragmentation that undermines effectiveness:

Lost Momentum: Breakthroughs require sustained attention. When couples return seven days later, they've lost connection with insights from the previous session. Each week begins with reconstruction rather than building forward.

Diluted Focus: Weekly sessions allow couples to avoid sustained engagement with difficult patterns. They can explore challenging territory for 50 minutes, then return to familiar dynamics for six days. This intermittent engagement prevents the sustained discomfort required for genuine change.

Crisis Management versus Transformation: Weekly formats naturally drift towards crisis management. Couples arrive with the week's emergencies, consuming session time with reactive problem-solving rather than transforming underlying patterns.

Open-Ended Drift

Traditional therapy's lack of defined structure or endpoint creates problems for couples' work:

Unclear Progress: Without defined goals or timeframes, couples cannot assess whether therapy is working. This ambiguity allows ineffective approaches to continue indefinitely while couples grow increasingly discouraged.
Dependency Development: Open-ended therapy can create relational dependency on the therapeutic relationship rather than building the couple's capacity for autonomous functioning.
Financial Burden: Ongoing weekly sessions create significant cumulative costs. Couples making modest progress may continue indefinitely, unable to determine if continued investment is warranted.

The Evidence for Intensive Work

Research increasingly validates intensive approaches for relationship therapy:

Intensive formats (weekend workshops, multi-day retreats, extended sessions) show effect sizes equivalent to or exceeding traditional weekly therapy.
Couples report higher satisfaction with intensive formats, particularly appreciating the ability to achieve sustained focus without weekly interruptions.
Intensive work demonstrates particular effectiveness for high-conflict couples and relationships with complex trauma histories.
Long-term follow-up studies show gains from intensive work maintain comparably to traditional therapy, while requiring significantly less total therapeutic time.

These findings aren't surprising. Intensive formats overcome the four structural limitations that constrain traditional approaches. Extended sessions allow deeper work, coordinated co-therapy prevents triangulation, concentrated scheduling maintains momentum, and defined structure creates clarity.

Why Practitioners Don't Use Better Approaches

Despite evidence supporting intensive work, most practitioners continue using traditional formats. This innovation-implementation gap stems from practical barriers:

Training Limitations: Graduate programmes teach weekly individual/couples therapy. Practitioners receive little training in intensive formats, leaving them feeling unprepared despite knowing better approaches exist.

Practice Constraints: Therapists working in agencies or group practices face scheduling limitations. Extended sessions don't fit standard office hours or insurance structures.

Economic Concerns: Weekly sessions provide predictable revenue streams. Intensive formats require different business models that feel risky without guidance.

Lack of Frameworks: Knowing intensive work is effective differs from having practical frameworks for implementation. Practitioners need specific guidance for session structure, assessment processes, and intervention sequencing.

Professional Isolation: Implementing new approaches alone feels daunting. Practitioners need communities of practice, supervision, and collegial support.

The Evidence Base for Duo Coaching: Embracing Complexity in Relational Research

Any honest examination of the evidence base for relationship therapy must begin with an uncomfortable acknowledgment: the gold standard of randomised controlled trials, so effective in pharmaceutical research, becomes fundamentally problematic when applied to the living, breathing complexity of human relationships. This is not a failure of rigour but rather a recognition that relational interventions exist within an entirely different epistemological domain.

My doctoral research at Middlesex University, *The Phenomenology of Relationships*, involved an extensive critical examination of the existing research literature on relationship therapy efficacy. What emerged from this systematic review was a sobering picture of the field's evidential foundations—or rather, their fragility.

The challenges are manifold and interconnected. First, there is the observer effect—what we might call the therapeutic equivalent of Schrödinger's cat. The moment a therapist enters a relational system, that system changes. There can be no pristine observation because observation itself is intervention. Second, the notion of a control group becomes ethically and practically untenable; we cannot meaningfully compare couples receiving therapy with those denied it, nor can we assume that any two couples—or any two therapists—are sufficiently comparable to draw valid conclusions. Each therapeutic encounter is, in essence, a unique phenomenon. Third, confirmation bias permeates outcome measurement: couples who invest time, money, and emotional energy in therapy are predisposed to attribute subsequent improvements to the therapeutic process, regardless of the myriad other factors that may have contributed to change. Fourth, the scarcity of longitudinal studies means we have precious little understanding of whether therapeutic gains endure, and even where such studies exist, the passage of time introduces countless confounding variables that make attribution nearly impossible.

These conclusions did not emerge from theoretical speculation but from rigorous engagement with the published research itself. Study after study, when examined through a critical lens, revealed methodological limitations that their authors often acknowledged only in passing, if at all. The field has, perhaps understandably, been reluctant to confront the implications of these limitations head-on.

This is not to suggest that relationship therapy lacks value—clinical experience and client testimony consistently suggest otherwise. Rather, it is to acknowledge that the evidence base for all relationship therapy, including the most established modalities, rests on foundations far less solid than practitioners sometimes claim. My doctoral research led me to conclude that intellectual honesty demands we hold our claims to efficacy with appropriate humility, even as we continue the vital work of supporting couples in distress.

Intuitive Inquiry as Methodological Foundation

The Duo Coaching Framework was born not from laboratory conditions but from the crucible of clinical practice, refined through what qualitative researchers term *intuitive inquiry*—a methodology that honours the researcher's embodied knowledge while maintaining systematic rigour. Developed by Rosemarie Anderson, intuitive inquiry recognises that in fields involving human consciousness and relationship, the practitioner's accumulated wisdom, pattern recognition, and felt sense constitute valid and valuable forms of knowing.

This approach aligned naturally with the phenomenological orientation of my doctoral work, which emphasised the primacy of lived experience over abstracted measurement. Phenomenology asks not "what can we prove?" but "what is the essential nature of this experience?"—a question far better suited to the intimate complexities of couple relationships than the reductive demands of controlled trials.

This is not to privilege intuition over evidence but to acknowledge that in relational work, intuition *is* a form of evidence—one that emerges from thousands of hours of clinical observation, from the therapist's own relational experiences, and from the ongoing dialogue between theoretical understanding and practical application. The Duo Coaching Framework represents the crystallisation of such inquiry: an approach developed through careful attention to what works, what resonates, and what creates lasting change in the couples who entrust themselves to this process.

Building an Emerging Evidence Base

While acknowledging these epistemological constraints, practitioners of Duo Coaching are committed to building the most robust evidence base possible within these limitations. This includes systematic collection of client feedback, tracking of presenting issues and outcomes, documentation of session processes, and ongoing refinement of the framework based on accumulated clinical learning. The extended session format (3.5 hours rather than traditional 50-minute appointments) and the co-therapy model create unique conditions for observation and intervention that merit careful documentation and analysis.

What we can say with confidence is this: the Duo Coaching Framework draws upon established theoretical foundations and phenomenological approaches to relationship—while offering an innovative delivery model that addresses many of the limitations inherent in traditional relationship therapy. Its efficacy, like that of all relational interventions, is best understood not through the lens of controlled trials but through the careful accumulation of clinical wisdom, client testimony, and the ongoing refinement that comes from practitioners committed to reflective practice.

The conclusions of my doctoral research were not cause for despair but for liberation—permission to develop approaches grounded in clinical reality rather than constrained by methodological frameworks ill-suited to our work. Duo Coaching stands as one such approach: theoretically informed, phenomenologically grounded, and refined through the only laboratory that ultimately matters—the sacred space where couples come to heal.

The Path Forward

Recognising these limitations isn't about abandoning traditional approaches entirely. Weekly therapy serves important functions for many clients. However, for couples facing complex challenges—high conflict, infidelity, trauma histories, or communication breakdown—traditional formats prove inadequate.

The Duo Coaching Framework addresses these limitations systematically:

Extended sessions (3.5 hours) overcome time constraints, allowing deep work without artificial interruptions

Co-therapy model eliminates triangulation, providing balanced support while accessing blind spots

Concentrated scheduling maintains momentum, with sessions spaced two to four weeks apart for sustained engagement

Structured framework provides clarity, with defined assessment, intervention sequence, and completion process

The following chapters provide everything you need to explore this approach: theoretical foundations, practical tools, session structure, assessment frameworks, intervention strategies, and business implementation guidance. You'll discover how to overcome the innovation-implementation gap that keeps practitioners trapped in inadequate formats.

Your couples deserve approaches that actually work. You deserve frameworks that enable effective practice. The structural limitations of traditional therapy aren't your fault, but continuing to use formats you know are inadequate becomes your responsibility. Let's explore the alternative.

Coming Next: Chapter 3—The Duo Coaching Framework

Now that you understand what doesn't work and why, you're ready for the solution. Chapter 3 introduces the Duo Coaching Framework—a systematic approach specifically designed to overcome every limitation you've just explored.

You'll discover six integrated elements that create conditions for profound relationship transformation: co-therapy partnerships that eliminate triangulation while accessing blind spots, extended 3.5-hour sessions that allow deep work without artificial interruption, concentrated scheduling that maintains momentum, structured assessment that provides clarity, comprehensive frameworks that guide couples through complexity, and between-session support that prevents crisis spirals.

This isn't theory—it's a proven framework built from working with hundreds of couples over years of practice refinement. Chapter 3 shows you exactly how these elements work together to transform relationship outcomes. The alternative you've been seeking begins here.

> The pessimist sees difficulty in every opportunity. The optimist sees opportunity in every difficulty.
>
> —Winston Churchill

Chapter 3

The Duo Coaching® Framework

A Systemic Approach for Relationship Transformation

The relationship is not just a place to be comfortable. It is a crucible for becoming.
Neil Wilkie, *Relationship Inspirations*

A Framework Born from Necessity

The Duo Coaching Framework didn't emerge from academic theorising or research laboratories. It was born from personal frustration, refined through hundreds of hours with real couples, and validated through consistent outcomes that traditional approaches struggled to achieve.

In *Reinventing*, I shared my own experience as a relationship therapy client—sitting across from well-intentioned therapists who provided empathy and insight but couldn't help my partner and me create the transformation our relationship desperately needed. That frustration became the catalyst for reimagining what relationship therapy could become when designed around couples' actual needs rather than professional convenience.

What emerged wasn't a new therapeutic modality but a comprehensive framework—a systematic methodology that addresses each of the structural limitations we explored in Chapter 2 while integrating the best elements of established therapeutic traditions.

The Six Core Elements

The Duo Coaching Framework rests on six foundational elements that work synergistically to create conditions for transformation:

Co-therapy Partnership: Two Therapists Working Together

The Innovation: Rather than one therapist working alone with two clients, Duo Coaching employs two therapists (typically male and female) working collaboratively with each couple.

Why This Matters: Remember the triangulation trap from this chapter? Two therapists fundamentally change the therapeutic dynamic:

DOI: 10.4324/9781003715627-5

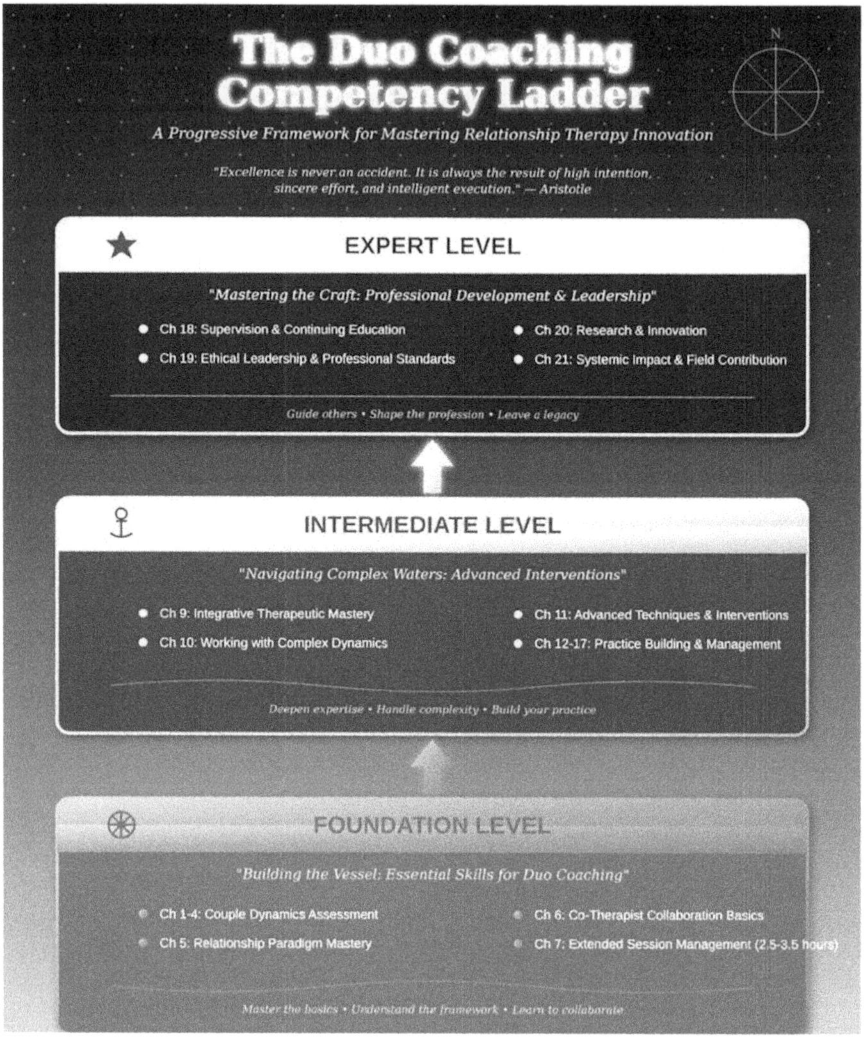

Infographic 2 The Framework at a Glance: How Duo Coaching Works in Practice.

Natural Balance With two therapists present, neither partner can easily feel that the therapeutic environment favours one over the other. The balanced energy helps both partners experience the space as fair and supportive.

Complementary Perspectives What one therapist misses, the other often catches. Male therapists may notice dynamics with male clients that female therapists miss, and vice versa. Together, we create more complete awareness of what's actually happening in the relationship system.

Reduced Burnout Intensive relationship work is emotionally demanding. Two therapists can support each other, preventing the exhaustion that leads to reduced effectiveness in traditional solo practice.

Modelling Healthy Partnership Two therapists working collaboratively demonstrate respectful disagreement, collaborative problem-solving, and balanced communication—providing a living model of what couples are trying to create.

The Co-Therapy Relationship The relationship between co-therapists becomes a crucial element of the therapeutic container. My co-therapist, Maria, and I have worked together for over eight years, developing non-verbal communication systems, complementary intervention styles, and deep professional trust that allows us to work fluidly even in complex, emotionally charged sessions.

This isn't about casual collaboration—it requires dedicated partnership development, regular debriefing, and willingness to address differences constructively.

Extended Sessions: Time for Complete Emotional Cycles

The Innovation

- Initial session: 3.5 hours
- Subsequent sessions: 2.5 hours
- Typically six sessions over three to four months

Why This Matters: This chapter detailed how 50-minute sessions create compression effects that abort emotional cycles just as they reach transformative potential. Extended sessions change everything:

Hour 1: Moving Past Defences Sufficient time to move beyond surface presentations and protective postures into authentic exploration of underlying issues. Couples begin to drop their rehearsed narratives and access genuine feelings.

Hour 2: Deeper Pattern Work Space to explore family-of-origin influences, attachment dynamics, and unconscious relationship contracts. This depth work requires sustained focus impossible in shorter timeframes.

Hour 3+: Breakthrough and Integration Time for couples to experience breakthrough moments, practice new patterns, and consolidate learning—all within the therapeutic container where support is immediately available.

Natural Rhythm Respected These timeframes weren't arbitrarily chosen—they reflect the natural rhythm of how profound emotional processing actually occurs. We're not imposing structure; we're creating space for natural processes to unfold.

Managing Energy Extended sessions require different energy management. We build in brief breaks, vary intensity levels, and shift between different types of work to maintain engagement without overwhelming couples.

Finite Timeline: Productive Urgency

The Innovation: Typically six sessions over three to four months, with clear outcomes established from the start.

Why This Matters: The drift problem this chapter identified—couples attending weekly sessions indefinitely without clear progress—is eliminated through defined timelines:

Maintained Momentum: Knowing the work has a beginning, middle, and end creates focus and urgency without pressure. Couples don't settle into comfortable patterns of weekly attendance without meaningful change.

Integration Time: Weekly or bi-weekly sessions (rather than daily or twice-weekly) provide time between sessions for couples to practise new patterns, integrate insights, and return with questions about real-world application.

Outcome Accountability: Clear timelines mean everyone—couple and therapists—remains accountable for progress. If approaches aren't working, we adjust rather than continuing ineffective interventions indefinitely.

Natural Completion: Six sessions typically provide sufficient depth for most couples while preventing dependency. Complex cases may extend to eight to ten sessions, but the principle of finite work remains.

Success Criteria: From session one, we establish what success looks like. Not vague aspirations like "better communication" but concrete, observable changes: "We make financial decisions together without arguing" or "We have intimate connection at least twice weekly."

Integrative Approach: Selecting Optimal Tools

The Innovation: Drawing from 15+ therapeutic modalities to select whatever approach best serves each unique couple at each moment.

Why This Matters: Remember the single-modality constraint from this chapter? Relationships are multidimensional, requiring different approaches for different dimensions:

The Integration Principle Rather than forcing every couple through the same theoretical lens, we assess what each couple actually needs and select accordingly:

- **Cognitive work** when thought patterns create relationship barriers
- **Emotional processing** when unexpressed feelings block connection
- **Behavioural interventions** when practical skills are missing
- **Psychodynamic exploration** when family-of-origin patterns repeat
- **Systemic understanding** when circular dynamics maintain problems
- **Somatic work** when body-based trauma affects intimacy

Primary Modalities Used

- Emotionally Focused Therapy
- Psychodynamic Approaches
- Neuro-Linguistic Programming
- Gottman Method
- Attachment Theory
- Systems Theory
- Gestalt Therapy
- Mindfulness-Based Approaches

- Hypnotherapy
- Internal Family Systems
- Solution-Focused Brief Therapy
- Narrative Therapy
- Imago Relationship Therapy
- Family Constellation Work

Real-Time Selection Integration isn't about eclecticism—randomly mixing approaches. It's about skilled assessment of what's needed moment-to-moment and selecting the most effective intervention from a comprehensive toolkit.

Your Existing Training Whatever your therapeutic background, it becomes part of your integrative foundation rather than a limitation. Cognitive behavioural therapists learn to access emotions; psychodynamic practitioners develop behavioural interventions; person-centred counsellors gain structured assessment tools.

The Duo Coaching Academy provides comprehensive training in integrative therapeutic approaches, with supervision in real-time intervention selection and skilled integration of multiple modalities.

"Me, You, Us" Focus: Individual and Systemic Integration

The Innovation: Explicit attention to three dimensions simultaneously:

- **Me**: Individual patterns, growth areas, and self-development
- **You**: Understanding your partner's unique perspective and needs
- **Us**: The co-created relationship system and its dynamics

Why This Matters: Traditional couple therapy often focuses exclusively on the "us" while neglecting individual foundations. But you cannot create a strong relationship between two people who haven't developed strong relationships with themselves.

Individual Foundation (Me) Each partner explores:

- Personal patterns brought from family of origin
- Individual mental health and well-being
- Self-awareness and emotional regulation
- Personal values and life vision
- Individual growth areas and aspirations

Partner Understanding (You) Each partner develops:

- Genuine curiosity about partner's inner world
- Understanding of partner's needs and fears
- Appreciation of partner's strengths and struggles
- Empathy for partner's perspective
- Recognition of partner as a separate person, not an extension of self

Relationship System (Us) The couple works on:

- Communication patterns and skills
- Shared vision and values
- Conflict resolution approaches
- Intimacy and connection
- Practical partnership management
- Co-created relationship identity

The Balance Healthy relationships require both individual wholeness and genuine partnership. Too much "me" creates parallel lives; too much "us" creates enmeshment and identity loss. The framework maintains this crucial balance.

Between-Session Support: Real-Time Guidance

The Innovation: 24/7 availability (within reason) for text, email, or brief phone call contact between sessions.

Why This Matters: Relationship crises don't wait for weekly appointments. When couples can access guidance as challenges emerge, they:

Prevent Damage Accumulation Rather than letting conflicts spiral for days or weeks until the next session, couples get real-time support to navigate difficulties constructively.

Practice with Support As couples implement new patterns, questions and challenges arise. Brief contact provides course correction before bad habits re-establish.

Maintain Momentum Connection between sessions keeps the therapeutic work alive rather than letting it fade until the next appointment.

Build Confidence Knowing support is available reduces anxiety and helps couples take risks trying new approaches.

Boundaries and Reality This doesn't mean constant availability or becoming couples' 24/7 on-call therapist. It means brief, focused contact when genuinely needed—typically two to three brief exchanges between sessions that prevent hours of circular arguing or unnecessary suffering.

How the Elements Work Together

These six elements aren't independent features—they create a synergistic system where each element enhances the others:

Co-therapy + Extended Sessions Two therapists can maintain therapeutic presence through long sessions better than one, preventing fatigue that reduces effectiveness.

Extended Sessions + Finite Timeline Longer individual sessions mean fewer total sessions needed, making finite timelines feasible while maintaining sufficient depth.

Finite Timeline + Clear Outcomes Defined endpoints require clear success criteria, preventing drift while maintaining accountability.

Integrative Approach + Co-therapy Two therapists bring broader combined expertise, enabling more sophisticated integration of multiple modalities.

"Me, You, Us" + Extended Sessions Time to work on all three dimensions within single sessions, creating integrated rather than fragmented understanding.

Between-Session Support + Finite Timeline Intensive support during defined period creates concentrated transformation rather than extended dependency.

What Makes Duo Coaching Different: A Comparison

Traditional Weekly Therapy versus Duo Coaching

Aspect	*Traditional Approach*	*Duo Coaching Framework*
Session Length	50 minutes	2.5–3.5 hours
Therapist Structure	Single therapist	Two therapists (co-therapy)
Timeline	Open-ended	Finite (typically 6 sessions)
Approach	Single modality	Integrative (15+ modalities)
Focus	Often "Us" only	"Me, You, Us" explicitly
Between Sessions	No contact	24/7 support available
Outcomes	Process-focused	Clear success criteria
Momentum	Can drift	Maintained urgency

When Duo Coaching Is Most Effective

The framework particularly excels with:

Complex Cases Multiple interacting stressors (Chapter 2 complexity) requiring intensive, multifaceted intervention.

Relationship Damage Betrayals, infidelity, or accumulated resentments needing intensive repair work beyond what weekly sessions can provide.

Crisis Situations Immediate, focused intervention when couples are at breaking point and can't wait for weekly appointments to create momentum.

Previous Therapy Failures Couples who have tried traditional approaches without success often respond to the intensity and different structure.

High-Functioning Couples Partners with strong individual skills but relationship challenges benefit from focused intensive work rather than extended weekly sessions.

Essential Conditions for Success

The framework's effectiveness requires specific conditions from both couples and therapists:

From Couples

Genuine Commitment Both partners must genuinely want the relationship to work, not just attend to avoid divorce consequences.

Clarity About Outcomes Willingness to articulate specific, observable changes they want to create.

Self-Examination Readiness to examine their own contributions to problems rather than focusing solely on partner's faults.

Emotional Availability Some capacity to access and express vulnerable feelings, not just intellectual understanding.

Investment Willingness Commitment to investing time, energy, and resources in an intensive process.

From Therapists

Co-therapist Partnership Established working relationship with complementary skills and mutual professional respect.

Diverse Skill Set Competency in multiple therapeutic modalities, not just depth in one approach.

Outcome Focus Comfort with clear success criteria and accountability for results.

Stamina and Presence Ability to maintain therapeutic effectiveness through extended sessions.

Flexibility Willingness to work outside traditional scheduling and contact patterns.

Your Implementation Journey Begins

Understanding the framework intellectually is the first step. Implementation requires:

Foundation Skills (Part of this section):

- Session structure and management
- Co-therapist collaboration basics
- Outcome clarification processes
- Essential assessment competencies

Intermediate Skills (Previewed, detailed in Academy):

- Advanced modality integration
- Complex case management
- Specialised population adaptations
- Crisis intervention protocols

Expert Skills (Academy intensive training):

- Training and supervising others
- Innovation and adaptation

- Research and contribution
- Professional leadership

This chapter provides the conceptual foundation. Chapter 5 introduces the Relationship Paradigm—your practical assessment and intervention tool for implementing the framework effectively.

Common Questions and Concerns

"How can I afford two therapists?" While Duo sessions cost more, couples typically need fewer total sessions (6 vs. 20–30+ in traditional therapy), often making total investment comparable or less.

"Won't long sessions exhaust couples?" We manage energy carefully with breaks, varied intensity, and different types of work. Most couples report sessions "flew by" and they wanted more time, not less.

"What if I don't have a co-therapist?" Chapter 6 provides detailed guidance on finding and developing co-therapy partnerships. Many practitioners start by adapting some elements (extended sessions, finite timelines) before adding co-therapy.

"Do I need training in 15 modalities?" Start with your existing expertise and add strategically. The Academy provides structured training in key integrative approaches, but even incorporating three to four modalities significantly enhances effectiveness.

"What about couples who can't afford intensive work?" Not every couple needs or can afford intensive intervention. Traditional weekly therapy remains appropriate for many situations. The framework expands options rather than replacing all traditional work.

Integration and Self-reflection

Foundation Level Skills Addressed in This Chapter

Framework Comprehension: Understanding all six core elements (co-therapy, extended sessions, finite timeline, integrative approach, "Me-You-Us" focus, between-session support) and how they work synergistically

Systematic Thinking: Recognising how Duo Coaching elements create a coherent system rather than isolated techniques

Outcome Orientation: Understanding the importance of clear success criteria and measurement

Structural Innovation Awareness: Grasping how framework design addresses traditional therapy limitations

Reflection Questions

1 Which of the six core elements resonates most with you as addressing limitations you've experienced in traditional couple therapy?

2 How does the finite timeline framework (six sessions) challenge or align with your current therapeutic philosophy?
3 What concerns or excitement arise when you consider working with a co-therapist?
4 How might the "Me, You, Us" focus change your current approach to couple work?
5 What would need to shift in your practice structure to accommodate 2.5–3.5 hour sessions?

Self-assessment

Rate your current understanding of the Duo Coaching Framework

Trust your gut response. What number first comes to mind when you consider how ready you feel to take this further?

Score	*Interpretation*
1–2	Need more clarity on core elements and their integration
3–4	Grasping individual elements but unclear how they work together
5–6	Solid conceptual foundation ready to explore implementation
7+	Strong understanding ready to begin planning framework adoption

Practice Exercise

Select a current couple client (or past case you remember well). For each of the six core elements, reflect on:

- Co-therapy: How might having a co-therapist change the therapeutic dynamics with this couple?
- Extended sessions: What additional work could you accomplish with 2.5 hours instead of 50 minutes?
- Finite timeline: How might knowing you have exactly six sessions change your treatment planning?
- Integrative approach: What modalities beyond your primary orientation might benefit this couple?
- "Me, You, Us" focus: Are you currently balancing individual and relationship work, or focusing primarily on one?
- Between-session support: How might brief contact between sessions prevent crisis or maintain momentum?

This exercise helps you envision how the framework would function with real couples, building your implementation readiness.

Coming Next: Chapter 4—Transdisciplinarity in Relationship Work

The Duo Coaching Framework provides structure, but relationships exist as complex systems across multiple interconnected domains. Chapter 4 expands your vision beyond single-modality thinking into transdisciplinary integration.

You'll discover Nora Bateson's concept of "warm data"—the transcontextual information revealed through spatial dynamics, energetic patterns, and temporal rhythms that single perspectives miss. Learn how relationships function simultaneously across individual psychology, interpersonal dynamics, family systems, cultural contexts, and temporal dimensions, with changes in one domain cascading throughout the system.

Chapter 4 deepens your understanding of why intensive co-therapy works: You're not just combining two therapists or extending session time—you're creating conditions for accessing the systemic complexity that shapes relationship reality. This transdisciplinary foundation prepares you for the comprehensive assessment tool coming in Chapter 5.

"The Duo Coaching Framework doesn't replace your therapeutic expertise—it enhances it by providing the structural conditions where transformation becomes not just possible, but probable."

Chapter 4

Transdisciplinarity in Relationship Work

Integrative Thinking for Complex Relationship Systems

Image 5 School of Fish.

"Moving as One: The Intelligence of Collective Motion"

> The larger the number of perspectives we can bring to bear on a problem, the more likely it is that we will achieve a solution that works.
>
> —Gregory Bateson

Integrative Thinking for Complex Relationship Systems

Why This Chapter Matters

For Your Practice

Relationships are too complex for single-modality approaches. A couple presenting with "communication problems" may actually be dealing with attachment wounds, family-of-origin patterns, career transitions, and cultural conflicts—all at once. Transdisciplinary thinking gives you the frameworks to see and work with this complexity without feeling overwhelmed.

DOI: 10.4324/9781003715627-6

For Your Clients

When you can work across multiple contexts simultaneously, couples experience faster breakthroughs and more lasting change. Instead of spending months working on communication skills that don't stick because underlying patterns aren't addressed, you can intervene at multiple levels at once.

The Bottom Line

This chapter transforms how you SEE couples, which transforms what becomes possible in your work with them.

Core Transdisciplinary Concepts

Concept	*What It Means*	*Why It Matters in Practice*
Warm Data (Nora Bateson)	Transcontextual information revealed through: • Spatial dynamics (positioning, distance) • Energetic patterns (aliveness, deadness) • Temporal rhythms (pacing, timing) • Somatic communication (body language, breathing) vs. Cold Data: Quantitative measures like questionnaire scores and demographics	What you observe in the first five minutes often tells you more than questionnaires: Example: Couple sits far apart, one faces door, other stares at floor → Safety issue, not just communication problem You learn to read: • Power dynamics • Attachment styles in action • Defensive structures • What remains unspoken
Multiple Contexts	Relationships exist simultaneously across: • Individual Context (trauma, attachment, goals) • Interpersonal Context (communication, intimacy) • Family Context (family-of-origin, parenting) • Social Context (culture, community, class) • Temporal Context (life stage, history, future)	Change in one context creates ripples throughout: Example: Career promotion → • Individual: Identity shift • Interpersonal: Power dynamics shift • Family: Financial changes • Social: Status changes • Temporal: Life timeline accelerates You must address ALL affected contexts, not just the obvious one
The Hidden Third (Basarab Nicolescu)	Emergent properties belonging to the RELATIONSHIP itself, beyond individual partners:	Powerful therapeutic questions: • "What does your RELATIONSHIP need right now?"

(Continued)

Concept	*What It Means*	*Why It Matters in Practice*
	• Shared rhythms and synchronicities • Unique couple culture (language, rituals, humour) • Collective wisdom • Shared emotional fields • Joint creative capacity • Relationship "personality"	• "If your partnership could speak, what would it say?" • "What wants to emerge between you?" This shifts from individual complaints to relationship awareness Example: "It needs us to stop starving it. We feed everything else but never feed our connection."
Systems Thinking (Circular Causality)	Relationships operate through CIRCULAR causality, not linear: Linear: A causes B • Fix A to solve B Circular: A influences B, which influences C, which influences A • Continuous feedback loops • Multiple intervention points	Example Pattern: John's work stress → criticism of Mary → Mary withdraws → John feels more alone → increases work stress → more criticism → deeper withdrawal ... Instead of blaming John OR Mary, you: • Help them see the pattern • Interrupt the cycle • Create new patterns • Address underlying needs

Why It Matters: From Theory to Practice

Clinical Scenario

Sarah and Tom come to you saying, "We have communication problems." Traditional approach: teach communication skills.

Transdisciplinary Lens Reveals

- Individual Context: Sarah's promotion triggered imposter syndrome (individual therapy need)
- Interpersonal Context: Tom feels abandoned, withdraws (attachment pattern)
- Family Context: They moved near Tom's aging parents (family-of-origin activation)
- Social Context: Sarah's new status creates tension with old friends (identity shifts)
- Temporal Context: Promotion accelerated timeline for children (life planning pressure)

Communication skills alone won't address this complexity. You need interventions across all five contexts.

THIS IS WHY TRANSDISCIPLINARY THINKING MATTERS: You see the whole system, not just one piece.

Warm Data versus Cold Data: What to Observe

Cold Data (Traditional Assessment)	*Warm Data (Living Patterns)*
What Questionnaires Tell You: • How long together • Demographic characteristics • Relationship satisfaction scores • Stated problems and goals • Individual symptom checklists • Diagnostic categories **USEFUL but INCOMPLETE**	What You Observe in the Room: Spatial Dynamics: • How couples position themselves • Distance they maintain or close • Whether they face each other, you, or avoid eye contact • How spatial relationship changes as emotions shift Energetic Patterns: • Quality of aliveness or deadness between them • Moments when energy increases/decreases • Whether energies complement, compete, or disconnect • Emotional temperature and fluctuations Temporal Rhythms: • Pace of communication • Whether they interrupt, wait, or speak simultaneously • How timing affects the ability to connect • Rhythm of conflict and repair cycles Somatic Information: • Breathing patterns (synchronise or diverge) • Facial expressions and micro-expressions • Posture and gesture patterns • Physical tension and relaxation responses This reveals the TRUTH of their relationship

Case Example: Reading the Unspoken

Cold Data: Marcus and Elena's questionnaires showed moderate relationship satisfaction with communication as primary concern.

Warm Data: Elena sat rigidly upright, hands clasped tightly, eyes fixed on therapist. Marcus slumped in a chair, body angled away, one foot pointing towards the door. When Elena spoke, Marcus's jaw visibly tightened. When Marcus shared, Elena's breathing became shallow and rapid.

DIAGNOSIS: Not a communication problem—a SAFETY problem. Elena felt under threat (protective defences activated). Marcus felt trapped (preparing for escape). No communication technique would work until safety concerns were addressed.

The Five Contexts: Understanding the Relationship Ecosystem

Context	*What to Explore*	*Common Interventions*
1 Individual Context	• Personal histories and trauma • Attachment styles and nervous system patterns • Individual goals, values, and life purpose • Mental health and physical well-being • Career pressures and personal development needs • Identity and self-concept	• Individual therapy referrals when needed • One-to-one sessions within couple work • Timeline therapy for past wounds • Parts work for internal conflicts • Values clarification exercises
2 Interpersonal Context	• Communication patterns and conflict styles • Sexual and intimate connection • Power dynamics and decision-making • Shared goals and divergent priorities • Quality of friendship within romance • Pursuit-distance patterns	• Communication skills training • Gottman Method interventions • Emotionally Focused Therapy (EFT) attachment work • Imago dialogue • Intimacy-rebuilding exercises
3 Family Context	• Family-of-origin patterns and influences • Intergenerational trauma and resilience • Extended family relationships and pressures • Parenting challenges and decisions • Blended family dynamics • Sibling position effects	• Genogram work • Family-of-origin exploration • Boundary-setting with extended family • Parenting alignment work • Intergenerational pattern interruption
4 Social Context	• Cultural background and expectations • Religious or spiritual influences • Community connections and support systems • Friend networks and social pressures • Economic circumstances and class dynamics • Work cultures and environments	• Cultural genogram • Values clarification across cultures • Social support mapping • Community resource connection • Addressing discrimination impacts
5 Temporal Context	• Life stage and developmental transitions • Relationship history and significant events • Future goals and vision alignment • Seasonal patterns and anniversary reactions • The larger arc of their life together • Transition points (marriage, children, retirement)	• Life timeline work • Future visioning exercises • Dream boards and bucket lists • Lifecycle stage education • Narrative therapy approaches

The Interconnection Principle

CRITICAL INSIGHT: These contexts don't operate independently—they form a complex web of mutual influence.

Change in One Area Creates Ripple Effects Throughout the System

Individual therapy for one partner → affects relationship dynamic
Family-of-origin healing → influences current partnership patterns
Career changes → impact relationship priorities and daily rhythms
Community involvement → affects couple identity and values
Spiritual development → transforms meaning-making and connection

Why This Matters in Practice

If you only work at the interpersonal level (teaching communication skills), you'll miss:

- Individual trauma patterns sabotaging connection
- Family-of-origin dynamics driving current conflicts
- Social/cultural factors creating invisible pressure
- Life stage transitions requiring adaptation

Effective intervention requires working across MULTIPLE contexts simultaneously.

Common Relationship System Patterns

Recognising these circular patterns helps you interrupt them effectively:

Pattern Name	*How It Works (Circular Causality)*	*Intervention Points*
Pursue-Withdraw	Partner A seeks connection → Partner B creates distance • Partner A pursues harder • Partner B withdraws further • Partner A feels more desperate • Partner B feels more trapped • Cycle intensifies	• Help both see the pattern • Teach pursuer to make softer bids • Help withdrawer recognise bids vs. demands • Address attachment wounds • Create structured connection time
Blame-Defend	Partner A criticises • Partner B defends • Partner A feels unheard, criticises more • Partner B defends more strongly • both escalate • no resolution • resentment builds • next conflict starts from higher baseline	• Teach soft start-ups • Practice repair attempts • Develop self-soothing skills • Address underlying hurt beneath criticism • Build culture of appreciation

(Continued)

Pattern Name	*How It Works (Circular Causality)*	*Intervention Points*
Parent-Child	Partner A becomes responsible • Partner B becomes dependent • Partner A feels burdened, takes more control • Partner B feels incompetent, becomes more dependent • Partner A resents, criticises • Partner B regresses further • inequality deepens	• Name the pattern explicitly • Redistribute responsibilities • Address family-of-origin roles • Build "child's" competence • Help "parent" relinquish control
Competitor-Competitor	Partner A achieves success → Partner B feels threatened, competes • Partner A feels unsupported, achieves more • Partner B escalates competition • both focus on winning rather than connecting • relationship becomes battleground	• Shift from competition to collaboration • Celebrate each other's wins • Create shared goals • Address underlying insecurity • Define success as "we" not "me"
Overwhelmed-Detached	• Partner A hyper-focuses on problems • Partner B detaches to cope • Partner A feels alone, intensifies focus • Partner B needs more space • Partner A pursues with anxiety • Partner B shuts down completely • Emotional distance grows	• Help overwhelmed partner regulate • Teach detached partner engagement • Create anxiety tolerance • Build emotional literacy • Practice co-regulation

Working with the Hidden Third: Practical Applications

Most therapy focuses on individual needs or interpersonal negotiations. But some of the most powerful therapeutic moments occur when you address the RELATIONSHIP as a living entity with its own requirements.

Questions That Access the Hidden Third

Traditional Questions (Focus on Individuals)	*Hidden Third Questions (Focus on Relationship)*
• What do YOU need? • What do YOU want from your partner?	• What does your RELATIONSHIP need right now? • If your partnership could speak, what would it say?

(Continued)

Traditional Questions (Focus on Individuals)	*Hidden Third Questions (Focus on Relationship)*
• How can YOU get your needs met? • What would make YOU happy? • What changes do YOU want to see? These keep focus on individual positions	• What wants to emerge between you that hasn't been born yet? • How does your relationship want to grow and evolve? • What is your relationship calling you both towards? • What does "we" need (not just "I" or "you")? These shift to relationship-level awareness

Interventions That Strengthen the Hidden Third

Couple Rituals: Create rituals that honour the relationship itself (weekly date night, annual relationship review, celebration of "us")

Shared Visioning: Processes that access collective wisdom beyond individual desires (dream boards together, bucket lists as a couple)

Joint Creative Projects: Activities requiring collaboration (cooking together, home projects, travel planning)

"We" Consciousness: Practices that cultivate awareness of partnership along-side individual identity

Relationship Celebrations: Honouring the relationship's unique qualities and contributions

Case Example: When the Relationship Speaks

David and Maria had been focusing on individual complaints for months without progress. When their therapist asked, "What does your relationship need from both of you right now?" the energy shifted.

After silence, Maria said: "It needs us to stop starving it. We feed our careers, our kids, our friends, but we never feed our connection."

David added: "It wants to play again. We used to have so much fun together."

This shift from individual positions to relationship awareness opened new possibilities. They began asking what their partnership needed before making decisions, gradually rebuilding shared purpose.

Integration Summary: Putting It All Together

Traditional Single-Modality Approach	*Transdisciplinary Integrative Approach*
Couple says: "We have communication problems"	Couple says: "We have communication problems"

(Continued)

Traditional Single-Modality Approach	*Transdisciplinary Integrative Approach*
You assess using: Questionnaires (cold data) You diagnose: Communication skills deficit You intervene: Teach speaker-listener technique Result: Skills don't stick because underlying patterns are not addressed Focus: Single context (interpersonal) Time to change: Slow or ineffective	You assess using: Warm data + cold data + multiple contexts You diagnose: Sarah's promotion (individual) triggered Tom's abandonment fears (attachment), activated family-of-origin dynamics (family context), shifted social status (social), accelerated life timeline (temporal) You intervene across multiple levels: • Individual: Sarah's identity work • Interpersonal: Attachment repair • Family: Boundary-setting • Social: Status transition support • Temporal: Life planning alignment • Hidden Third: "What does our relationship need?" Result: Sustainable change because whole system was addressed Focus: All five contexts + relationship itself Time to change: Faster and more lasting

Why Transdisciplinary Thinking Is Essential

The Complexity Challenge

Modern relationships face unprecedented complexity. Single-modality approaches—no matter how skilfully applied—cannot address this complexity effectively.

What Transdisciplinarity Offers

A way to SEE the whole system, not just one piece
Multiple intervention points instead of one
Ability to work at the level that will create the most change
Integration of best practices from multiple modalities
Recognition of relationships as living systems
Faster, more sustainable transformation

"You cannot solve complex problems with simple solutions. You need approaches as sophisticated as the challenges couples face. Transdisciplinary thinking gives you that sophistication."

Practical Next Steps for Your Practice

1 **Start Observing Warm Data:** In your next session, notice spatial dynamics, energy, timing, and body language BEFORE focusing on verbal content.
2 **Map the Five Contexts:** For your next couple, sketch out what's happening in all five contexts. Notice the ripple effects.

3 **Ask Hidden Third Questions:** Try "What does your relationship need?" and notice how it shifts the conversation.
4 **Identify Circular Patterns:** Look for pursue-withdraw, blame-defend, or other patterns. Help couples see the cycle.
5 **Intervene at Multiple Levels:** Don't just teach communication skills. Address individual wounds, family patterns, social context, and life stage simultaneously.

Reflection Questions

1 When you observe a couple in session, how much attention do you currently pay to "warm data" (spatial dynamics, energy, body language) versus the content of what they're saying?
2 Think of a current or recent couple. Can you identify what's happening across all five contexts (individual, interpersonal, family, social, temporal)? Where might you be missing important information?
3 How comfortable are you asking "Hidden Third" questions that address the relationship itself rather than individual partners' positions?
4 Which circular patterns (pursue-withdraw, blame-defend, parent-child, competitor-competitor, overwhelmed-detached) do you encounter most frequently? How effectively do you help couples see and interrupt these cycles?
5 What would need to shift in your current theoretical orientation to embrace genuinely transdisciplinary thinking rather than single-modality practice?

Self-assessment

Rate your current understanding of transdisciplinary relationship work:

Trust your gut response. What number first comes to mind when you consider how ready you feel to take this further?

Score	*Interpretation*
1–2	New to these concepts; primarily work from single-modality perspective
3–4	Understand individual concepts but unclear how to integrate them clinically
5–6	Solid grasp of warm data, multiple contexts, and systems thinking; beginning to apply in practice
7+	Confident working across contexts and reading warm data; ready to deepen integration skills

End of Part I

You now understand why conventional approaches fall short and what makes intensive co-therapy different. The theoretical foundation is in place. But understanding why something works is not the same as knowing how to do it. In Part II, we turn from theory to practice—building the core skills you'll use in every session.

Part II: Core Clinical Skills (Chapters 5–8)

With the theoretical foundation in place, we turn to the essential competencies every Duo Coach needs. Here you'll develop the framework fundamentals: the Relationship Paradigm, finding and working with a co-therapist, session structure, and taking your first steps towards implementation. These chapters build the skills you'll draw upon in every session.

Coming Next: Chapter 5—The Relationship Paradigm Framework

Transdisciplinary thinking reveals relationship complexity, but how do you assess it systematically? Chapter 5 introduces the Relationship Paradigm—your practical compass for understanding the 12 dimensions that determine relationship health.

This comprehensive framework maps everything from communication patterns and emotional intimacy to conflict resolution, sexual connection, shared vision, and resilience capacity. You'll learn to identify precisely where couples thrive and where they struggle, creating clear pathways for intervention rather than wandering through unfocused exploration.

More than assessment, the Relationship Paradigm becomes a therapeutic tool couples use to understand themselves. They move from "we're broken" to "here's exactly where we need development"—a shift that transforms hopelessness into agency. Chapter 5 gives you the map that guides every subsequent intervention.

Part II

Foundation Level Implementation

Core Principles and Essential Skills

Chapter 5

The Relationship Paradigm Framework

Your Practical Compass for Relationship Health

> My Relationship Paradigm framework has 6 key elements: Communication, Connection, Commitment, Fun, Growth and Trust. This is the foundation of a relationship. If trust starts to be doubted then the strength of the whole relationship will start to dissipate.
>
> —From *Reinventing*

Beyond Vague Aspirations

When Rebecca and Tom arrived for their first Duo Coaching session, Emma said: "We just need better communication." James nodded: "Yeah, we want to feel more connected."

These desires are genuine and understandable. But they're also beautifully vague—offering no clear direction for intervention, no way to measure progress, and no understanding of what specifically needs to change.

Twenty minutes into the session, after using the Relationship Paradigm assessment, the picture became crystal clear:

Emma's Ratings

Communication: 3/10
Connection: 2/10
Commitment: 8/10
Fun: 1/10
Growth: 4/10
Trust: 7/10

James's Ratings

Communication: 6/10
Connection: 5/10
Commitment: 8/10
Fun: 3/10
Growth: 5/10
Trust: 8/10

DOI: 10.4324/9781003715627-8

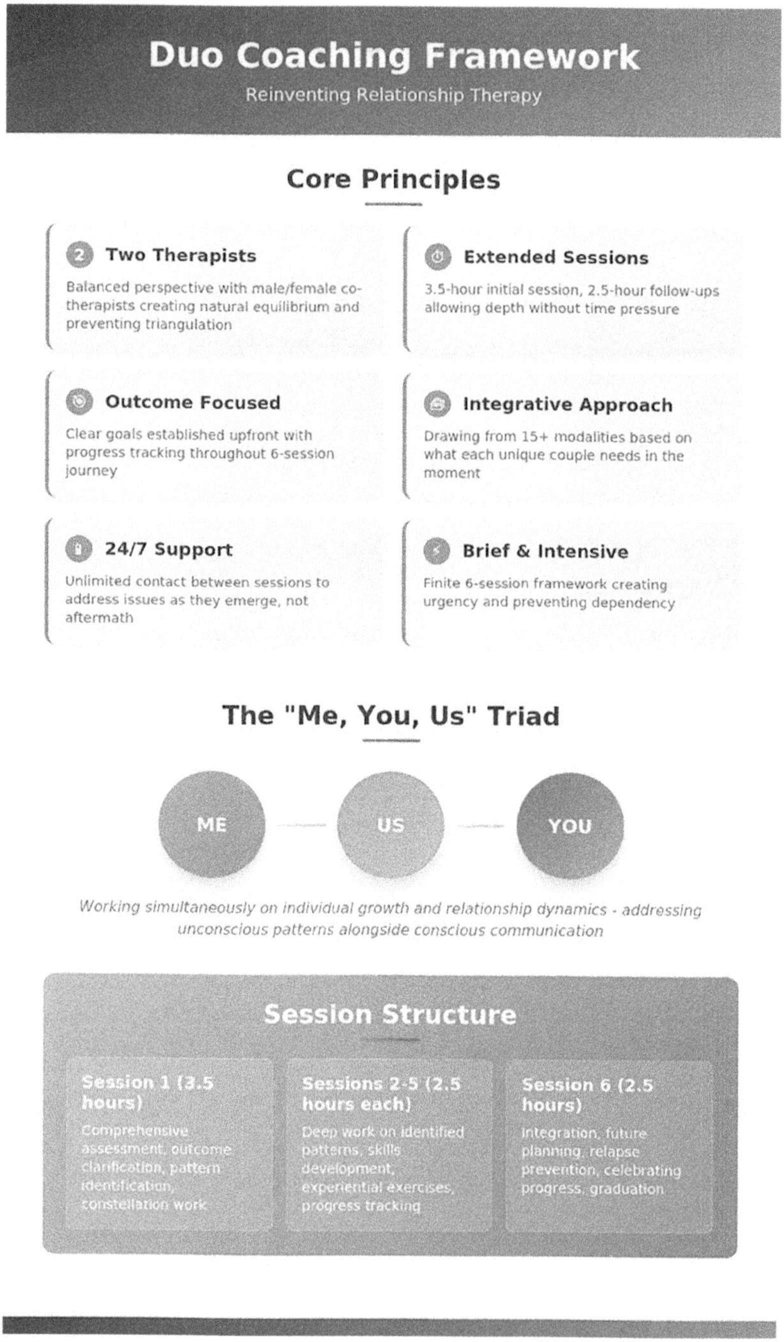

Infographic 3 The Relationship Paradigm: Six Elements, Three Perspectives, One Whole.

Suddenly, "better communication" became specific: Emma felt unheard and dismissed (rating 3), while James thought they communicated adequately (rating 6). The real crisis wasn't communication—it was Connection (Emma at 2, James at 5) and Fun (Emma at 1, James at 3). They'd become business partners managing children and household, with zero playfulness or intimacy.

This specificity changed everything. Instead of six months of vague "communication work," we could focus intensively on rebuilding connection and reintroducing fun—addressing what actually needed attention.

This is the power of the Relationship Paradigm.

The Six Essential Elements

The Relationship Paradigm identifies six dimensions present in thriving relationships. Like a medical diagnostic tool that measures vital signs, it provides concrete data about relationship health rather than vague impressions.

Communication: The Bridge Between Worlds

What It Actually Means

Communication extends far beyond exchanging information. It encompasses:

Expressing thoughts, feelings, and needs clearly
Being heard and understood by your partner
Navigating differences without contamination spreading throughout the relationship
Repair attempts that successfully de-escalate conflicts
Non-verbal communication that matches or contradicts words

Healthy versus Unhealthy Communication

Healthy (7–10)	*I Unhealthy (1–3)*
Can express vulnerability safely	Criticism and defensiveness dominate
Listens to understand, not just respond	Stonewalling or dismissive responses
Ruptures are repaired quickly	Days of silence after conflicts
Adjusts style to partner's needs	Insists partner adapts to their style
Conflict leads to deeper understanding	Conflicts create distance and resentment

The Platinum Rule: Effective communicators move beyond the golden rule ("treat others as you would like to be treated") to the platinum rule: "Treat others as they would like to be treated." They adapt their communication style to match their partner's needs.

Remember: "The meaning of any communication is the response it gets." If your partner consistently misunderstands you, the issue may not be with their listening but with how you're communicating.

Assessment Questions

Can you express difficult feelings without your partner becoming defensive?
Do you feel heard and understood when you share concerns?
Can you navigate disagreements without damaging the relationship?
Do you understand your partner's communication needs and preferences?

Connection: The Invisible Threads That Bind

What It Actually Means

Connection encompasses all the ways partners make contact:

Physical touch and affection throughout the day
Emotional vulnerability and authentic sharing
Full presence when together (not distracted by devices)
Shared experiences that create memories and meaning
Sexual intimacy that feels connecting rather than mechanical
Rituals of greeting, parting, and daily togetherness

Dr. John Gottman's Research: His work on "bids for connection" shows that partners in healthy relationships respond to each other's small attempts at connection (a comment, a touch, a shared observation) around 86% of the time. In relationships heading towards divorce, that number drops below 33%.

The Daily Deposits: Connection isn't maintained through occasional grand gestures but through hundreds of small daily interactions—the kiss goodbye in the morning, the text checking in during the day, the touch while passing in the kitchen, the genuine interest in each other's experiences. These are what I term Micro-Connections. The opposite are Micro-Disconnections that can cause sclerosis in the relationship system.

Common Connection Killers

Screens competing for attention during couple time
Parallel parenting without couple connection
Exhaustion leaving no energy for intimacy
Unresolved resentments creating emotional walls
Taking each other for granted and neglecting daily rituals

Assessment Questions

Do you have at least 10–15 minutes of undistracted couple time daily?
Does physical affection feel natural and wanted by both partners?
Do you feel emotionally close and understood?
Is sexual intimacy satisfying for both partners?

Commitment: Aligned Vision and Shared Investment

What It Actually Means

Commitment encompasses more than staying together:

Clarity about what both partners want from the relationship
Aligned vision for the future (children, location, lifestyle, values)
Active investment of time, energy, and resources
Prioritisation of the relationship amid competing demands
Reliability and follow-through on agreements
Willingness to work through difficulties rather than exit

The Clarity Principle: Many couples assume they're committed because they're together, but they've never actually discussed what commitment means to each of them or what future they're building together.

Common Commitment Patterns

Strong Commitment (7–10): Clear shared vision, active daily investment, relationship prioritised appropriately, willingness to work through challenges, both partners pulling in the same direction.

Ambiguous Commitment (4–6): Unclear about long-term vision, one partner is more invested than the other, competing priorities (work, extended family) undermine the partnership, commitment questioned during conflicts.

Crisis Commitment (1–3): One foot out the door, considering alternatives, minimal investment in relationship health, vision completely misaligned, staying for external reasons (children, finances) rather than genuine desire.

Assessment Questions

Can you articulate what you're building together?
Do you both prioritise the relationship appropriately?
Are you confident your partner is fully committed?
Do you invest time and energy in relationship health?

Fun: Vitality, Playfulness, and Joy

What It Actually Means

Fun provides the vitality that makes relationships resilient:

Playfulness and ability to be silly together
Shared laughter and humour
Novel experiences that create excitement

Leisure activities you genuinely enjoy together
Spontaneity rather than rigid routines
Lightness that balances life's inevitable heaviness

Why Fun Matters More Than You Think

Fun isn't frivolous—it's essential. Couples who maintain playfulness and joy have better conflict resolution, higher satisfaction, and greater resilience during difficult periods. Fun creates positive emotional deposits that buffer against stress and inevitable difficulties.

The Fun Erosion Pattern

Many couples start with abundant fun—dating adventures, spontaneous weekends, playful teasing. Then life intervenes: careers intensify, children arrive, responsibilities multiply. Fun becomes "something we'll do when things settle down." But things never settle down, and fun disappears entirely.

Eventually, partners become roommates managing logistics—coordinating schedules, dividing household tasks, discussing children, and bills. The relationship that began with laughter and adventure becomes a joyless partnership of burden-sharing.

Rebuilding Fun

The good news: Fun is often the easiest element to improve because it doesn't require deep psychological work or difficult conversations. It just requires deliberate attention and prioritisation.

Assessment Questions

When did you last laugh together genuinely?
Do you have activities you enjoy as a couple?
Can you be playful and silly together?
Do you create novel experiences or rely entirely on routine?

Growth: Individual and Relationship Evolution

What It Actually Means:

Growth prevents stagnation at both individual and relationship levels:

Individual Development: Each partner continuing to learn, develop, and evolve
Relationship Evolution: The partnership adapting to changing circumstances and stages
New Experiences: Trying new things together that challenge and expand
Self-awareness: Ongoing reflection and personal insight

Mutual Support: Partners encouraging each other's growth
Positive Challenges: Setting goals and working towards aspirations together

The Stagnation Trap

Relationships naturally move from excitement to stability. But stability can become stagnation—partners stop growing individually, the relationship becomes predictable and boring, conversations cover only logistics, and life feels like endless repetition of the same routines.

Stagnant relationships aren't necessarily unhappy—they're just flat. Partners often describe feeling "fine" but lacking vitality, purpose, or excitement about the future.

Individual versus Relationship Growth:

Both dimensions matter. Individual growth keeps partners interesting to each other—new skills, perspectives, and experiences create ongoing attraction and conversation. Relationship growth ensures the partnership evolves rather than calcifying—adapting to new life stages, developing deeper intimacy, and building shared purpose.

The Balance: Strong commitment provides safety for individual growth (knowing your relationship is secure allows risk-taking), while individual development energises the partnership by keeping partners dynamic and evolving.

Assessment Questions

Are you continuing to develop and learn new things?
Does your partner support your individual growth?
Is your relationship evolving or stuck in patterns?
Do you have shared goals you're working towards?

Trust: The Foundation Supporting Everything

What It Actually Means

Trust forms the bedrock upon which all other elements rest:

Reliability: Doing what you say you'll do, when you say you'll do it
Transparency: Openness about thoughts, feelings, and actions
Consistency: Being the same person across contexts and situations
Accountability: Taking responsibility for mistakes and working to repair damage
Fidelity: Honouring agreements about exclusivity and boundaries
Respect: Treating your partner with consideration and dignity

The Foundation Effect

Trust functions differently from other elements. When trust is strong, partners interpret ambiguous situations generously, give the benefit of the doubt, and feel safe being vulnerable. When trust is damaged, even positive interactions in other areas feel tentative and fragile—fun feels forced, communication becomes guarded, and commitment feels uncertain.

Trust Builds Slowly, Breaks Quickly

Trust develops through thousands of small, consistent actions over time—kept promises, transparent communication, reliable follow-through. But it can shatter in moments through betrayal, deception, or broken agreements.

Trust Recovery

Rebuilding trust after damage requires:

Full acknowledgment of the breach and its impact
Complete transparency about what happened and why
Genuine accountability without excuses or minimisation
Behavioural changes that address underlying causes
Patience for the natural rebuilding process
Consistent demonstration of new patterns over time

Trust recovery can't be rushed. The betrayed partner needs time to observe consistent new behaviour before feeling safe again.

Assessment Questions

Can you rely on your partner to keep their word?
Do you feel safe being vulnerable with your partner?
Is your partner transparent about their life and feelings?
Do you trust your partner's fidelity and loyalty?

How the Elements Interact

The Relationship Paradigm isn't six separate dimensions—it's an integrated system where elements influence each other:

Communication and Connection Feed Each Other

Poor communication creates emotional distance; emotional distance makes communication more difficult. Conversely, a strong connection makes communication easier, and good communication deepens the connection.

Connection and Fun Support Each Other

Playful interactions create emotional connection; feeling connected makes couples more willing to be spontaneous and playful together.

Commitment and Growth Enable Each Other

Strong commitment provides safety for individual growth; personal development keeps partners interesting and reinforces commitment.

Trust Enables Everything

When trust is strong, all other elements flourish. When trust is damaged, every other element becomes tentative and fragile.

Understanding These Interactions Helps You

Recognise why working on one element often improves others
Understand why some persistent problems require addressing multiple elements simultaneously
Avoid focusing on symptoms (communication) when the real issue is elsewhere (trust or connection)

Using the Paradigm in Practice

Initial Assessment Process

Step 1: Individual Rating

Each partner privately rates the relationship on each element (1–10 scale):

1–3: Crisis level requiring immediate attention
4–6: Concerning but manageable with focused effort
7–8: Functioning well with room for improvement
9–10: Excellent and satisfying

Step 2: Comparison Discussion

Partners share ratings and explore differences:

Large discrepancies reveal important perception gaps
Consistent low ratings indicate priority intervention areas
High ratings identify strengths to leverage

Step 3: Pattern Recognition

Look for common patterns:

Crisis Pattern: Multiple elements rated 1–3
Imbalance Pattern: Large rating differences between partners
Stagnation Pattern: Everything rated 5–7 (not crisis, not thriving)
Foundation Issue: Trust rated low, undermining other elements

Step 4: Priority Setting

Based on assessment, identify one to two elements for immediate focus rather than trying to address everything simultaneously.

Common Relationship Patterns

The Crisis Couple

Multiple elements rated 1–3, typically after major betrayal or accumulated damage. Priority: Crisis intervention and trust rebuilding before addressing other elements.

The Passion Paradox

High Connection and Fun (7–9) but low Commitment and Trust (4–6). Relationships feel exciting but lack security for long-term sustainability. Priority: Building consistent trustworthiness and aligned vision.

The Communication Crisis

Low Communication (1–4) dragging down all other areas. When partners can't express needs or navigate differences, every element suffers. Priority: Specific communication skills before addressing other areas.

The Stagnation

Moderate scores (5–7) across all elements; not in crisis but not thriving. Partners feel like roommates living parallel lives. Priority: Revitalisation through intentional growth experiences and fun.

The Individual Imbalance

Significant score differences suggesting partners live in different relationship realities. Priority: Understanding and bridging perceptual gaps before focusing on specific elements.

Intervention Planning

The Relationship Paradigm guides intervention selection:

For Communication Issues (Low Scores)

Structured communication exercises
Active listening training
Conflict resolution protocols
Understanding communication style differences

For Connection Deficits (Low Scores)

Daily connection rituals establishment
Physical affection rebuilding
Emotional vulnerability exercises
Quality time prioritisation

For Commitment Ambiguity (Low Scores)

Vision alignment conversations
Values clarification exercises
Decision-making frameworks
Future planning activities

For Fun Absence (Low Scores)

Novel experience creation
Playfulness exercises
Hobby exploration together
Laughter and levity restoration

For Growth Stagnation (Low Scores)

Individual goal-setting
Shared challenge identification
Learning experiences together
Personal development support

For Trust Damage (Low Scores)

Trust rebuilding protocols
Transparency agreements
Accountability structures
Repair and forgiveness work

For comprehensive intervention protocols for each Relationship Paradigm element, including detailed exercises, structured programmes, and specialised approaches for complex cases, the Duo Coaching Academy provides level-specific training modules with ongoing supervision.

Progress Measurement

The Relationship Paradigm provides objective progress tracking:

Baseline Assessment: Initial ratings establish the starting point

Mid-Work Check: Typically after three sessions, couples rate again to assess progress and adjust focus

Completion Assessment: Final ratings demonstrate change and identify ongoing attention areas

Follow-Up: Three to six months post-completion, couples rate again to assess sustainability

This measurement provides concrete evidence of change rather than vague impressions, maintaining motivation and accountability.

The "Me, You, Us" Integration

Notice how the paradigm visually connects "You" and "Me" to create "Us." This representation emphasises a crucial truth: *healthy relationships require both individual wholeness and genuine partnership.*

The Balance

Too Much "Me": Parallel lives, minimal partnership, connection suffers
Too Much "Us": Enmeshment, identity loss, eventual resentment
Healthy Balance: Strong individuals creating strong partnership

Each Element at Three Levels

Communication

Me: Can I express my needs clearly?
You: Do I understand my partner's needs?
Us: Can we navigate differences productively?

Connection

Me: Am I emotionally available?
You: Do I respond to my partner's bids for connection?
Us: Do we create meaningful togetherness?

Commitment

Me: Am I clear about what I want?
You: Do I understand my partner's vision?
Us: Are we building a shared future?

Fun

Me: Can I experience joy and playfulness?
You: Do I contribute to my partner's enjoyment?
Us: Do we create fun together?

Growth

Me: Am I continuing to develop?
You: Do I support my partner's growth?
Us: Is our relationship evolving?

Trust

Me: Am I trustworthy and reliable?
You: Can I trust my partner?
Us: Have we built a foundation of mutual trust?

Your Foundation Competency: Paradigm Mastery

As a foundation-level practitioner, mastering the Relationship Paradigm means:

Assessment Competency

Conducting initial assessments smoothly
Facilitating productive comparison discussions
Recognising common patterns quickly
Identifying priority intervention areas

Intervention Planning

Selecting appropriate interventions for each element
Understanding when to address multiple elements
Knowing when element imbalances require rebalancing
Recognising when trust work must precede other interventions

Progress Tracking

Using re-assessment to measure change
Adjusting interventions based on progress
Celebrating improvements to maintain motivation
Identifying areas needing ongoing attention

This competency forms the foundation for everything that follows in Duo Coaching implementation.

Integration and Self-Reflection

Foundation Level Skills Addressed in This Chapter

Paradigm Understanding: Comprehensive knowledge of all six elements and their interactions

Assessment Competency: Ability to conduct and interpret Relationship Paradigm assessments
Pattern Recognition: Identifying common relationship patterns from assessment results
Intervention Planning: Selecting appropriate interventions based on paradigm results

Reflection Questions

Which Relationship Paradigm element do you think is most commonly deficient in your current caseload?
How might using the paradigm assessment change your initial sessions with couples?
Can you identify which pattern (Crisis, Passion Paradox, Stagnation, etc.) best describes two to three current clients?
What additional skills do you need to use the paradigm confidently as both assessment and intervention guide?

Self-assessment: Rate your current Relationship Paradigm competency:
Trust your gut response. What number first comes to mind when you consider how ready you feel to take this further?

Score	*Interpretation*
1–2	Need more practice with assessment and interpretation
3–4	Grasping concepts but need experience applying them
5–6	Solid foundation ready to use paradigm in practice
7+	Strong competency ready to train others in paradigm use

Practice Exercise: Take a current couple client and retrospectively rate them on each element (as you perceive their relationship). Then consider: What pattern do they represent? What would be your priority intervention areas? How might this change your treatment approach?

"The Relationship Paradigm transforms vague relationship dissatisfaction into specific, measurable, achievable goals—providing both couples and therapists with clear direction for transformative work."

Coming Next: Chapter 6—Finding and Working with a Co-therapist

You understand the framework and assessment tools, but implementing Duo Coaching requires something many practitioners find daunting: a co-therapy partnership. Chapter 6 demystifies this crucial element with practical guidance for finding, vetting, and building effective therapeutic partnerships.

Discover the essential qualities that predict co-therapy success beyond mere competence—complementary styles, compatible values, emotional maturity, and collaborative capacity. You'll learn structured approaches for trial sessions that reveal compatibility before committing, communication protocols that prevent misunderstandings, and conflict resolution processes that strengthen rather than damage partnerships.

Chapter 6 also addresses the fears that keep practitioners isolated: What if we disagree in session? How do we handle different theoretical orientations? What about revenue sharing and liability? Practical answers replace anxiety with confidence. Your co-therapy partnership begins here.

Chapter 6

Finding and Working with a Co-therapist

Building and Maintaining Effective Partnerships

Image 6 Two Sailboats Repeated.

"Companionship at Sea: No Vessel Sails Alone"

> What we seek from clients is openness and honesty without which we cannot help. We have a wide range of tools and techniques and will use whatever is going to get the best results for each couple and each individual.
>
> —From *Reinventing*

The Heart of Duo Coaching: Why Two Therapists Transform Everything

After 15 years of co-therapy practice with hundreds of couples, I can say with certainty that finding the right therapeutic partner will transform not only your

DOI: 10.4324/9781003715627-9

effectiveness with couples but your entire professional experience. The co-therapy relationship isn't simply an add-on to traditional therapy or a luxury for couples who can afford extra professional attention. The presence of two skilled therapists working in harmony creates qualitatively different therapeutic possibilities that cannot be replicated through single-therapist approaches.

This isn't a theoretical preference—it is a practical reality learned through direct experience of both models.

Why Traditional Solo Practice Falls Short

Working alone with couples, even with exceptional skill, creates inherent limitations that affect therapeutic outcomes:

The Triangulation Trap

With one therapist and two clients, someone always risks feeling like the odd one out. Despite your best intentions to remain neutral, couples will unconsciously attempt to recruit you as an ally in their relationship dynamics.

I remember my own experience as the male partner sitting with a female therapist. No matter how professionally neutral she remained, I felt somehow marginal—that she naturally understood my partner's perspective better than mine. This wasn't her fault; it was the geometry of the situation. One therapist, two clients, three points creating an inevitable triangle where someone feels outside.

The Overwhelm Factor

Simultaneously tracking two individual histories, their joint dynamics, managing your own countertransference responses to both partners, and selecting appropriate interventions can overwhelm even the most experienced practitioners.

Solo couple therapists must:

Track both partners' verbal and non-verbal communication
Monitor the interaction patterns between them
Manage their own emotional responses to each individual
Notice what's happening in the therapeutic relationship with both
Select and implement interventions
Maintain therapeutic balance and neutrality
Track time and session structure

It's like being a one-person orchestra—technically possible, but inevitably something gets less attention than it deserves.

The Gender Balance Challenge

Many couples benefit from having both male and female perspectives available, particularly when working through issues related to gender roles, communication styles, or sexual intimacy.

When Jennifer talked about feeling invisible in her marriage, having Maria present added a dimension I couldn't provide alone. When Michael described his experience of being criticised, I could offer understanding from lived male experience that complemented Maria's perspective. Neither perspective is inherently superior—together they create a fuller understanding.

The Modelling Deficit

Couples in distress often lack examples of healthy collaboration, respectful disagreement, and effective communication. A single therapist cannot model partnership dynamics—you can talk about them, but you can't demonstrate them in action.

When couples watch Maria and me navigate differences in therapeutic approach, respectfully disagree about directions to take, support each other's contributions, and coordinate our efforts towards shared goals, they're witnessing a healthy partnership. This modelling often teaches more powerfully than any words we could offer.

What Co-therapy Makes Possible

Balanced Attention and Reduced Triangulation

With two therapists, each partner can feel they have someone who might particularly understand their perspective, dramatically reducing the likelihood that either will feel marginalised or misunderstood.

This doesn't mean creating "his therapist" and "her therapist"—we work as a unified team. But inevitably, certain moments find one partner feeling more understood by one therapist, other moments by the other. This natural flow prevents the fixed triangulation that single-therapist work can create.

Enhanced Observation and Assessment

Four eyes and ears notice different aspects of couple dynamics. While one therapist focuses on verbal content, the other might observe non-verbal communication. While I'm tracking one partner's breakthrough, Maria might notice the other's response. This enhanced observation leads to richer understanding and more targeted interventions.

Maria might lean towards me during a session and quietly say, "Notice Michael's hands—they're clenched even though his words sound calm." That observation shifts my awareness, allowing intervention I would have missed working alone.

Real-time Consultation

The presence of a colleague allows for subtle consultation during sessions—a glance, a gesture, or a brief sidebar that enriches your understanding and responsiveness without interrupting the therapeutic flow.

Maria and I have developed non-verbal communication so refined that a raised eyebrow can mean "I'm noticing something here—shall we explore this?" A slight head tilt might indicate "I think we need to shift direction." This real-time collaboration enhances responsiveness beyond what either could achieve alone.

Live Modelling of a Healthy Partnership

Two therapists working together demonstrate respectful disagreement, mutual support, collaborative problem-solving, and effective communication in real-time. Couples witness healthy partnership dynamics rather than just hearing about them.

Couples frequently comment on what they learn from watching us work together:

"You two don't always agree, but you figure it out respectfully."
"I love how you build on each other's ideas rather than competing."
"You obviously trust each other—that's what we want to create."

This modelling happens without deliberate teaching—it emerges naturally from authentic professional partnership.

Shared Therapeutic Load

Instead of carrying the entire responsibility for therapeutic progress, co-therapists share the holding, the noticing, the responding. When one therapist needs to step back to process what's emerging, the other maintains the therapeutic connection.

When sessions become emotionally intense—which they often do in three-and-a-half-hour containers—we can support each other as well as the couple. The loneliness of solo practice, that sense of carrying everything yourself, gets replaced by genuine collaboration.

The Creation of Liminal Space

Perhaps most remarkably, co-therapy creates a quality of liminal space that neither therapist could achieve alone. There's something about the dynamic between two therapists working in harmony that generates profound safety and possibility.

Couples consistently tell us they feel able to share things they've never spoken aloud—not just to us, but to each other. Secrets held for decades, vulnerabilities they thought were too dangerous to express, truths they believed would end their relationship.

This threshold space we co-create seems to suspend ordinary rules of interaction, allowing couples to access parts of themselves and their relationship that remain hidden in everyday life. Perhaps it's the modelling of healthy partnership they witness between us, or the sense that they're held by something larger than any individual perspective. Whatever creates it, this liminal space consistently enables the authentic expression and emotional risk-taking that transformation requires.

Finding Your Co-therapist: Essential Considerations

Finding the right co-therapy partner is as important as finding the right life partner—perhaps more so, given the professional responsibilities involved. This section guides you through the essential considerations.

Core Qualities to Seek

Shared Vision and Values

Before anything else, you need alignment on fundamental questions:

What's your philosophy about relationships and how they change?
What do you believe creates lasting transformation?
How do you understand the therapist's role?
What ethical principles guide your work?

Maria and I discovered immediate alignment on core values: relationships can transform profoundly when provided proper support; couples contain their own wisdom for healing; our role is facilitating rather than fixing; extended time and multiple perspectives create possibilities unavailable in traditional models.

Without this foundational alignment, technical skills matter little.

Complementary Rather Than Identical Skills

You're not seeking a clone of yourself but someone whose skills complement yours. Different backgrounds create richness; identical training creates redundancy.

My background in business, coaching, and eclectic therapeutic approaches complements Maria's foundation in integrative counselling and Relate training. Her attention to emotional process balances my focus on practical outcomes. Together, we create a more complete therapeutic response than either could offer independently.

Personal Chemistry and Mutual Respect

You'll spend extended time in intimate professional space with this person. Do you genuinely like and respect them? Can you imagine weathering disagreements constructively? Do you feel energised or drained by their presence?

When Maria and I first met, there was immediate ease—conversation flowed naturally, our communication styles meshed, and we found ourselves genuinely enjoying the exploration of how we might work together. That personal chemistry has sustained us through challenging cases and difficult moments.

Emotional Maturity and Self-awareness

Co-therapy requires people who can:

Accept feedback without defensiveness
Acknowledge mistakes and limitations
Share credit and responsibility
Manage their own emotional responses
Communicate about difficulties directly

Look for evidence of ongoing personal development work—therapy, supervision, spiritual practice, whatever creates genuine self-awareness and emotional regulation capacity.

Commitment to the Partnership

Co-therapy requires significant commitment:

Regular meeting time for case discussion and planning
Coordination of complex schedules
Shared professional development
Working through inevitable conflicts
Long-term stability rather than short-term convenience

Ensure potential partners understand and accept these requirements before beginning.

Practical Considerations

Licensing and Professional Background

Consider what licensing or registration requirements exist in your jurisdiction. Some locations require both practitioners to hold specific credentials; others allow more flexibility. Understanding legal requirements prevents future complications.

Gender Considerations

While not absolutely essential, having male-female co-therapy teams offers advantages for most couples. Same-gender teams can work beautifully, particularly with same-gender couples or when working within specific cultural contexts where gender balance has different meanings.

Availability and Schedule Compatibility

Extended sessions demand coordinated availability. Can you both commit to 3.5-hour blocks? Do your schedules align sufficiently for regular joint sessions? What happens when one partner has other commitments?

Financial Arrangements

How will fees be divided? What about preparation time, case discussion, and professional development? Clear financial agreements prevent later resentment.

Geographic Proximity

Ideally, co-therapists live within a reasonable distance, allowing face-to-face collaboration and shared physical space. Remote co-therapy is possible but loses important elements of the partnership dynamic.

The Courtship Phase: Testing Compatibility

Don't rush into a formal co-therapy partnership. Create a careful courtship process that tests compatibility before full commitment.

Initial Exploratory Conversations

Begin with extended conversations exploring:

Professional backgrounds and training
Philosophy about relationships and therapy
Previous co-therapy experience (if any)
What you hope to create through partnership
Concerns or reservations about co-therapy work
Practical considerations and constraints

Take time—several meetings over weeks or months—to ensure alignment runs deep.

Observing Each Other's Work

If possible, observe each other working. Attend each other's workshops, observe individual sessions (with appropriate consent), or collaborate on low-stakes projects before committing to couple work together.

Starting with a Trial Case

Begin your partnership with one or two couples, treating this as a trial period. After each session, debrief thoroughly:

What worked well in our collaboration?
Where did we struggle to coordinate?
What did couples notice about our partnership?
Do we want to continue working together?

Honest assessment during trial phases prevents deeper investment in partnerships that won't ultimately serve.

Supervision and Third-Party Perspective

Consider engaging a supervisor experienced in co-therapy to observe your early work together and provide feedback about partnership dynamics, strengths, and areas needing development.

Maria's Perspective: Transitioning to Duo Coaching

In Maria's own words:

It was February 2017 when I received an email out of the blue from Neil, stating that we hadn't met but as a counsellor in the area could he bounce a thought off me. I was then introduced to Duo Coaching, a very different dynamic of having two therapists working with a couple and offering a very intensive programme of coaching and counselling. I was intrigued.

As a Relate Counsellor and Supervisor working within a 50-minute systemic model with back-to-back clients in Southampton, this approach seemed both exciting and daunting.

He asked if I had the capacity and desire to do more relationship counselling and could there be synergy in us working together? It would take some rearrangement of working hours and childcare, but I could have the capacity. Whether there was synergy was yet to be seen.

The First Meeting: Anticipation and Discovery

I agreed to meet with Neil on 13 March 2017. I was somewhat anxious driving to Brockenhurst after a Group Supervision meeting in Winchester—counselling has always been individual work for me, so the thought of working with someone else was rather daunting, and I didn't know what to expect.

Neil was engaging, enthusiastic, and highly experienced. His calm and considered manner made it a comfortable meeting, and I came away with a feeling of really being able to help and support couples in their counselling journey to a greater extent than I had been achieving. We agreed to meet again that week, and I was offered the opportunity to join Neil as the second member of Duo Coaching on 17 March 2017.

The First Session: Everything I Thought I Knew Was Challenged

Our first clients arrived the following week for a 3½ hour initial session. It felt such a long time, and I had many imposter syndrome moments sitting next to Neil while he expertly navigated the couple through their relationship history and offered exercises to help them understand what and who were important. I was able to watch and learn and soon realised how beneficial the allowance of extra time enabled clients to move forward more than the traditional 50-minute model.

We were able to learn so much about the couple and how they had come to the impasse in their relationship. They both had the chance to reveal their perspective on events and the impact of them. The extended time meant we could go deep into their histories, explore patterns without rushing, and begin transformation work in that first session rather than spending weeks building foundation.

Learning to Navigate Together

The transition from solo practice to co-therapy partnership required learning new skills I hadn't anticipated:

Sharing Therapeutic Space: I'd been trained to hold space alone—learning to share that holding with another practitioner felt vulnerable initially. What if we disagreed? What if I missed something Neil saw? What if couples preferred his style to mine?

Real-Time Coordination: Solo practitioners can follow their intuition without negotiation. Co-therapy requires constant awareness of your partner's direction and subtle coordination. Neil and I developed non-verbal communication that allows seamless collaboration, but this took time and attention to develop.

Different Modalities: Neil's eclectic approach drew from modalities I hadn't trained in—NLP (Neuro Linguistic Programming), Clean Language, constellation work. Rather than seeing this as threatening, I learned to view it as expansion. He opened doors to techniques that enhanced my existing skills rather than replacing them.

Deeper Vulnerability: Working alongside another practitioner meant my limitations became visible. Neil witnessed when I struggled, when interventions didn't land, when I needed support. Initially uncomfortable, this visibility ultimately created professional growth I couldn't have achieved alone.

The Rewards: Why I'd Never Return to Solo Practice

Eight years later, I can't imagine returning to the single-therapist model. What co-therapy has given me—and through me, our clients—far exceeds what I left behind:

Enhanced Effectiveness: We simply achieve better outcomes. Couples transform more completely, more quickly, more sustainably than anything I accomplished working alone.

Professional Growth: Neil's different background continuously teaches me new approaches. Our case discussions deepen my understanding. The partnership itself models what I'm trying to help couples create.

Shared Joy and Challenge: The loneliness of solo practice has been replaced by genuine collaboration. When work is hard, I have a partner. When breakthroughs happen, we celebrate together. The work feels sustainable in ways it never did alone.

Continuous Learning: Every session teaches me something new—about relationships, about therapy, about myself. The presence of another skilled practitioner creates learning opportunities unavailable in solo work.

Yes, there's a learning curve. Yes, you'll question your competence more often than feels comfortable. But the results—for both your clients and your own professional fulfilment—justify the effort.

Neil's Perspective: The Power of Shared Navigation

My partnership with Maria has transformed not just our effectiveness with clients, but my entire experience as a practitioner.

Before co-therapy, I carried the full weight of each couple's journey alone—responsible for tracking every dynamic, catching every subtle shift, holding space for both partners while maintaining therapeutic balance. It was like single-handed sailing in challenging waters: possible, but exhausting and limiting. You can only be in one place at a time, see from one perspective, respond to one element while potentially missing others.

Working with Maria has revealed what becomes possible when two skilled practitioners navigate together. While I'm focused on one partner's breakthrough, she's tracking the other's response. When I'm following one line of exploration, she's noticing patterns I might miss. We can literally be in different places in the room simultaneously, creating multiple perspectives on the same dynamic. It's like having depth perception for relationship work—seeing dimensions that remain invisible to single-vision approaches.

Perhaps most powerfully, our different backgrounds and perspectives create richness of response that neither of us could achieve alone. Maria's integrative counselling foundation complements my more eclectic, business-informed approach. Her attention to emotional process balances my focus on practical outcomes. Together, we create a more complete therapeutic response than either could offer independently.

Building and Maintaining the Partnership

Finding the right co-therapist is just the beginning. Maintaining an effective partnership requires ongoing attention and care.

Regular Partnership Meetings

Schedule dedicated time separate from case discussions to focus on the partnership itself:

How is our working relationship?
What's working well in our collaboration?
Where are we struggling?
What do we each need more or less of?
How are we managing the practical aspects of our partnership?

These meta-conversations prevent small issues from becoming larger problems.

Clear Communication Protocols

Before Sessions: Brief pre-session discussions ensure alignment on approach, goals, and any particular concerns.

During Sessions: Develop non-verbal signals for real-time communication. We use:

Eyebrow raise: "I'm noticing something—shall we explore?"
Slight head tilt: "I think we need to shift direction"
Hand gesture: "I'd like to intervene here"

After Sessions: Immediate post-session debriefs capture fresh observations and coordinate follow-up planning.

Managing Disagreements Constructively

Co-therapists will disagree—about assessment, intervention choices, case conceptualisation, and practical matters. How you handle disagreement determines partnership success or failure.

Principles for Healthy Disagreement

Never disagree openly in front of couples (save it for debrief)
Assume good intentions even when perspectives differ
Focus on what serves the couple rather than who's right
Be willing to try your partner's approach when uncertain
Learn from outcomes rather than defending original positions

When Maria and I disagree about direction, we often explicitly tell couples: "Maria sees this one way, I see it slightly differently. Let's try both and see what serves you better." This transparency models healthy disagreement while serving the couple.

Sharing Credit and Responsibility

Ego can poison co-therapy partnerships. Both therapists must be willing to:

Share credit for successes equally
Take responsibility for challenges jointly
Celebrate partner's contributions genuinely
Acknowledge partner's insights publicly
Support partner when they're struggling

This requires emotional maturity and genuine commitment to partnership over personal recognition.

Managing Power Dynamics

Co-therapy partnerships often involve different levels of experience, training, or public recognition. The more experienced or prominent practitioner must actively work to:

Create space for partner's contributions
Defer to partner's expertise when appropriate
Avoid dominating session time or decision-making
Share leadership rather than establishing hierarchy

The less experienced practitioner must:

Bring full presence and contribution despite insecurity
Speak up when intuition suggests different direction
Trust their own perceptions and skills
Grow into equal partnership rather than remaining junior

Ongoing Development Together

Strong partnerships invest in shared development:

Attend trainings and workshops together
Read and discuss relevant literature
Engage in shared supervision
Practice new techniques with each other before using with clients
Celebrate learning and growth as partners

This shared development creates a common language, aligned understanding, and continuous partnership evolution.

When Partnerships End or Evolve

Not all co-therapy partnerships last forever. Health issues, relocations, career changes, or simply growing in different directions can end even successful partnerships.

Recognising When Partnership Isn't Working

Signs that partnership needs reassessment:

Increasing tension or resentment
Difficulty communicating about difficulties
Couples noticing friction between therapists
One or both partners dreading sessions together
Consistent disagreement about fundamental approaches
Loss of respect or trust

When these signs emerge, honest conversation about partnership viability serves everyone better than struggling forward.

Ending Partnerships with Grace

If partnership must end:

Have honest conversations about reasons
Create transition plans for existing couples
Maintain professional respect regardless of reasons
Learn from the experience rather than assigning blame
Leave door open for future collaboration if appropriate

My partnership with my first co-therapist, Cathy, ended when health issues required her to step back. Though difficult, we navigated the transition with mutual respect, ensuring couples received continued care while honouring her need to prioritise health.

Finding New Partners After Partnership Ends

The transition to a new co-therapy partner requires similar care as initial partnership development. Existing clients need reassurance about continuity while new partnership dynamics develop.

The Co-therapy Relationship as a Model

Perhaps the most powerful aspect of co-therapy is what it models for couples. They witness two people with different perspectives, backgrounds, and approaches working together respectfully and effectively towards shared goals. In a world where collaboration often feels impossible and differences seem irreconcilable, your co-therapy partnership becomes a living demonstration that unity doesn't require uniformity.

Your willingness to share power, credit, and responsibility models the very partnership dynamics your clients are trying to create in their own relationships. The vulnerability required to work this closely with another professional, accepting feedback and acknowledging limitations, demonstrates the courage that intimate partnership requires.

Conclusion: The Foundation of Transformation

Finding and developing the right co-therapy partnership may be the most important decision you make in implementing the Duo Coaching Framework. Take the time to do it thoughtfully, invest in developing it consciously, and trust that the right partnership will enhance not only your professional effectiveness but your personal understanding of what makes relationships truly work.

The couples you serve together witness something powerful beyond therapeutic technique—they see genuine partnership in action. They learn not through instruction but through observation that two people can work together effectively, disagree respectfully, support each other genuinely, and create something together that neither could achieve alone.

In the next chapter, we'll explore the practical considerations of setting up your Duo Coaching practice—the physical space, legal framework, and business structure that support your co-therapy partnership and serve couples seeking transformation.

> The feedback, support, and shared responsibility create conditions for taking therapeutic risks and exploring innovative approaches that would feel too daunting to attempt alone.
>
> —From *Reinventing*

From Strangers to Partners: The Courtship Process

You've learned the theory of co-therapy partnerships—what to look for, how to assess compatibility, why complementary styles matter. But what does the actual formation process *feel* like? How do two skilled therapists navigate the awkwardness, uncertainty, and vulnerability of building a working relationship?

Let's rewind to the beginning of Maya and James's partnership—before Susan and David, before their rupture and repair, before any clients at all. Let's watch them navigate the delicate courtship process that every co-therapy partnership must undergo.

This is where professional relationships begin: with curiosity, caution, and tentative hope.

INTERLUDE: MAYA & JAMES *The Beginning*

The Duo Coaching Academy Training (Day 1)

Maya

The training room is full of therapists—about twenty people arranged in a circle. Maya scans the room during introductions, assessing. Old habit from years of practice: Who's here? What are their styles? Anyone interesting?

Her eyes land on a man across the circle. Late thirties, good posture, expensive notebook. When it's his turn, he introduces himself: "James Crawford. Background in organizational psychology, executive team coaching. Curious about bringing systemic approaches to couples work."

Too corporate, Maya thinks. *Probably all structure, no soul.*

James

He notices her during the break. She's talking animatedly with another participant, hands moving as she speaks. Lots of warmth, lots of emotional language. When she introduces herself to the group, she says: "Maya Kapadia. Integrative counseling background—Person-Centred, Gestalt. I work phenomenologically. Trust what emerges."

Too feelings-focused, James thinks. *Probably all intuition, no framework.*

They don't speak to each other all day.

The Duo Coaching Academy Training (Day 2)

The Pairing

The trainers announce: "Today we're doing demonstration work. You'll be paired randomly. One pair will work with a role-play couple while the rest observe."

Maya and James get paired together. Of course.

They sit next to each other awkwardly. The trainers (a seasoned Duo Coaching pair) role-play a couple in crisis—20 years together, drifted apart, considering separation.

"You have thirty minutes," the trainers say. "Show us what you'd do."

Maya

Her heart is racing. She's never worked with a co-therapist before. And this guy—all structure and systems—is going to want to plan everything out, control the process.

But there's no time to plan. The role-play starts.

She follows her instinct. Leans towards the "wife": "Tell me about when you first met. What drew you to him?"

A story unfolds. Beautiful, tender. Maya holds the space, asks gentle questions.

Then James speaks, and she tenses, waiting for him to interrupt the flow.

James

He watches Maya work. She's good at this—creating emotional safety, drawing out vulnerability. The "wife" is opening up in ways that surprise him.

But he's noticing the pattern. The circular dynamic. The way the "husband" withdraws when the "wife" pursues.

He leans forward. "I'm noticing something. When she reaches toward you emotionally, you step back. And when you step back, she reaches more. It's like a dance you both know really well."

The "husband" nods slowly. "Yeah. That's … that's exactly it."

Maya glances at James. Something passes between them—recognition.

The Breakthrough

What happens next surprises them both. They find a rhythm.

Maya draws out the emotion: "What's the loneliest moment been for you?"

James names the pattern: "You're protecting each other from disappointment by not asking for anything."

Maya reflects the grief beneath: "There's such loneliness in that protection."

James clarifies the direction: "So what do you both actually want? Not what you don't want—what do you want?"

The role-play couple (their trainers) both tear up. One says, quietly: "That was really powerful. You two found something together that neither could have found alone."

After, the group applauds. Maya and James sit in stunned silence.

James

"That was …" James doesn't know how to finish the sentence.

"I know," Maya says. "I couldn't have done that alone."

"Neither could I."

A long pause. Then James says: "Want to get coffee after this?"

The Coffee Meeting (One Week Later)

The Awkward Beginning

They meet at a café near Maya's practice. Small talk about the training, about the weather. Then silence.

James clears his throat. "So. I've been thinking about what happened. When we worked together."

"Me too."

"I think …" He chooses words carefully. "I think we're very different. But maybe that's the point?"

"Maybe." Maya wraps her hands around her chai. "I was ready to dislike you on Day 1. Thought you'd be too rigid, too cognitive."

"I thought you'd be too emotional. Too unstructured."

They both laugh, a bit.

"But when we actually worked together," Maya continues, "your structure gave me freedom. I could follow the emotion because you were holding the framework."

"And your emotional attunement meant I didn't have to," James says. "I could see the patterns because you were holding the feelings."

Another silence, but this one feels different. Possibility.

The Vulnerable Questions

"Can I ask you something?" Maya says. "What scared you during the training?"

James is surprised by the directness. Considers his answer. "The bit where we had to notice our own parts. I realised I use competence to avoid vulnerability."

Long pause. "You?"

"I realised I can feel everyone's pain except my own."

Longer pause. They're both sitting with that.

"Maybe we need each other more than we realised," James says quietly.

The Practical Reality

"Okay, so if we were actually going to do this," Maya says, "we'd need to figure out logistics. Room space, fees, how we split income, scheduling …"

"Partnership agreement," James says. "Clear from the start."

"And supervision. I'd want us to have joint supervision, not just our individual supervisors."

"Agreed." James pulls out his notebook. "Should we make a list?"

Maya smiles. "Of course you have a notebook."

"Always."

They spend the next hour sketching out possibilities:

Could they share Maya's practice space three days a week?
50/50 fee split seems fair

Both keep their individual practices alongside Duo work
Monthly partnership check-ins built in from the start
Joint supervision at least monthly

"This is feeling real," Maya says.

"It is." James looks at her. "Are you scared?"

"Terrified. You?"

"Same."

"Good," Maya says. "If we weren't scared, we probably wouldn't be taking it seriously enough."

Their First Practice Session (Two Weeks Later)

The Set-Up

James arrives at Maya's practice room. She's rearranged the furniture—four chairs in a gentle arc, water glasses ready, tissues positioned.

"This feels very official," he says.

"Mock couple therapy," Maya reminds him. "We're going to practice on ourselves before we inflict ourselves on real clients."

"Harsh but fair."

They've asked two colleagues to role-play a couple for them. Married ten years, communication breakdown, considering counselling. Standard presenting issue.

The Awkwardness

It's clunky at first. They both go to speak at the same time. Stop. Gesture for the other to continue. More awkward silence.

James tries a structured opening. "Let's start with each of you telling us about the relationship. How you met, what drew you together …"

Maya jumps in with emotion. "And what it's like for you right now, being here together …"

They're talking over each other. Not flowing.

The role-play couple looks confused.

The Breakthrough (Again)

But then, about 20 minutes in, something clicks.

James asks a question. Maya lets it breathe. Waits.

Maya makes a reflection. James builds on it and adds structure.

He names a pattern. She explores the feeling underneath.

By the end of the hour, they're moving together like they've done this for years.

The Debrief

After the colleagues leave, Maya and James sit in silence.

"That was painful at first," James admits.

"So painful. We were stepping on each other."

"But then ..."

"Then it worked," Maya finishes. "Like the training. We found the rhythm."

"We need to practise more," James says. "A lot more. Get comfortable with the coordination."

"Agreed. But James ..." Maya looks at him. "I think this could actually work. Like, really work."

"Yeah," he says. "I think so too."

Their Agreement (One Month Later)

The Document

They're sitting with a two-page partnership agreement James drafted. Maya's been reading it carefully.

"This is thorough," she says.

"Too thorough?"

"No. Actually ... it makes me feel safe. Everything's explicit. No assumptions."

The agreement covers:

Financial arrangements: 50/50 split, separate billing, how expenses are shared

Decision-making: Consensus required for taking on new couples; either can veto

Disagreements: Commitment to address them in supervision, not let them fester

Communication: Weekly check-ins, immediate post-session debriefs

Exit strategy: How they'd wind down the partnership if needed, with six months' notice

"The exit strategy feels pessimistic," Maya says.

"Or realistic," James counters. "Better to agree now, before we're in conflict."

"That's actually very wise."

The Commitment

"So," James says. "Do we do this? Actually commit to building a co-therapy practice?"

Maya takes a breath. "I think we do. But can we agree on something else, not in the document?"

"What?"

"That we'll be honest with each other. About what's working, what isn't, when we're frustrated, when we're scared. No British politeness protecting us from truth."

James smiles. "I can do that. Scary, but I can do it."

"And one more thing," Maya says. "Can we acknowledge this is a relationship? Not romantic, obviously, but a real relationship. With all the vulnerability and maintenance that requires."

"It is a relationship," James agrees. "Maybe the most important professional relationship either of us will have."

They both sit with that.

Then James extends his hand. "Partners?"

Maya shakes it. "Partners."

Preparing for Susan and David (Three Months Later)

The Night Before

James texts Maya at 10 PM: *"I've prepared too much for tomorrow, haven't I?"*

Maya replies: *"I haven't prepared enough."*

James: *"We balance each other."*

Maya: *"We do. See you at 9:30 to set up?"*

James: *"I'll bring coffee. You make the chai."*

The Morning of

They're in the practice room at 9:30. James is arranging his notes. Maya is checking the pebbles bowl for the third time.

"What if we can't help them?" Maya asks.

"Then we'll fail together," James says. "Come on, your chai's getting cold."

They sit for a moment in comfortable silence. Three months ago, they were strangers who thought they wouldn't like each other. Now they're about to embark on the most intensive work either has attempted.

"Ready?" James asks.

"No," Maya says. "But let's do it anyway."

The buzzer rings. Susan and David have arrived.

What This Demonstrates about Partnership Formation

Maya and James's journey from strangers to partners illustrates the essential phases every co-therapy relationship must navigate:

Phase 1: Initial Assessment and Judgment (Day 1)

Both made quick judgments based on surface impressions
Both were wrong in their assumptions
First impressions rarely capture the full person
Your learning: Don't dismiss potential partners too quickly

Phase 2: Unexpected Discovery (Day 2)

Working together revealed what talking couldn't
Their differences became complementary under pressure
The "stereo effect" emerged naturally
Your learning: Try working together before deciding compatibility

Phase 3: Exploratory Conversation (Coffee Meeting)

Moved beyond logistics to vulnerability
Shared fears and growth edges
Discovered mutual need beneath the differences
Your learning: Ask deep questions early—"What scared you? What do you struggle with?"

Phase 4: Practical Planning

Created clear agreements about money, decisions, boundaries
Built in maintenance structures (check-ins, supervision)
Addressed "what if this fails?" proactively
Your learning: Romance is for romantic relationships; professional partnerships need clear contracts

Phase 5: Practice and Refinement

Started clunky, found rhythm through repetition
Learned each other's signals and timing
Built confidence before working with real clients
Your learning: Practice extensively in low-stakes situations first

Phase 6: Commitment with Eyes Open

Acknowledged this as a real relationship requiring maintenance
Named the vulnerability inherent in partnership

Committed despite fear, not without fear
Your learning: Good partnerships embrace uncertainty together

Critical Success Factors

Notice what made Maya and James's partnership successful from the start:

Complementary styles recognised as strength, not weakness

Structure + intuition = stereo effect
Neither tried to make the other "more like me"

Vulnerability about fears and limitations

James admitted using competence to avoid vulnerability
Maya admitted feeling everyone's pain except her own
This honesty created safety

Explicit agreements before starting

Clear financial arrangements
Decision-making processes
Exit strategy if needed
Regular maintenance built in

Willingness to practise before real stakes

Mock sessions with colleagues
Learning coordination in safety
Building rhythm before clients arrived

Commitment to ongoing communication

Weekly check-ins
Immediate post-session debriefs
Joint supervision
Permission to name difficulties

What They Got Right (That Many Partnerships Miss)

They acknowledged partnership as relationship: Too many co-therapists treat the partnership as merely logistical—a business arrangement, not a relational one. Maya and James understood from the beginning: This is a relationship requiring vulnerability, maintenance, repair, and ongoing attention.

They planned for endings: The exit strategy in their agreement wasn't pessimistic—it was realistic. Knowing how to end well gave them freedom to commit fully.

They built in maintenance structures: They didn't wait for problems to emerge before creating support systems. Weekly check-ins and monthly supervision were built in from day one.

They practiced before performing: Many partnerships jump straight to clients. Maya and James invested time practicing coordination, building trust, finding rhythm—all before the pressure of real clients.

They named their fears: Instead of projecting confidence they didn't feel, they admitted: "I'm terrified." This honesty created an authentic connection.

Your Partnership Formation Checklist

Based on Maya and James's journey, use this checklist as you build your own co-therapy partnership:

Initial Assessment Phase

Work together in practice situations before committing
Notice complementary strengths, not just differences
Ask vulnerable questions: What do you struggle with? What activates you?

Agreement Phase

Create written partnership agreement covering finances, decisions, communication
Include exit strategy (how to end well if needed)
Build in regular maintenance structures from the start

Practice Phase

Minimum three to five practice sessions with mock couples before real clients
Debrief thoroughly after each: What worked? What felt clunky?
Develop your non-verbal communication signals

First Client Phase

Choose moderate-complexity couple (not your hardest case)
Debrief after every session for the first three clients
Seek supervision focused on partnership dynamics, not just case content

Ongoing Maintenance

Weekly or bi-weekly partnership check-ins separate from case discussions
Monthly joint supervision
Annual partnership review: How are we doing? What needs adjustment?

The Journey Continues

You've now seen Maya and James at three points in their journey:

This chapter: The beginning—strangers becoming partners
Chapter 11: The crisis—rupture and repair three months in
Chapter 21: Years later—mature partnership supervising others

Each phase teaches different lessons. The beginning teaches courage—the willingness to try despite uncertainty. The crisis teaches humility—the necessity of doing your own work. The maturity (which you'll see in the final chapters) teaches sustainability—how to maintain and deepen partnership over the years.

For now, remember James and Maya in that practice room before Susan and David arrived:

"What if we can't help them?"

"Then we'll fail together."

That's partnership—not the absence of fear, but the willingness to face it together.

Integration and Self-reflection

Foundation Level Skills Addressed in This Chapter

Partner Selection: Identifying co-therapists with complementary skills and compatible approaches

Collaborative Communication: Developing effective coordination and real-time responsiveness

Rupture and Repair: Managing inevitable tensions and misalignments productively

Professional Growth: Learning from partnership challenges to strengthen practice

Reflection Questions

What qualities and skills do you most need in a co-therapist?
What do you offer a partnership?
How comfortable are you with direct, honest communication about session dynamics and concerns?
What would make it difficult for you to work with a co-therapist? How might you address this?
How do you typically handle professional disagreements or tensions with colleagues?

Self-assessment: How ready are you to work effectively in co-therapist partnership?

Trust your gut response. What number first comes to mind when you consider how ready you feel to take this further?

Score	*Interpretation*
1–2	Need significant development in collaborative skills before partnership
3–4	Developing partnership capacity with structured support

(*Continued*)

Score	*Interpretation*
5–6	Strong collaborative skills with effective communication
7+	Masterful partnership dynamics with ability to navigate complexity

Next Steps: Begin conversations with potential co-therapists. Practice honest communication about your working style and needs. Seek supervision support during partnership formation and challenges.

Note: *The co-therapy relationship stands at the absolute centre of the Duo Coaching Framework. Finding the right therapeutic partner may be the most important decision you make in implementing this approach—one that transforms not only your effectiveness with couples but your entire professional experience. The partnership requires as much attention, care, and ongoing development as the couple relationships you serve together. When two therapists create therapeutic space collaboratively, couples witness genuine partnership in action—perhaps the most powerful intervention of all.*

Coming Next: Chapter 7—Session Structure and Process

Finding your co-therapist is the first step; working together effectively requires a structured process. Chapter 7 provides detailed frameworks for managing 3.5-hour intensive sessions from opening to closure.

You'll discover the rhythm of extended sessions: how to create safety that allows vulnerability, when to intensify therapeutic pressure and when to ease it, how to navigate co-therapy coordination in real-time, techniques for maintaining energy through extended work, and strategies for bringing couples to completion rather than merely stopping when time expires.

Chapter 7 transforms theory into practice with session-by-session guidance, intervention timing, and the moment-to-moment decision-making that separates adequate from transformative intensive work. The practical implementation you need awaits.

Chapter 7

Session Structure and Process

Managing Intensive Sessions

Image 7 Curling Ocean Wave.

"The Wave Builds: When Force and Form Come Together"

> In a relationship, there is no reality—only perception. Both perceptions can be very different, yet equally correct.
>
> —From Duo Coaching practice

From Theory to Practice

You now understand why extended sessions create transformation (Chapter 3), how the Duo Coaching Framework addresses structural limitations (Chapter 4), and how to use the Relationship Paradigm for assessment (Chapter 5). But what actually happens minute-by-minute in a 3.5-hour first session? What do you DO with all that time? How does the session flow naturally rather than feeling forced or exhausting?

This chapter provides the authentic structure of Duo Coaching sessions as they actually unfold in practice—not an idealised template, but the real rhythm and content that creates transformation for couples.

You cannot be a Duo Coaching Practitioner until you have gone through the Duo Coaching Academy training and accreditation process. You can consider introducing some of these ideas into your own practice, if they are adopted with care.

DOI: 10.4324/9781003715627-10

Managing Intensive Sessions and Collaborative Practice

Session 1: Building Foundation Through Story and Understanding (3.5 Hours)

Phase	*Time*	*Focus*	*What Happens/Key Activities*
Phase 1: Arrival and Safety Building	15–20 minutes	Creating psychological safety and transitioning into a therapeutic space	• Warm welcome and environmental comfort • Explanation of session structure and expectations • Initial relationship building with both therapists • Ground rules and confidentiality clarification • Permission to take breaks as needed Psychological Purpose: Couples arrive anxious, guarded, uncertain. They're assessing safety and deciding how open to be. Co-Therapist Coordination: One therapist leads the welcome, while the other observes couple dynamics, body language, and interaction patterns. Natural switching after 10–15 minutes ensures balanced initial contact.
Phase 2: Relationship Stories	90 minutes (45 minutes each)	Understanding each partner's perception of the relationship journey	The Critical Opening Question: "Tell us about when you first met. How did your relationship begin?" This reveals: • Did they fall in love instantly or gradually? • How does each describe initial attraction? • What drew them together initially? Anchoring Positive Memory: Before exploring problems, anchor them to hopeful beginnings: • What did you feel when you first met? • What intrigued you about them? • What made you want to see them again?

(Continued)

Phase	*Time*	*Focus*	*What Happens/Key Activities*
			Purpose of Positive Anchoring: • Reminds them positive feelings existed • Activates neural pathways associated with connection • Provides contrast to current distress • Offers hope that feelings can be rekindled The Journey From Then to Now: Each partner tells their version from first meeting to present, including: • Moments of deep connection and joy • Times they felt proud of their partnership • Challenges navigated successfully • Milestones and celebrations • Disappointments, hurts, and turning points Fundamental Principle: "In a relationship, there is no reality—only perception." Both perceptions are true—for that person. Different doesn't mean one is lying or mistaken.
Phase 3: Individual Histories	30–45 minutes	Understanding unconscious patterns from past	Childhood and Upbringing: • Family emotional climate and communication patterns • Parental relationship model • Position in sibling order and family roles • Significant childhood events or trauma • Messages received about love, relationships, emotions Previous Relationships: • Significant past relationships and their endings • Patterns across relationships • Unhealed wounds from previous partnerships • Lessons learned (or not learned)

(*Continued*)

Phase	*Time*	*Focus*	*What Happens/Key Activities*
			Significant Life Events: • Losses, traumas, major transitions • Career or financial stresses • Health challenges • Events that shaped current relationship capacity Why This Matters: Unconscious patterns established in childhood and previous relationships continue operating in current partnership. Understanding these patterns helps couples recognise when they're responding to ghosts from the past.
Break	5–10 minutes	Physical needs and therapist consultation	Essential for: • Bathroom and movement • Nervous system regulation • Therapist consultation about what's emerging
Phase 4: Pebbles Constellation	30–45 minutes	Mapping internal worlds spatially through embodied exercise	The Setup: Provide large, clear surface and collection of small objects (pebbles, shells, buttons) The Instructions: "Choose a pebble to represent yourself and place it where it feels right. Then choose pebbles to represent the important people and things in your life, and place them where they need to be. Don't think too much—trust your intuition." What Emerges: • Spatial representations of their internal "maps of the world" • What matters to them • How close or distant important elements feel • What comes between them and their partner The Power of Seeing: When both constellations are placed side-by-side: • Distance between partner pebbles mirrors emotional distance • Objects between partners reveal what creates distance (work, children, phones, resentments)

(*Continued*)

Phase	*Time*	*Focus*	*What Happens/Key Activities*
			• Size differences show perceived power dynamics • Orientation (facing towards/away) shows engagement level This reveals patterns words cannot access
Phase 5: Relationship Paradigm Assessment	20–30 minutes	Quantifying current relationship health across six elements	The Six Elements: Each partner rates 1–10: 1 Communication Ability to express thoughts/feelings and be heard 2 Connection Emotional, physical, and day-to-day togetherness 3 Commitment Alignment on goals and willingness to invest 4 Fun Joy, playfulness, and positive experiences 5 Growth Individual and couple development 6 Trust Confidence in partner's reliability, integrity, honesty What the Numbers Reveal: • Where they agree vs. differ in perceptions • Which elements are strongest (build on these) • Which elements need immediate attention • Priorities for subsequent sessions
Break	5–10 minutes	Integration pause	Allows couples to process what's been revealed before final phase
Phase 6: Outcome Clarification and Homework	10–20 minutes	Establishing vision for change and beginning practice	Outcome Clarification: • What would success look like? • If your relationship improved, what would be different? • What specific changes would you notice? • How would you know transformation had happened? Standard Homework Assignments: Logbook 1: Bids for Connection (ALWAYS assigned) • Notice when partner makes bids for attention/connection • Track your responses (turn towards, away, against) • Practice turning towards bids

(*Continued*)

Phase	*Time*	*Focus*	*What Happens/Key Activities*
			Additional Homework (based on Paradigm scores): • If Connection very low: Exercises 3 and 4 (Ten Things I Love/ Respect) • If Fun very low: Schedule one fun activity before next session • If Communication low: Practice speaking/listening exercise Between-Session Support: • Explain 24/7 availability for crises or questions • Text or phone support protocol • Next session scheduling (typically two to three weeks)
Closing	10 minutes	Grounding and preparing to leave	• Brief summary of what emerged in session • Validation of their courage in sharing • Hope and encouragement about path forward • Practical reminders about homework • Ensuring they leave grounded, not overwhelmed Critical Principle: Every session must end "in a good place"—emotionally contained and hopeful rather than raw and overwhelmed

Co-therapist Coordination Throughout Session 1

Coordination Point	*How It Works*
Pre-Session Planning (30 minutes before)	• Review pre-session questionnaires together • Note any red flags or safety concerns • Agree on who leads which phases • Establish signals for consultation needs • Set intention for the session • Self-care check-in for both therapists
During Arrival Phase	• One leads welcome, one observes • Switch after 10–15 minutes for balance • Note couple's interaction patterns • Assess anxiety levels and defensiveness

During Story-Telling	• One facilitates questions, one tracks patterns
	• Non-verbal signals:
	  • Raised hand: "I notice something important"
	  • Eye contact + nod: "Follow this thread"
	  • Slight head shake: "Let's redirect"
	• Switch roles between the two partners
	• Both track differences in perception

During Breaks	• Compare observations and insights • Discuss what's emerging • Adjust second half plan if needed • Support each other emotionally • Quick decision-making about direction • Energy check-in for therapists
During Pebbles	• One facilitates, one observes partner reactions • Track what each partner chooses and places • Note emotional responses to exercise • Jointly facilitate comparison discussion
During Closing	• Both contribute to summary • Ensure both partners feel heard • Jointly explain homework • Tag-team encouragement and hope-building
Post-session Debrief (15–30 minutes after)	• Share observations and intuitions • Discuss couple dynamics and patterns • Note areas for subsequent sessions • Process emotional impact on therapists • Document key insights • Plan for Session 2 • Celebrate what went well

Sessions 2–6: The Transformation Journey (2.5 Hours Each)

Session	*Primary Focus*	*Typical Structure*	*Key Interventions*
Session 2: Deepening Understanding	Build on Session 1 insights with experiential work and skill development	• Opening and Homework Review (20–30 minutes) • Drawing Exercise (45–60 minutes)	Drawing Exercise: Reveals different visions and how to integrate them

(Continued)

Session	*Primary Focus*	*Typical Structure*	*Key Interventions*
		• Life as it is now • Life as they'd like it to be • Break (5 minutes) • Communication Practice (50–60 minutes) • Planning and Homework (10 minutes)	Communication Skills: • Interactive Listening • Speaker-Listener technique • Soft start-ups • Validation practice
Session 3: Core Pattern Work	Address deeper patterns beyond surface behaviours	• Opening and Progress (20–30 minutes) • Deep Pattern Work (60–75 minutes) • Break (5 minutes) • Integration and Practice (40–50 minutes) • Homework and Planning (10min)	Content varies by needs: • Values if priorities unclear • Timeline Therapy for past wounds • One-to-One Work if individual issues blocking progress • Parts Negotiation for internal conflicts Session 3 is often the most intense—deep work happening

Session 4: Challenge and Growth	Push growth edges while maintaining safety; address avoided topics	• Opening and Integration (20–30 minutes)
		• Challenge Work (40–60 minutes)
		  • Intimacy/sexuality
		  • Financial conflicts
		  • Parenting disagreements
		  • Avoided conversations
		• Break (5 minutes)
		• Practice and Application (40 minutes)
		• Future Visioning (20 minutes)
		Homework and Planning (10 minutes)
			Addressing difficult topics:
			• Intimacy and sexuality work
			• Financial communication
			• Parenting approach alignment
			• Extended family boundaries
			Future Visioning:
			• Dream Boards
			• Bucket Lists
			• Shared vision creation

Session 5: Consolidation	Consolidate gains and prepare for independence	• Opening and Celebration (10–20 minutes) • Paradigm Re-Rating (compare to Session 1) (5 minutes)	Focus areas: • Deepening intimacy work if needed • Advanced communication skills

(*Continued*)

Session	Primary Focus	Typical Structure	Key Interventions
		• Remaining Work (60–75 minutes) • Break (5 minutes) • Maintenance Planning (40–50 minutes) • Session 6 Preparation (10–20 minutes)	• Conflict resolution practice • Addressing setbacks Maintenance Planning: • What practices continue? • Early warning signs to watch • When to seek help
Session 6: Completion and Launch	Formal completion, celebration, and empowerment for the future	• Journey Review (20 minutes) • Final Assessment (30 minutes) • Maintenance Protocols (30–40 minutes) • Break (5 minutes) • Visioning and Commitment (30–40 minutes) • Celebration and Completion (30 minutes)	Completion work: • Final Paradigm ratings vs. baseline • Celebrating transformation • State of Union as permanent practice • Crisis management strategies • Future relationship vision Should feel celebratory, not sad. Leave the door open for booster sessions if needed.

Common Patterns across All Sessions

Pattern Element	How It Works

Opening Phase (Every Session)	Standard structure:
	• Welcome and reconnection (5–10 minutes)
	• Homework review (15–20 minutes)
	  • What did you notice?
	  • What was difficult?
	  • What insights emerged?
	• Energy and readiness check
	• Set intention for today's session

Strategic Break Timing	Breaks serve multiple purposes: For Couples: • Physical needs (bathroom, water, movement) • Nervous system regulation • Integration time for intense material • Pause before shifting to a new topic For Therapists: • Compare observations • Consult about direction

(Continued)

Pattern Element	*How It Works*
	• Adjust plans based on what's emerging • Support each other emotionally Timing Guidelines: • After 60–90 minutes of intensive work • Before major transitions • When emotional intensity peaks • When you sense fatigue (theirs or yours)
Homework Assignment (Every Session)	Standard Components: 1 Explain the Exercise: • What it is and why it matters • How to do it (demonstrate if possible) • When to do it (daily, weekly, etc.) 2 Address Potential Obstacles: • What might get in the way? • How will you make time for this? • What support do you need from each other? 3 Check Understanding: • Have them explain it back • Answer questions • Clarify expectations 4 Between-Session Support: • Text/phone availability if questions arise • When to reach out vs. wait for next session
Closing Phase (Every Session)	Standard structure: 1 Integration (10–15 minutes): • What stood out most today? • What are you taking away? • What feels different? 2 Homework Clarity (5–10 minutes): • Review assignments • Answer questions • Build motivation 3 Encouragement (5 minutes): • Acknowledge their work • Offer hope and support • Look forward to next session Critical: Every session ends "in a good place"—grounded, hopeful, not raw or overwhelmed
Flexibility Within Structure	While structure provides framework: • Allow natural stopping points rather than rigid timing • If major breakthrough happens, follow it • Adjust plans based on what couples bring • Watch for fatigue and adjust pacing • Some couples move faster, some slower • Honour emotional rhythms over clock The structure serves the couple, not the other way around.

Key Principles for Managing Intensive Sessions

Respect Natural Rhythms

Couples open up at their own pace. Extended time allows natural unfolding rather than forcing artificial constraints. Don't rush to "cover everything"—trust the process.

Balance Structure and Spontaneity

Have a plan but hold it lightly. The best sessions often diverge from plans when following what emerges. Structure provides safety; spontaneity allows responsiveness.

End Every Session "In a Good Place"

Never leave couples emotionally raw or overwhelmed. The last 15–20 minutes should provide containment, hope, and grounding. They need to be able to drive home safely and function the rest of the day.

Use Breaks Strategically

Breaks aren't just bathroom stops—they're therapeutic tools. They allow integration, nervous system regulation, and therapist consultation. Don't skip breaks to "save time."

Co-therapist Partnership Is Everything

Pre-session planning, in-session coordination, break consultations, and post-session debriefing make the work possible. Invest in the partnership.

Honour Both Partners Equally

Track airtime, emotional attention, and validation carefully. Both partners must feel heard and understood by both therapists. Co-therapy helps ensure balance.

Homework Is Essential, Not Optional

Change happens between sessions through practice. Homework completion predicts success. If couples aren't doing homework, explore why—it's diagnostic information.

Different Perceptions Are Both True

In a relationship, there is no single reality—only perceptions. Both partners' perceptions are valid. Help them understand each other's experience without needing to agree who's "right."

"The structure creates safety. The extended time creates space. The co-therapy creates balance. Together, they allow transformation to unfold naturally rather than forcing change artificially."

Between-Session Work: The Engine of Transformation

Why Work Outside the Counselling Room Matters

Transformation does not happen in the counselling room alone. Even with extended sessions and the power of two therapists, couples spend perhaps 16 hours with us across a complete programme. They spend thousands of hours with each other. If nothing changes between sessions—if couples simply arrive, do the work, and return to old patterns the moment they leave—progress will be limited at best, illusory at worst.

Between-session work is where insight becomes embodied, where understanding transforms into changed behaviour, where the couple begins to become their own therapists. It requires commitment, energy, and time. It asks couples to prioritise their relationship not just during sessions, but throughout their daily lives. This investment signals something profound: that they are willing to do what it takes to create lasting change.

The most successful couples in Duo Coaching are those who engage fully with between-session work. They arrive at each session having reflected, experimented, discovered, and sometimes struggled. They bring questions born of genuine exploration rather than theoretical curiosity. They have tested new approaches in the laboratory of their actual relationship. This creates momentum that carries through the entire programme and, crucially, continues long after our work together ends.

A Framework for Between-Session Exploration

Between-session work in Duo Coaching is not random homework assigned to fill the time between meetings. It follows a purposeful structure, tailored at the end of each session to address the specific needs that have emerged. The Duo Coaching Academy contains over 200 resources designed for between-session work, allowing practitioners to select precisely the right exercise for each couple at each stage of their journey.

These resources fall into distinct domains, each addressing different aspects of relationship understanding and growth:

Understanding Heritage

Every person arrives in a relationship shaped by their history. The parenting they received—whether nurturing or critical, authoritative or permissive, present or absent—creates templates for how relationships work. Their emotional education matters profoundly: How comfortable were they taught to be with pride and accomplishment, with love and affection, with anger, with sadness, with fear? These early lessons often operate beneath conscious awareness, yet they shape every interaction.

Attachment styles formed in childhood frequently create recurring patterns in adult relationships. A partner who learned that closeness leads to pain may withdraw precisely when intimacy deepens. One who learned that needs go unmet may pursue with increasing desperation. Understanding these patterns—not as flaws but as adaptations that once made sense—opens the door to conscious choice rather than unconscious repetition.

Between-session work in this domain helps individuals explore their heritage and, crucially, understand its ongoing impact on their current relationship. This is archaeological work—excavating the foundations upon which their relationship patterns were built.

Self-understanding

How well do you truly know yourself? This deceptively simple question opens vast territory for exploration. Some individuals discover they sit somewhere on the spectrum of neurodiversity, a recognition that reframes years of relationship friction. Others examine their natural orientation—do they focus primarily on their own needs, on others' needs, or do they struggle to find balance between the two?

Within relationships, people unconsciously adopt roles and fill familiar systemic positions. The caretaker, the pursuer, the distancer, the peacekeeper, the rebel—these roles may have originated in the family of origin and transferred seamlessly into partnership. Between-session work invites individuals to examine these roles: which serve them, which constrain them, and which they might consciously choose to release?

Deeper self-understanding work invites individuals to articulate who they truly are—not who they think they should be, not who their partner wants them to be, but their authentic self. This culminates in work that asks profound questions: How do you want to be remembered? What do you want loved ones to say about you when you are gone? This future-framing exercise helps individuals align their current choices with their deepest values.

Understanding Your Partner

Long-term relationships create a dangerous illusion: The belief that we know our partner completely. We mistake familiarity for understanding, prediction for perception. Yet our partners continue to grow, change, and surprise us—if we remain curious enough to notice.

Between-session work in this domain challenges couples to examine how well they truly know each other. Do they understand what their partner genuinely needs—not what they assume, not what would be convenient, but what actually matters to their partner? Do they know their partner's dreams, fears, and unspoken longings? Do they understand how their partner experiences love, and are they offering love in ways their partner can receive?

Perhaps most importantly, this work cultivates what might be called epistemological humility—the recognition that what we see may not be the complete picture. It invites partners to meet each other afresh, setting aside accumulated assumptions to perceive the person actually before them, not the mental image they have constructed over the years.

Connection and Communication

How do two people actually connect? This domain explores the mechanics and the mystery of communication between partners. It examines the language each person uses—not just what they say, but how they say it, what remains unsaid, and what gets lost in translation between two different internal worlds.

Partners often process information and experience life in fundamentally different ways. One may think in words, another in images. One may need to talk through problems, another to retreat and reflect. One may process emotions quickly, another slowly. Understanding these differences—and developing shared language for navigating them—transforms frustrating miscommunications into opportunities for deeper understanding.

Living in Harmony

Beyond the relationship itself lies the question of how well each partner is living their whole life. Are their fundamental needs being met—for meaning, for growth, for contribution, for joy? Do their individual lives complement each other, or are they pulling in incompatible directions?

Between-session work in this domain invites couples to examine whether they are living in alignment with their values, both individually and together. It explores the practical architecture of shared life: how time, energy, and attention are allocated, and whether that allocation reflects what matters most.

Focusing on the Good

Relationships in difficulty develop a negativity bias. Partners become exquisitely attuned to what is wrong, what is missing, what their partner has failed to do. The good becomes invisible, taken for granted, while the problematic looms large.

Between-session work deliberately counters this bias. It trains couples to notice what is working, to hunt for the good stuff, to share with each other daily what went well. This is not naive positivity or denial of real problems—it is deliberate rebalancing of attention.

Structured rituals support this rebalancing. A weekly "state of the union" meeting creates space for couples to reflect on what has gone well in their relationship, alongside an honest examination of what needs attention. This ritual establishes a rhythm of conscious relationship tending rather than crisis-driven reaction.

Small interactions carry enormous weight in relationships. The power of hello and goodbye, the warmth of small acknowledgments, the micro-moments of connection that punctuate daily life—these are the heartbeat of relationship health. Between-session work heightens awareness of these small interactions and their cumulative impact.

Creating a Shared Future

Where are they going together? Many couples have never articulated a shared vision of their future. They drift, making decisions reactively rather than in service of a conscious direction.

Between-session work in this domain invites couples to dream together. What do they want to experience? What do they want to create? What legacy do they want to leave? Bucket lists, dream boards, and structured visioning exercises help couples articulate and align their aspirations. This shared vision then becomes a compass for decision-making and a source of motivation when difficulties arise.

Navigating Disagreement

Every couple disagrees. The question is not whether conflict exists, but how it is navigated. Between-session work helps couples understand the unmet needs that drive recurring disagreements. It builds capacity for genuine resolution where possible and graceful acceptance where perspectives genuinely differ.

The goal is not to eliminate disagreement—that would require eliminating individuality. The goal is to transform disagreement from a source of escalation and disconnection into an opportunity for deeper understanding and creative problem-solving.

Ongoing Reflection: The Logbook

Threading through all between-session work is the practice of keeping a logbook. This ongoing record captures what is happening, how each partner is feeling, what is changing, what is difficult, what is improving. The logbook creates continuity between sessions and provides rich material for reflection.

More than a diary, the logbook is a tool for developing self-awareness. It helps individuals notice patterns they might otherwise miss. It provides evidence of progress during moments of discouragement. It becomes a shared reference that both partners and therapists can draw upon.

Tailoring Between-Session Work

At the end of each Duo Coaching session, practitioners select between-session work specifically tailored to what has emerged. This is not a standardised curriculum but a responsive, personalised programme. A couple grappling with the legacy of one partner's dismissive upbringing will receive different work than a couple struggling to articulate a shared vision for their future.

The Duo Coaching Academy provides practitioners with a comprehensive library of over 200 resources spanning all the domains described above. These resources have been developed and refined over years of clinical practice, each designed to facilitate specific types of exploration and growth.

Practitioners trained through the Duo Coaching Academy learn not only what resources exist but how to select and sequence them effectively. They develop clinical judgment about pacing—when to introduce challenging material and when to consolidate gains. They learn to read couples' readiness and to adjust expectations accordingly.

The Invitation

Between-session work is an invitation, not a command. Couples who engage fully accelerate their progress. Those who struggle with between-session work are not failing—they are providing important clinical information about their capacity, their resistance, or their competing demands.

When couples resist between-session work, this becomes grist for the mill. What gets in the way? Is it practical—genuine lack of time—or is it protective? What does avoidance of this particular work reveal about their relationship dynamics? Sometimes the most valuable session focuses not on new material, but on understanding why the between-session work did not happen.

Ultimately, between-session work prepares couples to continue their growth long after formal sessions end. The goal of Duo Coaching is not to create dependency on therapists but to develop couples' capacity to be their own relationship healers. Between-session work builds that capacity, session by session, until couples have internalised the questions, the practices, and the commitment that sustain relationship health across a lifetime.

Domains of Between-Session Work

Domain	*Focus*	*Purpose*
Understanding Heritage	Parenting styles, emotional education, attachment patterns	Recognising how the past shapes current relationship dynamics
Self-understanding	Neurodiversity, roles, authentic identity, life purpose	Developing deep self-knowledge as foundation for intimacy
Understanding Partner	Needs, dreams, love languages, epistemological humility	Seeing the partner clearly, beyond accumulated assumptions
Connection and Communication	Language, processing styles, translation between worlds	Building shared understanding and effective dialogue

(Continued)

Domain	Focus	Purpose
Living in Harmony	Values alignment, needs fulfilment, life architecture	Creating complementary rather than competing individual lives
Focusing on the Good	Gratitude practices, rituals, small interactions	Rebalancing attention towards what is working
Creating a Shared Future	Vision, dreams, bucket lists, legacy	Aligning aspirations and creating shared direction
Navigating Disagreement	Unmet needs, resolution, acceptance	Transforming conflict into opportunity for understanding
Ongoing Reflection	Logbook, pattern recognition, progress tracking	Developing self-awareness and continuity between sessions

Detailed resources for between-session work are available to practitioners trained through the Duo Coaching Academy, which provides comprehensive materials for each domain along with guidance on selection, sequencing, and clinical application.

From Theory to Practice: A Complete First Session

You've now learned the structure, timing, and essential elements of Session 1. But what does this actually look like when four human beings sit in a room together for three and a half hours? What's happening inside each person as the session unfolds?

Let's follow Susan and David Harper's first session with Maya Kapadia and James Crawford. We'll see it from all four perspectives—not just what's said in the room, but what each person is thinking, feeling, and experiencing internally.

This is where theory becomes practice. This is where the work lives.

INTERLUDE: SUSAN & DAVID'S FIRST SESSION

Four Perspectives on Beginning

The Arrival (10:00 Am)

Maya

She's checked the room three times. Tissues positioned just so. Water glasses filled. The chairs—she's gone with the gentle arc formation, not quite facing each other, not quite side-by-side. Allows choice. James arrives carrying his leather notebook, and she notices he's wearing the blue trainers today. Good. Approachable.

"Chai?" she offers.

"God, yes." He sits, and she catches his nervousness. They're both trying to look calmer than they feel.

The buzzer. Her stomach flips. *Here we go.*

When Susan and David walk in, Maya notices everything at once: Susan makes herself small coming through the doorway. David checks his phone before pocketing it. They don't touch. There's at least two feet of space between them. Susan's hands are clasped tight. David's jaw is set.

They're terrified. Defended. Please let us help them.

James

The couple walks in and James's organisational psychology brain kicks in automatically: Power differential. David leads, Susan follows. His body language says *I'm here under duress.* Her body language says *I'm here because I have to be, but I've already given up.*

He stands, offers his hand. "James Crawford." David's handshake is firm, performative. Susan's is soft, brief.

Maya's doing the warm welcome—offering tea, water. James watches her work. She's good at this, the settling. He tends to want to jump straight in, get to the point. Learning to trust the preamble.

David sits first, chooses the chair nearest the door. Interesting. Susan takes the one furthest from him. They've created the maximum possible distance in the arc.

Three and a half hours with this much defence—Oh!

SUSAN

The room is nicer than she expected. Warm. There are plants. The woman—Maya—has kind eyes, but Susan's been disappointed by kind eyes before. The man—James—is more neutral, assessing. She prefers that. Less chance of false hope.

David's already in business mode. Handshake, polite smile, the charm he uses with clients. She knows this performance. She's lived with it for years.

Maya offers tea. "I've got proper chai if you'd like?"

Susan almost says yes—she loves chai—but stops herself. Don't get comfortable. Don't trust this. "Just water, thank you."

She sits. Realises she's chosen the chair furthest from David. Good. Let them see. Let them know this is real.

David

Professional room. Professional people. This'll be like every other therapy attempt—two hours of Susan explaining everything he does wrong, therapist nodding sympathetically, him defending himself, nothing changes. But fine. He said he'd try. He's here. Box ticked.

The man—James—seems alright. Bit young maybe. The woman is doing the hospitable thing, offering drinks. He accepts water. Keep it simple.

He chooses a seat. Susan predictably goes to the opposite end. Point made.

His phone vibrates in his pocket. Site issue probably. He'll check it in the break. There is a break in these things, right? Three and a half hours. Jesus. He's got the Birmingham thing tomorrow, still needs to review the contracts tonight.

Get through this. Be reasonable. She can't say you didn't try.

Contracting (10:15 Am)

James

Right. Structure. He needs structure.

> So, we work a bit differently than you might have experienced before. Three and a half hours, both of us in the room. Maya and I work as a team – we might notice different things, offer different perspectives. We'll take a short break halfway through.

David nods. Business-like. Susan's looking at her hands.

"We're not here to referee or take sides. We're here to help you both understand what's happening between you, and to explore whether this relationship is something you want to repair, and if so, how."

Did that sound too formal? Maya, help me here.

Maya leans forward slightly. "What we've found is that having two therapists means you're both truly held. You both get to be fully heard. Neither of you is the problem – the pattern between you is what we're curious about."

Better. Softer. James watches Susan's shoulders drop slightly.

"So maybe we start with what brought you here? What made you pick up the phone?"

Susan

The pattern between you. That phrase catches something. Not *his* problem. Not *her* problem. The *pattern.*

Maya's question hangs in the air. What brought them here?

David will answer. He always answers first. Takes control of the narrative.

But he's quiet. Looking at her. Waiting.

Oh God, they want me to speak.

"I …" Her voice sounds strange. "I called. Because I realised I didn't want to be married anymore, but I also didn't want to just … give up. Without trying one more thing."

It's out. The truth. She risks a glance at David. His face is carefully neutral, but something flickers. Hurt? Anger? Relief?

"I feel like we're just … housemates. Polite strangers. And I'm tired of being lonely in my own marriage."

David

Lonely. She's said this before, but hearing it here, in front of witnesses, lands differently.

"I didn't know you felt like a housemate," he says, and it comes out more defensive than he meant. "I thought we were … I work hard so you and the kids can have—"

"We know you work hard, David." Susan's voice has an edge now. The edge that means *here we go again.*

James interrupts, gently but firmly. "David, can I pause you there?"

David stops. Looks at him.

"I notice you went straight to explaining, defending. What was it like to hear Susan say she's lonely?"

What kind of question is that? "I … what do you mean?"

"Just – when she said those words, 'I'm tired of being lonely in my own marriage' – what happened inside you?"

David's jaw tightens. This is the therapy bullshit he hates. Feelings. Always bloody feelings.

But something in James's face—no judgment, just … curiosity—makes him pause.

"I suppose … I felt like I'd failed. Again."

Maya

There. The first crack in David's armour. She saw his jaw tighten, the defence rising, but then … something softened. *I felt like I'd failed.*

James caught it too. She can see him letting it breathe.

"Failed?" Maya asks softly. "Say more about that?"

David shifts in his chair.

> Everything I do is to provide for them. The house, the schools, the holidays. I'm building something. For us. For our future. And I hear that I'm doing it wrong, that it's not enough, that I'm failing at the one thing I thought I was getting right.

Susan makes a small sound—not quite a laugh, not quite a sob.

Maya turns to her. "Susan? What's happening for you hearing David say that?"

Susan looks up, and there are tears now.

> I don't want the bigger house, David. I don't want the fancier holidays. I want *you*. I want you to come home and ask how my day was. I want you to touch me like you used to. I want to feel like I matter to you as much as the Birmingham meeting.

There it is. The chasm between them.

The Break (11:45 Am)

James

David's stepped outside to check his phone. Susan's in the bathroom. James and Maya have 15 minutes.

"Christ," James says, running his hand through his hair. "Did you catch what happened when she mentioned his PA?"

"Emma." Maya nods. "His whole body changed. And Susan's face—"

"She knows. Or suspects." James is pacing slightly. "And the way he deflects every emotion into 'I'm providing' – it's a bloody fortress."

"But it cracked," Maya says. "When you asked what it was like to hear her loneliness. That was good."

"We need to get underneath the affair question."

"Not yet." Maya's firm on this. "They're not ready. Susan's barely holding on. If we push too hard—"

"She'll leave."

"She'll leave." Maya looks at James. "Are you okay? You seem …"

"Activated," he admits. "The way he checked his phone, the dismissiveness – reminds me of my dad. I need to watch that."

Good. He's noticing it. They're growing.

Susan

She splashes water on her face in the bathroom. Looks at herself in the mirror. Red eyes. Blotchy skin. *Attractive.*

That moment when David said he felt like a failure—something in her softened despite herself. She'd forgotten that he might actually be hurting too. That his absence might be about his own pain, not just indifference to hers.

But then. *Then.* When she'd mentioned Emma in passing—"you have more conversations with Emma than with me"—the way he'd frozen. The way he'd recovered too quickly.

He's lying about something.

Her phone buzzes. Lucy: "How's it going? x"

She doesn't know how to answer.

David

Three emails need answering. The Birmingham contracts aren't ready. Site issue in Manchester needs his call.

But he's standing in the corridor of a therapy office, and all he can think about is Susan's face when she said *I want you to touch me like you used to.*

When did he stop? When did work become easier than home?

(He knows when. When Emma joined the company two years ago, work suddenly became fun again. Someone who laughed at his jokes, asked his opinion, looked at him like he was interesting. Nothing happened. Nothing *physical.* But Susan said lonely, and he realises—he's lonely too. Just been filling it with something else.)

He opens his phone. Email from Emma: "Hope the thing goes okay. We're all rooting for you."

He deletes it without responding.

After the Break (12:00 Pm)

Maya

They're back. Susan's eyes are red but clearer. David's put his phone in his bag this time. Small thing, but Maya notices.

"Before we broke," James says,

> we were starting to hear about what each of you *wants*. Susan, you said you want David present, asking about your day, touching you. David, you said you want to feel like you're not failing. Can we stay with that? What else do each of you want?

David speaks first this time, and his voice is different. Quieter. "I want to come home and not feel like I'm walking into a courtroom. Like everything I do will be used as evidence that I'm a shit husband."

Susan flinches.

Maya intervenes: "David, can you say that without the blame? What do you *want*, not what you don't want?"

He thinks. "I want … I want to come home and feel welcome. I want to feel like Susan's pleased to see me, not just cataloging my failures."

Susan's crying now, properly.

> I used to be pleased. I used to wait for you. But you'd come home and barely see me. You'd eat dinner on your phone. You'd go to bed after I

was asleep. You'd leave before I woke up. How am I supposed to stay pleased when you're choosing *not to be there*?

David

It hits him like a punch. *Choosing not to be there.*

Is that what he's been doing?

He thinks about the early mornings, slipping out before she wakes. Tells himself it's to not disturb her. But maybe … maybe it's also to avoid the heaviness. The disappointment in her eyes.

"I didn't …" he starts. Stops. "I didn't realise I was choosing that."

James: "What would it be like to choose differently?"

And David doesn't have an answer. Because he doesn't know if he can. If it's too late. If Susan even wants him to anymore.

Susan

She's seeing something she hasn't seen in years: David uncertain. David without the answers.

Maybe that's all she needed. Not solutions. Not promises. Just … this. Him not knowing either. Them both in the dark together instead of her alone in it.

"I don't know if we can come back from this," she hears herself say. "I don't know if I have it in me to try again and fail again."

"That's honest," Maya says. "And that honesty is important. You don't have to know yet. That's part of what these sessions are for – to explore whether there's a way forward you both can live with."

James

He glances at Maya. They've got 90 minutes left. The affair question is sitting in the room like unexploded ordnance. They need to address it, but carefully.

"Can I name something?" James says. "There's been a lot about work, about absence. And Susan, you mentioned Emma – David's PA. I'm curious about that."

The room temperature drops five degrees instantly.

David's defences slam back up. "There's nothing—"

"I'm not accusing," James says steadily. "I'm noticing that when her name came up, something changed in this room. And I'm wondering if there's something there that needs light on it."

Susan's looking at David with an expression James can't quite read. Hope? Dread?

"David?" Maya's voice is gentle. "What's happening right now?"

The Hour That Follows

David

*F*ck.*

He could lie. He's been lying by omission for two years. But sitting here, with Susan's tear-stained face, with these two people who somehow feel … safe … he can't.

"Nothing physical happened," he says, and his voice sounds hollow even to himself. "But … there was an emotional … connection. With Emma. It made work feel less heavy. She was easy to talk to. And I …"

He can't look at Susan. "I let it go too far. The conversations. The texts. The— I let myself feel things I shouldn't have felt."

Silence.

Then Susan's voice, very small: "Are you in love with her?"

Susan

She's asked the question she's been terrified to ask for months. Her heart is hammering so hard she can barely hear.

David's face is anguished. "No. No, I'm not. But I … I used her to avoid dealing with us. With how hard we'd become. And that's not fair to you, or to her, or to anyone."

He admitted it. Finally. Finally.

She doesn't know what she feels. Rage? Relief? Grief? All of it.

"You made me feel crazy," she whispers. "I knew something was wrong, and you kept saying I was imagining things, being paranoid—"

"I know. I'm sorry. I'm so sorry."

Maya: "Susan, what do you need right now?"

What does she need? "I need … I need to know it's over. The— whatever it was with her. I need to know you've ended it."

David

"I have," he says immediately. "Three weeks ago. Before you even mentioned therapy. I realized—I realized I was destroying everything that mattered for something that wasn't even real."

Susan's face: She wants to believe him. She doesn't know if she can.

Maya

The room is raw now. All the defences stripped. Both of them exposed, hurting, uncertain.

This is the liminal space. The place between the old pattern and whatever might come next. This is where the work lives.

She looks at James. He nods slightly. *They're ready for the next question.*

"So here you both are," Maya says.

> David, you've been building a fortress of work to avoid the pain of failing at home. Susan, you've been managing the loneliness by managing everything else, keeping busy, keeping small. And somewhere in there, you both forgot how to reach for each other.

She pauses. "The question is: do you *want* to remember? Not 'can you' yet – just *do you want to*?"

Susan

Does she want to?

The woman who walked in here three hours ago would have said no. Would have said it's too late, too broken, too much water under the bridge.

But this woman, sitting here now, having seen David's face crack open, having heard him say *I'm sorry* with something real behind it …

"I think I might," she says. "I'm terrified. But I think I might."

David

He looks at Susan. Really looks at her. Sees the woman he fell in love with under all the years of hurt and distance.

"I want to," he says. "I don't know how. But I want to try."

James

"Then that's where we begin," James says. "Not with fixing everything. Not with promises. But with this tiny, terrifying willingness. That's enough for today."

The Pebbles Constellation (1:00 Pm)

Maya

"There's an exercise we'd like to invite you to do," Maya says, showing two large wicker baskets filled with pebbles—all different sizes, shapes, colours, textures. Stones from beaches around the world.

"These are just stones, but they can help you see things about yourself and your situation that words sometimes can't quite reach."

David looks sceptical. Susan looks curious.

"Here's what we'd like you to do," James says carefully. "Each of you will do this at the same time, without watching what the other person is doing. Use the carpet or anywhere else."

"The instruction is this: Choose one pebble to represent yourself, and place that where that needs to be."

Pause. Let it land.

"Then choose other pebbles to represent other important people or things in your life right now, and place those where those need to be."

Susan: "What do you mean, where they need to be?"

James repeats the instruction exactly: "Choose one pebble to represent yourself and place that where that needs to be. Then choose other pebbles to represent other important people or things in your life right now, and place those where those need to be."

"Just trust yourself," Maya adds gently. "There's no right or wrong."

David

This feels strange. But also … something about the simplicity of it appeals to him. No talking, no explaining, just … placing stones.

He reaches into the bowl. His hand hovers over several before closing around a large, dark, solid stone. *That's me.* He places it off-centre in his space.

Another stone. Rough, grey. He places it close to the first one.

A smooth stone. Smaller. He places it at the far edge of his area.

A jagged stone, small. Goes between two others.

One more. Light coloured, worn smooth. Far corner.

He sits back. Looks at what he's created. *Oh.*

Susan

She's drawn to a large, smooth stone immediately. *Me.* Places it in the centre of her space.

Another stone, similar but slightly smaller, goes right next to it. Almost touching.

A beautiful polished stone—something about it speaks to her. She places it in the far corner, almost off the table.

A sharp, dark stone. Her hand hesitates before placing it between the centre stones.

One more. Pale, worn. She places it reaching towards David's area—then stops, realises she's not supposed to be looking at his. Adjusts it.

Done.

Maya

"Okay," Maya says softly. "You can look at each other's now."

Both David and Susan turn slightly, seeing what the other has created. There's a long silence.

"David," James says, "would you be willing to talk us through yours? Starting with – which one represents you?"

David

He points to the large dark stone in the centre-left. "This is me."

"And the others?"

He touches the rough grey stone near it. "This is … work. My business. It's very close to me."

The smooth stone at the far edge. "This is Susan. She's … far away."

The jagged small stone is between the first two. "This is … I don't know how to say it. Guilt? Failure? Something painful."

The light stone in the corner. "This is … maybe who I used to be? Someone lighter. But he's far away too."

"And where is 'you' in relation to these?" Maya asks.

David looks. "I'm between work and guilt. And Susan and the lighter version of me are both … out of reach."

Susan

She's crying silently, looking at his constellation.

"Susan," Maya says gently, "would you share yours?"

Susan points to the large smooth stone. "This is me."

"And this one?" James points to the similar stone right next to it.

"This is … everything I manage. The household, the kids, all of it. It's almost part of me now. Can barely tell the difference."

The beautiful polished stone in the corner. "This is who I used to be. The teacher. The person with her own life. She's very far away."

The sharp stone between the centre ones. "This is anger. I keep it close but hidden."

The pale stone reaching outward. "This is … hope, maybe? Or something that wants to reach toward David but doesn't know if it can."

James

"Look at both constellations together," James says. "What do you notice?"

Long silence. Then David: "We both have a version of ourselves that's far away. Your teacher. My lighter self."

"And," Susan says quietly, "you put me at the edge. I put hope reaching toward you. We're …" she stops.

"You're both reaching and distant at the same time," Maya observes.

Maya (The Ideal Future)

"Now," Maya says, "here's the second part. We'd like you to create your ideal future. You can move any pebbles, add new ones from the bowl, take pebbles away. Just create what your ideal future would look like."

"At the same time again?" David asks.

"Yes. Don't watch each other. Just create yours."

David

He sits for a moment, looking at his stones. Then reaches for the smooth stone that represents Susan. Moves it closer. Not right next to him, but … closer.

Takes the light stone—his former self—and moves it in towards the centre too.

The rough grey stone—work—he moves it back slightly. Still there, but not so dominant.

The jagged guilt stone. He picks it up, hesitates, then makes it smaller by choosing a tinier stone to replace it.

Then he reaches into the bowl. Finds a blue-grey stone, smooth and calming. Places it near the centre.

"What's that one?" James asks.

"I don't know yet," David says. "But it needs to be there."

Susan

She looks at her constellation. The polished stone—her former self—she moves it towards the centre. Not all the way, but closer.

The sharp anger stone—she doesn't remove it, but she moves it slightly back. Still there, but not so central.

Her "self" stone and the "managing everything" stone—she creates space between them. They're still close, but distinct now.

The hope stone—she moves it more decisively towards where David's area is.

Then she adds a new stone from the bowl. A warm, rose-coloured one. Places it near the centre.

"And that one?" Maya asks.

"I don't know what to call it," Susan says. "But it feels important."

James

"David, talk us through your ideal future."

"Susan's closer. Work is still there but not consuming me. The guilt is smaller. And this new stone – I think it's about being present. Actually being here, not always racing ahead."

"Susan?"

teacher in me comes back – not all the way, but she's part of my life again. Anger's still there but not hidden in the middle of everything. And this new stone … I think it's belief. Belief that this could actually work.

Maya (The Crucial Question)

"So," Maya says, "you've both created an ideal future. It's different from where you are now. David, for you to get from where you are now to this ideal future – what needs to happen?"

David

He stares at the stones. The question lands heavy.

"Susan needs to come closer … that means I need to make different choices. Come home earlier. Actually be present when I'm there. Stop choosing work over her."

"What else?"

"The guilt needs to get smaller. Which means … I need to forgive myself? Or maybe make amends properly. Stop carrying it like a weight."

"And the present stone – the new one?"

"I need to learn how to be here. To stop. To rest. To just … be."

Susan

"Susan," James asks, "what do you need to have happen to get you to your ideal future?"

She looks at her stones. "The teacher needs to come back. Which means I need to actually do the course. Stop waiting for permission. Take up space."

"What else?"

"Anger needs to move back – which means I need to let it out safely. Say what I feel. Not hide it and then explode."

"And the belief stone?"

"I need to risk hoping again. Even though I'm scared. Even though I might get hurt."

James

"Look at what you both need," James says carefully. "David needs to be more present, to choose home over work. Susan needs to reclaim her own life, her own passion. These aren't in conflict – they actually support each other."

"If David creates more space," Maya adds, "Susan has room to grow. If Susan reclaims herself, David has someone real to come home to, not just the household manager."

Both are quiet, taking this in.

"Can I ask," David says slowly, "can we keep the stones? Like, take photos? So we remember?"

"Of course," Maya says. "In fact, we'll do this again in our final session. See where the stones have moved."

Susan

She looks at David's constellation again. Then at hers. "When you moved me closer," she says to David, "I felt something. Like maybe you do still want me there."

"I do," he says, and his voice cracks. "I really do."

After They Leave (1:45 Pm)

Maya

The door closes behind Susan and David. Maya and James sit in silence for a long moment.

"Bloody hell," Maya says finally.

"Yeah." James is pale. "That was … intense."

"Did we do okay?"

"I think so?" He's not sure. "The affair stuff – was it too soon?"

"It was *there*," Maya says. "We couldn't not address it. And I think … I think they needed it named."

They start the debrief. What they noticed. What worked. What they'd do differently. Where their own stuff got activated.

"When he admitted the emotional affair," James says, "I felt this wave of anger at him. For lying to her, for making her doubt her reality. Had to breathe through it."

"I know," Maya says. "I felt protective of her. Had to remind myself – he's hurting too. They're both trapped in this pattern."

"We did okay," James says finally. "They're coming back. That's something."

What You Just Witnessed

Susan and David's first session demonstrates every element we've discussed:

The Four-Layer Assessment Unfolding Naturally

Initial enquiry and individual consultations happened before this session

Relationship Paradigm scores revealed communication at 2/10, connection at 1/10

Their relationship stories showed divergent narratives and perception gaps

The pebbles constellation made invisible patterns visible

The Phases of Session 1 in Practice

Arrival and contracting (15 minutes)

The emotional breakthrough around loneliness and failure (45 minutes)

The affair disclosure and its impact (60 minutes)

The pebbles constellation revealing spatial relationships and hidden dynamics (90 minutes)

Outcome clarification through the "what needs to happen" question (30 minutes)

Co-therapist Coordination

James providing structure and naming patterns

Maya holding emotional space and following energy

Their silent communication and mutual support

Both getting activated (James by David's dismissiveness, Maya by Susan's pain) and managing it

The Transformation Beginning

From defended strangers to tentatively willing partners

From "I don't love you anymore" to "I think I might want to try"

From invisible patterns to visible constellations

From hopelessness to the smallest seed of possibility

This is what Session 1 creates: not solutions, but *foundation*. Not promises, but *willingness*. Not certainty, but *enough* to take the next step.

In Chapter 11, we will explore what happens in Sessions 2–6 as Susan and David—and Maya and James—continue their journey.

Integration and Self-reflection

Foundation Level Skills Addressed in This Chapter

Extended Session Management: Maintaining therapeutic focus and effectiveness throughout 2.5–3.5 hour sessions, structuring time to include multiple emotional cycles and breakthrough opportunities

Energy Management: Managing both practitioner and couple energy levels throughout intensive sessions, creating natural breaks that maintain momentum while preventing exhaustion

Session Structure and Rhythm: Facilitating relationship story-telling, conducting pebbles constellations, and transitioning smoothly between session phases

Co-therapist Collaboration Basics: Non-verbal communication, tag-teaming interventions, balanced participation, and effective debriefing

Safety and Crisis Response: Recognising safety concerns, managing emotional intensity, and implementing appropriate crisis protocols

Documentation Systems: Note-taking during sessions, session summaries, and between-session support tracking

Reflection Questions

1 What concerns arise for you about maintaining therapeutic focus and energy for 2.5–3.5 hours? How might you prepare yourself physically and mentally?
2 Have you experienced facilitating experiential exercises like pebbles constellations? What skills would you need to develop?
3 How confident do you feel in your ability to track session flow while remaining present with couples' emotional experiences?
4 Reflect on the principle "there is no reality—only perception." How comfortable are you holding two contradictory versions of events without needing to determine who is "right"?
5 What natural breaks or rhythm changes might work in your practice space for extended sessions?
6 How would you manage a couple in emotional crisis during an extended session? What safety protocols would you need?
7 What co-therapist communication systems (verbal and non-verbal) could you imagine developing with a partner?

Self-assessment

Rate your current readiness for managing extended intensive sessions:

Score	*Interpretation*
1–2	Need significant development in session management and stamina
3–4	Understanding concepts but uncertain about practical implementation
5–6	Solid foundation with some experience in extended sessions or experiential work
7+	Strong competency ready to begin managing full intensive sessions

Practice Exercise

To build your readiness for extended sessions, try this progressive practice:

Week 1–2: Extend Current Sessions

With one to two current couple clients, extend one session from 50 to 90 minutes. Notice: What becomes possible with the extra time? How do you manage energy? Where are natural break points?

Week 3–4: Practice Story-Telling Facilitation

Ask a couple to tell their relationship story from beginning to present, listening for patterns. Practice asking: "What drew you together? When did things change? How do you each experience that?"

Week 5–6: Try Pebbles Constellation

Introduce a simple constellation exercise: "Choose objects to represent you, your partner, and your relationship. Place them where they need to be." Observe what emerges. Practice Clean Language questions: "And when you see that arrangement, what do you notice?"

Week 7–8: Extend to Two Hours

With couples showing progress, offer a two-hour session. Structure it: 90-minute work + 10-minute break + 20-minute integration. Document what worked and what challenged you.

This graduated practice builds your competency systematically while serving your current clients effectively.

Coming Next: Chapter 8—Start Your Implementation Journey

You now understand how to structure and manage intensive sessions, but knowledge alone doesn't transform practice. Chapter 8 bridges the gap between understanding Duo Coaching and actually implementing it, providing a practical roadmap for your first steps.

Discover how to assess your current practice readiness, identify the specific changes needed for intensive work, create a realistic implementation timeline, prepare your first intensive couples, and navigate the psychological barriers that keep practitioners trapped in familiar patterns. You'll learn which elements to implement first (and which to defer), how to pilot intensive work while maintaining your existing practice, and strategies for managing the discomfort of professional growth.

Chapter 8 recognises that changing how you practice feels risky. Rather than demanding wholesale transformation, it offers graduated pathways that build confidence through successful experience. Your implementation journey—moving from knowing to doing—begins here.

"Managing extended sessions isn't about doing more of the same—it's about creating the spaciousness where complete emotional cycles can unfold and transformation becomes inevitable."

Chapter 8

Start Your Implementation Journey

Practical First Steps and Academy Preparation

Image 8 Lone Sailboat at Dawn with Moon.
"Between Night and Day: The Quiet Before Transformation Begins"

> What story are you writing together? What would you like the next chapter to hold? The pen is in your hand.
>
> *Neil Wilkie, Relationship Inspirations*

From Understanding to Action

You've completed the foundation section of this book. You understand why change is needed (Chapter 1), the complexity you're addressing (Chapter 2), why traditional approaches fall short (Chapter 3), and the Duo Coaching Framework structure (Chapter 4). You've learned the Relationship Paradigm tool (Chapter 5), how to manage extended sessions (Chapter 6), and what foundation-level competency looks like in practice (Chapter 7).

Now comes the crucial question: How do you actually begin?

DOI: 10.4324/9781003715627-11

This chapter provides your practical roadmap from current practice to Duo Coaching implementation, addressing the real-world challenges of transition while building towards Academy training for advanced competencies.

Assessing Your Current Position

Practice Structure Audit

Before making changes, understand where you are. The audit below covers four domains—complete it honestly before proceeding.

Domain	*Key Questions*
Current Session Format	What is your typical session length? How many couple sessions weekly? Do you work solo or with colleagues? What cancellation/rescheduling flexibility do you have?
Financial Model	What is your current couple session fee? Average number of sessions per couple? Total revenue per couple? Can you sustain lower session volume if individual sessions cost more?
Physical Space	Is your space suitable for 2.5–3.5-hour sessions? Comfortable seating for extended work? Private, interruption-free environment? Bathroom facilities accessible? Space for two therapists plus couple?
Theoretical Foundation	What is your primary therapeutic orientation? What other modalities are you competent in? Where would additional training be beneficial?
Professional Support	Do you have access to supervision? Are there colleagues interested in co-therapy? Can you connect with other relationship therapists for consultation?

Readiness Assessment

Rate yourself honestly (1–5) on both foundation competencies and personal readiness:

Foundation Competencies	*Personal Readiness*
Understanding of Relationship Paradigm and assessment use	Commitment to professional development and learning
Ability to conduct extended sessions (90+ minutes)	Willingness to work outside traditional constraints
Comfort with integrative approaches	Openness to supervision and feedback
Capacity to work collaboratively with co-therapist	Energy and stamina for intensive work
Business flexibility to adapt practice structure	Patience with your own learning curve

Interpreting your scores: If you scored 4–5 on most items, you're ready to begin implementation with support. If you scored 3 on many items, you need additional preparation and skill-building before full implementation. If you scored 1–2 on multiple items, focus on foundation development through Academy training before attempting implementation.

The Graduated Implementation Approach

Don't try to transform your entire practice overnight. Use this graduated approach:

Phase 1: Extend Time (Months 1–2)

Rather than jumping to co-therapy and 3.5-hour sessions, begin by simply extending session length with current couple clients.

Identify two or three couples who would benefit from extended time and propose a pilot: "I'm experimenting with 90-minute sessions instead of 50 minutes to allow deeper work. Would you be interested?" Schedule these sessions and charge proportionally—if your 50-minute session is £100, a 90-minute session would be £180.

Notice what becomes possible with additional time: more complete emotional cycles, deeper exploration without rushing, better integration of insights, and reduced need to "contain" just as breakthrough emerges. This phase builds your stamina for extended work and your confidence before adding co-therapy complexity.

Phase 2: Find Your Co-therapist (Months 2–4)

While practising extended sessions, identify a potential co-therapist partner. Look among colleagues in your professional network, at professional association meetings (BACP, UKCP), in local supervision groups, at continuing education workshops, or through online practitioner communities.

What matters in a co-therapist? Seek complementary skills—different theoretical backgrounds create richer integration. Look for compatible values, similar ethical standards, and a client-centred philosophy. Gender balance is ideal (though same-gender partnerships can work). Professional maturity matters: You need sufficient experience to work collaboratively without ego. And don't forget geographic proximity—practical logistics matter.

Begin with an exploratory conversation: "I'm interested in developing a co-therapy partnership using the Duo Coaching approach. Would you be open to exploring whether we might work well together?" Then trial your collaboration: co-facilitate a workshop or group, observe each other's clinical work (with permission), conduct mock couple sessions to test compatibility, and have honest conversations about working styles and expectations.

Phase 3: Pilot Duo Coaching (Months 4–6)

Once you have a co-therapist partner and experience with extended sessions, you're ready to pilot. Select a couple of moderate complexity—not your most challenging case—where both partners are motivated and emotionally available, and willing to participate in a new approach.

Offer a six-session programme at a reduced "pilot" rate. Start with Session 1 at 2.5 hours (shorter than the eventual 3.5), with Sessions 2–6 at 2 hours (building up to 2.5). Make the agreement explicit: "We're developing this approach and welcome your feedback."

Co-therapist coordination is essential: 30-minute pre-session planning before each session, 30-minute post-session debrief after, regular check-ins about partnership dynamics, and honest feedback about what's working and what needs adjustment. Document everything—session notes with extra detail, what interventions worked or didn't, partnership dynamics and coordination, couple feedback and outcomes, and your own learning and questions.

Phase 4: Expand and Refine (Months 6–12)

With successful pilot experience, begin gradual expansion: add one or two more Duo Coaching couples per quarter, extend session lengths to the full 3.5/2.5-hour format, charge full professional rates (pilot pricing ends), and develop efficient systems and protocols.

Continue your ongoing development through regular supervision focused on Duo Coaching work, continuing education in modalities where you need depth, case consultation with other Duo Coaching practitioners, and refinement of your co-therapist partnership. Build your evidence base by tracking outcomes using Relationship Paradigm assessments, collecting client feedback and testimonials, documenting success rates and completion rates, and building case studies for learning and marketing.

Finding and Developing Your Co-therapist Partnership

The Co-therapist Relationship

This professional partnership is crucial. Invest in building it well through a clear partnership agreement covering four key areas:

Area	*Key Questions to Address*
Professional Boundaries	How will you handle disagreements about cases? What's the protocol if one therapist needs to miss a session? How do you protect confidentiality when discussing cases? What happens if the partnership needs to end?
Financial Arrangements	How are fees split? (50/50 is standard) Who handles billing and administration? How are cancellations managed financially? What about unpaid sessions or no-shows?

(*Continued*)

Area	*Key Questions to Address*
Clinical Decision-Making	How do you resolve different treatment opinions? Who has final say on safety concerns? How do you handle one partner's discomfort with an intervention? When do you seek outside supervision or consultation?
Communication Protocols	How often do you meet for partnership check-ins? What's the process for giving each other feedback? How do you handle between-session couple contacts? What documentation does each therapist maintain?

Developing Non-verbal Communication

Set aside time to develop your non-verbal communication system before you need it.

Practice Exercise 1: Silent Observation. Watch couples therapy video together, practising signalling each other when you notice dynamics. Develop subtle gestures for common observations, then debrief about what signals worked.

Practice Exercise 2: Mock Sessions. Role-play couple sessions, practising intervening, supporting, and handoffs using only non-verbal cues to coordinate. Refine your signal system based on experience.

Practice Exercise 3: Live Observation. Observe each other's actual couple sessions (with permission), practising signalling from the observer position. Debrief about what you noticed and how signals worked, building trust in each other's clinical judgement.

Common Implementation Challenges

Challenge	*Solutions*
"I can't find a co-therapist"	Start with extended individual sessions while searching. Join the Duo Coaching Academy to connect with potential partners. Advertise in professional newsletters or associations. Consider virtual co-therapy if no local partners are available. Adapt some elements (extended sessions, finite timeline) solo while building towards co-therapy.
"Extended sessions don't fit my schedule"	Reserve specific days for Duo Coaching intensive work. Offer a limited number of Duo Coaching slots monthly. Charge premium rates, making fewer sessions financially viable. Consider this a specialised service, not an entire practice transformation.
"Couples can't afford intensive work"	The total investment is often comparable to extended weekly therapy. Payment plans make intensive work accessible. Offer a sliding scale for financial hardship cases. Remember: some couples *can't afford* ineffective traditional therapy that takes longer.

(Continued)

Challenge	*Solutions*
"I don't feel competent enough"	That's why Academy training exists. Begin with foundation-level cases, not the most complex. Use supervision extensively during development. You're more competent than you think—every expert was once a beginner.
"My professional community questions this approach"	Share research supporting intensive formats. Invite colleagues to observe (with permission). Present case studies demonstrating effectiveness. Connect sceptics with satisfied clients. Stand confidently in evidence-based innovation.

Preparing for Academy Training

Foundation Level Preparation

Before enrolling in Academy training, ensure you have the necessary grounding across four areas:

Area	*Readiness Indicators*
Clinical Experience	At least 10–15 extended (90+ minute) sessions conducted. Some form of co-therapy attempted (even informal). Relationship Paradigm assessment used with multiple couples. Documented outcomes showing benefits of longer sessions.
Theoretical Grounding	Completed reading of "Reinventing" and "Practitioners." Familiar with at least three to four therapeutic modalities. Understand attachment theory basics. Comfortable with systems thinking.
Professional Development	Current supervision arrangement. Regular continuing education participation. Professional liability insurance appropriate for intensive work. Professional association membership (BACP, UKCP, etc.).
Practical Readiness	Co-therapist partner identified (or in development). Practice space suitable for extended sessions. Business model accommodating intensive format. Time available for training and implementation.

Academy Training Pathway

Foundation Course covers comprehensive Relationship Paradigm mastery, detailed session protocols and timing, advanced co-therapist communication systems, outcome measurement and tracking, business model development, cultural adaptation basics, and supervision in live practice.

Intermediate Specialisation (future development) addresses complex case management protocols, detailed infidelity recovery process, trauma-informed intensive work, cultural competency development, specialised population training, and advanced modality integration.

Expert Level (advanced contribution) involves training and supervising other practitioners, research and outcome documentation, innovation and technique development, community leadership and impact, and certification and quality assurance.

Your First 90 Days: Action Plan

Month 1: Foundation Building

Weeks 1–2: Complete your practice structure audit, identify two or three couples for extended session pilot, research potential co-therapist partners, and review the Practitioner's Guide and relevant sections of "Reinventing."

Weeks 3–4: Propose extended sessions to selected couples, schedule your first 90-minute sessions, reach out to three to five potential co-therapist candidates, and join a Duo Coaching community or professional network.

Month 2: Skill Development

Weeks 5–6: Conduct your first extended sessions, document experiences and learning, have initial conversations with co-therapist candidates, and begin supervision focused on intensive work.

Weeks 7–8: Continue extended session practice, select your preferred co-therapist partner candidate, develop your partnership agreement, and plan your first co-facilitated experience.

Month 3: Integration

Weeks 9–10: Co-facilitate a workshop or group with your partner, practise mock couple sessions together, develop your non-verbal communication system, and prepare for your first Duo Coaching pilot couple.

Weeks 11–12: Launch your first Duo Coaching pilot case with intensive pre-session planning, conduct your first 2.5-hour co-therapy session, and complete a detailed post-session debrief and learning capture.

Beyond 90 Days: Continue developing through practice, supervision, and Academy training.

Your Implementation Checklist

Foundation Skills	*Business Readiness*
Comfortable conducting 90+ minute sessions	Financial model supports intensive work
Using Relationship Paradigm for assessment	Practice space suitable for extended sessions

(Continued)

Foundation Skills	*Business Readiness*
Tracking outcomes objectively	Scheduling accommodates longer appointments
Managing energy through extended work	Insurance/liability coverage appropriate
Co-therapist partner identified	Marketing materials communicate new offering

Professional Development	*Quality Assurance*
Regular supervision arranged	Outcome measurement system in place
Academy training enrolment planned	Client feedback collection process
Continuing education in key modalities	Case documentation protocols
Peer consultation group or network	Regular co-therapist partnership reviews
Professional community support	Ethical practice standards maintained

The Courage to Begin

Change is uncomfortable. Implementing a new approach while maintaining your existing practice requires courage, commitment, and patience with yourself during the learning process.

Remember: Every expert was once a beginner who took the first uncertain steps. Couples need what you're learning—their desperation deserves your courage. You're not alone—the Academy and practitioner community provide support. Small steps compound—each extended session builds competency. Progress over perfection—you'll refine through practice.

Rebecca and Tom (Chapter 5) tried traditional therapy, and it failed them. Duo Coaching gave them their relationship back. There are thousands of couples like them waiting for practitioners brave enough to offer something different.

Will you be one of those practitioners?

Integration and Self-reflection

Foundation Level Skills Addressed in This Chapter

This chapter has addressed four key foundation skills: Practice Assessment (honest evaluation of current structure and readiness), Implementation Planning (clear graduated approach to change), Partnership Development (framework for finding and building co-therapist relationships), and Challenge Navigation (solutions for common implementation obstacles).

Reflection Questions

1 What is your biggest concern about implementing Duo Coaching in your practice?
2 Do you have a potential co-therapist partner in mind? If not, where will you look?
3 What is your realistic timeline for beginning foundation-level implementation?
4 When will you enrol in Academy training to develop advanced competencies?

Looking Ahead: Part II Preview

You've completed the Foundation Level section. Congratulations!

Part II provides previews of intermediate and expert competencies: Chapters 9–17 address complex cases, specialised populations, and advanced practice building; Chapters 18–21 cover expert-level training, contribution, and professional leadership. These chapters build your awareness of advanced competencies and prepare you for Academy training where you'll develop these skills through supervised practice.

The transformation of relationship therapy begins with individual practitioners willing to think differently, work innovatively, and commit to excellence in service of the couples who trust us with their most precious relationships.

Your journey begins now.

Reflection Questions

Having completed the Practice Structure Audit, what is your most significant structural barrier to implementing Duo Coaching?

Do you have a potential co-therapist partner in mind? If not, where specifically will you look, and what qualities matter most to you?

Which phase of the graduated implementation approach feels most achievable to begin within the next month? What's your first concrete step?

What psychological barriers (fear of failure, discomfort with change, perfectionism) might keep you from taking action despite intellectual understanding?

What support would you need to maintain momentum through the inevitable discomfort of the learning curve?

Self-assessment

Rate your readiness to begin your implementation journey:

Trust your gut response. What number first comes to mind when you consider how ready you feel to take this further?

Score	*Interpretation*
1–2	Significant barriers to address before implementation can begin; focus on foundation development
3–4	Some readiness but key elements missing (co-therapist, space, time, or confidence)

(Continued)

Score	*Interpretation*
5–6	Practical foundations largely in place; ready to begin Phase 1 with appropriate support
7+	Clear pathway and resources identified; prepared to commence graduated implementation

End of Part II

You've developed the fundamental framework: the Relationship Paradigm, the co-therapist partnership, session structure, and a pathway to begin. These are your tools. In Part III, we put them to work—walking through what actually happens when four people sit down together and begin the work of transformation.

Part III: Session-by-Session Implementation (Chapters 9–11)

This is the heart of this book. These chapters walk you through what actually happens in the room—session by session, moment by moment. You'll learn to integrate multiple therapeutic approaches, respond to whatever emerges, and establish your practice. Theory becomes lived experience here.

Coming Next: Chapter 9—Integrative Therapeutic Mastery

You've begun implementing Duo Coaching structure and process, but couples require more than format—they need interventions drawn from multiple therapeutic traditions. Chapter 9 explores how to integrate diverse modalities fluidly within intensive sessions rather than remaining confined to single-approach constraints.

Discover how Emotionally Focused Therapy, Gottman Method, Internal Family Systems, Somatic Experiencing, Cognitive-Behavioural approaches, and Psychodynamic perspectives each illuminate different relationship dimensions. You'll learn to recognise which modality serves specific moments, how to shift between approaches seamlessly, when theoretical integration strengthens versus confuses intervention, and how co-therapy partnerships enable modality flexibility that single practitioners cannot achieve.

Chapter 9 liberates you from single-modality limitations without creating theoretical chaos. You'll develop the integrative sophistication that separates competent from masterful relationship therapy. Your therapeutic repertoire expands here.

> The couples walking through your door tomorrow deserve practitioners who've done the work you've done in these eight chapters - understanding why change is needed, learning new frameworks and tools, and committing to implementation despite uncertainty. You are becoming that practitioner.

Part III

Intermediate Level Competencies

Advanced Interventions and Complex Cases

Chapter 9

Integrative Therapeutic Mastery

Blending Multiple Modalities Fluidly

In the beginner's mind there are many possibilities, but in the expert's there are few.
—Shunryu Suzuki

Image 9 Nautical Chart with Sextant and Dividers.
"The Navigator's Table: Instruments for Charting an Unknown Sea"

DOI: 10.4324/9781003715627-13

The Myth of Theoretical Purity

When I began my training as a relationship therapist, there was an unspoken expectation that I would choose my theoretical allegiance—would I be a systemic practitioner, a psychodynamic therapist, an attachment-based specialist? The assumption was that excellence required depth in a single approach rather than breadth across multiple traditions.

But relationships didn't read the textbooks. They arrived in my therapy room messy, complex, and stubbornly resistant to fitting neatly into any single theoretical framework.

Consider Lauren and Daniel, who came to see us in their third year of marriage. David had grown up in a household where emotions were dangerous—his father's rage could explode without warning, and survival meant becoming invisible. Emma's family, by contrast, had prized verbal expression and direct communication above all else. When conflict emerged in their relationship, David would shut down completely, triggering Emma's escalating pursuit, which, in turn, confirmed David's belief that emotional expression led to danger.

A purely systemic approach might have helped them understand their interaction patterns. Attachment theory could have illuminated David's avoidant strategies and Emma's anxious pursuit. Narrative therapy might have helped them rewrite their relationship story. Solution-focused work could have identified exceptions and built on existing strengths.

But here's what I discovered: They needed all of these. And they needed them not sequentially, but sometimes within the same session, even within the same conversation.

The Case for Integration

The argument for integrative practice in relationship therapy isn't about theoretical fashion or professional flexibility—it's about effectiveness. Relationships operate simultaneously across multiple dimensions: historical patterns and present-moment interactions, conscious intentions and unconscious drives, individual psychology and systemic dynamics, verbal communication and embodied experience.

No single theoretical tradition adequately addresses this complexity. Each lens illuminates certain aspects while leaving others in shadow. The question isn't whether to integrate, but how to integrate thoughtfully, coherently, and effectively.

What Integration Is Not

Before exploring what effective integration looks like, let's clarify what it's not:

Integration is not eclecticism. Simply mixing techniques from different approaches without understanding their theoretical foundations creates confusion rather than coherence. It's like speaking a sentence with words from multiple languages—technically possible, but unlikely to communicate clearly.

Integration is not theoretical relativism. The position that "all approaches are equally valid" ignores genuine differences in evidence, effectiveness, and theoretical coherence. Some approaches work better for certain presentations; some rest on more robust foundations than others.

Integration is not abandoning depth for breadth. Superficial familiarity with many approaches serves couples less well than genuine competence in several complementary traditions.

Integration is not ignoring contraindications. Some approaches work beautifully together; others create tension or contradiction. Thoughtful integration requires understanding not just when to combine approaches but when not to.

What Integration Is

Effective integration in relationship therapy involves:

Theoretical coherence: Understanding how different approaches complement rather than contradict one another, creating a conceptual framework that makes sense of diverse interventions.

Principled selection: Choosing interventions based on what couples bring rather than practitioner preference, remaining responsive to emerging needs while maintaining clear therapeutic direction.

Genuine competence: Developing real skill in multiple approaches rather than superficial technique-borrowing, respecting the depth and complexity of different therapeutic traditions.

Flexible application: Moving fluidly between modalities as situations require, matching interventions to immediate needs while maintaining overall therapeutic coherence.

Ongoing learning: Recognising that integration is a developmental process requiring continuous study, practice, and refinement rather than a fixed endpoint.

Decision Flowcharts, Vignettes, and Comparison Tables

The Integration Challenge

No single therapeutic tradition adequately addresses relationship complexity. Each lens illuminates certain aspects while leaving others in shadow. The question isn't WHETHER to integrate, but HOW to integrate thoughtfully, coherently, and effectively.

This chapter provides practical tools for:

- Deciding which modality to use when
- Understanding how different approaches complement each other
- Seeing integration in action through real examples

Core Therapeutic Modalities: At-a-Glance Comparison

Modality	*Core Focus*	*Key Strengths*	*Limitations*	*Best Used When …*
Psychodynamic	Unconscious processes, early attachment, historical patterns	• Deep understanding of patterns • Reveals hidden motivations • Addresses root causes • Explains "irrational" reactions	• Can get stuck in past • May delay practical solutions • Requires time and insight capacity	• Patterns repeat despite effort • Reactions seem disproportionate • Defences block intimacy • Family-of-origin issues intrude
Systems Theory/ Family Therapy	Circular causality, interaction patterns, homeostasis	• Reveals couple dynamics • Reduces individual blame • Shows pattern maintenance • Identifies intervention points	• Can underemphasise individual psychology • May miss emotional depth • Pattern focus can feel cold	• Stuck in rigid patterns • Solutions worsen problems • Family interference present • Power dynamics need illumination
Attachment Based (EFT)— Emotionally Focused Therapy	Emotional bonds, attachment injuries, felt security	• Powerful emotional access • Research-supported • Creates lasting change • Addresses core needs	• May underemphasise skills • Requires emotional capacity • Less focus on systemic patterns	• Emotional distance present • Attachment injuries block trust • Pursue-withdraw patterns • Insecure attachment evident
Cognitive-Behavioural (CBT)	Skills, thoughts, behaviours, practical change	• Concrete tools • Immediate application • Measurable progress • Skill-building focus	• May miss deeper dynamics • Skills don't address "why" • Can feel surface level	• Basic skills lacking • Cognitive distortions present • Behavioural change needed • Couples want practical tools

(Continued)

Modality	*Core Focus*	*Key Strengths*	*Limitations*	*Best Used When …*
Narrative Therapy	Stories, meaning-making, re-authoring	• Externalises problems • Reduces shame/blame • Opens new possibilities • Honours culture/context	• Can feel abstract • May avoid concrete change • Requires narrative capacity	• Problem-saturated narratives • Cultural stories constrain • Can't imagine alternatives • Need to reduce blame
Solution-Focused Brief Therapy	Exceptions, strengths, preferred future	• Hope-building • Resource-focused • Quick progress possible • Counteracts negativity	• May miss important problems • Can feel superficial • Not deep enough for trauma	• Overwhelmed by problems • Small changes could help • Strengths need recognition • Quick wins possible
Somatic/Body Centred	Embodied experience, nervous system, physical patterns	• Accesses non-verbal truth • Regulates nervous system • Bypasses defences • Grounds in present moment	• Requires body awareness • Can feel uncomfortable • May not address cognition	• Words fail or defences block • Trauma stored in body • Dysregulation present • Need grounding/presence

Decision Flowchart 1: Which Modality to Start With?

Use this flowchart when beginning work with a new couple:

START: What's the presenting issue?

↓

SAFETY CHECK:
Is there active danger (violence, severe mental health crisis, substance abuse)?
→ **YES:** REFER for individual treatment first. Safety before couples work.
→ **NO:** Continue assessment

↓

EMOTIONAL ACCESSIBILITY:
Can both partners access and express emotions?
→ **NO (One or both shut down/defensive):** Start with ATTACHMENT-BASED work (EFT) to create safety and emotional accessibility
→ **YES:** Continue assessment

↓

PATTERN CLARITY:
Do they understand their interaction patterns?
→ **NO:** Start with SYSTEMS THEORY to reveal circular causality and patterns
→ **YES:** Continue assessment

↓

SKILL LEVEL:
Do they have basic communication skills?
→ **NO:** Start with CBT for concrete skill-building
→ **YES:** Skills aren't the issue—go deeper

↓

HISTORICAL PATTERNS:
Do patterns repeat despite understanding and skills?
→ **YES:** Use PSYCHODYNAMIC work to explore unconscious processes and family of origin
→ **NO:** Focus on current dynamics

↓

NARRATIVE CONSTRAINTS:
Are problem-saturated stories blocking possibilities?
→ **YES:** Use NARRATIVE THERAPY to re-author stories
→ **NO:** Stories aren't the constraint

↓

Remember: This is a STARTING POINT. Most couples need MULTIPLE modalities as work progresses.

Decision Flowchart 2: When to Switch Modalities Mid-Session

Use this when your current approach isn't creating movement:

STUCK POINT: Current intervention isn't working

↓

WHAT'S HAPPENING?

1. Intellectualising (talking ABOUT rather than experiencing):
→ Switch to SOMATIC work: "Notice what you're feeling in your body right now"
→ OR switch to ATTACHMENT work: "What are you most afraid of in this moment?"

2. Blame cycle escalating:
→ Switch to SYSTEMS view: "Let's look at the pattern you're both caught in"
→ OR switch to NARRATIVE: "The problem isn't either of you—it's this pattern between you"

3. Emotional flooding/overwhelm:
→ Switch to SOMATIC: "Let's pause and ground ourselves in the present"
→ OR switch to SOLUTION-FOCUSED: "When has this NOT happened? What was different?"

4. Lost in problem focus:
→ Switch to SOLUTION-FOCUSED: "What would be different if this improved?"
→ OR switch to NARRATIVE: "Tell me about a time when you felt connected"

5. Skills exist but aren't used:
→ Switch to PSYCHODYNAMIC: "What stops you from using what you know?"
→ OR switch to ATTACHMENT: "What's the fear beneath this pattern?"

6. Defensiveness blocking everything:
→ Switch to ATTACHMENT: Soften into vulnerable emotions underneath
→ OR switch to NARRATIVE: Externalise to reduce shame

Key Principle: When one modality creates resistance, try another door into the same room.

Brief Clinical Vignettes: Integration in Action

These vignettes show how skilled practitioners move fluidly between modalities within single sessions.

VIGNETTE 1 Lauren and Daniel—Multiple Modalities in 20 Minutes

Presenting Pattern: Daniel shuts down when conflict emerges; Lauren escalates in pursuit.

SYSTEMS LENS (Minutes 1–5):
Therapist: "Let me show you what I'm seeing. Lauren, when you feel disconnected, you move toward Daniel with questions and concern. Daniel, what happens for you when Lauren moves toward you?"

Daniel: "I feel cornered. Like I need to escape."

Therapist: "And Lauren, what happens when Daniel pulls away?"

Lauren: "I panic. I need to know we're okay."

Therapist: "So the more Lauren pursues, the more Daniel withdraws. And the more Daniel withdraws, the more Lauren pursues. Neither of you wants this—you're both caught in it."

[Systems lens helped them SEE the pattern without blame]

PSYCHODYNAMIC EXPLORATION (Minutes 6–10):
Therapist: "David, you said you feel cornered. What does that remind you of?"

David: [long pause] "My dad. His rage could come out of nowhere. The safest thing was to become invisible."

[Psychodynamic lens revealed WHY the pattern exists]

ATTACHMENT WORK (Minutes 11–15):
Therapist: "So when Emma moves toward you, some part of you experiences danger, even though Emma isn't your father. Emma, what's happening for you as you hear this?"

Emma: [softening] "I didn't know. I thought he just didn't care."

Therapist: "Emma, can you tell David what you need from him when you feel disconnected?"

Emma: "I just need to know you're there. That we're okay."
[Attachment lens accessed vulnerable emotions and needs]

CBT SKILL-BUILDING (Minutes 16–20):
Therapist: "Let's practice something different. David, when Emma needs reassurance, what could you do that doesn't feel like danger to you?"
David: "I could … just hold her hand? Say 'I'm here'?"
Therapist: "Yes! Emma, would that help you feel connected?"
Emma: "That would be perfect."
[CBT gave them a concrete skill to practice]

INTEGRATION SUMMARY:
In 20 minutes, the therapist used FOUR modalities seamlessly:

- Systems: Revealed the pattern
- Psychodynamic: Explored historical roots
- Attachment: Accessed vulnerable emotions
- CBT: Provided concrete alternative behaviour

Each modality built on the previous, creating a coherent understanding and practical change.

VIGNETTE 2 Sarah and Tom—Career Transition Complexity

Presenting Issue: Sarah's promotion created tension. Tom withdrew. Communication broke down.

NARRATIVE THERAPY (Opening):
Therapist: "Tell me the story of Sarah's promotion. What was that like for you both?"
Sarah: "It should have been celebratory, but it felt like … the beginning of something breaking."
Tom: "Everyone was so proud of her. I was proud too, but also …"
[Narrative approach surfaced the competing stories]

SYSTEMS LENS:
Therapist: "So Sarah's promotion didn't just affect work—it rippled through your whole relationship. What else changed?"
Tom: "She's busier. We moved closer to my parents because we could afford it now. My mom is … involved."
Sarah: "And suddenly I'm in a different social circle at work. My old friends feel distant."
[Systems view showed cascading effects across multiple contexts]

PSYCHODYNAMIC:

Therapist: "Tom, you said you felt proud but also … something else. What was that 'also'?"

Tom: [long pause] "Left behind. My brother was always the successful one. I was just … Tom. And now Sarah is moving up and I'm …"

[Psychodynamic work revealed sibling position and identity wound]

SOLUTION-FOCUSED:

Therapist: "When have you navigated a big transition well together? What did you do then that worked?"

Sarah: "When we moved to this city. We made it an adventure. We explored together."

Therapist: "What would it look like to make THIS transition an adventure you explore together?"

[Solution-focused approach identified resources and exceptions]

INTEGRATION SUMMARY:

The therapist moved between modalities based on what emerged:

- Narrative: Honoured their stories
- Systems: Revealed complexity
- Psychodynamic: Uncovered deeper wounds
- Solution-focused: Built on past successes

VIGNETTE 3 Marcus and Elena— When Words Fail

Presenting Pattern: Both highly articulate, but talking ABOUT their issues without connecting.

CBT ATTEMPT (What Didn't Work):

Therapist taught speaker-listener technique. Both did it perfectly—mechanically. No emotional movement.

SOMATIC SHIFT:

Therapist: "I notice you're both excellent at talking. Let's try something different. Marcus, as you sit here right now, what do you notice in your body?"

Marcus: [surprised] "My chest is tight. I'm … holding my breath."

Therapist: "What happens if you breathe into that tightness?"

Marcus: [breathing, tears forming] "I'm scared. I'm so scared we're losing this."

[Somatic work bypassed intellectual defences]

ATTACHMENT:

Therapist: "Elena, what's it like to see Marcus's fear?"

Elena: [reaching for his hand] "I didn't know you were scared. I thought you didn't care anymore."

[Attachment work connected them emotionally]

INTEGRATION SUMMARY:
Sometimes the most sophisticated intervention is switching modalities when one doesn't fit. CBT skills were premature—they needed emotional connection first through somatic and attachment work.

Integration Decision Matrix: Which Modalities Work Together?

Some modalities complement each other beautifully; others create tension. Use this matrix:

Modality Combination	*Integration Level*	*How They Work Together*
Systems Theory + Attachment (EFT)	✓✓✓ EXCELLENT	Systems reveals the PATTERN (pursue-withdraw) Attachment reveals WHY (attachment fears drive it) Use together: Show pattern, then explore emotional drivers
Psychodynamic + Systems	✓✓✓ EXCELLENT	Psychodynamic reveals HISTORICAL roots Systems shows how history plays out in CURRENT patterns Use together: Explore family of origin, then track how it shows up now
Narrative + Solution-Focused	✓✓✓ EXCELLENT	Narrative externalises problems and re-authors stories Solution-focused identifies exceptions and strengths Use together: Challenge problem-saturated stories, highlight exceptions
Somatic + Attachment	✓✓✓ EXCELLENT	Somatic accesses embodied emotions Attachment provides a framework for understanding them Use together: Notice body sensations, explore attachment meanings
CBT + Any Other Modality	✓✓ GOOD	CBT provides practical skills Other modalities address WHY skills aren't used Use together: Explore depth, then teach concrete skills

(Continued)

Modality Combination	*Integration Level*	*How They Work Together*
Narrative + Psychodynamic	✓✓ GOOD	Both explore meaning-making and stories Narrative more present-focused, Psychodynamic more historical Use together: Explore family stories, help re-author current narrative
Solution-Focused + Psychodynamic	⚠ USE WITH CAUTION	Tension between future focus and historical exploration Solution-focused can feel superficial after deep work If combining: Use in different phases, not simultaneously
CBT + Narrative	⚠ USE WITH CAUTION	CBT's focus on "fixing" can conflict with narrative's non-pathologising stance If combining: Use narrative to reduce shame, then teach skills

Your Integration Quick Reference Guide

When Couples Present With ...

Communication Breakdown: Start: Systems (reveal pattern) → Add: CBT (teach skills) → If stuck: Psychodynamic (explore why)

Emotional Distance: Start: Attachment (access emotions) → Add: Systems (understand pattern) → If stuck: Somatic (body work)

Repetitive Conflicts: Start: Systems (identify cycle) → Add: Psychodynamic (explore roots) → Add: CBT (alternative behaviours)

Feeling Stuck/Hopeless: Start: Solution-focused (find exceptions) → Add: Narrative (re-author story) → If needed: Attachment (emotional connection)

Intellectualising: Start: Somatic (embodied experience) → Add: Attachment (emotional access) → Then: Systems or Psychodynamic

Trauma History: Start: Somatic (regulate nervous system) → Add: Attachment (create safety) → Carefully add: Psychodynamic (process)

Power Struggles: Start: Systems (circular causality) → Add: Narrative (externalise) → Add: Psychodynamic (underlying needs)

Loss of Hope: Start: Solution-focused (exceptions, strengths) → Add: Narrative (new story) → Add: Attachment (emotional reconnection)

Core Integration Principles

1 Start where the couple is, not where your training is
2 Use multiple lenses to see the whole picture

3 Switch modalities when you hit resistance
4 Build on strengths of each approach
5 Stay coherent—explain your shifts
6 Depth before skills (usually)
7 Multiple doors into the same room

Remember: Integration is an art developed through practice. Start with one or two complementary modalities and expand as you gain confidence.

These advanced techniques from Chapter 11 provide additional powerful tools for integration:

Advanced Techniques: At-a-Glance Comparison

Technique	*Core Focus*	*Key Strengths*	*Limitations*	*Best Used When …*
NLP (Neuro-Linguistic Programming)	Unconscious patterns, language, represen-tational systems, anchoring	• Accesses unconscious patterns • Quick pattern interruption • Language precision • Resource anchoring • Reframing perspectives	• Can feel manipulative if not transparent • Requires specialised training • May bypass necessary emotional processing	• Stuck patterns need interruption • Perceptual shifts needed • Resources need accessing • Language patterns maintaining problems
Timeline Therapy	Past trauma healing, future visioning, releasing limiting decisions	• Resolves past trauma efficiently • Releases limiting decisions • Creates future vision • Works with unconscious time coding • Gentle trauma processing	• Requires specific training • Not suitable for severe trauma without preparation • Some couples find it too abstract	• Past wounds blocking present • Limiting decisions identified • Need future vision clarity • Pattern roots in specific events
Parts Negotiation (Internal Family Systems)	Internal conflicts, protective parts, self-compassion	• Reduces internal conflict • Increases self-compassion • Honours all aspects of self • Resolves ambivalence • Explains contradictory behaviours	• Can feel strange initially • Requires psychological mindedness	• Internal conflicts evident • "Part of me wants, part doesn't" • Self-criticism blocking progress • Contradictory behaviours present

(Continued)

Technique	*Core Focus*	*Key Strengths*	*Limitations*	*Best Used When …*
Constellation Work (Pebbles and Human)	Spatial representation, systemic dynamics, embodied awareness	• Bypasses verbal defences • Reveals hidden dynamics • Accesses intuitive knowing • Shows perceptual differences • Creates visual metaphors	• Requires space and materials • Can feel unfamiliar • Interpretation requires skill	• Words failing to capture reality • System dynamics need revealing • Perceptual differences evident • Need embodied understanding
Clean Language	Client's own metaphors, non-leading questions, self-generated insights	• Honours client's own language • Avoids therapist projection • Develops client metaphors • Self-generated insights • Respectful and collaborative	• Requires learning specific questions • Can feel formulaic initially • May be too slow for crisis	• Client using metaphors naturally • Want to avoid leading • Need client-generated solutions • Exploring constellations or imagery

Additional Clinical Vignettes: Advanced Techniques in Action

VIGNETTE 4 Timeline Therapy—James and the Abandonment Pattern

Presenting Issue: James panics when Sarah travels for work, creating conflict before every trip.

PATTERN RECOGNITION (Systems):
Sarah announces trip → James becomes critical/demanding → Sarah feels guilty/resentful → Distance increases → Confirms James's abandonment fears

ROOT EXPLORATION:
Therapist: "When did you first feel this kind of panic about someone leaving?"

James: "I was seven. My mom left for a week—emergency with her sister. My dad didn't cope well. I remember feeling … terrified she wouldn't come back."

TIMELINE INTERVENTION:
Therapist: "If you could go back to that seven-year-old James, knowing what you know now—that Mom always comes back, that Sarah always comes back—what would you tell him?"

James: [emotional] "That it's okay. She loves you. She always comes back. You're safe."

Therapist: "Imagine telling him that. Really feeling him hear it and believe it. What shifts?"

James: [tears, then visible relaxation] "He can breathe. He doesn't have to be so scared."

INTEGRATION:
Timeline work rapidly resolved the root fear. Next session, James reported: "When Sarah mentioned her next trip, I felt the old panic start … but then I remembered seven-year-old me knowing she comes back. The panic just … faded."

VIGNETTE 5 Parts Negotiation—Emma's Push-Pull with Intimacy

Presenting Issue: Lauren initiates intimacy then pushes Daniel away. "I don't understand myself."

PARTS IDENTIFICATION:
Therapist: "It sounds like part of you wants closeness and part of you wants protection. Can you sense both of those parts?"

Emma: "Yes! Part of me wants to be close to David. But another part … gets scared and shuts down."

PARTS DIALOGUE:
Therapist: "Let's talk to each part. First, the part that wants closeness—what does she want?"

Emma: "She wants to feel loved. Safe. Connected."

Therapist: "And the part that pushes away—what is she protecting you from?"

Emma: "Being hurt again. Like when my ex … When I trusted and he betrayed that."

PARTS NEGOTIATION:
Therapist: "So one part wants love and the other wants safety. These aren't enemies—they both care about you. Can you thank the protective part for trying to keep you safe?"

Emma: [softening] "She was just trying to help."

Therapist: "And can you help her see that David isn't your ex? That she can relax a bit because you're safer now?"

Emma: [to protective part] "It's different now. You can ease up a little."

OUTCOME:
Understanding her internal conflict reduced Emma's shame about the push-pull pattern. She began recognising when her protective part activated and could choose different responses.

VIGNETTE 6 Clean Language and Pebbles—Making the Invisible Visible

Context: Rachel created her pebbles constellation. Clean Language helps her explore it.

RACHEL'S CONSTELLATION:
She placed a large rough pebble (herself), a small smooth pebble (Tom) far away, and several medium pebbles between them.

CLEAN LANGUAGE EXPLORATION:
Therapist: "And what kind of pebble is that?" [pointing to herself]

Rachel: "It's big and rough. Like … I take up too much space."

Therapist: "And when you take up too much space, what happens next?"

Rachel: "Tom gets smaller. Like he disappears."

Therapist: "And where is 'disappears'?" [spatial question]

Rachel: [pointing to small pebble far away] "There. Where I can't reach him."

Therapist: "And what would need to happen for him to come closer?"

Rachel: [long pause, insight dawning] "I'd have to get smaller. But … I don't want to get smaller. I want to be me AND have him close."

BREAKTHROUGH:
Using Rachel's own metaphor ("take up space") and Clean Language questions, she discovered her unconscious belief: she could be herself OR be close to Tom, not both. This belief could now be challenged.

Clean Language let Rachel generate this insight herself rather than the therapist interpreting her constellation.

Expanded Decision Flowchart: Including Advanced Techniques

When basic modalities aren't creating movement, consider these advanced techniques:

SITUATION: Pattern identified but won't shift

Ask: Is there a specific past event driving this?
→ **YES:** Use TIMELINE THERAPY to resolve the root event
→ **NO:** Continue assessment

Ask: Is internal conflict evident ("part of me wants … but part of me …")??
→ **YES:** Use PARTS NEGOTIATION to resolve internal conflict
→ **NO:** Continue assessment

Ask: Are words failing to capture their experience?
→ **YES:** Use CONSTELLATION WORK (pebbles) to make invisible visible
→ **NO:** Continue assessment

Ask: Do they use metaphors naturally ("it's like a wall between us")?
→ **YES:** Use CLEAN LANGUAGE to develop their metaphors
→ **NO:** Continue assessment

Ask: Are unconscious patterns driving the behaviour?
→ **YES:** Use NLP techniques (reframing, anchoring, pattern interruption)

Advanced Techniques Integration Matrix

Technique Combination	*Integration Level*	*How They Work Together*
Constellation + Clean Language	*✓✓✓ EXCELLENT*	*Constellations create visual metaphors* *Clean Language explores them without leading* *Combines beautifully in Session 1 assessment*
Timeline + Attachment (EFT)	✓✓✓ EXCELLENT	Timeline resolves root events Attachment work rebuilds felt security Use Timeline first to clear trauma, then EFT for reconnection
Parts + Somatic	✓✓✓ EXCELLENT	Parts work identifies conflicts Somatic work notices where parts live in body Both honour internal multiplicity
NLP + Systems	✓✓ GOOD	Systems reveals pattern NLP interrupts and reframes it Use Systems for understanding, NLP for intervention
Timeline + CBT	⚠ USE CAREFULLY	Timeline addresses historical roots CBT teaches present skills Use Timeline first, then CBT skills won't be blocked by past wounds

Integration Summary
You now have tools from:

- Core modalities (this chapter): Psychodynamic, Systems, Attachment, CBT, Narrative, Solution-Focused, Somatic
- Advanced techniques (Chapter 11): NLP, Timeline Therapy, Parts Negotiation, Constellation Work, Clean Language

The art of integration is knowing:

1 WHICH tool to use
2 WHEN to use it
3 HOW to combine tools coherently

Start with core modalities, add advanced techniques as your competence grows, always following what the couple brings into the room.

Integration within Duo Coaching

The Duo Coaching Framework particularly supports integrative practice through several structural features:

Extended sessions allow movement between modalities without artificial time pressure. You can explore psychodynamic patterns, then shift to skills practice, then facilitate attachment repair—all within one session's natural flow.

Two therapists bring complementary expertise. One therapist might maintain systemic focus while the other works with individual emotional process. The interplay between therapists models integration in action.

Structured assessment (Chapter 14) using the Relationship Paradigm helps identify which modalities different couples need most, creating principled rather than random integration.

Outcome focus provides accountability for integration—if approaches aren't creating change, frameworks must shift rather than couples being blamed for "resistance."

Moving Forward

This chapter has introduced core modalities and integration principles. Subsequent chapters will explore specific techniques and interventions from different traditions, showing how they combine within actual practice.

Remember: Integration isn't about becoming expert in everything, but about thoughtfully expanding your range to serve couples more effectively. Start where you are, build on your strengths, and add carefully chosen dimensions over time.

The goal isn't theoretical purity but practical effectiveness—helping couples create the relationships they long for by drawing wisely from the rich traditions that relationship therapy has developed.

Integration and Self-reflection

Foundation Level Skills Addressed in This Chapter

Theoretical Understanding: Grounding in multiple therapeutic modalities and their relationship applications

Integration Capacity: Ability to blend approaches coherently based on couple presentation
Clinical Responsiveness: Selecting appropriate modalities based on emerging needs rather than practitioner preference
Professional Development: Commitment to proper training before implementing new approaches

Reflection Questions

Which two to three therapeutic modalities form your current foundation? How do they complement each other?
When have you noticed your primary approach reaching its limits with certain couples? What did you do?
How do you decide in the moment which modality or intervention to use? What guides your choices?
What new modality would most strengthen your current practice? What training would you need?

Self-assessment: How confident are you in integrating multiple therapeutic modalities responsively?

Trust your gut response. What number first comes to mind when you consider how ready you feel to take this further?

Score	*Interpretation*
1–2	Need foundational training in core modalities before integration
3–4	Developing ability to blend approaches with supervision
5–6	Solid integration capacity across 3–4 modalities
7+	Fluid mastery across diverse approaches with coherent personal framework

Next Steps: Identify your next strategic modality addition. Seek proper training and supervision rather than technique-borrowing. Focus on deepening existing competencies before expanding breadth.

Note: *This competency assessment and reference list are designed to support practitioners in their professional development journey towards integrative therapeutic mastery. It is not exhaustive but represents foundational and essential resources for developing competence across multiple modalities within the Duo Coaching Framework.*

Coming Next: Chapter 10—Working with What Comes into the Room

Therapeutic modalities provide tools, but real couples bring messy complexity that doesn't match textbook presentations. Chapter 10 teaches you to work with what actually emerges—the unconscious patterns, defensive structures, attachment wounds, and systemic dynamics that shape every interaction.

You'll learn to recognise the subtle signals that reveal deeper patterns: how bodies speak what words conceal, when silence communicates more than speech, how couples unconsciously recreate childhood dynamics, and why some conflicts repeat endlessly despite apparent resolution. More crucially, you'll discover interventions that address these underlying patterns rather than surface symptoms.

Chapter 10 develops your capacity to sense the unspoken, name the unnamed, and work with relationship dynamics at their source. This is where therapeutic artistry emerges from foundational competence.

Chapter 10

Working with What Comes into the Room

Complex Dynamics and Unconscious Patterns

Image 10 Three Sailboats in Line.

"Sailing in Company: Three Boats, One Horizon"

> In the room there is not just me, Maria and the couple. The couple bring in ghosts from their pasts and the session is often an attempt to give a body to the ghost so we can all see them and have a conversation with them.
>
> —From *Reinventing*

The Invisible Presence: What Couples Actually Bring

When couples walk into your therapy room, they carry far more than their presenting complaints about communication or intimacy. They bring the accumulated weight of their histories—family patterns spanning generations, previous relationship wounds, cultural messages about love and partnership, unprocessed traumas, and unconscious contracts that may have outlived their usefulness.

Understanding and working with these invisible influences is what separates surface-level relationship counselling from the profound transformation possible

DOI: 10.4324/9781003715627-14

through the Duo Coaching Framework. This chapter will teach you to recognise, assess, and work therapeutically with the full complexity of what couples actually bring to your sessions.

The Ghosts in the Room

Recognising the Invisible Guests

Every couple brings what I call "ghosts" into the therapy room—powerful influences from their past that continue to shape present relationship dynamics. These aren't metaphysical entities but psychological and emotional patterns that operate largely outside conscious awareness yet profoundly affect the current partnership.

I remember Sarah and James, who came to us struggling with what they called "trivial arguments." They'd fight about dishwasher loading, thermostat settings, weekend plans—seemingly minor issues that somehow escalated into relationship-threatening conflicts. But in their second session, when James described how Sarah had reorganised the garage without consulting him, his voice carried an intensity far beyond the situation.

"It's not about the garage," he said, tears suddenly forming. "My mother controlled everything in our house. Everything. My father had no say. And when Sarah moves my tools around …" His voice trailed off, but the ghost had revealed itself—his mother's controlling presence, still operating 30 years later through James's hypervigilance about being controlled.

Types of Ghosts We Encounter

Parental Relationship Models

The template for intimate partnership is largely established through observing parents or primary caregivers. Every couple brings these templates—often unconsciously—into their current relationship:

- How love was expressed (or not expressed) between parents
- Patterns of conflict resolution or conflict avoidance
- Power dynamics and decision-making structures
- Communication styles and emotional expression norms
- The relationship between individual needs and partnership needs

When Rachel described feeling invisible in her marriage to Tom, exploration revealed her mother had been perpetually overwhelmed and emotionally unavailable. Rachel had learned that expressing needs was burdensome. Tom, meanwhile, whose parents had maintained elaborate facades of perfection, found genuine emotional expression terrifying. Their relationship enacted patterns neither had chosen consciously but both had inherited completely.

Family-of-Origin Roles and Rules

Each partner carries implicit rules about relationships learned in their family system. These rules operate as unquestioned assumptions until brought into conscious awareness:

- "Good partners don't express anger directly"
- "Love means anticipating the other person's needs"
- "Conflict is dangerous and should be avoided"
- "Strong people don't need support from others"
- "Emotions are private and shouldn't be shared"

The therapeutic challenge isn't just identifying these rules but helping couples recognise they have choices about which rules to keep, modify, or discard entirely. What served them in their families of origin may not serve their current partnership.

Previous Relationship Traumas

Unhealed wounds from past relationships create defensive patterns in current partnerships:

- Betrayal trauma leading to hypervigilance about partner's loyalty
- Abandonment wounds creating clingy or distancing behaviours
- Abuse history affecting ability to trust or set boundaries
- Sexual trauma impacting intimate connection and pleasure
- Divorce trauma creating fear of commitment or legal entanglement

When Marcus couldn't explain his panic when Elena was 15 minutes late, we eventually discovered his previous partner had announced she was leaving during what he thought was a routine dinner date. Now any unpredictability triggered survival responses. Elena wasn't just late—she was activating Marcus's entire trauma response system.

Intergenerational Trauma Patterns

Trauma can be transmitted across generations through family systems, creating patterns that persist long after original events:

- War trauma affecting multiple generations' capacity for emotional connection
- Immigration and displacement creating attachment disruptions
- Systemic oppression and discrimination internalised across generations
- Family secrets and shame passed down without conscious awareness
- Loss and grief that was never adequately processed

The ghost of intergenerational trauma operates differently—it's often a felt sense of danger, unworthiness, or disconnection without clear origin in either partner's direct experience. When couples describe feeling "something's wrong but we don't know what," intergenerational patterns often lurk beneath.

Working Therapeutically with Ghosts

Making the Invisible Visible

The first step in working with ghosts is helping couples recognise their presence. This requires:

Gentle Inquiry: "When you feel that intensity, does it remind you of anything from your past? Where have you felt this before?"
Connecting Present to Past: "What you're describing about needing constant reassurance—I'm wondering if that connects to something in your childhood?"
Externalising Patterns: "It sounds like there's a rule operating here about anger. Where did that rule come from?"
Somatic Awareness: "Notice what's happening in your body right now. Does that sensation have a history?"

Giving Ghosts a Voice

Sometimes the most powerful intervention is allowing ghosts to speak. I might say: "James, would you be willing to speak from your mother's perspective for a moment? What would she say about control and partnership?"

This isn't psychodrama or role-play but creating space for implicit patterns to become explicit. When ghosts have voices, couples can have actual conversations with them, challenge them, and choose whether to grant them continued influence.

Creating New Narratives

Once ghosts are recognised, couples need help creating new narratives that honour their histories without remaining imprisoned by them:

"Your father's way of showing love was through criticism. You learned to equate caring with critique. But Sarah's love language is different. Can we help you recognise care even when it doesn't look like what you learned?"

Understanding Warm Data: Reading What Lies Beneath

Beyond Cold Data: What Numbers Can't Capture

Traditional therapeutic assessment relies heavily on what Nora Bateson calls "cold data"—questionnaire scores, diagnostic categories, demographic information, and other quantifiable measures. While useful, cold data misses the most crucial dimension of relationship dynamics: the living, breathing, ever-changing patterns of connection that emerge between people.

Warm data, by contrast, is transcontextual information produced through communication forms both direct and indirect. It's the quality of energy between partners, the micro-expressions that reveal authentic feelings, the way couples position themselves in space, the rhythm of their interactions, and the emotional atmosphere they co-create.

Consider what happens when you first meet a couple:

Cold Data Tells You

- How long they've been together
- Their demographic characteristics
- Their scores on relationship satisfaction measures
- Their stated problems and goals

Warm Data Reveals

- The emotional climate between them
- Power dynamics and alliance patterns
- Attachment styles in action
- Defensive structures and vulnerabilities
- The story their bodies tell about their relationship
- What remains unspoken but powerfully present

Learning to Read Warm Data

Developing sensitivity to warm data requires expanding your perceptual awareness beyond verbal content to include multiple channels of information:

Spatial Dynamics

How couples position themselves speaks volumes:

- Do they sit close or far apart?
- Do they face each other, you, or avoid eye contact entirely?
- How does their spatial relationship change as emotions shift?
- Who controls the physical space between them?

When Priya and Amir first arrived, they sat at opposite ends of the sofa, bodies angled away from each other. Amir's crossed arms and legs created a fortress. Priya's body leaned slightly towards him—reaching but not quite daring to bridge the distance. Before they spoke a word, the warm data revealed their dance: Priya pursuing connection, Amir defending against intrusion.

By their fourth session, they sat closer, bodies more open. At one point, when discussing a difficult topic, Priya instinctively reached for Amir's hand. He didn't pull away. The warm data was showing me their transformation before any questionnaire could capture it.

Energetic Patterns

The quality of aliveness or deadness between partners tells crucial stories:

- Is there vitality and energy, or flat affect and disconnection?
- When does energy increase or decrease during sessions?
- Do their energies complement, compete, or remain disconnected?
- What's the emotional temperature, and how does it fluctuate?

I remember sitting with Julia and Michael, both describing their relationship in neutral, reasonable tones. The content seemed fine—no major conflicts, shared interests, mutual respect. But the room felt dead. No spark, no friction, no juice. The warm data was screaming what they couldn't yet articulate: they'd created safety at the cost of aliveness.

Temporal Rhythms

The pace and timing of interactions reveal attachment patterns and emotional regulation capacities:

- Do they interrupt, wait patiently, or speak simultaneously?
- How does timing affect their ability to connect?
- Can they synchronise their rhythms or do they remain perpetually out of sync?
- What's the rhythm of their conflict and repair cycles?

David would launch into rapid-fire explanations whenever anxiety rose. Karen would slow down, speaking deliberately, pausing between thoughts. Their temporal mismatch created constant friction—David experienced Karen's pace as withholding; Karen experienced David's speed as overwhelming. Neither was wrong; they were simply operating in different temporal zones.

Somatic Information

Bodies carry truth that minds often obscure:

- How do breathing patterns synchronise or diverge?
- What do facial expressions and micro-expressions reveal?
- How do posture and gestures change with emotional content?
- Where is physical tension held, and when does it release?

When Sophie talked about trusting Oliver again after his affair, her words said "I forgive you," but her body screamed otherwise—shoulders hunched defensively, arms wrapped around her torso, breath shallow and rapid. The warm data revealed what she couldn't yet acknowledge: forgiveness was aspiration, not accomplishment.

Case Example: Reading the Unspoken

When Marcus and Elena first entered the therapy room, their questionnaires indicated moderate relationship satisfaction with communication as their primary concern. But the warm data told a different story:

Elena sat rigidly upright, hands clasped tightly in her lap, eyes fixed on me. Marcus slumped in his chair, body angled away from Elena, one foot pointing towards the door. When Elena spoke, Marcus's jaw visibly tightened. When Marcus shared his perspective, Elena's breathing became shallow and rapid.

The warm data revealed what the questionnaires couldn't: this wasn't a communication problem—it was a safety problem. Elena felt under threat and had activated protective defences. Marcus felt trapped and was preparing for escape.

Naming what the warm data showed changed everything: "I'm noticing you're sitting very still, Elena, almost frozen. And Marcus, your body seems ready to bolt. Before we talk about communication, can we talk about what's making this room feel unsafe right now?"

The relief was visible. Finally, someone saw beneath the surface presentation to the terror driving their patterns.

The Multiple Contexts Couples Inhabit

Cultural and Societal Influences

Couples don't exist in isolation—they're embedded in cultural contexts that profoundly shape their relational possibilities:

Cultural Narratives About Love

Western cultures often promote romantic narratives that set couples up for disappointment:

- The soulmate myth ("there's one perfect person for me")
- The passion imperative ("if the spark dies, the relationship has failed")
- The self-sufficiency story ("we shouldn't need anyone else")
- The happiness mandate ("relationships should make us happy")

When couples believe these narratives unconsciously, normal relationship challenges feel like evidence of failure rather than opportunities for growth.

Gender Role Expectations

Despite decades of feminist progress, traditional gender expectations still operate powerfully:

- Who initiates emotional conversations?
- Who takes responsibility for relationship maintenance?
- How are power and decision-making distributed?
- What expressions of emotion are acceptable for each partner?

Sarah and Tom struggled with his emotional unavailability until we explored how Tom's father had taught him that "real men don't discuss feelings." The cultural ghost of toxic masculinity was operating through Tom without his conscious awareness.

Socioeconomic Pressures

Financial stress and economic uncertainty create relationship pressures that require acknowledgment:

- How does work stress spill into partnership?
- What's the impact of economic precarity on relational security?
- How do class backgrounds create different expectations?
- What's possible when survival pressures dominate?

Technology and Digital Intrusions

Modern couples navigate technological dimensions that previous generations never encountered:

- Social media creating comparison and insecurity
- Digital connection reducing face-to-face presence
- Pornography reshaping sexual expectations
- Work intrusion through constant connectivity
- The paradox of connection and isolation in digital age

These aren't just "issues to discuss" but fundamental forces reshaping what relationships are and can be.

The Hero's Journey: Understanding the Transformation Process

The Call to Adventure

Couples arrive in therapy answering a call—usually reluctantly. Something in their relationship has become untenable, forcing them to venture beyond familiar territory. Like Joseph Campbell's hero, they stand at the threshold, uncertain whether to turn back or step into the unknown.

The presenting problem—"we fight too much" or "we've lost connection"—is rarely the actual call. The deeper call is towards growth, authenticity, and fuller aliveness that their current patterns prevent. Your role is helping them recognise this deeper call while honouring their fear about answering it.

The Road of Trials

The middle phase of couple therapy mirrors the hero's trials—facing internal demons, confronting uncomfortable truths, developing new capacities, and learning to trust the process. This phase is rarely linear. Couples advance, retreat, advance again.

Your task is maintaining faith in the journey when couples lose faith in themselves. The trials aren't obstacles to overcome but necessary initiations into deeper relational maturity.

The Return with Treasure

Successful couple therapy ends not with perfection but with integration—couples returning to ordinary life with new awareness, skills, and capacity for connection. They've faced their dragons, rescued parts of themselves they'd abandoned, and brought treasures back to their relationship.

The treasure isn't just technique or insight but transformed identity—they've become people capable of the relationship they desire.

Working with What Comes In: Practical Approaches

Creating Safety for Revelation

Before couples can explore ghosts and patterns, they need safety. This requires:

Normalising Complexity: "Every couple brings these invisible influences. You're not broken—you're normal."
Reducing Shame: "These patterns made sense once. They protected you. We're not here to judge them but to see if they still serve you."
Honouring Resistance: "Part of you doesn't want to look at this. That part makes sense. Can we go slowly?"
Celebrating Courage: "Showing up here and being willing to explore this—that takes real bravery."

Balancing Depth and Action

Working with what comes into the room requires holding tension between depth exploration and practical change. Too much focus on patterns without intervention creates therapy that illuminates but doesn't transform. Too much focus on skills without addressing underlying patterns creates change that doesn't last.

The art is knowing when to dive deeper and when to surface with practical tools. Extended Duo Coaching sessions allow both within single sessions—you can explore the ghost of James's controlling mother, then practice actual communication tools for negotiating household decisions.

Using Both Therapists Strategically

Having two therapists allows one to track warm data while the other focuses on content, one to explore historical patterns while the other maintains present focus, one to hold emotional intensity while the other provides grounding.

Maria and I developed a rhythm where she often tracked somatic and energetic patterns while I followed content and narrative. She might interject: "I'm noticing Mark's breathing just changed. Can we pause here?" This dual awareness catches what single practitioners miss.

Common Challenges in Working with What Comes In

Over-Intellectualising

Some couples (and therapists) prefer talking about patterns to actually experiencing them. The ghost stays safely abstract rather than becoming felt reality. Guard against this by continuously bringing awareness back to present-moment experience:

"You're describing your mother's criticism beautifully. But right now, as you talk about it, what are you feeling in your body?"

Becoming Archaeologists Rather Than Therapists

It's possible to get so fascinated by historical exploration that you forget couples came for help with their current relationship. Pattern recognition serves present change, not historical accuracy.

Missing Cultural Humility

Your cultural lens affects what you see and don't see. Remain curious about how cultural contexts you don't share shape the couples before you. Ask rather than assume.

Neglecting Strengths and Resources

When focusing on what's wrong—the ghosts, traumas, and patterns—don't miss what's right. Couples bring resilience, love, commitment, and resources alongside their challenges. Make sure warm data tracking includes noticing moments of connection, successful repair, and genuine care.

Moving Forward

This chapter has explored the rich complexity couples bring into therapy beyond their presenting concerns. In the next chapter, we'll examine advanced techniques and interventions that help you work effectively with this complexity, transforming invisible patterns into conscious choices and creating lasting change in relationship dynamics.

Remember: couples come seeking help with symptoms—poor communication, lack of intimacy, constant conflict. But underneath symptoms lie the ghosts, the patterns, the warm data, and the transformative journey waiting to unfold. Your willingness to see and work with this fuller reality makes genuine transformation possible.

> The couple bring with them shadows from the past and unrealised ghosts that are anchoring them to the rocks and preventing them from moving forward in the right direction. Diving below the surface and freeing the snagged anchors requires several different approaches as they need to understand what is below both of their surfaces.
>
> — From *Reinventing*

Integration and Self-reflection

This competency assessment evaluates your ability to recognise and work therapeutically

Foundation Level Skills Addressed in This Chapter

Present-Moment Awareness: Tracking what couples bring rather than following predetermined agendas

Unconscious Pattern Recognition: Identifying family-of-origin influences and repetition compulsions

Defence Mechanism Navigation: Working skilfully with resistance and protective strategies

Process versus Content Distinction: Focusing on how couples interact, not just what they discuss

Reflection Questions

1. How comfortable are you diverging from session plans when couples bring urgent material?
2. Can you identify repeating patterns from family of origin in your current couples? How do you address these?
3. When have you encountered strong resistance or defensiveness? How did you respond?
4. What helps you notice the process (how couples interact) rather than just content (what they say)?

Self-assessment: How skilled are you at working with what couples bring into the room?

Trust your gut response. What number first comes to mind when you consider how ready you feel to take this further?

Score	*Interpretation*
1–2	Need foundational training in psychodynamic and systemic approaches
3–4	Developing awareness of patterns with supervision support
5–6	Strong capacity to follow couples' material responsively
7+	Expert ability to recognise and work with unconscious dynamics fluidly

Next Steps: Practice distinguishing process from content in sessions. Develop awareness of your own countertransference reactions. Seek supervision when encountering complex unconscious patterns.

Note: *This competency assessment addresses intermediate-to-advanced level skills in couple therapy. Working with invisible influences, unconscious patterns, and complex dynamics requires ongoing training, supervised practice, and personal development. The references provided represent essential foundational knowledge for developing these competencies within the Duo Coaching Framework.*

Coming Next: Chapter 11—Setting Up Your Practice

You've developed therapeutic mastery, but transforming how you practice requires addressing practical realities: business structures, pricing strategies, scheduling systems, and marketing approaches that support intensive work. Chapter 12 provides comprehensive guidance for building a sustainable Duo Coaching practice.

You'll discover business models that work for intensive formats, pricing frameworks that reflect value while remaining accessible, scheduling strategies that protect your energy, space requirements for extended sessions, insurance and liability considerations, and marketing language that attracts ideal clients while managing expectations.

Chapter 11 addresses the fears that keep practitioners trapped in traditional formats: What if couples can't afford intensive work? How do I fill a schedule with fewer, longer sessions? What about insurance reimbursement? Practical solutions replace anxiety with implementation confidence. Your practice transformation begins here.

Chapter 11

Setting Up Your Practice

Business Models and Logistical Framework

> The room in which we operate is in a very different environment to the counselling rooms that I have experienced… We had no idea what would happen when the clients arrived if, indeed, they would. The first contact was in 2009 and clients came in through the door in my house to a professionally set up counselling room, depersonalised and a very safe spacious environment.
>
> —From *Reinventing*

Image 11 Bold Anchor.

"Holding Ground: The Anchor That Keeps the Vessel Safe"

DOI: 10.4324/9781003715627-15

Creating the Container: Physical and Professional Infrastructure for Transformation

When I first started Duo Coaching in 2009, I converted a room in my house into a professional therapy space. The process taught me that physical environment profoundly impacts therapeutic outcomes. Couples can sense when they're in a space designed specifically for their needs. The environment either supports or hinders the vulnerable work of relationship healing.

This chapter will guide you through every practical consideration for establishing your Duo Coaching practice.

Physical Space: Room Design for Duo Sessions

Rethinking the Traditional Therapy Room

Most counselling rooms are designed for 50-minute individual sessions with a single therapist. Duo Coaching requires spaces that can comfortably accommodate two practitioners and a couple for several hours while maintaining the intimacy and safety essential for vulnerable relationship work.

Essential Space Requirements

Element	*Minimum*	*Optimal*	*Purpose*
Floor space	4m × 4m (16m^2)	5m × 6m (30m^2)	Basic functionality vs. comfortable movement
Ceiling height	2.4m	2.7m+	Prevents cramped feeling during extended sessions
Clear floor area	2m × 2m	3m × 3m	For constellation work and movement exercises
Storage	Basic cupboard	Dedicated area	Materials, refreshments, client belongings

Flexible seating is essential: comfortable chairs that support good posture for extended periods, with the ability to reconfigure for different exercises—facing each other, forming circles, or individual work. Consider adding an optional sofa for couples who prefer sitting together, floor cushions or mats for constellation work, and small side tables for water, tissues, and personal items.

Ideally, there should also be a second room available of it is appropriate to break out into separate 121 sessions during the main sessions.

Movement and activity space should allow for standing exercises and movement-based interventions, room to separate partners for individual work when needed, and an area where co-therapists can step aside for brief consultations.

Environmental Design Elements

Element	*What to Aim For*	*Why It Matters*
Lighting	Natural light, warm adjustable artificial lighting, table/floor lamps, dimmer switches	Harsh overhead lighting creates clinical atmosphere that inhibits vulnerability; softening light during emotional work helps couples feel safer
Acoustics	Sound insulation, carpeting/rugs, soft furnishings, optional background sound system	When couples know they're completely private—that no one outside can hear them—they become dramatically more willing to express difficult truths
Climate	Reliable heating/ventilation, individual comfort adjustments (throws, fans), fresh air circulation, accessible temperature controls	Nothing disrupts therapeutic momentum like couples being uncomfortably hot or cold for three hours
Aesthetics	Neutral calming colours, minimal artwork, natural elements (plants, natural materials), professional yet homely appearance	The goal is professional warmth—a space that feels safe and containing without being clinical or cold

Practical Amenities and Equipment

Refreshment facilities are essential for extended sessions. Ensure easy access to fresh water for both clients and therapists, facilities for tea, coffee, or light refreshments during breaks, a small fridge for storing water and healthy snacks, and a quiet kettle or coffee machine that won't disrupt sessions. The ability to offer tea during a brief pause can help couples ground themselves when work becomes intense.

Technology and equipment should include a clock positioned where therapists can see it without clients feeling time pressure, high-quality tissue boxes placed discreetly but accessibly, an optional flip chart or whiteboard for visual exercises, audio recording equipment if couples consent to session recording, and a mobile phone on silent for emergency contact.

Storage solutions maintain professional atmosphere: a secure filing system for client records and assessment materials, storage for therapeutic materials (constellation pebbles, art supplies), coat storage and a personal belongings area for clients, and professional resources accessible but not intrusive.

Accessibility should accommodate diverse needs, including wheelchair accessible entrance and facilities, accessible toilet facilities within reasonable distance, a hearing loop system if working with hearing-impaired clients, and clear pathways with obstacle-free movement areas.

Case Example: The Evolution of Practice Space

Phase 1—Starting Out (2009)

When I began Duo Coaching, I converted a ground-floor room in my house with separate external access into a professional therapy space. The initial setup involved removing all personal items and domestic furniture, adding sound insulation between the therapy room and main house, creating a small refreshment area, installing professional lighting and comfortable seating, and ensuring accessible facilities and parking.

Client feedback: Couples reported feeling "safe and private" in the space while appreciating the "professional yet warm" atmosphere that felt less intimidating than clinical settings.

Phase 2—Practice Growth (Current)

As the practice matured and client demand grew, I transitioned to high-quality dedicated office space designed specifically for intensive couple work. The professional office now includes a reception area creating a professional first impression and transition space, plus two therapy rooms allowing for breakout sessions when individual work is needed, one-to-one consultations during couple sessions, flexibility for co-therapist coordination, and separate spaces for different types of work.

Benefits of the dual-room setup: the ability to work with partners individually without leaving the building, co-therapist consultation space during sessions, professional reception demonstrating an established practice, enhanced flexibility for different therapeutic needs, and clear separation of waiting/transition and therapy spaces.

Virtual Considerations: Online Duo Coaching Best Practices

The Necessity of Virtual Options

Post-pandemic reality and geographical limitations mean that effective virtual Duo Coaching capabilities are essential for serving couples who cannot access in-person sessions. While in-person work offers significant advantages, well-executed virtual sessions can still facilitate profound transformation.

Technology Requirements

Category	*Requirements*
Platform capabilities	High-quality video/audio for four participants simultaneously, stable connection for two- to three-hour sessions, screen sharing for assessment tools and exercises, breakout room functionality for individual consultations, recording capabilities (with consent)

(Continued)

Category	Requirements
Recommended platforms	Zoom Professional (reliable multi-participant support), Microsoft Teams (excellent business integration), Google Meet (simple interface, good accessibility), or specialist GDPR-compliant therapy platforms
Equipment standards	HD webcams with wide-angle capability, professional-quality microphones, ring lights or professional lighting, minimum 50 Mbps internet speed, secondary internet connection, and device backup

Virtual Session Adaptations

Virtual sessions require specific modifications. Structure sessions slightly shorter (2.5 hours instead of 3.5) due to screen fatigue, with more frequent breaks every 45–60 minutes. Allow for enhanced pre-session technology testing and modified closing procedures to ensure clients feel grounded before disconnecting.

Standard Technique	Virtual Adaptation
Constellation work	Online whiteboard tools for spatial representation
Movement exercises	Adapted for limited camera view and domestic spaces
Breakout consultations	Platform breakout rooms for individual or co-therapist work
Resource sharing	Email follow-up with session summaries and homework materials

Technical protocols should include a 15-minute technology check before each session, backup phone numbers and alternative platforms, guidance for clients about ensuring private space, and end-to-end encryption with GDPR-compliant recording practices.

Environment Guidelines

Guide clients to prepare a private room where they won't be interrupted for several hours, comfortable seating with both partners visible on camera, good lighting that illuminates faces clearly, stable internet with backup options, and a quiet environment with minimal background noise.

For your own setup, ensure a professional or branded virtual background, excellent lighting and camera positioning, high-quality audio equipment, a separate workspace free from domestic interruptions, and emergency contact protocols for client crisis situations.

Case Example: The Rural Couple Success

James and Emma lived in rural Scotland, three hours from the nearest major city, making in-person Duo Coaching impractical. We conducted their entire six-session programme virtually: a technology testing session one week before the first session, constellation pebbles sent by post for spatial work, breakout rooms for individual partner work, and detailed written summaries after each session.

Despite never meeting in person, James and Emma reported transformation comparable to in-person clients. The key was thorough preparation, excellent technology, and adapted techniques that honoured virtual limitations while leveraging virtual advantages—like recording key moments for later review.

Business Structure and Legal Considerations

Duo Coaching Certification and Trademark

Important: The Duo Coaching name, framework, and approach are protected intellectual property. The "Duo Coaching" name and methodology can only be used by practitioners who have been certified through the Duo Coaching Academy.

Certification requires completion of the Academy training programme, demonstrated competency in the framework and methodology, ongoing adherence to Duo Coaching standards and ethics, and maintenance of certification through continuing education. This protects the integrity and quality of the approach, ensures couples receive care from properly trained practitioners, maintains consistent standards, and provides accountability and a professional standards framework.

If you are not certified: You may use the principles and approaches described in this book to enhance your relationship therapy practice, but you may not use the "Duo Coaching" name or trademark, market yourself as a "Duo Coach," claim certification or association with Duo Coaching, or use Duo Coaching branding or materials. Instead, describe your practice using generic terms such as "intensive couples therapy," "extended-session relationship work," "co-therapy approach to couples," or "integrative relationship therapy."

For information about Duo Coaching Academy certification, visit: www.duocoachingacademy.com

Partnership Options

Structure	*Characteristics*	*Best For*
Simple Partnership	Shared responsibility and liability with joint income; straightforward to establish but no personal asset protection	Practitioners comfortable with shared risk
Limited Liability Partnership (LLP)	Protected personal assets with business flexibility; more complex to establish but provides important protections	Established practices with significant client base
Separate Practices	Individual practices with collaboration agreements; each practitioner maintains independence; coordination required for shared clients	Those valuing independence

(Continued)

Structure	*Characteristics*	*Best For*
Company Structure	Limited company with both practitioners as directors; most complex but maximum protection and tax efficiency	Practices reaching substantial income levels

Financial Arrangements

Fee division options include equal split (both therapists receive 50% regardless of experience differences), proportional split (reflecting different experience levels or client acquisition), or hourly rate (each therapist paid for actual hours worked).

Expense sharing should cover room rental or mortgage proportions, equipment and materials costs, professional development and training, marketing and advertising expenses, and insurance and legal costs.

Administrative responsibilities need a clear agreement: who handles bookings and scheduling, who manages invoicing and payments, who maintains records and correspondence, and how these responsibilities are compensated.

Insurance Requirements

Type	*Coverage*
Professional Indemnity	Covers claims of professional negligence (essential)
Public Liability	Covers accidents or injuries on premises
Employers' Liability	Required if employing administrative staff
Building and Contents	If owning or renting dedicated space

Ensure your policies specifically cover co-therapy arrangements, verify coverage for virtual/online sessions, confirm extended session times don't affect coverage, and check whether both practitioners need separate policies.

Professional Registration and Compliance

Required registrations vary by jurisdiction. The following table provides guidance for practitioners in the UK and US:

Requirement	*UK*	*US*
Professional body membership	BACP (British Association for Counselling and Psychotherapy), UKCP (UK Council for Psychotherapy), BPS (British Psychological Society)	AAMFT (American Association for Marriage and Family Therapy), APA (American Psychological Association), ACA (American Counseling Association), NASW (National Association of Social Workers)

(Continued)

Requirement	*UK*	*US*
Licensing/ Accreditation	Accreditation appropriate to qualifications; voluntary register with Professional Standards Authority	State licensing required (LMFT, LCSW, LPC, Licensed Psychologist); requirements vary by state
Data protection registration	ICO (Information Commissioner's Office) registration; GDPR compliance	HIPAA compliance required; state privacy laws may also apply
Business registration	HMRC registration; Companies House if limited company	IRS (federal tax); state business registration; local business licenses may apply
Insurance	Professional indemnity insurance	Malpractice/liability insurance; verify coverage for co-therapy and extended sessions

Required registrations include professional body membership (BACP, UKCP, etc.), accreditation appropriate to your qualifications, data protection registration (ICO in the UK), and business registration with HMRC.

Compliance requirements encompass GDPR data protection protocols, professional standards and codes of ethics, continuing professional development commitments, and supervision arrangements.

Marketing and Client Acquisition

Building Your Client Base

Website and online presence: Establish a professional website explaining the Duo Coaching approach with clear information about session structure, costs, and outcomes. Include testimonials from satisfied clients (with consent), a blog or resources demonstrating expertise, and online booking or inquiry systems.

Professional networking involves building relationships with individual therapists who can refer couples, connections with family law solicitors, partnerships with relationship organisations, and presentations at professional conferences.

Community presence can include workshops on relationship topics, media interviews or articles, social media presence with valuable content, and partnerships with local venues or organisations.

Pricing Strategies

When setting fees, consider the extended session time (3.5 hours vs. traditional 50 minutes), the involvement of two practitioners instead of one, the intensive approach requiring fewer total sessions, the value delivered through profound transformation, and regional market rates and client demographics. Clients will appreciate that this is a very different approach to standard and will expect premium pricing.

Pricing Model	*Description*
Per Session	Clear fee for each extended session
Package Pricing	Discounted rate for committing to full six-session programme, with support between sessions
Sliding Scale	Reduced rates for couples with financial constraints
Deposit Systems	Partial payment securing session times

Initial Consultation Approach

Consider offering a free or low-cost initial consultation: a 30–60 minute exploratory conversation to assess fit between couple needs and the Duo Coaching approach; explain the process, costs, and expectations clearly; and give couples the opportunity to assess the therapists before committing. Both partners should speak individually by phone before the joint consultation.

Administrative Systems

Essential Systems

System	*Key Components*
Scheduling and calendar management	Digital calendar systems both therapists can access, buffer time between sessions for debrief, advance scheduling of six-session programmes, reminder systems for upcoming appointments
Record keeping	Secure GDPR-compliant client management system, session notes accessible to both co-therapists, assessment and outcome measure storage, backup systems for data security
Financial management	Invoicing and payment processing systems, expense tracking and reimbursement procedures, tax preparation documentation, regular financial reviews
Communication systems	Professional email addresses, secure messaging for client communication, internal communication system for co-therapists, emergency contact protocols

Growth and Development Planning

Practice Expansion Considerations

As your practice matures, several growth pathways become available:

Additional co-therapy teams—training and mentoring other practitioner partnerships, creating associate relationships, and building a team of Duo Coaching practitioners.

Specialist programmes—developing expertise in specific populations or issues, creating specialised offerings (affair recovery, premarital, etc.), and building reputation for particular relationship challenges.

Training delivery—teaching the Duo Coaching approach to other professionals, developing certification or training programmes, and contributing to the professional knowledge base.

Research contributions—systematic outcome measurement, contributing to the evidence base, and publishing findings and approaches.

Quality Assurance Systems

Outcome measurement should include systematic tracking of client satisfaction and relationship improvement, pre- and post-assessment comparisons, long-term follow-up with former clients, and continuous improvement based on feedback.

Professional standards require regular review of practices against professional body requirements, staying current with ethical guidelines, ensuring continuing competence through ongoing development, and peer review and consultation.

Creating the Foundation for Transformative Work

The investment in creating proper foundations pays dividends in client outcomes, professional satisfaction, and practice sustainability. Couples can sense when they're in an environment designed specifically for their needs, and practitioners work more effectively when supported by robust systems and clear frameworks.

Remember that practice setup is an iterative process. Begin with the essentials and develop sophistication over time as your experience and client base grow. What matters most is creating an environment where couples feel safe to be vulnerable, and practitioners feel supported to do their best work.

Start where you are, with what you have, and build thoughtfully from there. Some of the most effective Duo Coaching happens in converted spare rooms and home offices. The physical environment matters, but what matters most is the quality of presence and expertise you bring to the work.

> We are flexible and aware enough to be able to make, in the moment, changes of direction and re-contracting … We need to work on what is consciously presented, the unconscious and unsaid, the interplay and energy between the couple and all the warm data that is being picked up.
>
> —From *Reinventing*

Integration and Self-reflection

This competency assessment evaluates your ability to establish, develop, and maintain the new practice.

Foundation Level Skills Addressed in This Chapter

This chapter has addressed four key skills: Business Model Selection (choosing practice structure appropriate to your situation), Financial Planning (creating sustainable pricing and resource allocation), Space and Logistics (establishing functional practice environment), and Professional Systems (implementing efficient administrative processes).

Reflection Questions

1 Which business model best fits your current situation and goals (solo, group, hybrid)?
2 What pricing structure would make your practice both sustainable and accessible?
3 What space considerations are essential for effective Duo Coaching sessions?
4 Which administrative systems would most streamline your practice operations?

Self-assessment

How prepared are you to establish sustainable practice structures?

Score	*Interpretation*
1–2	Need significant business planning support before implementation
3–4	Developing practical systems with guidance
5–6	Solid practice infrastructure with effective operations
7+	Sophisticated business model with efficient systems

Next Steps: Create a detailed business plan addressing model, pricing, space, and systems. Seek consultation on financial sustainability. Establish essential administrative infrastructure before client intake.

End of Part III

You've now seen the work from the inside: session by session, moment by moment, rupture and repair. This is no longer abstract—you know what Duo Coaching looks like in practice. Part IV builds on this foundation, developing the advanced competencies that transform capable practitioners into masterful ones.

Part IV: Professional Development (Chapters 12–17)

Competent practice requires more than session skills. These chapters address advanced techniques, assessment processes, session planning, common challenges, complex cases, and knowing when to refer. This is where foundational competence deepens into professional mastery.

Coming Next: Chapter 12—Advanced Techniques and Interventions

Working with what comes into the room requires recognising patterns; transforming those patterns requires advanced interventions. This chapter equips you with sophisticated techniques for challenging cases that standard approaches cannot reach.

Discover powerful interventions for breaking repetitive cycles, accessing attachment wounds safely, resolving trauma that blocks intimacy, navigating affairs and betrayal, addressing sexual disconnection, and working with personality differences that create chronic friction. Each technique includes clear protocols, timing considerations, contraindications, and integration strategies.

Chapter 12 bridges intermediate competence and expert mastery. These aren't introductory tools—they're the interventions you reach for when couples present complexity that demands your highest skill. Your advanced toolkit awaits.

Part IV

Intermediate Level Practice Building

Implementation and Professional Development

Chapter 12

Advanced Techniques and Interventions

Specialised Tools for Challenging Cases

> The invitation of 'Reinventing' is to expand rather than replace, to integrate rather than discard, and ultimately to engage in a collaborative evolution of how we conceptualise and facilitate relationship therapy.
>
> —From *Reinventing*

Beyond the Fundamentals: Sophisticated Tools for Complex Dynamics

I remember the moment I realised my basic therapeutic toolkit wasn't sufficient. Emma and Richard had been working with me for three months. We'd improved their communication, they'd learned conflict resolution skills, they understood their attachment patterns. Yet something fundamental remained unchanged—a quality of deadness between them that no amount of talking seemed to touch.

In frustration, I asked Emma to choose objects in the room to represent herself, Richard, and their relationship. Without thinking, she picked up a paperweight for herself, a pen for Richard, and placed them at opposite ends of my desk facing away from each other. Then she placed a tissue box between them—large, opaque, completely blocking their view of each other.

"What's that?" I asked, pointing to the tissue box.

"My mother," Emma said quietly. "She's always between us."

That simple spatial representation revealed what months of conversation hadn't touched. Emma's intrusive mother wasn't just an occasional annoyance—she was the organising principle of their entire relationship system. We needed interventions that could work at that deeper, systemic level.

This chapter introduces you to the advanced techniques that can access and transform relationship dynamics at this profound level.

Working with the Unconscious: Building a Comprehensive Therapeutic Repertoire

The Duo Coaching Framework demands that therapists develop a sufficiently wide repertoire of modalities to address the full spectrum of relationship challenges.

DOI: 10.4324/9781003715627-17

While many therapeutic approaches focus primarily on what clients consciously present, our experience consistently demonstrates that the keys to transformation often lie deep within the unconscious mind.

Throughout our work, we've observed that many relationship patterns trace back to what might retrospectively seem like minor childhood experiences—yet these were formative traumas at the time they occurred. A parent's offhand remark, delivered innocuously but received as a verdict on the child's worth. A teacher's casual criticism that planted seeds of inadequacy. These moments, often forgotten consciously, become embedded in the unconscious architecture that shapes adult relationships.

The unconscious mind doesn't distinguish between major and minor traumas; it registers impact and meaning. A five-year-old told they're "too much" or "not enough" doesn't contextualise this feedback—they internalise it as fundamental truth. These seeds fester, influencing partner selection, conflict patterns, and emotional responses decades later, while the individual remains unaware of their origins.

This is why Duo Coaching requires therapists to be proficient in modalities that access unconscious material. Timeline therapy allows us to trace current patterns back to their formative moments. Parts negotiation helps clients dialogue with conflicting internal voices that operate below conscious awareness. Hypnotherapy creates the relaxed, focused state where unconscious material becomes accessible and malleable.

These aren't optional skills—they're essential to the Duo Coaching repertoire. Surface-level interventions may produce temporary relief, but lasting transformation requires working at the level where the patterns were formed: in the unconscious mind.

Creating Liminal and Transformative Spaces

The physical and psychological environment of Duo Coaching sessions serves two interconnected functions that are fundamental to the work's effectiveness.

The Liminal Space

Before therapy can truly begin, clients must cross a threshold—moving from their everyday consciousness into a space where deep work becomes possible. This liminal space is not metaphorical; it's a carefully constructed experience that begins before clients enter the therapy room.

Creating this threshold requires attention to multiple elements. The physical environment itself must signal safety and possibility—comfortable, private, free from the intrusions of ordinary life. The pre-session briefing establishes expectations and permissions, helping clients understand they're entering a different kind of conversation. And crucially, both therapists must be fully present in the room before clients arrive, their own energy settled and open, creating a field of welcome that clients can feel the moment they step through the door.

This liminal space communicates at an unconscious level: "You are safe here. You can be honest here. What emerges here will be held with care." Without this carefully constructed threshold, clients remain partly defended, partly performing, unable to access the vulnerability that transformation requires.

The Transformative Space

Within the session itself, a second kind of space must be maintained—what we call the transformative space. This is where the actual work of change occurs, and it requires both therapists and clients to be oriented towards possibility rather than problem-rehearsal.

The transformative space is created through where therapists place their attention. Rather than simply witnessing or analysing patterns, we're actively holding the intention that change is not only possible but expected. Our attention creates a field of potential—we're not just observers but participants in the transformation itself.

Clients sense this orientation. When therapists genuinely believe in and expect transformation, clients become open to it in ways that surprise even themselves. They move from "this is how we've always been" to "perhaps this could be different." This shift from fixed to malleable, from problem to possibility, is what makes the space truly transformative.

Both the liminal and transformative spaces require conscious cultivation. They don't happen automatically; they emerge from the therapists' intentional creation and maintenance of particular conditions—physical, psychological, and relational.

The Energetic Dimension: Recognising and Working with Subtle Shifts

There is an aspect of Duo Coaching work that some may find unconventional, yet it's too significant to leave unaddressed: the energetic dimension of therapeutic encounters.

Einstein reminded us that at the most fundamental level, everything is energy. In the therapy room, we're not just exchanging words and witnessing emotions—we're participating in a dynamic energetic field. Experienced therapists know the moment when something shifts. The air seems to change. The quality of presence alters. Sometimes the hairs on the back of your neck stand up. Something significant has just occurred, even if you can't yet articulate what.

These energetic shifts often precede conscious awareness. Before a client speaks their breakthrough realisation, before tears come, before the body visibly relaxes—there's an energetic movement in the room. As therapists, we become attuned to these subtle changes. We can't always explain their source, and perhaps we don't need to. What matters is that we recognise them and understand their significance.

This isn't about adopting any particular spiritual framework or belief system. Different therapists will interpret these experiences through different lenses—some may see them as intuitive reading of micro-expressions and body language, others as energetic sensitivity, still others as the natural result of deep empathic attunement. The interpretation matters less than the recognition.

What we ask of Duo Coaching therapists is openness to this dimension of the work. Be aware that these shifts occur. Notice when you feel them. Understand that your role includes creating the conditions where energy can move—where what's been stuck can become unstuck, where what's been rigid can become fluid.

This energetic awareness serves the practical work of transformation. When you sense a shift, you know to pause, to create space, to allow something important to emerge. You learn to trust these subtle signals as much as the explicit content of what's being said.

The therapy room is not just a physical space but an energetic container. Our work is to tend that container with the same care we bring to our words and interventions.

Constellation Work: Making the Invisible Visible

Pebble Constellations for Individual Couples

Constellation work, originating in family systems therapy, recognises that relationships operate according to invisible organising principles. By externalising these patterns spatially, we can see and work with dynamics that remain hidden in purely verbal therapy.

The Power of Spatial Representation

Something remarkable happens when we move from talking about relationships to representing them spatially. The analytical mind quiets, and a different kind of knowing emerges—embodied, intuitive, systemic. Couples often gasp when they see their relationship laid out in pebbles or objects because the representation shows truth their words couldn't access.

Basic Pebble Constellation Protocol

1 **Setup**: Provide a large, clear surface (desk, table, or floor) and a variety of small objects (pebbles, buttons, shells—anything that can represent people or elements). I strongly prefer pebbles as they are organic, have infinite variety and clients just love picking them up and feeling them.
2 **Initial Instruction**: "Choose a pebble to represent yourself and place it where it needs to be."
3 **Expansion**: "Now choose other pebbles to represent important people or things in your life and place them where they need to be."
4 **Spontaneous Placement**: Allow clients to place objects without planning or explanation—trust their unconscious knowing.
5 **Exploration**: Once complete, explore the arrangement using Clean Language questions.

Clean Language Integration with Constellations

Combining constellation work with David Grove's Clean Language questioning creates powerful exploration:

- "And when you see that arrangement, what do you notice?"
- "And is there anything else about the distance between those pebbles?"
- "And what would that pebble like to have happen?"
- "And if that could happen, what difference would that make?"

Movement and Change

After exploring the current constellation:

1. "And knowing what you know now, is there anything that wants to move?"
2. Allow organic movement without forcing or directing
3. Explore each movement: "And when [pebble] moves there, what happens to [other pebbles]?"
4. Continue until the system feels complete or resolved

Constellation Applications in Relationship Work

Current Relationship Assessment

Understanding present dynamics through spatial representation:

- How close or distant are partners represented?
- What comes between them (work, children, extended family)?
- How do their orientations towards each other and the world appear?
- What patterns of connection, hierarchy, or exclusion emerge?

Case Example: The Distance between Us

When Michael created his constellation, he placed himself and Jennifer about three feet apart, both facing slightly away from each other. Between them, he placed multiple small pebbles—"the kids," "my job," "her mother," "money worries," "the house."

"No wonder we can't connect," Jennifer said, seeing it laid out. "Look at all the stuff between us. And we're not even facing each other."

The constellation revealed what needed to happen: some of those "between" elements needed to move (the kids behind them, symbolising united parenting), some needed to shrink (her mother, moved to the periphery), and they needed to rotate towards each other. The visual clarity created immediate shifts in how they organised their relationship.

Family-of-Origin Exploration

Constellations powerfully reveal how current relationships mirror or react to family-of-origin patterns:

- How does current relationship mirror parental relationship arrangements?
- What positions did each partner hold in their families?
- What family loyalties or exclusions affect the relationship?

Case Example: The Constellation Revelation

James and Susan both said they wanted "more connection" but couldn't specify what that meant. Their pebble constellations revealed the real issue:

James's Constellation: Placed himself and Susan close together but facing outward in the same direction, like crew members on a ship looking at the horizon.

Susan's Constellation: Placed herself and James facing each other with comfortable space between, like partners in conversation.

The Discovery: James wanted partnership (facing same direction together towards shared goals); Susan wanted intimacy (facing each other in emotional connection). They'd been trying to create connection in incompatible ways.

The Solution: Creating arrangements that honoured both needs—sometimes facing outward together for shared adventures, sometimes facing each other for intimate connection.

Human Constellations: When Groups Are Available

While pebble constellations provide powerful insights in individual couple sessions, human constellations—when groups are available—offer an entirely different dimension of therapeutic possibility. Working with representatives allows couples to access collective unconscious wisdom and experience their relationship dynamics through embodied knowing that transcends intellectual understanding.

The Phenomenon of Representing Knowledge

In human constellations, people representing partners or family members often experience sensations, emotions, and impulses that accurately reflect the represented person's experience—even when they know nothing about that person's history. This phenomenon, while controversial in academic circles, consistently provides profound insights in clinical practice.

When and How to Use Human Constellations

Group constellation work requires additional training beyond basic Duo Coaching and should only be offered by practitioners with proper certification. However, understanding the principles helps you recognise when referral to constellation specialists might benefit couples.

The Therapist's Journey: When Partnerships Need Their Own Work

You've now learned the advanced techniques that access deep transformation—constellation work, parts negotiation, timeline therapy, Gestalt approaches, and clinical hypnotherapy. These are powerful tools.

But here's a truth that's rarely discussed in training programmes: Learning to use these techniques with couples is inseparable from doing your own work as a co-therapy partnership.

The co-therapist relationship itself will activate your patterns, trigger your defences, and require its own healing. You cannot guide couples through transformation you haven't attempted yourself.

Let's return to Maya and James. Three sessions into working with Susan and David, their partnership hits a crisis point. What happens next demonstrates both the vulnerability and the necessity of therapists doing their own constellation and parts work.

This is where theory becomes deeply personal.

> You've now learned how constellation work makes the invisible visible, and how parts negotiation resolves internal conflicts. But these aren't just techniques for couples. They're essential tools for your own growth as a practitioner and for your co-therapy partnership. Let's see what this looks like when the therapists themselves need healing …

INTERLUDE: MAYA and JAMES *When the Therapists Need Healing*

The Rupture (After Session 3 with Susan and David)

Maya

They're in the debrief, and something's wrong. She can feel it. James is being polite, professional, but there's a distance that wasn't there before.

"That intervention you made," James says carefully, "when you reflected Susan's anger back to her—'you sound furious with him'—I thought we'd agreed to stay with the vulnerability underneath?"

Maya feels defensive immediately. "She *was* furious. I was naming what was true."

"But David shut down completely after that. Took us twenty minutes to get him back."

"That's not my fault—" Maya stops. Hears herself. Takes a breath. "Okay. You're right. I was following my instinct, but I didn't check with you first."

"It's not about checking," James says, but there's frustration in his voice. "It's about trust. I thought we were holding the space for vulnerability, and you went to confrontation. Made me feel like we're not on the same page."

James

He hates conflict. Especially with someone he respects. But this is the third session where Maya's gone off-plan, followed her intuition in ways that left him scrambling to catch up.

"I think," he says slowly, "we need to talk about how we're working together. Because right now, it feels like I'm providing structure and you're … I don't know, going rogue?"

Maya flinches at "rogue." "That's harsh."

"Maybe." He softens slightly. "But I'm feeling ungrounded. Like I don't know what you're going to do next."

"And I'm feeling constrained," Maya admits. "Like you want me to be more cognitive, more planned, and that's not how I work."

They sit in uncomfortable silence.

"We need help," James says finally.

"Supervision?"

"More than that. We need to do what we ask our clients to do. Our own pebbles work. Because we're stuck in a pattern."

Supervision with Rachel (Two Days Later)

Rachel

Rachel is in her 60s, warm but direct, trained in systemic therapy. She's been supervising both of them individually, but this is their first joint session.

"So," she says, once they've explained the rupture, "you're discovering that co-therapy brings up all your own relational patterns. Welcome to the hardest and most rewarding work you'll ever do."

She pulls out her own basket of stones—smooth river rocks, beach pebbles, each one unique.

"Let's see what's happening between you. Maya, start with your constellation. Not of the couple—of yourself in relationship to James as your co-therapist."

Maya's Constellation

Maya picks up stones, places them thoughtfully.

A large, smooth amber stone in the centre: "This is the Intuitive Therapist. The one who feels into the room, who trusts the emergent process."

A darker stone, placed close: "The Protector. She doesn't want to be controlled, told how to work. She's had enough of that in her marriage."

A small, clear stone, placed at a distance: "The Collaborative One. She wants to work with James, values him. But she's scared."

"Scared of what?" Rachel asks.

"Scared of being diminished. Scared of being the 'emotional' one while he's the 'smart' one. Scared of being … less than."

James looks surprised. "I've never thought of you as less than—"

"I know," Maya says quickly. "This isn't about what you think. It's about my pattern."

She places one more stone—rough, reddish. Between the Intuitive Therapist and the Collaborative One. "The Resentful One. She's angry that she has to justify her instincts, prove they're valid. She wants to just *work* without defending herself."

James's Constellation

His turn. He picks up stones, places them carefully.

A grey, solid stone: "The Structure Holder. The one who keeps us on track, holds the framework."

Another stone, darker, placed very close: "The Anxious One. Terrified of chaos, of not knowing what's coming, of losing control of the process."

A smooth white stone, placed further away: "The Trustful One. The part that wants to let go, trust Maya's instincts, be more spontaneous."

"And that one's far away," Rachel observes.

"Because it's scared," James admits. "If I let go of structure, what if it all falls apart? What if I'm not needed?"

He places a final stone—small, dark. Near the Anxious One. "The Critical One. The one that judges Maya for being 'too emotional,' judges himself for being 'too rigid.' Always finding fault."

Rachel

"Look at these two constellations together," Rachel says. "What do you notice?"

Silence. Then Maya: "My Protector and your Anxious One are in the same position. Both terrified, both defending."

"And," James adds, "we both have a new part. The Resentful One and the Critical One—they're both keeping us stuck."

"Exactly," Rachel says. "You're in a classic pattern. Maya, your fear of being diminished makes you prove your autonomy by going rogue. James, your fear of chaos makes you grip tighter to structure. You're each triggering the other's core wound."

Maya

"My ex-husband," Maya says slowly, "was also a therapist. He was always subtly correcting me, suggesting I was too soft, too feeling-focused. I started either defending everything I did or just … doing it without telling him. To avoid the criticism."

"And I'm not your ex-husband," James says gently.

"I know. But my Protector doesn't know that yet."

James

"My dad," James says, not looking at either of them,

> left when I was twelve. Just … left. Walked out one day. And I remember thinking if I'd been better, more organised, held things together better, maybe he'd have stayed. So I became the boy who held everything together. The Structure Holder.

"And when I deviate from the plan," Maya says, understanding flooding in, "your Anxious One thinks the structure's failing. Thinks you're failing."

"Yeah."

Rachel

"So here's your work," Rachel says.

> The same work you're asking Susan and David to do. Can the Protector and the Anxious One start to soften? Can they trust that the other person isn't the enemy? Can the Trustful One and the Collaborative One come closer to the centre?

"How?" Maya asks.

> The same way you guide your couples. Slowly. With noticing. With communication. James, when you feel your Anxious One activated—'Oh god, what's Maya doing, this is chaos'—can you name it? Out loud? 'I'm feeling anxious about where this is going, can we pause?'

James nods slowly.

> And Maya, when your Protector rises up—'I'll do what I want, I don't need to explain myself'—can you catch it? Can you say, 'I'm having an instinct here, let me share it with you before I act on it'?

"That feels vulnerable," Maya admits.

"It *is* vulnerable," Rachel says. "That's why it works. You're modelling for each other what you're asking your couples to do."

Their Own Pebbles Work: Creating the Ideal Future

Rachel

"Now," Rachel says, "create your ideal future. What needs to be different?"

They work silently, moving stones, adding new ones.

Maya (Ideal Future)

She moves the Collaborative One much closer. Not merged with her, but nearby.

Creates space between herself and the Intuitive Therapist stone. "Still connected, but I can see it as separate from me."

The Protector stone—she makes it smaller, moves it back.

Adds a new stone. Smooth, blue. "This is … communication. Sharing my process before I act on it."

James (Ideal Future)

He creates distance between himself and the Structure Holder stone. "It's still there, but it's not all of me."

Moves the Trustful One significantly closer.

The Critical One—he removes it entirely, then hesitates. Puts a tiny version back. "It doesn't disappear. But it gets quieter."

Adds his own new stone. Green, warm. "This is … I don't know. Ease? Being okay with not knowing?"

Rachel (The Crucial Question)

"Maya—what do you need to have happen for you to get from here to here?"

Maya studies her stones. "I need to let the Collaborative One come closer. Which means … I need to risk being vulnerable. Sharing my instincts before I act, even when I'm not sure. Trusting James won't diminish them."

"And?"

"The Protector needs to step back. Which means dealing with my fear of being controlled, being made small. Recognising James isn't my ex-husband."

Rachel

"James?"

> Structure needs to not be all of me. Which means I need to find other sources of value—not just being the organised one. And I need to let trust come closer. Risk letting go, trusting Maya's process even when it scares me.

"What else?"

"The Critical One needs to quiet down. Which means … working on my own stuff. The perfectionism, the fear of my father's abandonment. Not putting that on Maya."

Rachel

She sits back, looks at both constellations.

"You're mirror images," she says. "Maya's merged with intuition, James merged with structure. Maya's pushed collaboration away, James has pushed trust away. And both of you have protection mechanisms keeping you safe but separate."

"The good news," she continues, "is you both know what needs to happen. The stones told you. Now it's about doing it. Slowly. With noticing. Exactly what you ask your couples to do."

Their Practice (The Following Week)

Maya

They're preparing for Session 4 with Susan and David. Maya feels an intuition rising—she wants to focus this session on Susan's rage, really let it out.

The old pattern would be: just do it, see what happens.

Instead: "James, I'm having an instinct. Can I share it?"

He looks up, surprised by the shift. "Please."

"I think Susan's Angry One needs more space. I want to invite her to really express it—safely, but fully. Let David witness it without defending. But I know that might feel chaotic to you."

James breathes. Notices his Anxious One rising. "Yeah, I'm nervous. What if David walks out? What if it's too much?"

"Valid concerns," Maya says.

> What if we structure it? Set a container—'Susan, we're going to give you ten minutes where the only job is to let the Angry One speak. David, your only job is to listen.' That way it's held but also free?

James relaxes. "That could work. And I can be watching David, make sure he doesn't flood. If he does, I can call a pause."

"Perfect. We're doing it—the stereo effect. I'm holding the emotion, you're holding the structure."

"We're learning," James says, and smiles.

James

That evening, he texts Maya: "Thank you for the supervision. For being willing to do the work."

She replies: "Thank you for trusting me enough to share your instincts before acting. Makes me feel like we're a team."

He realises: That's all his Collaborative One ever wanted. To feel like a team.

Their Growth (Three Months Later)

Maya

Session 6 with Susan and David—their final session. As they're wrapping up, Susan says something that makes Maya tear up:

"Watching you two work together taught us as much as anything you said. The way you disagreed respectfully, supported each other, navigated differences—that's what we're learning to do."

After Susan and David leave, Maya and James sit in silence.

"We did it," Maya says. "Our first couple. And they made it."

"*We* made it," James corrects. "Our partnership. We could have crashed at Session 3. But we did our own work."

"The hardest session of all was the one with Rachel," Maya admits. "Seeing my stones. Admitting my Protector was running the show."

"Same," James says. "Seeing how my Anxious One was choking the life out of our partnership."

"But we're different now," Maya observes. "The Collaborative One is much closer. I check in with you before following instincts. And it doesn't feel like weakness anymore. It feels like strength."

"And my Trustful One has come home," James says. "I can let go now. Trust the process. Trust you. Trust us."

Their Supervisor, Rachel (Email That Week)

Subject: Your Growth

Maya and James,

I wanted you to know—watching your partnership evolve over these months has been one of the joys of my supervising work. You came to me stuck in a painful pattern, each triggering the other's deepest wounds.

What you did next—the willingness to do your own constellation work, to see your patterns, to make yourselves vulnerable—that's the mark of truly excellent therapists.

But more than that: You modeled for Susan and David what repair looks like. They watched you navigate difference, communicate through difficulty, maintain respect even in disagreement. That was as therapeutic as any intervention you made.

The work continues, of course. Your Protector and Anxious One are still there, waiting in the wings. But now you know them. You can catch them earlier. You have tools for repair.

This is what mastery looks like—not the absence of struggle, but the capacity to work with it.

Keep going. The field needs partnerships like yours.

Rachel

What This Demonstrates About Advanced Techniques

Maya and James's journey illustrates several critical principles about the advanced techniques you're learning:

Constellation Work Reveals What Words Cannot

Notice how their verbal discussions about "not being on the same page" were circular and unproductive. But their pebbles constellations immediately revealed:

- The spatial relationship between their parts
- How merged they were with their protective patterns (Intuitive Therapist and Structure Holder)
- How far away their collaborative capacities had moved
- The protective mechanisms (Protector, Anxious One) maintaining the distance

The stones made the invisible visible. This is why constellation work is so powerful—it bypasses cognitive defences and shows truth.

Parts Work Addresses Internal Conflicts First

Before Maya and James could negotiate *between* them, they each needed to negotiate *within* themselves:

- Maya's Protector versus Collaborative One
- James's Anxious One versus Trustful One

Their external conflict was actually two internal conflicts playing out in relationship. This pattern repeats constantly in couples work—what looks like "couple conflict" is often two people's internal parts in collision.

The "What do you need to have happen?" Question Creates Direction

Notice how this question (the cornerstone of clean language constellation work) moved them from problem to solution:

- Not "What's wrong?"
- Not "Whose fault is this?"
- But "What needs to happen to get from here to where you want to be?"

This shifts from analysis to action, from blame to agency.

Transformation Requires Actually Doing the Work

Rachel didn't just talk about their patterns. She guided them through the actual constellation work—choosing stones, placing them, exploring what emerged, creating ideal futures, identifying what needed to happen.

The same applies to your couples. Don't just *talk about* parts or patterns. Do the actual experiential work. Let them move stones, speak from different chairs, timeline their past. Talking about transformation is not transformation.

Therapist Healing Enhances Client Outcomes

After Maya and James did their own work, their effectiveness with Susan and David increased dramatically. Why?

- They stopped projecting their partnership struggles onto the couple
- They could model healthy repair in real time
- Their complementary styles became true collaboration rather than competition
- Susan and David absorbed the modelling without it being "taught"

Your own healing is not separate from your clinical competence. It is your clinical competence.

Patterns Return—That's Normal

Three months later, Maya notes: "The Protector and Anxious One are still there, waiting in the wings."

This is crucial. Constellation and parts work don't make difficult patterns disappear forever. They:

- Make you aware of the patterns
- Give you tools to catch them earlier
- Create pathways for quicker repair
- Reduce the intensity and duration of activation

Mastery isn't absence of struggle. It's skilful navigation of struggle.

Your Own Work

Before you can masterfully guide couples through advanced techniques, you must:

Experience These Techniques Yourself

- Receive your own constellation work
- Do your own parts negotiation
- Process your own timeline
- Understand these tools from the inside

Do Constellation Work on Your Co-Therapy Partnership

- What parts of you show up in this partnership?
- What's the spatial relationship between collaboration and self-protection?
- What needs to happen for your partnership to flourish?

Maintain Ongoing Supervision Focused on Partnership Dynamics

- Not just case consultation
- But relationship work between co-therapists
- Processing ruptures as they happen
- Celebrating repairs and growth

Normalise That You're Learning

- You will make mistakes
- Your partnership will hit rough patches
- You'll trigger each other's wounds
- This is part of the work, not a deviation from it

A Note on Vulnerability

Some practitioners resist doing their own constellation and parts work. Common defences:

- "I've done enough therapy"
- "This is different—I'm the therapist, not the client"
- "I understand the theory, that's sufficient"
- "My issues don't affect my clinical work"

All of these are forms of the same protection: fear of being seen, of being vulnerable, of discovering uncomfortable truths.

But consider: If you can't tolerate your own vulnerability, how will you hold space for your clients' vulnerability? If you can't face your own patterns, how will you help couples face theirs?

The Work Begins with You

Moving Forward

In the chapters ahead, we'll continue exploring advanced techniques. But never forget Maya and James's lesson: These aren't just tools you use *on* couples. They're pathways of transformation you walk *with* couples—and sometimes, before couples.

Rachel's words are worth remembering: "The work continues. Your Protector and Anxious One are still there, waiting in the wings. But now you know them. You can catch them earlier. You have tools for repair."

This is what we're building—not perfect therapists, but aware ones. Not partnerships without conflict, but partnerships with repair capacity. Not techniques we wield from a distance, but practices we embody.

As Maya and James discovered, constellation and parts work are foundational. But they're not the only advanced techniques that catalyse transformation. Let's continue exploring the tools that will expand your therapeutic range.

Now let's continue exploring the specific advanced techniques that catalyse deep transformation …

Working with Both Conscious and Unconscious Processes

Throughout our work, we've observed that many relationship patterns trace back to what might retrospectively seem like minor childhood experiences—yet these were formative traumas at the time they occurred. A parent's offhand remark, delivered innocuously but received as a verdict on the child's worth. A teacher's casual criticism that planted seeds of inadequacy. These moments, often forgotten consciously, become embedded in the unconscious architecture that shapes adult relationships.

Duo Coaching recognises that while couples consciously present with communication problems or intimacy issues, the roots of these difficulties frequently lie deep within the unconscious mind. A comprehensive therapeutic approach must therefore work at multiple levels—addressing both what couples can articulate clearly and what operates beneath their awareness.

This requirement for depth work necessitates facility with a broad spectrum of modalities. We cannot rely solely on conscious processing through discussion and skill-building. We must also access the unconscious patterns, implicit memories, and automatic responses that drive relationship dynamics outside couples' awareness.

The NLP Umbrella: Accessing Unconscious Patterns

Neuro-Linguistic Programming (NLP) provides a comprehensive framework for working with unconscious processes. Within the Duo Coaching context, we draw upon several specific NLP methodologies:

Timeline Therapy allows couples to revisit formative experiences and release emotional charge that continues affecting present relationships. When David freezes during conflict, timeline work helps him identify the moment he learned that expressing needs brought danger—usually tracing back to a specific childhood incident with his volatile father. By processing that original experience, he can separate past danger from present safety.

Change Personal History techniques enable couples to rewrite the meaning of past events. Emma's belief that "I'm too much" for partners originated in her mother's exasperated sighs. Through Change Personal History work, Emma can revisit those moments with adult resources, recognising her mother's overwhelm wasn't about Emma being defective but about her mother's limited capacity.

Parts Negotiation addresses internal conflicts that sabotage relationships. James has a part that wants intimate connection and another part protecting him from vulnerability after past betrayals. Rather than suppressing either part, we facilitate negotiation between them, finding ways both parts' needs can be honoured—creating internal alignment that allows external connection.

The Empty Chair technique (drawn from Gestalt therapy but enhanced through NLP) enables couples to have conversations with people not physically present—critical parents, former partners, even younger versions of themselves. When Sarah speaks to the "chair" representing her critical father, expressing feelings she never could as a child, her partner Michael witnesses her vulnerability in ways that create profound empathy.

Clean Language and Clean Space, developed by David Grove, provide precision questioning that accesses clients' metaphorical landscapes without therapist contamination. When Michael describes feeling "like I'm walking on eggshells," we use Clean Language to explore that metaphor: "And what kind of eggshells?" "And where are those eggshells?" His unconscious mind reveals the complete pattern—he's walking on eggshells in a dark room, never knowing when he'll crack one and wake the sleeping tiger. This metaphor contains the entire dynamic with more precision than cognitive discussion could access.

Symbolic Modelling extends Clean Language by helping couples build and transform their internal metaphorical representations. As Michael explores his eggshells metaphor over multiple sessions, he discovers the tiger is actually a frightened kitten—his partner's reactions aren't dangerous, just loud. The metaphor shifts, and with it, his physiological response.

What Actually Happens in Sessions: The Responsive Mix

Session 1 follows the structure detailed earlier: couples tell their stories, create pebbles constellations, complete the Relationship Paradigm assessment, and receive their first between-session assignments. But Sessions 2–6 become highly responsive to what each unique couple presents.

Some sessions focus heavily on communication coaching—we guide couples through actual conflicts in real-time, teaching them to express feelings without blame, listen without defensiveness, and repair ruptures as they happen. We don't just discuss communication; we create opportunities for them to practice while we're present to course-correct.

Other sessions dive deep into unconscious patterns. We might spend 90 minutes with one partner doing timeline work while the other witnesses their vulnerability, creating understanding impossible through discussion alone. Or we facilitate parts negotiations, helping couples recognise their internal conflicts before addressing external ones.

Many sessions include experiential exercises: drawing pictures of their relationship journey, writing "I am" poems revealing their self-concepts, creating visual representations of their fears or hopes. These exercises bypass cognitive defences, accessing material couples didn't know they knew.

The key principle: we respond to what presents rather than following predetermined protocols. If a couple arrives in acute crisis from the previous night's argument, we address that immediately. If they've had a breakthrough at home and arrive connected, we build on that momentum. The framework provides structure; clinical judgment provides responsiveness.

Between-Session Practice

Transformation doesn't happen only in sessions—it happens in the daily practice between sessions. The Logbook system provides couples with structured exercises tailored to their specific needs, current progress, and presenting issues. Actual assignments are selected responsively based on clinical judgment.

The Logbook isn't homework in the traditional sense—it's structured practice that extends therapeutic work into daily life. Couples don't just talk about connection in sessions; they practice connecting between sessions. They don't just discuss their patterns; they observe and document them in real-time.

This between-session practice transforms insight into integration, understanding into behaviour change, therapeutic conversation into lived relationship transformation.

Clean Language: The Power of Precision Questioning

David Grove's Clean Language methodology provides perhaps the most powerful tool for accessing couples' internal experience without imposing therapist assumptions or interpretations. This approach is particularly valuable in relationship work because it honours each partner's unique perceptual world while facilitating exploration and change.

Core Clean Language Principles

- Use client's exact words rather than paraphrasing or interpreting
- Ask questions that help clients develop their own metaphors and understanding
- Avoid adding content, suggestions, or interpretations
- Trust that clients contain the resources for their own healing
- Facilitate client discovery rather than therapist analysis

Essential Clean Language Questions

Developing Information

- "And what kind of [client's word] is that [client's word]?"
- "And is there anything else about [client's word]?"
- "And where is [client's word]?"
- "And whereabouts [location given by client]?"

Exploring Relationships between Elements

- "And is there a relationship between [X] and [Y]?"
- "And when [X], what happens to [Y]?"
- "And what's between [X] and [Y]?"

Moving Through Time and Sequence

- "And what happens just before [client's words]?"
- "And then what happens?"
- "And what happens next?"
- "And what would you like to have happen?"

Clean Language in Relationship Assessment

Exploring Relationship Metaphors

Many couples naturally use metaphors to describe their relationships. Clean Language helps develop these metaphors to reveal deeper understanding:

Client:	"Our relationship feels like we're ships passing in the night"
Clean Question:	"And ships passing in the night. And is there anything else about those ships?"
Client:	"They're going in different directions. And it's dark, so they can't really see each other."
Clean Question:	"And when ships are going in different directions in the dark, what would those ships like to have happen?"
Client:	"They'd need to ... maybe turn on their lights? Or change course toward each other?"

Notice how Clean Language questions help the client develop their own metaphor and discover their own solutions without therapist interpretation or advice.

Case Example: The Wall between Us

Sarah described feeling a "wall" between her and Tom. Rather than interpreting what the wall meant, I used Clean Language:

Me: "And there's a wall. And what kind of wall is that wall?"
Sarah: "It's ... it's thick. Very solid. Made of ... concrete or something."
Me: "And a thick, solid wall made of concrete. And is there anything else about that wall?"
Sarah: "It's ... I built it. Brick by brick. Every time he criticized me, I added another brick."
Me: "And you built it brick by brick. And when you built that wall, what did you want to have happen?"
Sarah: "I wanted to protect myself. To not feel the hurt."
Me: "And to not feel the hurt. And now, knowing what you know about that wall, what would you like to have happen?"
Sarah: "I'd like to ... maybe not tear it down completely. But maybe create a door? So I can choose when to open it?"

This exchange took three minutes and revealed more than months of conventional therapy. Sarah discovered her agency in creating the wall, understood its protective function, and generated her own solution—not demolishing defences but creating choice about when to open them.

NLP and Timeline Therapy: Rapid Change Techniques

NLP and Timeline Therapy offer tools for creating rapid, elegant change by working with how clients represent and organise their experiences internally.

Core NLP Principles for Relationship Work

Submodalities: How clients represent experiences internally (visual qualities, sounds, feelings) affects their emotional impact. Changing submodalities changes emotional response.
Anchoring: Creating associations between specific triggers and desired states allows couples to access resourceful states when needed.
Reframing: Changing the meaning attributed to behaviours or situations transforms emotional responses and behavioural options.
Modelling Excellence: Identifying and replicating the structure of successful relationship moments creates templates for future success.

Timeline Therapy Applications

Healing Past Relationship Wounds

Timeline therapy can help clients release emotions trapped in past experiences that contaminate current relationships:

Protocol

1. Identify the limiting emotion (hurt, anger, guilt, fear, sadness)
2. Float above the timeline to gain perspective
3. Go back to the first time this emotion was felt
4. Release the emotion from that event and all subsequent events
5. Return to present with the emotion's charge neutralised

Case Example: Breaking the Betrayal Pattern

Marcus carried rage from his first wife's affair that poisoned his current relationship with Elena. Traditional therapy had helped him understand the anger but hadn't resolved it. Timeline work allowed him to:

1. Identify the specific anger towards his ex-wife
2. Recognise that holding the anger hurt him more than her
3. Release the emotion from the original betrayal event
4. Return to present relationship without that contaminating rage
5. Respond to Elena based on her actual behaviour, not his previous trauma

Parts Work and Internal Negotiation

Often relationship conflicts reflect internal conflicts within partners. Parts work helps negotiate these internal conflicts, reducing external relationship tension.

Basic Parts Protocol

1. **Identify the Conflict**: "Part of me wants X, but part of me wants Y"
2. **Give Voice to Each Part**: Allow each part to fully express its positive intention
3. **Find Common Ground**: Discover the higher-level outcome both parts want
4. **Negotiate Agreement**: Create solutions that honour both parts' positive intentions
5. **Test Ecology**: Ensure the agreement works across all life contexts

Case Example: The Independence-Connection Conflict

David struggled with Susan's requests for more together time. Parts work revealed:

Independent Part: Feared losing himself, becoming controlled (positive intention: maintaining autonomy and identity)
Connection Part: Wanted deeper intimacy with Susan (positive intention: creating meaningful relationship)
Higher Intention: Being authentic and fulfilled while deeply connected
Agreement: Scheduled couple time honoured connection needs; protected solo time honoured autonomy needs; both parts felt respected

Gestalt Approaches: Present-Moment Awareness

Gestalt therapy's focus on present-moment awareness and unfinished business provides powerful interventions for relationship work.

The Empty Chair Technique

Having partners speak to empty chairs representing parts of themselves, each other, or significant others can access emotional truths that normal conversation misses.

Protocol

1 Set up empty chair representing the person/part to be addressed
2 Invite client to speak directly to the chair
3 Then switch positions—sit in the chair and respond as that person/part
4 Continue dialogue, switching positions, until resolution or new understanding emerges

Case Example: Speaking the Unspeakable

Jennifer couldn't tell her husband directly that his criticism devastated her. Speaking to an empty chair representing him, she found her voice:

> "When you criticize how I load the dishwasher, I hear my father telling me I'm stupid and incompetent. I know you're not my father, but that's what I feel. And I shut down because I'm afraid if I tell you how much it hurts, you'll think I'm too sensitive, just like my father did."

Hearing this (actually hearing it, not just having it reported), Michael's defensiveness dissolved. He hadn't realised the depth of impact his comments carried.

Awareness Continuum

Gestalt's awareness continuum helps couples notice present-moment experience:

"Right now, I'm aware of …"

This simple intervention pulls couples out of storytelling about the past or worrying about the future into the actual experience happening between them in the moment.

Case Example: Finding Each Other Now

Sarah and Tom spent entire sessions describing past conflicts. I interrupted: "Stop. Right now, Sarah, what are you aware of?"

Sarah: "I'm aware that my chest feels tight. And I'm aware I'm leaning away from Tom."

Me: "And Tom, right now, what are you aware of?"

Tom: "I'm aware I want to reach out to her. But I'm also aware I'm afraid she'll pull away."
Me: "And Sarah, are you aware of Tom wanting to reach out?"
Sarah: "No... really? You want to reach out?"

That present-moment awareness cut through months of historical narrative to the actual longing between them happening right now.

Clinical Hypnotherapy: Accessing Deeper Resources

Hypnotherapy offers tools for accessing unconscious resources, healing past wounds, and installing new patterns at levels beneath conscious awareness.

Resource State Access and Anchoring

Helping couples access and anchor positive states creates resources they can use when facing challenges:

Protocol

1. Identify desired state (calm, confident, loving, playful)
2. Help client recall a time they fully experienced that state
3. Deepen the state through sensory detail
4. Create an anchor (touch, word, image) associated with the state
5. Test the anchor's effectiveness
6. Apply to relationship situations needing that resource

Hypnotic Healing of Relationship Trauma

Some relationship wounds require work at deeper levels than conscious conversation can reach.

Case Example: Healing Sexual Trauma's Impact

Lisa's teenage sexual assault created automatic fear responses during intimacy with David, even though she felt safe with him consciously. Traditional talk therapy had helped her understand the trauma but hadn't fully resolved the automatic fear responses during physical intimacy.

Hypnotic Healing Process

1. In trance, Lisa accessed her strongest, most resourceful adult self
2. This resourceful self provided comfort and protection to her teenage self

3 New beliefs about safety and her right to pleasure were installed
4 Positive associations with intimacy were strengthened through resource state access
5 New automatic responses of safety and openness were installed for intimate moments

Couples Integration

1 David learned to recognise and respond supportively to Lisa's healing process
2 Both partners practiced new intimacy patterns through hypnotic rehearsal
3 Positive relationship memories were amplified and anchored
4 Post-hypnotic suggestions supported ongoing healing and connection

Integration Principles: When to Use Which Approach

Effective advanced work requires knowing not just how to use techniques but when to use them and how to sequence them for maximum impact.

Assessment-Driven Selection

Couple Characteristics

- Learning style preferences (visual, auditory, kinaesthetic)
- Comfort with emotional expression and vulnerability
- Previous therapy experience and theoretical preferences
- Cultural background and spiritual orientation
- Individual and relationship readiness for change

Presenting Issues

- Communication problems: Gestalt and NLP techniques
- Trust issues: Psychodynamic exploration and timeline healing
- Intimacy challenges: Hypnotherapy and somatic approaches
- Pattern recognition: Constellation work
- Future planning: NLP modelling and Clean Language visioning

Session Phase

- Opening phase: Clean Language for outcome setting and assessment
- Exploration phase: Psychodynamic and constellation work for understanding
- Change phase: NLP, Gestalt, and hypnotherapy for transformation
- Integration phase: Timeline work and anchoring for consolidation

Sequential Integration Strategies

Building Foundation to Advanced Work

Start with approaches that create safety and build towards more challenging interventions:

1 Clean Language for understanding and outcome setting
2 Psychodynamic exploration for insight and awareness
3 Gestalt work for present-moment experience
4 NLP and hypnotherapy for change installation
5 Constellation and timeline work for integration

Case Example: Integrated Treatment Planning

Marcus and Elena presented with communication difficulties, sexual disconnection, and recurring conflicts about family involvement.

Session 1: Clean Language outcome setting revealed different definitions of "good communication"; constellation work showed Marcus feeling crowded by Elena's family and Elena feeling unsupported by Marcus

Session 2: Psychodynamic exploration uncovered Marcus's family-of-origin pattern of emotional withdrawal and Elena's pattern of seeking security through family connection

Session 3: Gestalt work helped them experience present-moment contact without defensiveness; NLP parts negotiation resolved Marcus's internal conflict between independence and connection needs

Session 4: Timeline therapy helped Elena heal childhood insecurity that drove her need for family validation; hypnotherapy helped Marcus access and anchor feelings of love and connection

Session 5: Integration of all approaches through future modelling and resource installation; constellation work confirmed new relationship arrangement felt right to both partners

Ethical Considerations for Advanced Work

Informed Consent

Couples need clear information about advanced techniques:

- What the technique involves and why it's being suggested
- Potential benefits and risks of the intervention
- Alternative approaches that might achieve similar results
- Their right to decline or modify the suggested technique

Scope of Practice

Staying within professional competence boundaries:

- Referring to specialists when techniques exceed your training
- Avoiding techniques that require licenses you don't hold
- Coordinating with other professionals when complex issues arise
- Maintaining awareness of your competence limits

Cultural Sensitivity

Advanced techniques can carry cultural assumptions:

- Recognise that some techniques may not translate across cultures
- Adapt approaches to respect different worldviews
- Consult with cultural advisors when working outside your background
- Remain humble about what you don't know

Advanced Practitioner Development

Expanded Training Requirements

Advanced techniques require additional training beyond basic Duo Coaching:

- Constellation work training and supervision
- Clean Language and Symbolic Modelling certification
- Parts work and Internal Family Systems training
- NLP practitioner or master practitioner certification
- Clinical hypnotherapy training
- Ongoing continuing education

Supervision and Consultation

Advanced work requires ongoing supervision:

- Regular consultation with experienced practitioners
- Video review of advanced technique implementation
- Personal therapy or development work to understand techniques experientially
- Peer consultation groups for complex case discussion

Personal Practice

The most effective practitioners have personal experience with the techniques they use:

- Receiving constellation work yourself
- Being hypnotised and experiencing trance work

- Exploring your own timeline and internal parts
- Practicing Clean Language in personal development

The Art of Responsive Integration

The modalities described in this chapter represent a toolkit, not a cookbook. The art lies not in mastering individual techniques but in developing the sensitivity to know which approach will serve each unique couple in each specific moment.

Remember that integration serves the relationship, not your theoretical preferences. The goal is not to use every approach in every case but to have sufficient options to respond effectively to whatever couples present.

Start with genuine competence in a few approaches before expanding your range. Better to skilfully employ three techniques than superficially apply ten. As your experience deepens, you'll develop intuitive knowing about which interventions will create the most elegant change for each couple.

Trust your clients to guide you towards what they need. When you offer an intervention and feel resistance, respect that—perhaps timing isn't right, or another approach would serve better. When something lands powerfully, follow that energy.

Advanced work is called advanced not because it's more complex but because it requires refined judgment about when complexity serves and when simplicity suffices. Sometimes the most advanced intervention is a single Clean Language question that helps couples discover what they already know.

In our next chapter, we'll move from individual techniques to the crucially important task of finding and working effectively with a co-therapist—because even the most sophisticated interventions work best when delivered through a solid therapeutic partnership.

> These interventions go beyond symptom management to create fundamental shifts in how couples see themselves, each other, and their relationship possibilities.
>
> —From *Reinventing*

Integration and Self-Reflection

This competency assessment evaluates your proficiency with advanced therapeutic techniques.

Foundation Level Skills Addressed in This Chapter

- Advanced Intervention Mastery: Skilful use of specialised techniques (timeline therapy, parts work, empty chair, etc.)
- Timing and Readiness Assessment: Knowing when couples are prepared for deeper

- Safety and Containment: Managing emotional intensity during powerful experiential work
- Integration Support: Helping couples consolidate insights from advanced interventions

Reflection Questions

1 Which advanced techniques are you already trained in? Which require additional training for you?
2 How do you assess whether couples are ready for deeper experiential work?
3 When have you used an advanced intervention that created breakthrough? What made it effective?
4 What concerns arise for you about using powerful techniques? How do you manage safety?

Self-assessment: How competent are you in advanced therapeutic interventions?

Trust your gut response. What number first comes to mind when you consider how ready you feel to take this further?

Score	*Interpretation*
1–2	Need comprehensive training before implementing advanced techniques
3–4	Developing skills in one to two advanced approaches with supervision
5–6	Confident use of multiple advanced interventions appropriately
7+	Masterful integration of diverse specialised techniques responsively

Next steps: Seek proper training in any advanced techniques before implementation. Practice with supervision. Develop clear assessment protocols for readiness before using powerful interventions.

Coming Next: Chapter 13—Assessment and Intake Processes

Practice structure enables intensive work, but effective outcomes begin before the first session. Chapter 13 provides systematic assessment and intake processes that set couples up for success while protecting you from unsuitable cases.

Discover comprehensive assessment frameworks that evaluate readiness for intensive work, contraindications that predict poor outcomes, screening tools for safety concerns, preparation processes that prime couples for deep work, and intake procedures that establish clear agreements while managing expectations.

Chapter 13 ensures you work with couples who can benefit while referring those who need different interventions. Proper assessment prevents the frustration of investing intensive effort with couples unprepared for the work. Your foundation for success starts here.

Chapter 13

Assessment and Intake Processes

Systematic Client Evaluation and Preparation

Image 12 Real Photograph, Sextant on Nautical Chart.
"Reading the Chart Before You Leave Harbour"

> In a relationship, there is no reality—only perception. Both perceptions can be different, yet equally correct.
>
> —Neil Wilkie

Assessment as Foundation: Why It Determines Everything

The assessment process in Duo Coaching serves as far more than administrative gatekeeping—it's the foundation upon which all transformation rests. Unlike traditional therapy where couples can drift into weekly sessions without clear direction,

DOI: 10.4324/9781003715627-18

the intensive nature of Duo Coaching demands thorough preparation, precise understanding, and crystal-clear alignment before the first session begins.

After 15 years of intensive couple work, I've learned this truth: the quality of assessment directly predicts the success of the entire therapeutic journey. Couples who are properly assessed, well-prepared, and clearly aligned achieve remarkable transformation. Those who enter without adequate preparation often struggle despite the power of the approach.

This chapter guides you through developing assessment processes that ensure every couple who begins Duo Coaching is set up for success from the very first moment.

Four-Layer Assessment Framework Summary

Layer 1: Initial Enquiry (5–10 Minutes)

Purpose: Screening for basic suitability

Component	*Details*
Key Questions	• What's bringing you to seek help now? • How long have these difficulties been present? • Are both of you committed to doing this work together? • Have you tried couples therapy before? What was that experience like? • Is there any domestic violence, substance abuse, or severe mental health concerns?
Red Flags (May indicate unsuitability)	• Active domestic violence (physical, emotional, financial) • Severe untreated mental health issues requiring individual therapy first • One partner being coerced or pressured to attend • Active affairs with no intention to end them • Substance abuse requiring treatment before couple work • Legal proceedings (custody, divorce) creating immediate conflict
Green Flags (Indicating good fit)	• Both partners motivated and willing to invest time • Recognition that relationship requires work • Openness to intensive format • Ability to commit to multiple 3.5-hour sessions • Willingness to do between-session exercises
What to Explain	• The intensive nature of sessions (3.5 hours) • Typical commitment (six sessions over three to four months) • Co-therapy model with two practitioners • Between-session exercises and practice • Investment required (time, energy, finances)
Action	If suitable, proceed to Layer 2. If uncertain, request additional information.

Layer 2: Individual Pre-session Consultations (30 Minutes Each, by Phone)

Purpose: Build rapport, gather uncensored information, assess individual motivation and compatibility

Phase/Component	*Content and Focus*
Opening (5 minutes)	• Explain confidentiality boundaries • Create safety for honest sharing
Relationship Story (10–15 minutes)	Key Questions: • Tell me about your relationship. How did you meet? • What attracted you to your partner initially? • When did you notice things starting to struggle? • What's the most difficult aspect of your relationship right now? • What would be different if your relationship improved? Listen For: • Emotional quality (resentment, hope, despair, confusion) • Attachment to relationship vs. ambivalence about staying • Capacity for self-reflection vs. exclusive blaming • Awareness of own contributions to difficulties • Respect for partner despite frustrations
Specific Concerns (10 minutes)	• Is there anything happening that your partner doesn't know about? • Do you ever feel unsafe in the relationship—physically or emotionally? • Are there mental health or substance use concerns I should know about? • What are your biggest fears about doing this work? • What are your hopes if this works well?
Closing (5 minutes)	• Explain next steps • Send questionnaire • Confirm Session 1 date/time • Answer any questions about process

Assessment after Both Consultations

Assessment Criteria	*What to Evaluate*
Motivation Alignment	• Are both partners genuinely invested in improving the relationship? • Is one partner significantly more motivated than the other? • Are they seeking therapy to improve or to exit gracefully?

(*Continued*)

Assessment Criteria	*What to Evaluate*
Goal Compatibility	• Do their visions of "better" align reasonably? • Are there fundamental incompatibilities? • Can you envision interventions that would serve both partners' needs?
Safety Assessment	• Did either partner disclose abuse, coercion, or safety concerns? • Are there power imbalances that would make joint work unsafe? • Would individual therapy be more appropriate first?
Proceed Only If:	• Both partners demonstrate genuine willingness to work • No significant safety concerns • Goals are compatible enough to work towards together • Both partners understand and consent to intensive format

Layer 3: Pre-session Questionnaires

Component	*What It Reveals*
Duo Coaching Client Consultation Form	• Full personal background • Medical history • Any red flags • Perceived problems • The outcome they would like • How they will know they have achieved this
Relationship Paradigm Assessment (Six Elements)	1 Communication—Ability to express thoughts/feelings and be heard 2 Connection—Emotional, physical, and day-to-day togetherness 3 Commitment—Alignment on goals and willingness to invest 4 Fun—Joy, playfulness, and positive experiences together 5 Growth—Individual and couple development 6 Trust—Confidence in partner's reliability, integrity, honesty

Interpreting Paradigm Scores

Score Range/Pattern	*Interpretation*
Scores 7–10	Strengths to build upon and affirm
Scores 4–6	Areas needing attention and intervention
Scores 1–3	Crisis areas requiring immediate focus
Large gaps (3+ points difference)	Perception differences requiring exploration
Similar low scores	Shared awareness of problems—easier to address
One high, one low	May indicate denial, minimization, or different experiences

Layer 4: Session 1 Assessment (3.5 Hours)

Story-Telling Process (90 Minutes Total)

Assessment Component	*What to Listen for/Observe*
Phase 1: Individual Stories (45 minutes each) Diagnostic Questions	• Tell us how you met and what attracted you to each other • What were the early days like? When did you feel most connected? • When did you first notice something shifting or struggling? • What's been the most difficult period, and how did you get through it? • What brings you here now? What needs to change?
Content Patterns	• Idealisation vs. realistic appraisal of early relationship • Turning points where things shifted • Trauma or crisis events that changed the relationship • Cyclical patterns that repeat over time • External stressors (work, children, finances, health)
Process Patterns	• Emotional expression: Flat? Tearful? Angry? Resigned? • Self-awareness: Owns contributions or only blames partner? • Empathy capacity: Considers partner's experience or focuses on own? • Narrative coherence: Clear story or confused/contradictory? • Partner impact: Does partner soften while listening or harden further?
Phase 2: Synthesizing Stories	Co-therapists help identify: • Points of agreement: Where stories align • Points of divergence: Where perceptions differ dramatically • Shared pain: What both partners recognise as painful • Hidden strengths: Moments of resilience or connection to build upon

Pebbles Constellation

What Pebbles Reveal	*Interpretation Guide*
Spatial Relationships	• Distance between pebbles: How connected or separated they feel • Orientation (facing towards, away, side-by-side): Engagement level • Positioning (equal, hierarchical): Power dynamics • Relationship pebble placement: Shared space or separate from individuals?

(Continued)

What Pebbles Reveal	*Interpretation Guide*
Size and Characteristics	• Large vs. small pebbles: Perceived importance or power • Rough vs. smooth: How they experience self/partner • Colour choices: Emotional associations
Changes Over Time	• Where were these pebbles five years ago? • Where would you like them to be six months from now? • What needs to happen for them to move in that direction?

Safety and Contraindications: Green-Amber-Red Triage System

Category	*Indicators*
RED LIGHT DO NOT PROCEED	Absolute Contraindications: • Active physical violence or severe emotional abuse • One partner being coerced or forced to attend • Severe untreated mental illness requiring stabilization first • Active severe substance abuse requiring detox/treatment first • One partner in active affair with no willingness to end it • One or both partners already decided to divorce • Refer for individual therapy, safety planning, or other appropriate support
AMBER LIGHT CONDITIONAL PROCEED	Relative Contraindications: • Mild ambivalence but willing to try • Recent crisis (affair, major argument) but both committed to repair • Individual therapy ongoing but not conflicting • Financial constraints requiring payment plans • One partner more motivated but other willing to participate • Moderate depression/anxiety if manageable with support • Recent trauma requiring processing before couple work • Proceed with Session 1; reassess after to determine suitability
GREEN LIGHT PROCEED	All of the following present: • Both partners motivated and willing to work • No safety concerns • Capable of 3.5-hour sessions • Can commit to six-session series • Compatible goals (even if differ on how to get there) • Willing to do between-session work

Practical Implementation Checklists

Pre-session 1 Preparation

Area	*Items to Complete*
Initial Enquiry	• Basic suitability screening • Both partners motivated • No immediate red flags • Intensive format explained
Individual Consultations (30 minutes each)	• Each partner's relationship story heard • Individual motivations/concerns identified • Hidden issues explored • Safety assessed • Compatibility evaluated
Pre-session Analysis	• Paradigm scores reviewed and compared • Perception gaps identified • Attachment patterns understood • Primary pain points noted • Strengths identified • Session 1 focus areas planned • Potential homework exercises considered
Logistics	• Session 1 date/time confirmed with both partners • Location and directions provided • Co-therapist coordinated • Payment/contracting completed • Breaks and session structure explained

During Session 1 Assessment

Area	*Items to Complete*
Story-Telling	• Each partner shared full relationship narrative • Co-therapists observed content and process patterns • Couple dynamics during stories noted • Turning points and patterns identified
Pebbles Constellation	• Each partner created constellation individually • Spatial relationships and symbolism explored • Perception gaps revealed • Desired future state discussed
Integration and Planning	• Assessment findings synthesized • Primary treatment focus identified • Session 1 homework assigned • Session 2 planned based on assessment • Couple oriented to next steps

Post-Session 1 Reflection

Assessment Questions	*Planning Questions*
• Did anything emerge that changes suitability assessment? • Are both partners genuinely engaged in the work? • What are the core dynamics driving their difficulties? • What strengths can we build upon? • What interventions are most likely to help? • Is the six-session format realistic for their needs?	• What's the primary focus for Session 2? • Do we need to adjust our approach? • Are there any co-therapist dynamics we need to address? • What outcome are we working towards together?

Key Principle

Assessment in Duo Coaching isn't a one-time event completed before therapy "really begins"—it's an ongoing practice of understanding that continues throughout all six sessions.

The Quality of Assessment Determines the Quality of Everything That Follows

Integration Example—Emma and James

Assessment Layer	*Key Findings*
Initial Enquiry	Both motivated; relationship struggling for 2+ years; no safety concerns
Individual Consultations	Emma feels invisible and unheard; James feels criticized and inadequate
Questionnaires	Connection scored 2/10 (Emma) vs. 6/10 (James); Both scored Trust 3/10; Attachment patterns: anxious (Emma)/avoidant (James)
Session 1 Stories	Emma's narrative: "He's always working, never present"; James's narrative: "Nothing I do is good enough"
Pebbles Constellation	Emma placed pebbles far apart; James placed them close but Emma separate from relationship core

Integrated Diagnosis: Classic pursuit-distance pattern driven by anxious-avoidant attachment dynamic. Emma's bids for connection feel like demands/criticism to James, triggering avoidant withdrawal. James's withdrawal activates Emma's abandonment anxiety, intensifying pursuit. Connection and Trust eroded through this cycle. Fun eliminated. Both want closeness but behavioural pattern prevents it.

Treatment Implications

Interrupt pursuit-distance cycle through psychoeducation
Rebuild small connection moments (Logbook 1 homework)
Help James recognise Emma's bids for connection (not criticism)
Help Emma make softer bids James can receive
Later sessions: deeper attachment work, values alignment, intimacy rebuilding

From Assessment to Intervention: Exercise Selection

Matching Homework to Assessment Findings

What's the primary focus for Session 2?
Are they completing homework? If not, why?
Do we need to adjust our approach?
Are there any co-therapist dynamics we need to address?
What outcome are we working towards together?

Conclusion: Assessment as Ongoing Practice

Assessment in Duo Coaching isn't a one-time event completed before therapy "really begins"—it's an ongoing practice of understanding that continues throughout all six sessions. Each session reveals new layers of the couple's dynamics, strengths, and struggles. Skilled practitioners remain curious, flexible, and responsive to emerging information.

The assessment process described in this chapter—from initial enquiry through Session 1 story-telling and pebbles constellation—creates the foundation for transformation. When done with skill, care, and precision, assessment ensures that:

Couples are appropriately matched to the intensive approach
Safety concerns are identified and addressed
Both partners are motivated and aligned enough to do the work
Interventions are tailored to their specific needs
Homework exercises target their particular challenges
Co-therapists understand the relational dynamics at play

In our next chapter, we'll explore session planning and facilitation—the practical skills for guiding couples through transformative intensive sessions once assessment is complete.

> In a relationship, there is no reality—only perception. Both perceptions can be different, yet equally correct. Our work is to help couples understand each other's perceptions, find common ground, and create a shared reality they both want to live in.

Integration and Self-reflection

Foundation Level Skills Addressed in This Chapter

Comprehensive Assessment: Gathering complete picture of couple's presenting issues and history
Suitability Determination: Identifying couples appropriate for Duo Coaching versus requiring referral
Expectation Setting: Establishing clear understanding of process, commitment, and outcomes
Preparation Process: Using intake phase to begin therapeutic alliance and change process

Reflection Questions

What essential information do you need from couples before first session? How will you gather it?
How will you assess whether Duo Coaching is appropriate or if referral is indicated?
What expectations need explicit discussion during intake to prevent misalignment?
How can your intake process begin building therapeutic alliance and hope?

Self-assessment: How confident are you in conducting thorough, effective intake processes?

Trust your gut response. What number first comes to mind when you consider how ready you feel to take this further?

Score	*Interpretation*
1–2	Need significant training in assessment and intake procedures
3–4	Developing competence with structured guidance
5–6	Strong assessment skills with clear protocols
7+	Masterful intake process that serves both evaluation and preparation

Next Steps: Develop comprehensive intake protocols and documentation. Practice suitability assessments with supervision. Create clear materials explaining Duo Coaching approach and expectations.

Coming Next: Chapter 14—Session Planning and Management

Assessment identifies what couples need; effective outcomes require strategic session planning that sequences interventions purposefully. Chapter 14 provides frameworks for designing intensive session series that create progressive transformation rather than random exploration.

You'll discover how to sequence sessions for optimal impact, determine which issues to address when (and why order matters), balance couples' presenting concerns with deeper patterns requiring attention, coordinate co-therapist roles across multiple sessions, adapt plans based on emerging dynamics while maintaining therapeutic direction, and recognise when to intensify, when to consolidate, and when to pause.

Chapter 14 transforms you from a reactive therapist responding to whatever couples bring into a strategic architect designing pathways towards relationship health. This planning sophistication separates adequate from exceptional intensive work. Your session design mastery develops here.

Chapter 14

Session Planning and Management

Advanced Therapeutic Planning and Coordination

> Experience has shown that the first session needs to be about three and a half hours to explore how the couple have got to where they are right now ... Subsequent sessions are typically about two and a half hours long and are a mixture of the two of us working with the two of them on the 'us' issues of them as a couple.
>
> —From Duo Coaching practice

From Assessment to Action: Orchestrating Transformation across Six Sessions

You've completed comprehensive assessment (Chapter 14). You understand the couple's dynamics, patterns, and priorities. You've identified their Relationship Paradigm deficits. You know which exercises to assign. Now comes the crucial question: How do you orchestrate all this across six intensive sessions to create lasting transformation?

This chapter provides the practical frameworks, planning protocols, and coordination strategies that transform assessment insights into structured, progressive therapeutic work. You'll learn how to:

- Plan each session building on previous progress
- Coordinate seamlessly with your co-therapist
- Sequence interventions for maximum impact
- Track progress and adjust approaches
- Manage between-session support
- Document systematically for learning and accountability

Session planning isn't about rigid scripts—it's about creating flexible frameworks that guide couples through natural transformation stages while remaining responsive to what emerges.

DOI: 10.4324/9781003715627-19

Advanced Therapeutic Planning and Coordination

From Assessment to Action: Orchestrating Transformation across Six Sessions

The Six-Session Arc: Understanding the Journey

Phase	*Focus and Purpose*
Sessions 1–2: Foundation and Pattern Recognition	• Understanding current reality and how it developed • Recognising patterns rather than just symptoms • Building safety and therapeutic alliance • Beginning skill development
Sessions 3–4: Deep Work and Change	• Addressing core patterns and wounds • Challenging old behaviours and beliefs • Practicing new approaches with support • Navigating resistance and breakthroughs
Sessions 5–6: Integration and Independence	• Consolidating new patterns • Building maintenance systems • Preparing for independence • Celebrating transformation

Pre-session Planning: The Co-therapist Planning Protocol

Timing	*Activities and Focus*
48 Hours Before Session	Both therapists independently review: • Previous session notes and observations • Homework completion (or non-completion) • Between-session contacts or concerns • Relationship Paradigm progress tracking • Specific patterns emerging or persisting Email coordination questions: • What stood out for you from last session? • What progress or struggles have you noticed? • Which areas need priority attention this session? • What approaches do you think would be most effective?
Day of Session (30 minutes before)	Joint planning meeting covering: Session Intentions: • Primary outcomes for this session • Connection to overall six-session arc • Specific skills or insights to develop Progress Review: • What improved in the last session? • What homework was completed (or not)? • How has the couple's dynamic shifted?

(Continued)

Timing	*Activities and Focus*
	Intervention Planning: • Which exercises or approaches for this session? • How will we build on previous work? • Where might we encounter resistance? Role Coordination: • Who leads which interventions? • How will we signal need for consultation? • Break timing and structure Logistics Check (5 minutes): • Room setup and materials • Technology functioning • Emergency contacts confirmed • Self-care check-in for both therapists

Session 1: Foundation through Assessment (3.5 Hours)

Segment	*Time*	*Content and Focus*
Primary Outcomes		• Comprehensive understanding of couple's patterns • Both partners feeling heard and understood • Hope that transformation is possible • Clear direction for work ahead
Arrival and Safety	15–20 minutes	Creating safe space, setting expectations, building rapport
Relationship Stories	90 minutes	Individual histories (45–60minutes each)—how they met, turning points, current challenges
Individual Stories	30–45 minutes	Stories of childhood, upbringing, and previous relationships
Break	5–10 minutes	
Pebbles Constellation	30–45 minutes	Embodied assessment of relationship dynamics and perceptions
Outcome Clarification	10–20 minutes	What would success look like? What needs to change?
Integration and Homework	10 minutes	Synthesising insights, assigning homework, establishing between-session support
Planning Notes		• Allow flexibility in timing—natural stopping points more important than clock • Watch for fatigue around 2.5-hour mark • Ensure closing leaves couple grounded, not overwhelmed • Between-session support protocols clearly established

Session 2: Deepening Understanding (2.5 Hours)

Segment	*Time*	*Content and Focus*
Primary Outcomes		• Build on Session 1 insights with experiential work • Develop practical communication skills • Create positive experience of working together • Strengthen hope and motivation
Opening and Homework Review	20–30 minutes	• How did the week go? • What did Logbook 1 reveal about bids for connection? • Did they complete Exercises 3 and 4 (appreciation lists)? • What shifted or stayed the same?
Drawing Exercise	45–60 minutes	Each partner creates two drawings: • Drawing 1: Life as it is right now • Drawing 2: Life as they'd like it to be Explore what drawings reveal: • Identify gaps between current and desired • Understand different visions and how to integrate
Break	5 minutes	
Communication Practice	50–60 minutes	• Interactive Listening practice • Speaker-Listener technique with real issues • Soft start-ups instead of harsh criticism • Validation without necessarily agreeing
Planning and Homework	10 minutes	• State of the Union Meetings—introduce structure • Attunement—noticing and responding to bids • What Pleases Me/How Well Do You Know Each Other • Continue Bids Practice
Planning Considerations		• Drawing exercise very powerful but timing varies widely • Some couples finish quickly, others need full hour • Be prepared to adjust communication practice time accordingly • If major breakthrough happens, allow it—don't rush to finish "plan"

Session 3: Core Pattern Work (2.5 Hours)

Segment	*Time*	*Content and Focus*
Primary Outcomes		• Address deeper patterns beyond surface behaviours • Work with family-of-origin influences • Begin values alignment work • Possibly individual one-to-one work if needed
Opening and Progress	20–30 minutes	• Week review and homework discussion • Are State of Union meetings happening? • What's improving? What's still difficult? • Energy check: Where is each partner today?
Deep Pattern Work	45–60 minutes	Content varies based on couple's needs: • One-to-One Work if individual issues blocking couple progress
Break	5 minutes	
Integration and Practice	50–60 minutes	• Bringing individual insights into couple context • Practicing new understandings with real issues • Building on communication skills from Session 2 • Connection exercises if appropriate
Homework and Planning	10 minutes	• Continue State of Union/check-in practice • Specific exercises targeting their Paradigm deficits • Between-session support as needed
Planning Considerations		• Session 3 often the most intense—deep work happening • Watch for signs of overwhelm or shutdown • One-to-one is powerful but requires careful coordination • May reveal issues (affairs, trauma) requiring extended work

Session 4: Challenge and Growth (2.5 Hours)

Segment	*Time*	*Content and Focus*
Primary Outcomes		• Push growth edges while maintaining safety • Address avoided topics (often sex/intimacy) • Strengthen new patterns through practice • Build confidence in their capacity for change
Opening and Integration	20–30 minutes	• Review of progress across first three sessions • Celebration of improvements • Identification of remaining stuck areas • Energy assessment and readiness

(Continued)

Segment	*Time*	*Content and Focus*
Challenge Work	45–60 minutes	Addressing avoided or difficult topics: • Intimacy and sexuality if not yet addressed • Financial conflicts if money creating stress • Parenting disagreements if children involved • Extended family boundaries if in-law issues present • Difficult conversations they've been avoiding
Break	5 minutes	
Practice and Application	50–60 minutes	• Practicing difficult conversations with support • Role-playing challenging scenarios • Building skills for managing conflict constructively • Creating agreements about previously stuck issues
Future Visioning	20–30 minutes	• Creating shared vision for future • Aligning on goals and priorities • Homework assignment and support planning
Planning Considerations		• Session 4 often involves confronting what's been avoided • Requires strong therapeutic alliance from Sessions 1–3 • May need individual work before couple work on sensitive topics • Watch for defensive reactions—normalise and work through them

Session 5: Consolidation and Empowerment (2.5 Hours)

Segment	*Time*	*Content and Focus*
Primary Outcomes		• Consolidate gains from previous sessions • Build confidence in maintaining changes • Address remaining concerns or questions • Prepare for independence and completion
Opening and Progress Celebration	20–30 minutes	• Comprehensive review of journey so far • Celebrating specific improvements • Acknowledging hard work invested
Remaining Work	60–75 minutes	Content based on what still needs attention: • Deepening intimacy work if needed • Advanced communication skills • Conflict resolution practice • Addressing setbacks or concerns • Individual work supporting relationship gains
Break	5 min	

(*Continued*)

Segment	Time	Content and Focus
Maintenance Planning	40–50 minutes	• What practices need to continue? • How will they maintain State of Union meetings? • What early warning signs should they watch for? • When to seek help if issues emerge? • Creating ongoing support systems
Session 6 Preparation	10 minutes	• Setting intentions for final session • Identifying any remaining topics • Homework focused on maintenance • Continued practice of key skills
Planning Considerations		• Session 5 balances celebrating progress with addressing remaining issues • Avoid creating dependency—emphasise their competency • Some couples ready for completion; others need reassurance • Use this session to assess if six sessions sufficient or extension needed

Session 6: Completion and Launch (2.5 Hours)

Segment	Time	Content and Focus
Primary Outcomes		• Formal completion of the work • Comprehensive review of transformation • Solid maintenance plan established • Celebration and empowerment
Opening and Journey Review	20–30 minutes	Reflection on entire six-session journey: • What stands out most? • What surprised them? • How have they changed?
Comprehensive Assessment	10 minutes	• Final Relationship Paradigm ratings • Comparison with Session 1 baseline • Celebrating progress across all elements • Acknowledging remaining growth areas
Maintenance Protocols	40–50 minutes	• Exercises as permanent practice • Crisis management strategies • When to seek additional help • Support systems and resources • Preventive maintenance schedule
Break	5 minutes	
Visioning and Commitment	30–40 minutes	• Future relationship vision • Values and priorities clarification • Commitment to ongoing practices • Next chapter of their journey

(Continued)

Segment	*Time*	*Content and Focus*
Celebration and Completion	30–40 minutes	• Appreciation exchanges between partners • Acknowledgment from therapists • Formal completion ritual if desired • Meaningful goodbye and good wishes
Planning Considerations		• Session 6 should feel celebratory, not sad • Balance acknowledging progress with realistic expectations • Some couples struggle with ending—normalise this • Leave door open for informal updates and booster sessions if needed • Ensure they feel empowered, not abandoned

Between-Session Support and Management

Component	*Guidelines and Protocols*
24/7 Availability Protocol What It Means	• Couples have access to brief text or phone support • Not ongoing therapy between sessions • Crisis support and guidance for unexpected challenges • Clarification of homework or session agreements
Appropriate Contact Reasons	• Crisis situations requiring immediate guidance • Significant unexpected challenges or breakthroughs • Safety concerns that can't wait • Brief questions clarifying homework or exercises • Major life event affecting the work (job loss, illness, etc.)
Not Appropriate Contact	• Routine check-ins without specific need • Issues that can wait until next session • Individual complaints about partner • Requests beyond agreed scope • Dependency rather than genuine need
Response Protocol	Text Messages: • Response within 4–6 hours during business hours • Within 12 hours evenings/weekends unless urgent • Brief, supportive, action-oriented • Redirect to next session if not urgent Phone Calls: • For genuine crises or complex situations • Keep to 15–20 minutes unless emergency • Both therapists available if possible • Document contact and follow up in next session

Homework Compliance and Non-compliance

Situation	*Response Strategy*
When Homework Gets Done	In next session: • Review thoroughly—what did they learn? • Celebrate completion and insights gained • Build on homework for next exercises • Use homework as assessment of progress
When Homework Doesn't Get Done Explore Rather Than Shame	Questions to ask: • What got in the way of completing the homework? • Was the assignment unclear or overwhelming? • What would make homework more doable? • What does non-completion tell us about readiness or priorities?

Common Reasons for Non-completion	Logistical:
	• Too busy, forgot, couldn't find time together
	  • Problem-solve scheduling, simplify homework
	Emotional:
	• Too difficult, triggering, or uncomfortable
	  • Address fears, modify approach, build gradually
	Relationship:
	• One partner willing, other resisting
	  • Explore resistance, possible individual work needed
	Therapeutic:
	• Homework doesn't fit their learning style or needs
	  • Adjust approach, use different exercises
	Pattern:
	• Non-compliance is their relationship pattern
	  • Make non-compliance itself the therapeutic work

Modified Homework Approach (If consistently incomplete)	• Reduce quantity: one simple practice instead of multiple exercises • Increase accountability: daily text check-ins • Practice in-session: don't assign until they've practiced successfully with support • Address resistance: make non-completion the focus of therapeutic work

Co-therapist Coordination throughout the Arc

Coordination Activity	*Purpose and Process*
Weekly Check-Ins (Outside Session Time)	Even when not seeing couples, co-therapists stay connected: • 15-minute weekly call or meeting • How is partnership working?

(*Continued*)

Coordination Activity	*Purpose and Process*
	• Any concerns or tensions? • Celebrating successes together • Professional development coordination
After Challenging Sessions	Extended debrief when needed: • Longer processing time after difficult sessions • Sharing emotional impact of the work • Supporting each other through intensity • Learning from challenges together • Adjusting approaches for future
Monthly Partnership Reviews	Dedicated time to assess collaboration: • What's working well in our partnership? • Where are we struggling or out of sync? • How can we support each other better? • Professional development needs? • Relationship maintenance for partnership
Non-verbal Signals During Sessions	Agreed-upon signals: • Raised hand: "I'm noticing something important" • Eye contact + nod: "Go ahead, take the lead" • Slight head shake: "Let's redirect" • Hand on heart: "This is touching me emotionally" • Pointing to watch: "We need break soon"
Verbal Check-ins During Sessions	Natural consultation phrases: • "Maria, what are you noticing here?" • "Neil, would you add anything to what I'm observing?" • "Let's pause for a moment—I want to check something with my colleague" • "I'm curious what my co-therapist is picking up on"
Private Consultation During Breaks	Use break times to: • Compare observations and intuitions • Adjust second half based on first half • Coordinate who leads which interventions • Support each other emotionally if needed • Make quick decisions about direction

When to Extend beyond Six Sessions

Category	*Considerations*
Valid Reasons for Extension	Complexity Underestimated: • Multiple severe issues requiring more time • Trauma work needing additional sessions • Major crisis emerging mid-work (affair discovery, etc.) New facts emerge that were not disclosed up front (e.g.Affair)

(Continued)

Category	Considerations
	Significant Progress but Not Complete: • Core patterns shifted but integration incomplete • Skills developing but need more practice with support • Breakthrough in Session 5 or 6 opening new work External Disruptions: • Major life event interrupting work (illness, job loss, family crisis) • One partner's individual issue requiring pause in couple work • Circumstance beyond their control affecting progress
Extension Protocol	• Clear rationale discussed with couple • Specific outcomes for additional sessions • Typically two to four additional sessions maximum • Avoid drift into ongoing open-ended therapy • Maintain completion focus
When NOT to Extend	Slow Progress Without Clear Reason: • May indicate poor fit for Duo Coaching approach • Might need different intervention or individual work first • Extension won't solve fundamental misalignment One Partner Not Engaged: • Extension won't create motivation that's absent • Better to pause and reassess readiness • Individual work may be needed first Financial or Logistical Barriers: • If couple can't realistically commit to additional sessions • Better to complete well than extend incompletely • Can always return later if circumstances improve

Documentation and Outcome Tracking

Session Notes Template

Section	Content to Capture
Session Number and Date	Present: [Couple names] + [Therapist names]
Session Focus	Primary work of this session Key interventions used
Progress Observed	• What improved since last session? • What remained stuck or worsened? • Homework completion status
Key Moments	• Breakthroughs or insights • Challenging dynamics • Emotional shifts • Pattern recognition
Homework Assigned	• Specific exercises with rationale • Expected completion timeline • Support needed for completion

(Continued)

Section	*Content to Capture*
Co-Therapist Observations	• Separate notes from each therapist • Different perspectives on dynamics • Coordination effectiveness
Plans for Next Session	• Primary focus areas • Interventions to consider • Concerns to address
Relationship Paradigm Tracking	• Current ratings if reassessed • Observed progress on each element • Priority areas remaining

Outcome Measurement Timeline

Timing	*Measurements*
Baseline (Session 1)	• Initial Relationship Paradigm ratings • Specific presenting problems • Life satisfaction scores • Relationship happiness scale
Mid-Point (Session 3)	• Paradigm re-rating • Progress on presenting problems • Couple's perception of change • Adjustment of goals if needed
Completion (Session 6)	• Final Paradigm ratings • Outcome achievement assessment • Couple's satisfaction with process • Sustainability planning
Follow-up (three–six months post-completion)	• Email or phone check-in • Paradigm maintenance ratings • Challenges faced and managed • Booster session needs assessment

Session-by-Session Planning Framework

- Creating agreements about previously stuck issues

Progress Tracking Tool

Element	*Session 1*	*Session 3*	*Session 6*	*Notes*
Communication	Emma 3, James 6	Emma 5, James 7	Emma 7, James 8	Significant improvement
Connection	Emma 2, James 5	Emma 4, James 6	Emma 7, James 8	Major transformation
Commitment	Emma 8, James 8	Emma 9, James 9	Emma 9, James 9	Always strong
Fun	Emma 1, James 3	Emma 3, James 5	Emma 6, James 7	Good progress

(Continued)

Element	*Session 1*	*Session 3*	*Session 6*	*Notes*
Growth	Emma 4, James 5	Emma 6, James 6	Emma 7, James 7	Steady improvement
Trust	Emma 7, James 8	Emma 8, James 8	Emma 9, James 9	Stable and strong

- Paradigm maintenance ratings
- Challenges faced and managed
- Booster session needs assessment

Learning and Quality Improvement

Regular Case Review

Monthly with Supervisor or Peer Group

- Discuss challenging cases
- Review outcome data across multiple couples
- Identify patterns in successes and struggles
- Adjust approaches based on learning
- Celebrate effective work

Annual Practice Review

Comprehensive Analysis

- How many couples seen?
- What percentage completed six sessions?
- Average Paradigm improvement across elements
- Common presenting issues and outcomes
- Areas for professional development
- Practice improvements for next year

Conclusion: The Art of Orchestration

Session planning and management is the art of orchestrating multiple elements—assessment insights, therapeutic interventions, co-therapist coordination, homework progression, and between-session support—into a coherent journey that creates lasting transformation.

The Planning Paradox

- Plan thoroughly to create structure and direction
- Hold plans lightly to remain responsive to what emerges
- Trust the process while staying alert to needed adjustments
- Balance structure with spontaneity

What Skilled Practitioners Know

- The best plans change based on what couples bring
- Flexibility within structure creates safety
- Co-therapist coordination makes complexity manageable
- Documentation supports learning and improvement
- Each couple teaches something about the approach

Your Growing Mastery

As you gain experience planning and managing sessions:

- Interventions flow more naturally
- Co-therapist coordination becomes intuitive
- Pattern recognition accelerates
- Confidence in adjustments grows
- Trust in the process deepens

The couples you serve deserve practitioners who plan thoughtfully, coordinate skilfully, document systematically, and learn continuously. The session planning and management skills developed through this chapter transform assessment insights into structured transformation that changes lives.

In our next chapter, we'll explore common relationship challenges and how to adapt the Duo Coaching Framework for specific presenting issues—giving you practical protocols for the most frequent challenges couples bring.

"Planning creates the structure that allows spontaneity. Coordination enables responsiveness. Documentation supports learning. Together, they transform good intentions into lasting transformation."

Integration and Self-reflection

Foundation Level Skills Addressed in This Chapter

- Strategic Planning: Creating session structures that serve therapeutic goals
- Co-therapist Coordination: Effectively collaborating with partner throughout planning and delivery
- Time Management: Managing extended sessions skilfully with appropriate pacing
- Flexibility and Responsiveness: Adapting plans when couples' needs differ from expectations

Reflection Questions

1 How do you currently approach session planning? What works well and what needs refinement?
2 How would you coordinate with a co-therapist to create coherent session plans?

3 What challenges do you anticipate in managing 2.5–3.5-hour sessions effectively?
4 How comfortable are you with diverging from plans when couples' emergent needs require it?

Self-assessment: How skilled are you in planning and managing intensive sessions?

Trust your gut response. What number first comes to mind when you consider how ready you feel to take this further?

Score	*Interpretation*
1–2	Need foundational training in intensive session structures
3–4	Developing planning capacity with supervisory support
5–6	Strong planning and management skills with responsive flexibility
7+	Masterful session orchestration balancing structure and responsiveness

Next Steps: Develop planning templates with your co-therapist. Practice time management in extended sessions. Build comfort with flexible adaptation when indicated.

Coming Next: Chapter 15—Common Relationship Challenges

Session planning provides structure, but couples arrive with specific presenting issues: communication breakdown, conflict escalation, sexual disconnection, parenting disagreements, financial stress, in-law interference, and work-life imbalance. Chapter 15 offers protocols for the challenges you'll encounter most frequently.

Each common challenge receives comprehensive treatment: underlying patterns that perpetuate the problem, assessment questions that reveal depth beyond surface complaints, intervention sequences that create lasting change, typical resistance patterns and how to navigate them, and integration strategies that prevent relapse.

Chapter 15 serves as your clinical reference for everyday couple challenges. Rather than improvising interventions or hoping standard techniques work, you'll have proven protocols refined through hundreds of cases. Your confidence with common presentations grows here.

Chapter 15

Common Relationship Challenges

Specific Issue Protocols and Interventions

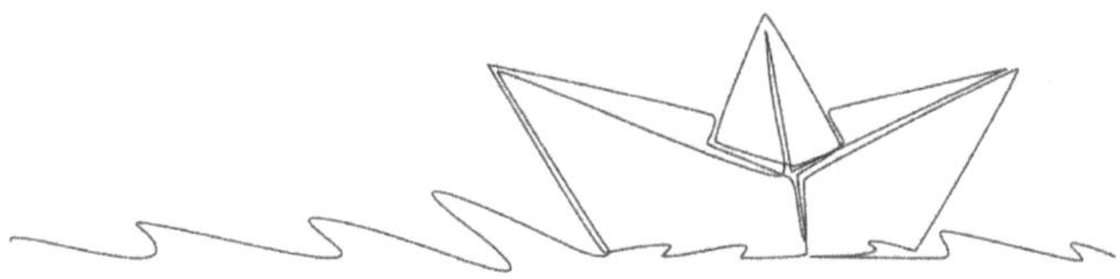

Image 13 Origami Paper Boat.

"Made from What's Already There: The Elegance of Something Simple That Floats"

> My insights from Duo Coaching, my life experiences and my research are that a couple bring with them shadows from the past and unrealised ghosts that are anchoring them to the rocks and preventing them from moving forward in the right direction.
>
> — From *Reinventing*

Beyond Surface Symptoms: Understanding Deeper Patterns

The presenting problems couples bring—communication difficulties, trust issues, sexual disconnection, parenting conflicts—are the visible manifestations of deeper patterns that developed over time. Our role is to help couples understand these underlying patterns while developing the skills and awareness needed to create lasting change.

This requires clinical sophistication that goes beyond technique application to include pattern recognition, cultural sensitivity, and the ability to work with multiple levels of human experience simultaneously.

Communication Breakdown: When Couples Can't Talk Constructively

The Myth of Communication Problems

"Communication problems" is the most frequently cited relationship complaint, yet it's also the most misunderstood. Couples often believe they need better

DOI: 10.4324/9781003715627-20

communication skills, when what they actually need is emotional safety, trust repair, or conflict resolution strategies.

I remember Kate and David, who came for help with "communication issues." They were both articulate professionals who communicated brilliantly at work. The problem wasn't that they couldn't communicate—it was that David shut down whenever Kate expressed hurt or disappointment, triggering Kate's anxiety and criticism, which reinforced David's withdrawal.

Teaching them communication techniques wouldn't solve their problem. David needed to understand that his shutdown pattern stemmed from childhood experiences where expressing emotion led to humiliation. Kate needed to recognise that her criticism came from fear of abandonment rather than David's behaviour. Once these patterns were revealed and addressed, their "communication" improved naturally.

The Real Issues Beneath Communication Complaints

Surface Complaint	*Underlying Dynamic*	*Key Intervention*
Emotional safety deficits	Partners don't feel safe being vulnerable, developing protective patterns that create the very disconnection they're trying to avoid	Build safety through explicit agreements about respectful communication, practice with low-stakes vulnerable sharing, develop time-out protocols, create positive emotional experiences to balance difficult conversations
Emotional suppression and conditioning	One or both partners learned early that expressing feelings was unsafe, shameful, or unwelcome—messages like "big boys don't cry" or "don't be so dramatic" created deeply ingrained patterns of shutting down or intellectualising rather than feeling	Explore the origins of emotional suppression without judgement, normalise the difficulty of unlearning decades of conditioning, build emotional vocabulary gradually, create explicit permission and safety for emotional expression, acknowledge that this is learning a new skill rather than fixing a flaw
Power imbalances and control	One partner holds more power or tries to control outcomes through communication manipulation	Make power dynamics explicit and discussable, create structured equal time, challenge controlling behaviours directly, sometimes require individual work first
Unresolved resentments	Years of unspoken hurts accumulated into walls preventing authentic communication	Structured sharing of accumulated resentments in safe container, teach distinction between expressing hurt and attacking, explore needs beneath criticisms

Safety Assessment Questions

- Do you feel safe expressing disagreement with your partner?
- Can you share vulnerable feelings without fear of being dismissed or attacked?
- Do you trust your partner's good intentions even during conflict?
- Can you ask for what you need without feeling selfish or demanding?

Emotional Expression Assessment Questions

- Growing up, what messages did you receive about expressing emotions?
- What happens in your body when you're asked to share how you feel?
- Have you learned that vulnerability is dangerous? What taught you this?
- What would you need to feel safe enough to express difficult emotions?

Power Imbalance and Control Assessment Questions

- Who usually gets the final say when you disagree?
- Do you feel you can express your opinion without being overridden or dismissed?
- Does one of you control more of the decisions about money, time, or social life?
- Do you ever feel you have to manage your partner's reactions or walk on eggshells?
- Are there topics you avoid raising because it's "not worth the battle"?
- When you argue, does one of you tend to dominate while the other withdraws or concedes?
- Do you feel your needs carry equal weight in the relationship?

Resentment Assessment Questions

- What have you never said because you feared the consequences?
- What disappointments have you swallowed rather than expressed?
- What needs have you given up on asking for?
- What criticisms do you repeat that mask deeper hurts?

Pursuit-Distance Patterns: The Most Common Dynamic

The most prevalent communication pattern is the pursuer-distancer dance, where one partner seeks connection while the other withdraws, each behaviour reinforcing the other.

The cycle: The pursuer feels disconnected and seeks closeness. Their seeking feels demanding to the distancer, who withdraws to protect autonomy or manage overwhelm. This withdrawal triggers the pursuer's anxiety, increasing pursuit. Increased pursuit reinforces the distancer's need for space. The cycle intensifies over time until both feel hopeless.

Partner	*What They Need to Recognise*	*New Behaviours to Practice*
Pursuer	Pursuit behaviour is driven by attachment anxiety; pursuit pushes away the connection they seek; underlying needs can be expressed differently; self-soothing capacity reduces pursuit urgency	Practice self-soothing and clear requests; recognise the cycle when it starts; take responsibility for their part
Distancer	Withdrawal triggers partner's attachment system; distance creates more pursuit, not less; underlying needs for autonomy can be negotiated; small moves towards connection prevent larger demands	Practice small moves towards connection; recognise the cycle when it starts; take responsibility for their part

Creating new patterns together: Regular connection rituals prevent cycle activation. Both partners learn to name the pattern when they notice it beginning, pause, and choose a different response.

Case Example: Breaking the Pursuit-Distance Cycle

Emma pursued, Simon distanced. She wanted emotional conversation; he needed space. Their pattern had intensified over eight years until both felt hopeless.

Intervention: We helped Emma understand her pursuit stemmed from childhood abandonment by her father—when Simon withdrew, her nervous system screamed that she was being left again. Simon's distance stemmed from growing up with an intrusive mother—Emma's pursuit felt suffocating, triggering his need to escape.

Neither was wrong. Both were responding to old wounds with strategies that made sense once but were now destroying their connection.

Outcome: Emma learned to soothe her abandonment fears and make clear requests rather than pursuing. Simon learned that small moves towards Emma—a text during the day, initiating a hug—prevented her pursuit far more effectively than distance ever had. "We were both trying to get to safety," Simon reflected. "We just finally learned we could be safe together."

Infidelity and Betrayal: The Toxic Triangle© Framework

Infidelity represents one of the most devastating challenges couples bring to therapy. The discovery of an affair creates profound trauma for the betrayed partner while simultaneously forcing critical decisions about the relationship's future. Yet when approached skilfully, affair recovery can paradoxically become a catalyst for relationship transformation deeper than what existed before the betrayal.

The betrayal creates an unavoidable stop in the relationship—the couple is aground, their vessel holed and taking on water. Some have hit the rocks at speed, sinking fast. Others have a slower leak, but a leak nonetheless. What they must not do is pretend it didn't happen and hope the memories will fade. They won't. Unfaced, they fester.

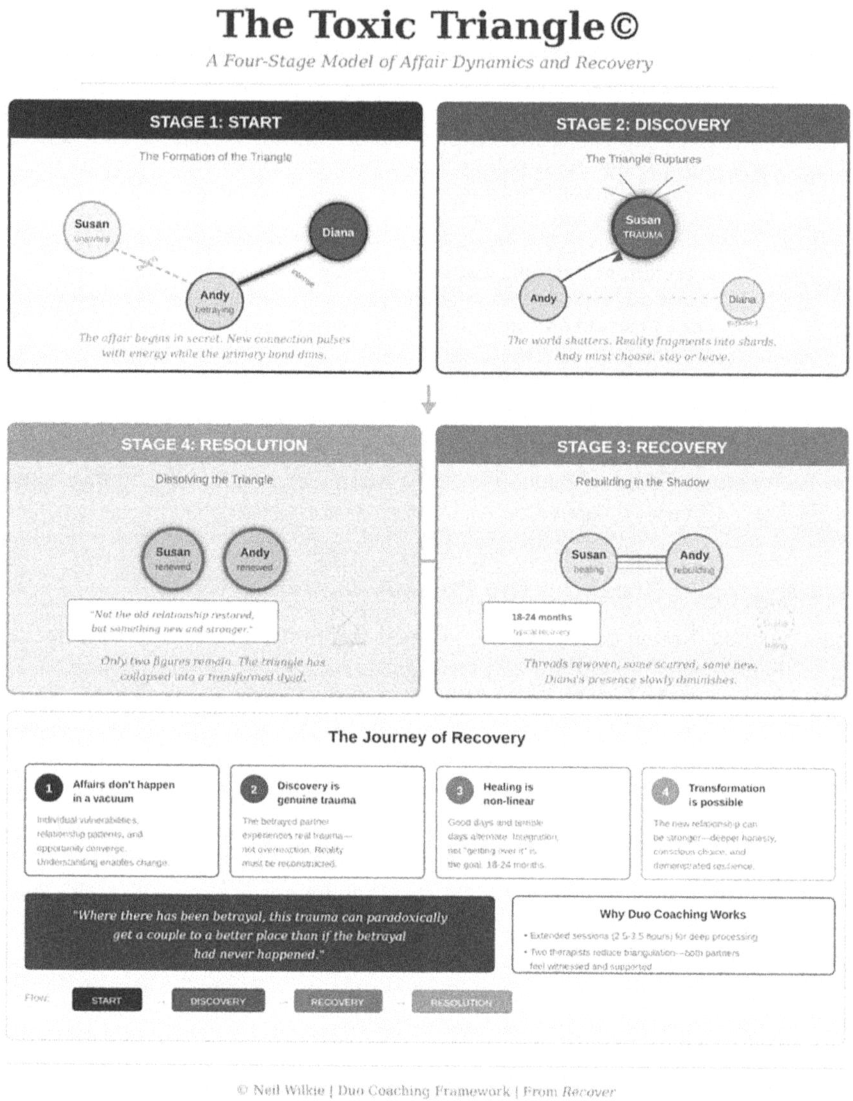

Infographic 4 The Toxic Triangle©: A Four-Stage Model of Affair Dynamics and Recovery.

Understanding the Toxic Triangle: A Four-Stage Model

The Toxic Triangle© framework provides a clear structure for understanding affair dynamics and recovery. This model recognises three figures: the betraying partner, the betrayed partner, and the affair partner. Recovery requires understanding how this triangle forms, ruptures, and ultimately resolves.

To illustrate this framework, I use three characters from my book Recover: Andy (the betraying partner), Susan (the betrayed partner), and Diana (the affair partner).

Stage 1: START—The Formation of the Triangle

Visual: Imagine two figures standing together, their connection represented by a fading thread between them. A third figure appears at the edge of the frame, luminous, drawing one partner's gaze. A new line begins to form—bright, electric, pulsing with forbidden energy—while the original connection dims to grey.

The affair begins in the space where unmet needs meet opportunity. Andy and Diana's connection grows strong, fuelled by novelty, excitement, and escape from the quiet disappointments of his relationship with Susan. What starts as friendship or professional connection crosses invisible lines. The secrecy itself becomes intoxicating—a private world where Andy feels seen, desired, alive in ways he'd forgotten were possible.

Meanwhile, Susan notices nothing, or notices only that Andy seems distracted, distant, preoccupied. She may reach for him and find him physically present but emotionally elsewhere. She doesn't yet know that elsewhere has a name.

What Creates Vulnerability to Affairs

Factor	*How It Operates*
Unmet needs	Emotional, sexual, or validation needs finding expression outside the primary relationship
Pre-existing disconnection	The relationship has been running on empty, both partners going through motions
Individual vulnerabilities	Attachment wounds, life transitions, identity crises creating susceptibility
Opportunity meeting vulnerability	The right person appearing at the wrong time, when defences are low

Therapeutic principle: Affairs rarely happen because someone is a "bad person" or the relationship is "bad." They happen within complex systems where individual vulnerabilities, relationship patterns, and opportunity converge. Understanding these factors doesn't excuse the betrayal—accountability remains essential—but understanding creates possibility for prevention and genuine transformation.

Stage 2: Discovery — The Triangle Ruptures

Visual: The triangle shatters. Susan stands centre frame, the ground cracking beneath her feet. The world she knew—her history, her future, her sense of reality—fragments into shards. Andy reaches towards her but is caught between two gravitational fields. Diana hovers at the periphery, suddenly visible, no longer a secret but a presence that cannot be unseen.

The moment of discovery is not a single event but an earthquake that keeps generating aftershocks. Susan finds a text, notices a lie, sees something she cannot unsee. In an instant, her entire reality restructures. Every memory is now suspect. Every "late night at work," every distracted dinner, every time he said "I love you"—all of it must be re-examined through this new, terrible lens.

What Susan experiences is genuine trauma, not overreaction. Her nervous system responds as it would to any life-threatening event: hypervigilance, intrusive thoughts, flashbacks, difficulty sleeping, appetite changes, inability to concentrate. She may oscillate between rage and despair, between wanting to know everything and wishing she could unknow what she's learned.

Andy faces a choice that will define everything that follows: stay and commit to the brutal work of repair, or leave. There is no middle ground, no keeping options open, no "figuring out his feelings" while Susan waits in agony. The affair relationship with Diana is fundamentally compromised—it cannot survive the light of day, though Andy may not yet fully understand this.

What the Betrayed Partner Experiences

Response	*Manifestation*
Trauma response	Shock, disbelief, physical symptoms, inability to process
Overwhelming emotions	Grief, rage, fear, numbness cycling unpredictably
Intrusive symptoms	Obsessive thoughts, mental movies, imagining details
Hypervigilance	Checking phones, needing to know whereabouts, scanning for lies
Shattered self-worth	"What's wrong with me?" "Why wasn't I enough?"
Reality questioning	"What else don't I know?" "Was anything real?"

What the Betraying Partner Must Do

Requirement	*Why It Matters*
Make a clear decision	Ambivalence is its own form of continued betrayal
End all contact with affair partner	Complete, verifiable, with no exceptions
Take full accountability	No minimisation, no "but you also ..."
Provide transparency	Answer questions honestly, even the painful ones
Understand the impact	Truly grasp what this has done to their partner

Stage 3: RECOVERY—Rebuilding within the Triangle's Shadow

Visual: Andy and Susan sit together, closer now but with visible wounds. Between them, the work of repair is happening—threads being rewoven, some scarred, some new. Diana's figure remains visible but has moved to the background, translucent, fading. She still occupies psychological space, but her presence is diminishing.

If Andy chooses to stay, the real work begins. This is not a matter of weeks but of months—typically 18–24 months minimum for the acute trauma to process, with ongoing integration beyond that.

Recovery requires Andy to demonstrate genuine remorse (not just regret at being caught), help Susan heal from trauma, end the relationship with Diana gently but irrevocably, answer questions honestly (often the same questions, repeatedly, as Susan's mind struggles to integrate the unthinkable), and accept the non-linear nature of healing.

Susan will have good days when the future seems possible, and terrible days when the betrayal feels as fresh as the moment of discovery. She may be preoccupied with Diana—comparing herself, wanting to know details, oscillating between curiosity and revulsion. This is normal. Diana still occupies psychological space in the triangle, and healing requires that presence to gradually dissolve.

Essential Recovery Work

Focus Area	*What It Involves*
Establishing safety	Complete transparency, access to devices/accounts, rebuilding predictability
Processing the affair's meaning	What was Andy seeking? What had been missing? What does this reveal?
Addressing underlying patterns	The relationship vulnerabilities that created susceptibility
Managing guilt productively	Andy staying present rather than collapsing into self-focused shame
Supporting trauma healing	Susan moving from acute trauma through grief towards integration

Timeline reality: Healing is non-linear. "Getting over it" is not the goal; integration and transformation are. Trust rebuilds slowly through consistent, trustworthy behaviour over time. The betrayed partner sets the pace for healing—pushing for faster recovery only delays it.

Stage 4: RESOLUTION—Dissolving the Triangle

Visual: Only two figures remain. Andy and Susan stand together, their connection renewed—different from before, bearing the marks of what they've survived, but strong. Perhaps stronger. Where Diana once stood, there is only empty space, no longer charged, no longer significant. The triangle has collapsed into a dyad. What was three is now, finally, two.

The final stage occurs when Diana is genuinely removed from the triangle—no longer occupying mental and emotional space for either partner. The fantasy is punctured. The affair, once so vivid and consuming, has become a memory that no longer has the power to destabilise.

A new relationship emerges between Andy and Susan—not the old relationship restored, but something built on fundamentally different foundations. Paradoxically, this new relationship may be stronger than what existed before:

Why Post-affair Relationships Can Be Stronger	*What Changed*
Forced honesty	Issues that were buried have been brought into the open
Examined patterns	Both partners have looked at their contributions
Deeper vulnerability	Honesty that once felt too dangerous is now essential
Conscious choice	The relationship is actively chosen, not continued by default
Demonstrated resilience	They now know they can survive and repair

The transformation principle: Where there has been betrayal, this trauma can paradoxically get a couple to a better place than if the betrayal had never happened. This doesn't mean the affair was "worth it" or "meant to be"—the pain is real and profound. But when couples can accept that the situation was in some way co-created and both desire a new and better relationship, transformation becomes possible.

The Duo Coaching Approach to Affair Recovery

The Toxic Triangle framework provides the conceptual map; now let's examine the clinical protocols for working through each stage. The intensive format of Duo Coaching is particularly well-suited to this work, providing extended time for deep emotional processing and the co-therapist partnership that reduces triangulation.

Three-Phase Recovery Protocol

Phase	*Toxic Triangle Stage*	*Sessions*	*Focus*
Phase 1: Crisis Stabilisation	Stage 2: Discovery	Sessions 1–2	Safety assessment, ending the affair, disclosure, containing the crisis
Phase 2: Understanding and Healing	Stage 3: Recovery (Early)	Sessions 2–4	Systemic understanding, trauma processing, accountability
Phase 3: Rebuilding and Transformation	Stages 3–4: Recovery to Resolution	Sessions 4–6	Creating new relationship, rebuilding trust, post-traumatic growth

Phase 1: Crisis Stabilisation (Sessions 1–2)

Safety Assessment Priorities

Domain	*Key Questions*
Psychological safety	Is the affair completely ended with no ongoing contact? Has full disclosure occurred? Can both partners be in the same room safely? Are there immediate mental health concerns?
Physical safety	Any concerns about violence? Substance abuse affecting judgement? Impulsive decisions threatening family welfare?

Essential Early Interventions

For the Betrayed Partner	*For the Unfaithful Partner*	*For the Couple*
Validation of trauma response	Taking full accountability	Agreement to postpone major decisions
Psychoeducation about recovery process	Complete transparency about details	Commitment to honesty moving forward
Support for overwhelming emotions	Understanding impact on partner	Crisis support protocols
Safety planning if needed	Ending affair with no contact	Agreements about telling others

Phase 2: Understanding and Healing (Sessions 2–4)

Rather than simple blame, explore contributing factors at multiple levels:

Level	*Factors to Explore*
Individual	Unmet needs in unfaithful partner; attachment wounds; life transitions or identity crises; mental health or addiction issues; character patterns
Relationship	Pre-existing disconnection; communication breakdown; sexual intimacy issues; power imbalances; unresolved conflicts
Situational	Opportunity and circumstance; external stressors; life transitions; cultural or peer influences

Healing the betrayed partner: Acknowledge discovery as traumatic event. Process shock, grief, rage, and fear. Use timeline work to heal trust wounds. Develop coping strategies for triggers. Explore what they need to feel safe again.

Accountability for unfaithful partner: Complete honesty about affair timeline and details. Answering questions truthfully even when painful. No trickle truth or minimisation. Genuine remorse versus self-focused guilt. Consistent transparency and patience with partner's healing process.

Phase 3: Rebuilding and Transformation (Sessions 4–6)

The goal isn't returning to the pre-affair relationship (which had vulnerabilities that contributed to the affair) but creating something new and stronger.

Rebuilding trust: Consistent transparency over time. Following through on commitments. Rebuilding emotional intimacy gradually. Restoring physical intimacy at the betrayed partner's pace.

Addressing contributing factors: Improving communication and emotional expression. Meeting needs within the relationship. Strengthening commitment. Developing prevention strategies.

Post-traumatic growth: Some couples emerge with deeper honesty and vulnerability, clearer communication, renewed commitment and appreciation, and greater emotional intimacy than they ever experienced before.

Case Example: Michael and Olivia—Recovery from Compound Betrayal

Michael discovered Olivia's eight-month affair through suspicious texts. Devastatingly, Olivia continued lying during the first weeks of therapy, minimising the affair as "emotional" when it had been fully physical. When complete truth emerged in Session 3, Michael faced double betrayal: the affair itself plus deception during recovery.

The crisis: "I've been trying to heal from the wrong wound," Michael said. "The affair was one betrayal. The lies during therapy were another. How do I trust someone who lied while supposedly rebuilding trust?"

The turning point: Olivia finally took complete accountability without excuses or minimisation. She provided full disclosure, answered every question honestly, and committed to radical transparency. Michael, despite devastating pain, chose to stay and rebuild—not the old marriage, but something entirely new based on complete honesty.

The outcome: Eighteen months later, both reported having deeper intimacy than ever existed before the affair. "We thought that level of honesty would be too dangerous," Olivia reflected. "We were wrong. Complete honesty is what made real intimacy possible for the first time."

Why Duo Coaching Is Particularly Effective for Affair Recovery

Advantage	*How It Helps*
Extended sessions	2.5–3.5 hours provides space for the betrayed partner to fully express pain without artificial time constraints; for the betraying partner to sit with their partner's pain rather than escaping it; for working through multiple layers in single sessions

(Continued)

Advantage	*How It Helps*
Co-therapist partnership	One therapist can hold the betrayed partner's trauma while the other holds the betraying partner's remorse; both partners feel witnessed and supported; therapeutic alliance remains balanced
Intensive interventions	Timeline therapy to process betrayal; parts work with the betraying partner's conflicted internal system; somatic work to address trauma in the body; empty chair work for the betrayed partner to express what they need to say

Practitioner Self-care in Affair Recovery Work

Working with infidelity is emotionally demanding. The pain is raw and intense, sessions may feel chaotic or hopeless initially, and your own relationship history and values will be activated.

Essential practices: Strong supervision with someone skilled in affair recovery. Personal therapy to process your own triggers. Clear boundaries around between-session communication. Realistic expectations for pace of healing. Celebrating small wins—couples showing up is itself a victory early on.

Sexual and Intimacy Issues

Sexual challenges in relationships are rarely just about sex. They're windows into attachment patterns, body image, trauma history, power dynamics, and the overall health of the emotional connection. Practitioners need comfort discussing sexuality explicitly while recognising its deeper meanings.

The Complexity of Sexual Issues

Presenting Complaint	*Often Reflects*
Desire discrepancy	Different attachment styles; relationship disconnection reducing desire; hormonal or health factors; responsive vs. spontaneous desire patterns
Performance concerns	Anxiety and pressure; health issues; porn-influenced expectations; relational factors affecting arousal
Intimacy avoidance	Past trauma affecting sexual comfort; body image issues; relationship resentments blocking desire; fear of vulnerability
Different preferences	Communication gaps about needs; shame around desires; mismatched expectations; porn influence

Assessment Framework

Medical factors: Always consider whether medical consultation is needed. Hormonal changes, medication effects, and health conditions can significantly impact sexual function.

Trauma history: Sexual trauma affects many adults and profoundly impacts intimate relationships. Assess sensitively and refer for specialised trauma therapy when needed.

Relationship context: Sexual issues often reflect broader relationship patterns. Improving emotional connection frequently improves sexual connection without directly addressing sex.

Intervention Approaches

For desire discrepancy: Psychoeducation about desire differences, particularly responsive versus spontaneous desire. Creating conditions for desire rather than demanding its appearance. Addressing relationship issues affecting desire. Negotiating frequency and initiation patterns.

For intimacy avoidance: Building emotional safety first. Gradual approach to physical intimacy at the pace of the more hesitant partner. Processing underlying fears or past experiences. Separating affection from sexual expectation.

For different preferences: Creating safety for honest conversation about desires. Exploring flexibility and willingness to please the partner. Addressing shame that blocks authentic expression. Finding mutually satisfying compromises.

Case Example: When "No Sex" Means Something Else

Rachel and James presented with "no physical intimacy for three years." Assessment revealed their sexual shutdown coincided with James's job loss and subsequent depression. Rachel had tried initiating but felt rejected. James felt too ashamed of his situation to be vulnerable.

Intervention: We addressed the underlying shame and disconnection first. As James processed his feelings about the job loss and Rachel shared her fears of abandonment, their emotional intimacy rebuilt. Physical intimacy followed naturally—not because we taught techniques, but because the emotional barriers had been removed.

Values and Life Direction Conflicts

Some couples present with fundamental differences in values, life goals, or direction that create ongoing conflict. These require careful assessment to determine whether differences are negotiable or represent genuine incompatibility.

Common Values Conflicts

Area	*Typical Tensions*
Children	Whether to have them; how many; timing; parenting philosophy
Career and ambition	Work-life balance; relocation for career; financial priorities

(Continued)

Area	*Typical Tensions*
Family of origin	Involvement level; boundary setting; holiday traditions
Religion and spirituality	Practice differences; raising children; moral frameworks
Lifestyle	Spending vs. saving; adventure vs. security; social life

Assessment Questions

Is this a values difference or a conflict avoidance issue? Have both partners been able to articulate their values clearly? Is there flexibility or are positions fixed? Can both partners' values be honoured through creative integration?

Intervention Approaches

Values clarification: Help each partner articulate what matters most and why. Explore the deeper needs beneath stated positions. Identify areas of overlap and genuine difference.

Creative integration: When values differ but the relationship is viable, find shared higher-level values, create agreements honouring both value sets, negotiate decisions respecting different priorities, and use differences as growth opportunities.

Case Example: Tom and Sarah—The Values Clash

Tom valued adventure, spontaneity, and living in the moment. Sarah valued security, planning, and building for the future. Their conflicts about money, travel, and lifestyle reflected deeper values differences.

Intervention: We explored underlying values without judgement and found a shared core value: both wanted lives they could look back on with satisfaction. We helped them create agreements honouring both values—planned adventures and secure foundations—and develop appreciation for how their partner's different values contributed to relationship strength.

Outcome: "We used to see our differences as incompatibility," Tom reflected. "Now we see them as complementary. Sarah keeps us grounded; I keep us adventurous. Together we create something neither could alone."

Parenting and Family Challenges

Children profoundly impact couple dynamics, often creating stress that reveals or exacerbates underlying relationship patterns.

Common Parenting-Related Challenges

Challenge	*What's Usually Underneath*
Disagreement about discipline	Different family-of-origin models; different values about authority and autonomy
Unequal division of childcare	Gender role expectations; invisible labour not being seen; resentment accumulation
Loss of couple identity	Children becoming sole focus; forgetting they were partners first
Extended family involvement	Boundary issues; competing loyalties; cultural expectations

Intervention Framework

Parenting team building: Create unified approach while respecting differences. Negotiate core values versus flexible methods. Develop decision-making protocols. Support each other publicly even when disagreeing privately.

Preserving couple identity: Protect couple time despite parenting demands. Maintain intimacy after children. Remember partnership predates and outlasts parenting. Develop support systems allowing couple connection.

Addressing labour inequities: Make invisible labour visible. Distinguish fair distribution from equal division. Appreciate different contributions. Adjust as needs change over time.

Modern Technology's Impact on Relationships

Contemporary couples navigate technological dimensions that previous generations never encountered.

Common Technology-Related Issues

Issue	*Impact on Relationship*
Social media	Comparison and insecurity; inappropriate connections; privacy violations
Digital distraction	Reduced face-to-face presence; phubbing (phone snubbing); divided attention
Pornography	Reshaping sexual expectations; secrecy and shame; impact on desire and arousal
Work intrusion	Constant connectivity; no boundaries between work and home; stress transfer
Privacy and transparency	Disagreements about device access; monitoring vs. trust

Intervention Approaches

Boundary development: Establish technology-free times and spaces. Create agreements about device use during couple time. Discuss transparency around accounts and communication. Set social media boundaries.

Reconnection practices: Prioritise face-to-face communication. Create physical presence without digital distraction. Address pornography's influence on sexual expectations. Design shared experiences not mediated by screens.

Conclusion: Seeing Beyond Symptoms to Patterns

The most important skill you can develop is seeing couples with compassion while maintaining clarity about what changes are needed for their relationship to thrive. This combination of empathy and clinical insight creates conditions where profound transformation becomes possible.

Remember that every couple is unique, even when surface problems appear similar. The frameworks and interventions outlined provide structure, but they must be adapted to each couple's specific needs, cultural background, and readiness for change.

The presenting problems couples bring are invitations to explore deeper. Your role is helping them understand the underlying patterns while developing skills and awareness needed to create lasting change.

> A great relationship needs two fulfilled individuals and an 'us' that is also fulfilled. Growth is needed to allow both people to flourish and cope with the changes of life.
>
> —From *Reinventing*

Integration and Self-reflection

Foundation Level Skills Addressed in This Chapter

This chapter has addressed four key skills: Issue-Specific Protocols (understanding specialised approaches for common challenges), Pattern Recognition (identifying underlying dynamics beneath presenting problems), Intervention Selection (choosing appropriate techniques for specific relationship issues), and Outcome Measurement (tracking progress in addressing targeted challenges).

Reflection Questions

1 Which common relationship issues do you feel most confident addressing? Which requires more development?
2 How do you distinguish between surface presenting problems and underlying patterns?
3 What interventions have you found most effective for specific challenges like communication breakdown or intimacy issues?
4 How do you know when your approach to a particular issue isn't working? What do you do then?

Self-assessment

Rate your competence in addressing common relationship challenges:

Trust your gut response. What number first comes to mind when you consider how ready you feel to take this further.

Score	*Interpretation*
1–2	Need comprehensive training in issue-specific protocols
3–4	Developing competence across several challenge areas with guidance
5–6	Strong capacity to address most common relationship issues
7+	Masterful intervention across diverse challenges with sophisticated pattern recognition

Critical Reminder

Presenting problems couples bring—communication difficulties, trust issues, sexual disconnection, parenting conflicts—are visible manifestations of deeper patterns that developed over time. The most important skill you can develop is seeing couples with compassion while maintaining clarity about what changes are needed for their relationship to thrive. This combination of empathy and clinical insight creates conditions where profound transformation becomes possible.

Remember that every couple is unique, even when surface problems appear similar. The frameworks and interventions outlined provide structure, but they must be adapted to each couple's specific needs, cultural background, and readiness for change. The presenting problems couples bring are invitations to explore deeper—your role is helping them understand the underlying patterns while developing skills and awareness needed to create lasting change.

Coming Next: Chapter 16—Complex Cases and Specialised Populations

Common challenges require solid protocols; complex cases demand specialised understanding. Chapter 16 addresses populations and presentations that test even experienced practitioners: intercultural relationships, interfaith couples, LGBTQ+ partnerships, age-gap relationships, neurodivergent individuals, chronic illness impact, addiction recovery, and blended family complexity.

You'll discover the unique dynamics each population brings, cultural competence considerations that prevent harmful assumptions, modified assessment approaches that honour diversity, intervention adaptations that respect difference, and common pitfalls practitioners encounter when working outside their cultural reference points.

Chapter 16 expands your practice capacity while teaching humility about limitations. You'll know when specialised consultation benefits couples and when referral serves them better. Your culturally responsive competence develops here.

Chapter 16

Complex Cases and Specialised Populations

Cultural, Sexual, and Identity Considerations

> My insights from Duo Coaching, my life experiences and my research are that a couple bring with them shadows from the past and unrealised ghosts that are anchoring them to the rocks and preventing them from moving forward in the right direction.
>
> —From *Reinventing*

Beyond Standard Cases: When Relationships Require Specialised Approaches

These situations test your clinical judgement, cultural competency, and ability to modify interventions while maintaining the integrity of the intensive approach. The challenge is knowing when to adapt and when to refer, when to proceed with caution and when to decline entirely.

High-Conflict Couples: De-escalation and Mediation Strategies

Understanding High-Conflict Dynamics

High-conflict couples present unique challenges because their relationship has become characterised by chronic anger, blame, and emotional reactivity that overwhelms their capacity for connection and growth.

What You See (Surface Presentations)	*What's Underneath (Underlying Dynamics)*
Arguments that escalate quickly and become personal attacks	Unresolved trauma creating hypervigilance and defensive responses
Inability to discuss any topic without conflict emerging	Personality disorders affecting emotional regulation and empathy
One or both partners becoming verbally abusive during disagreements	Addiction or mental health issues reducing impulse control

(Continued)

DOI: 10.4324/9781003715627-21

What You See (Surface Presentations)	*What's Underneath (Underlying Dynamics)*
Chronic state of anger, resentment, or emotional warfare	Family-of-origin models of conflict as normal relationship dynamic
Children or others becoming triangulated into couple conflicts	Negative cycle so entrenched that small triggers create major explosions
Both partners feeling like victims and viewing the other as perpetrator	Symmetrical escalation where each partner's defensive response triggers the other's
Communication patterns that reliably escalate rather than resolve issues	Attachment injuries creating hair-trigger reactivity to perceived criticism or rejection
External stressors (work, family, health, finances) overwhelming coping capacity	Insufficient emotional reserves; relationship becoming pressure valve for life stress

Modified Assessment Protocols for High-Conflict Couples

Safety assessment is the priority. Before proceeding, screen for immediate safety concerns and evaluate emotional safety:

Immediate Safety Screening	*Emotional Safety Evaluation*
Any history of physical violence or threats during conflicts?	Can both partners regulate their emotions enough for a productive conversation?
Do either partner fear for their physical safety during arguments?	Is there psychological abuse, intimidation, or threats occurring?
Are there weapons in the home or threats involving weapons?	Are children being exposed to frightening levels of parental conflict?
Have police ever been called during domestic disputes?	Can both partners commit to respectful communication during sessions?

If safety concerns exist, Duo Coaching may not be appropriate until individual safety planning and stabilisation occur.

Intervention Strategies for Manageable High-Conflict

Structure and ground rules are essential. High-conflict couples need more structure than typical couples: explicit agreements about respectful communication, clear consequences for rule violations (time-outs, session pausing), speaking time limits to ensure balance, no interrupting or talking over partner, and physical positioning that reduces escalation.

De-escalation techniques work best when applied early. Recognise the early signs of escalation—rising voice, body tension, dismissive gestures—and interrupt the pattern before it reaches explosive levels. Name what's happening ("I notice the intensity increasing here"), allow a brief pause for nervous system regulation, then return to the conversation with structure. Support individual regulation by teaching and practising breathing techniques during sessions, helping partners notice their own physiological arousal, creating signals for "I need a pause," normalising the need for regulation breaks, and practising returning to conversation after regulation.

Pattern interruption helps couples recognise and interrupt their escalation cycle. Map the typical sequence (trigger → response → escalation → explosion), identify early warning signs for each partner, develop alternative responses at each stage, practise new patterns in session before trying at home, and celebrate successful pattern interruptions.

Case Example: Mark and Janet—Breaking the Warfare Pattern

Mark and Janet fought constantly—about money, in-laws, parenting, household chores. Every conversation became a battlefield. Both felt victimised by the other. Their children were showing stress symptoms from the constant conflict.

Assessment revealed that Mark's father had raged regularly, so yelling felt normal to him. Janet's first husband had been violent, so she was triggered by raised voices. Both had legitimate grievances but couldn't discuss them productively, and external financial stress was amplifying all conflicts.

Intervention included individual work (Mark on rage patterns, Janet on trauma triggers), structured communication protocols with strict time limits, mandatory breaks when arousal reached a certain level, focus on one issue per conversation, and appreciation practices to balance negativity.

Outcome: Six months later: "We still disagree, but we don't destroy each other anymore. We've learned to fight fair—and more importantly, to repair after conflict."

Domestic Violence: When Couple Therapy Is Contraindicated

Recognising Domestic Violence

Domestic violence exists on a continuum from controlling behaviour to physical violence. Couple therapy can be dangerous when active domestic violence is present.

Warning signs include visible fear of partner in one person, physical injuries or history of violence, controlling behaviour limiting freedom or contact with others, economic control or isolation tactics, threats of violence or harm, and escalating patterns of intimidation.

Assessment questions (asked separately, never with both partners present): "Do you feel safe in your relationship?" "Has your partner ever hurt you physically?" "Are you afraid of your partner?" "Does your partner control aspects of your life?" "Has anyone ever called police for relationship violence?"

When Couple Work Is Inappropriate

Immediate Contraindications	*Why Couple Therapy Can Be Dangerous*
Active physical violence within past year	Creates illusion that relationship can be fixed without addressing violence
Fear present in either partner	May increase danger if victim becomes more assertive
Coerced participation in therapy	Abuser may use therapy content to further control or blame victim
Controlling behaviour preventing honest communication	Equalises responsibility when abuse is one partner's behaviour
Victim unable to speak freely without fear of consequences	May delay victim's recognition of danger and need for safety

Appropriate Response to Domestic Violence

Immediate actions: Conduct an individual consultation with the victim to assess safety and provide resources. Complete safety planning without the abuser present. Refer to domestic violence specialists. Document the disclosure (with permission). Make a clear statement that couple work is inappropriate while violence continues.

Safety Resources

When domestic violence is identified, practitioners must provide appropriate resources. The following services are available in each jurisdiction:

Safety Resources (UK)

Service	*Contact*
National Domestic Abuse Helpline	0808 2000 247 (24-hour, freephone)
Refuge	refuge.org.uk—Emergency accommodation and support
Women's Aid	womensaid.org.uk—Local services and live chat support
Men's Advice Line	0808 801 0327
Galop (LGBTQ+ support)	0800 999 5428
Respect (perpetrator programmes)	0808 802 4040

Safety Resources (US)

Service	*Contact*
National Domestic Violence Hotline	1-800-799-7233 (24-hour) or text START to 88788
National Coalition Against Domestic Violence	ncadv.org—Resources and local referrals
National Network to End Domestic Violence	nnedv.org—Safety planning resources
StrongHearts Native Helpline	1-844-762-8483 (for Native Americans)
The Hotline for Men	1-888-743-5754
The Network/La Red (LGBTQ+ support)	1-617-742-4911 or 1-800-832-1901

Long-term approach: Individual therapy for the victim to process trauma and develop a safety plan. Specialised treatment for the abuser (domestic violence programmes). Couple work is possible ONLY after violence has stopped for a significant period, the abuser has completed violence treatment, the victim feels genuinely safe, and specialist approval has been obtained.

Safety Resources: Sexual Assault and Abuse

For clients disclosing sexual assault or abuse:

Sexual Assault Resources (UK)

Service	*Contact*
Rape Crisis England & Wales	0808 500 2222
Rape Crisis Scotland	0808 801 0302
Survivors UK (male survivors)	0203 598 3898
NAPAC (childhood abuse)	0808 801 0331
The Survivors Trust	thesurvivorstrust.org—Directory of services

Sexual Assault Resources (US)

Service	*Contact*
RAINN (Rape, Abuse & Incest National Network)	1-800-656-4673 (24-hour) or online. rainn.org
National Sexual Assault Hotline	1-800-656-4673
1in6 (male survivors)	1in6.org—Online support groups
SNAP (Survivors Network of those Abused by Priests)	snapnetwork.org
Adult Survivors of Child Abuse	ascasupport.org

Child Protection Reporting

Mandatory reporting requirements differ between jurisdictions:

Jurisdiction	*Reporting Requirement*	*Contact*
UK	Report concerns to local authority children's services. In England, contact the local safeguarding children partnership.	NSPCC Helpline: 0808 800 5000 or local children's services
US	All states have mandatory reporting laws, though specific requirements vary. Most require reporting within 24–48 hours of suspicion.	Childhelp National Child Abuse Hotline: 1-800-422-4453 or contact state child protective services

Trauma-Affected Relationships: Specialised Approaches and Precautions

Understanding Trauma's Impact on Relationships

Individual trauma significantly affects relationship capacity in ways that require specialised understanding and modified intervention approaches.

Trauma Type	*Examples of Impact on Relationships*
Childhood trauma	Physical, sexual, or emotional abuse affecting trust and safety; neglect or emotional unavailability affecting attachment capacity; witnessing domestic violence affecting conflict tolerance; medical trauma affecting body trust and intimacy
Adult trauma	Sexual assault affecting intimacy and trust; military trauma affecting emotional regulation and hypervigilance; accident or medical trauma affecting sense of safety; work or financial trauma affecting stress management
Relationship trauma	Betrayal trauma from affairs or deception; attachment trauma from emotional abandonment; partner's addiction or mental illness affecting reliability; divorce or separation trauma affecting commitment capacity

Trauma-Informed Duo Coaching Adaptations

Modified consent and safety involves explicit discussion of potentially triggering content, clear agreements about breaks and pacing, permission to stop or redirect at any time, individual check-ins about readiness for difficult work, and awareness of trauma anniversaries or triggering dates.

Pacing adjustments include slower progression through intensive material, more frequent breaks for nervous system regulation, shorter initial sessions if extended time feels overwhelming, a graduated approach to vulnerability and emotional work, and respect for the trauma survivor's pace and timing.

Coordination with individual trauma therapy is often necessary. Trauma survivors frequently need individual therapy alongside couple work. Communication with the individual therapist (with client consent) ensures trauma work doesn't overwhelm couple work or vice versa. Sometimes couple work must be delayed until trauma stabilisation is achieved. Maintain clear division between individual trauma processing and couple sessions.

Case Example: Sarah and Tom—Healing from Sexual Trauma

Sarah's childhood sexual abuse created automatic shutdown during intimacy with Tom, even though she trusted him completely. Tom felt rejected and inadequate; Sarah felt broken and ashamed.

Trauma-informed approach: Individual trauma therapy for Sarah alongside couple work; psychoeducation for Tom about trauma responses; gradual reconnection at Sarah's pace with explicit consent at each stage; hypnotherapy to address automatic trauma responses; developing language for Sarah to communicate needs during intimacy.

Outcome: "For the first time in my life, I can be fully present during physical intimacy," Sarah reported after a year. "And Tom's patience and understanding made healing possible."

Addiction and Recovery: Working with Couples in Recovery

The Impact of Addiction on Relationships

Active addiction destroys relationships through lying, broken promises, financial damage, emotional unavailability, and betrayal of trust. But recovery creates different challenges requiring specialised understanding.

When Couple Work Is Inappropriate	*When Couple Work Can Proceed*
Active addiction preventing honest engagement	Addiction is in stable recovery (6+ months clean/sober)
Early recovery (first three to six months) requiring recovery focus	Individual working a recovery programme (AA, NA, therapy, etc.)
Addiction so severe that relationship issues can't be addressed	Both partners motivated for relationship repair
Partner's behaviour enabling continued use	Adequate support systems in place for recovery maintenance

Recovery-Informed Duo Coaching

Recovery priority maintained: Schedule couple sessions around recovery meetings. Recovery commitments take precedence over couple work. Crisis protocols should protect recovery first. Appreciate that recovery is ongoing individual work, and understand that recovery is the partner's responsibility, not the couple's.

Trust rebuilding after addiction requires complete accountability for addiction-related damage, understanding of the betrayed partner's trauma from the addiction period, gradual rebuilding with transparency and consistency, addressing underlying issues that contributed to addiction, and individual therapy for both partners processing addiction's impact.

Communication pattern changes include new patterns that support recovery rather than trigger use, honest expression of needs without enabling, conflict resolution that doesn't threaten sobriety, appreciation and celebration of recovery milestones, and family healing from addiction's impact on everyone.

Safety Resources: Addiction Support

For couples where addiction is a factor:

Addiction Resources (UK)

Service	*Contact*
FRANK (drug advice)	0300 123 6600 or text 82111
Alcoholics Anonymous UK	0800 917 7650
Al-Anon (families of alcoholics)	0800 0086 811
Drinkline	0300 123 1110
GamCare (gambling)	0808 802 0133
UKNA (Narcotics Anonymous)	ukna.org

Addiction Resources (US)

Service	*Contact*
SAMHSA National Helpline	1-800-662-4357 (24-hour, free, confidential)
Alcoholics Anonymous	aa.org or local directory
Al-Anon/Alateen	1-888-425-2666
Narcotics Anonymous	na.org
National Council on Problem Gambling	1-800-522-4700
Partnership to End Addiction	drugfree.org—1-855-378-4373

Case Example: Michael and Sarah—Rebuilding After Alcoholism

Michael's alcoholism had nearly destroyed their marriage—lying, financial irresponsibility, emotional unavailability, and a previous separation during his worst drinking period. Two years sober, they sought couple help.

Recovery-informed approach: Michael's AA participation and sponsor relationship were maintained. Sarah's Al-Anon involvement continued for her own healing. Individual therapy for Sarah addressed trauma from the addiction period. Trust was rebuilt gradually with financial transparency. New communication patterns supported both recovery and relationship.

Outcome: Three years later, Michael maintained sobriety, Sarah healed from addiction trauma, and their relationship became stronger than the pre-addiction period. "We're more authentic now," both reported.

Mental Health Complications: Coordinating Care

When Mental Health Affects Relationships

Mental health conditions significantly impact relationship functioning, requiring modified approaches and often coordination with psychiatric care.

Common mental health challenges in couples: Depression affecting energy, interest, and emotional availability. Anxiety creating need for reassurance or controlling behaviour. Post-Traumatic Stress Disorder (PTSD) creating hypervigilance, triggers, and emotional dysregulation. Bipolar disorder affecting stability and reliability. Obsessive-Compulsive Disorder (OCD) creating rigid patterns affecting the partner. Personality disorders affecting empathy and emotional regulation.

Assessment and Treatment Planning

Mental health screening should cover current diagnoses and treatment, medication management and stability, previous psychiatric hospitalisations, suicidal ideation or self-harm history, and impact on relationship functioning.

Proceed with Duo Coaching When	*Defer or Refer When*
Conditions are stable with treatment	Active mental health crisis requiring stabilisation
Medication effectively managing symptoms	Severe symptoms preventing relationship work
Individual therapy addressing mental health needs	Need for intensive individual treatment first
Both partners understand and can accommodate mental health needs	Risk of harm to self or others
Mental health doesn't prevent meaningful engagement	Lack of appropriate psychiatric care

Coordination with mental health providers (with client consent) includes communication with the psychiatrist or therapist; understanding medication effects and side effects; coordinating couple work with individual treatment; crisis protocols and emergency contacts; and regular assessment of mental health stability.

Safety Resources: Suicide and Mental Health Crisis

When clients present with suicidal ideation or mental health crisis, immediate resources should be provided:

Crisis Resources (UK)

Service	*Contact*
Samaritans	116 123 (24-hour, free) or email jo@samaritans.org
Crisis Text Line	Text SHOUT to 85258
CALM (Campaign Against Living Miserably)	0800 58 58 58 (5pm–midnight)
Papyrus (under 35s)	0800 068 4141 or text 07860 039967
SANE	0300 304 7000 (4:30pm–10:30pm)
NHS Mental Health Crisis	111 (option 2) or local crisis team
Mind Infoline	0300 123 3393

Crisis Resources (US)

Service	*Contact*
988 Suicide and Crisis Lifeline	988 (call or text, 24-hour)
Crisis Text Line	Text HOME to 741741
National Suicide Prevention Lifeline	1-800-273-8255 (still active, routes to 988)
Veterans Crisis Line	988 then press 1, or text 838255
Trevor Project (LGBTQ+ youth)	1-866-488-7386 or text START to 678-678
Trans Lifeline	1-877-565-8860 (US) or 1-877-330-6366 (Canada)
SAMHSA National Helpline	1-800-662-4357 (substance abuse and mental health)
NAMI Helpline	1-800-950-6264 (Mon–Fri, 10am–10pm ET)

LGBTQ+ Couples: Cultural Sensitivity and Unique Considerations

Understanding Unique Relationship Challenges

LGBTQ+ couples face all the same relationship challenges as heterosexual couples, plus additional stressors related to cultural context, family acceptance, and social discrimination.

Specific challenges include coming-out processes and different stages between partners, family acceptance and rejection issues, internalised homophobia or transphobia, lack of legal recognition or protections in some contexts, discrimination and minority stress, and limited relationship models and support.

Culturally Affirming Approach

Essential attitudes: Genuine affirmation of LGBTQ+ identities and relationships. Understanding of unique challenges without pathologising. Knowledge of community resources and support systems. Awareness of your own biases and commitment to ongoing education. Use of correct pronouns and terminology.

Addressing Specific Issues

Issue Area	*Considerations*
Coming-out disparities	Different stages between partners creating tension; family acceptance differences; workplace disclosure decisions; social context variations
Identity development	Individual journey with sexual orientation or gender identity; internalised negative messages; religious or cultural conflicts; integration of identity with other aspects of self
Family and social support	Dealing with family rejection or conditional acceptance; creating chosen family when biological family unsupportive; navigating heteronormative social structures; finding LGBTQ+ affirming community

Case Example: Jason and David—Coming-Out Disparities

Jason was completely out at work and with family. David was out to close friends only, with a religious family who knew about Jason but treated him as "roommate." Disagreement about adoption plans arose because David feared family reaction. Jason felt back "in the closet" visiting David's family.

Culturally affirming approach: Individual work for David on internalised homophobia and religious shame. Individual work for Jason on patience with David's coming-out process. Safety assessment for David coming out to family and workplace. Future planning honouring both partners' needs and fears. Connection with LGBTQ+ couples support groups.

Outcome: Eighteen months later, David had come out to family with mixed but gradually improving acceptance. The couple proceeded with adoption plans with a strong support system. Both reported feeling more authentic and connected.

Cross-Cultural Relationships: Navigating Different Value Systems

The Complexity of Cultural Integration

Cross-cultural relationships involve partners from different cultural, ethnic, religious, or national backgrounds navigating the integration of different worldviews, values, and family systems.

Common challenges include different communication styles and conflict approaches, varying expectations about gender roles and family structure, religious differences affecting values and practices, extended family involvement and expectations, cultural celebrations and traditions, language barriers, and immigration and visa issues.

Intervention Framework

Cultural exploration without judgement involves understanding each partner's cultural background and influences, exploring how cultural messages shape relationship expectations, recognising strengths each culture brings, and avoiding cultural stereotypes or superiority.

Negotiation of differences includes identifying which differences are manageable versus incompatible, creating a unique blend honouring both backgrounds, negotiating specific issues (child-raising, holidays, family involvement), and addressing power dynamics when one culture is dominant in society.

Family system navigation requires understanding extended family expectations from each culture, negotiating boundaries with families, creating agreements about family involvement, and supporting each other when facing family disapproval.

Cultural humility: Remember that you cannot be an expert in all cultures. Maintain humility, ask questions, admit what you don't know, and refer when cultural expertise beyond your competence is needed.

Advanced Clinical Judgement: When to Refer versus When to Adapt

Decision-Making Framework for Complex Cases

Safety Concerns Requiring Referral	*Manageable Concerns Requiring Adaptation*
Active domestic violence or threats of violence	History of violence with current safety and accountability measures
Active suicidal ideation or self-harm behaviours	Mental health conditions that are stable with treatment
Severe mental health crises requiring immediate intervention	Past trauma affecting relationship but not preventing engagement
Active substance abuse preventing meaningful relationship work	Mild substance use not impairing judgement or relationship work

Building Professional Competency for Complex Cases

Ongoing education and training should include trauma-informed therapy approaches, addiction and recovery counselling principles, mental health disorders and relationship impacts, cultural competency for diverse populations, and LGBTQ+ affirming practice.

Supervision and consultation include regular supervision with experienced practitioners, case consultation for complex cases, peer consultation groups, and professional development planning.

Professional network development means building referral resources: individual therapists specialising in trauma, addiction, and mental health; psychiatrists and medical professionals; cultural and identity specialists; legal and social service professionals; and domestic violence specialists.

Conclusion: Expanding Your Clinical Horizons

Working with complex cases and specialised populations expands clinical skills while deepening understanding of the resilience and adaptability of human relationships. These challenging situations often provide the most profound learning opportunities for both practitioners and couples.

The key to successful work with complex cases lies in maintaining core Duo Coaching principles—safety, respect, outcome focus, and relationship transformation—while adapting approaches to meet unique needs and circumstances. This requires ongoing professional development, cultural humility, and collaborative relationships with other professionals.

Remember that complexity doesn't negate the possibility of profound relationship transformation. Often, couples who have faced and overcome significant challenges develop a deeper appreciation, a stronger commitment, and a more authentic connection than those whose path was easier.

> Complexity doesn't negate the possibility of profound relationship transformation.
>
> —From *Reinventing*

Integration and Self-reflection

Foundation Level Skills Addressed in This Chapter

This chapter has addressed four key skills: Cultural Competence (working effectively across diverse cultural contexts and values), LGBTQ+ Affirmation (providing knowledgeable, affirming care for diverse sexual orientations and gender identities), Specialised Population Understanding (recognising unique needs of different couple types), and Scope Awareness (knowing when specialised expertise beyond your competence is required).

Reflection Questions

1. What cultural backgrounds and populations do you have lived experience with or specific training in?
2. How would you assess your current competence in working with LGBTQ+ couples? What development is needed?

3 Which specialised populations (interfaith, intercultural, neurodivergent, etc.) require additional training for you?
4 How comfortable are you recognising limitations and referring when cases exceed your expertise?

Self-assessment

How prepared are you to work with complex cases and diverse populations?

Trust your gut response. What number first comes to mind when you consider how ready you feel to take this further?

Score	*Interpretation*
1–2	Need substantial cultural competence development before working with diverse populations
3–4	Developing awareness with appropriate consultation and supervision
5–6	Strong competence with several populations, clear scope awareness
7+	Sophisticated cultural humility and broad population expertise

Next Steps: Pursue specific training in populations you'll serve. Develop consultation relationships with specialists. Create clear protocols for scope assessment and referral processes

Coming Next: Chapter 17—When to Refer and Professional Boundaries

Complex cases stretch competence, but some situations exceed the appropriate scope of practice. Chapter 17 provides clear guidance for recognising when couples need different resources, how to execute referrals that honour your therapeutic relationship, and maintaining professional boundaries that protect everyone involved.

You'll discover absolute contraindications for couple therapy (active domestic violence, severe untreated mental illness, substance abuse crisis), relative contraindications requiring modification (personality disorders, trauma activation, motivational disparity), when individual therapy must precede or accompany couple work, and how to present referrals without abandoning couples or damaging rapport.

Chapter 17 also addresses boundary challenges unique to intensive work: between-session contact limits, managing dependency, dual relationships in small communities, and social media complications. Knowing your limits isn't weakness—it's professional maturity that protects both couples and your practice.

Chapter 17

When to Refer and Professional Boundaries

Scope of Practice and Ethical Considerations

Image 14 Man with Long Telescope, Standing on Ground.
"Looking Further Than the Eye Can Reach"

> Not everything needs voicing, and timing matters. The question is whether the unsaid has become a permanent presence; a topic surrounded by electric fence, a truth everyone knows but no one speaks.
>
> Neil Wilkie, *Relationship Inspirations*

The Art of Professional Wisdom: Knowing Your Limits and Serving within Them

After 15 years of intensive couple work, I've learned that the most skilled practitioners are those who know their boundaries clearly and refer confidently when necessary. This chapter will guide you through developing the assessment skills, professional relationships, and ethical framework needed to make these crucial decisions with confidence.

DOI: 10.4324/9781003715627-22

Recognising Limitations: When Duo Coaching Isn't Appropriate

Understanding Scope of Practice

Duo Coaching is a powerful approach for relationship transformation, but it has specific parameters within which it works most effectively. Understanding these boundaries helps you serve couples appropriately while protecting both their well-being and your professional integrity.

Clear Contraindications for Duo Coaching

Category	*Specific Concerns*	*Action Required*
Active domestic violence	Physical violence or credible threats; escalating pattern of intimidation or control; partner expressing fear for physical safety; weapons involved in conflicts	Immediate referral to domestic violence specialists and crisis services
Current crisis requiring immediate intervention	Active suicidal ideation or recent suicide attempts; severe mental health crisis requiring hospitalisation; active psychotic episodes affecting reality testing; immediate child protection concerns	Emergency psychiatric care or crisis services take priority over relationship work
Active addiction preventing engagement	Intoxication during sessions or inability to remain sober; addiction so severe that relationship work is impossible; partner safety compromised by addiction-related behaviours; denial of addiction preventing honest engagement	Specialised addiction treatment before or alongside relationship work
Behavioural addictions	Gambling addiction causing financial crisis or deception; sexual addiction involving ongoing infidelity or high-risk behaviours; technology addiction preventing meaningful engagement; eating disorders requiring specialised medical intervention	Coordinate with addiction specialists rather than proceeding alone
Untreated severe mental illness	Active psychotic symptoms affecting reality testing; severe depression with suicidal ideation; manic episodes involving poor judgement or risky behaviours; personality disorders requiring intensive individual therapy first	Individual psychiatric treatment must precede couple work

(*Continued*)

Category	Specific Concerns	Action Required
Cognitive impairment	Dementia or neurological conditions affecting understanding; traumatic brain injury affecting emotional regulation; developmental disabilities requiring specialised approaches	Specialised services with appropriate expertise

Situations Requiring Specialised Expertise beyond Your Training

Situation	Examples	Refer To
Legal and custody issues	Contentious divorce proceedings; custody disputes requiring court intervention; legal domestic violence proceedings; financial fraud or criminal behaviour affecting relationship	Family law attorneys, mediators specialising in high-conflict divorce, custody evaluators, legal advocates
Medical and sexual health issues	Sexual dysfunction requiring medical evaluation; infertility issues requiring medical intervention; chronic illness significantly affecting relationship; sexual trauma requiring specialised therapy	Medical doctors, sex therapists with medical training, fertility specialists, trauma therapists
Cultural or religious complexity	Religious conflicts requiring theological expertise; cultural integration issues beyond your competence; immigration or visa issues; cultural practices you don't understand adequately	Religious counsellors from relevant traditions, culturally specific therapists, immigration attorneys, cultural consultants

Building Your Referral Network

Identifying Essential Referral Resources

A comprehensive referral network ensures couples can access specialised support when needed:

Category	Key Resources
Mental health specialists	Individual therapists specialising in trauma, addiction, and eating disorders; psychiatrists for medication evaluation and management; crisis intervention services and emergency psychiatric care; specialised therapists for personality disorders, psychosis, and severe depression

(Continued)

Category	*Key Resources*
Medical professionals	Primary care physicians for health issues affecting relationships; sexual health specialists and sex therapists; fertility specialists and reproductive medicine; pain management and chronic illness specialists
Legal and social services	Family law attorneys specialising in divorce and custody; mediators for high-conflict separations; domestic violence advocates and legal services; child protective services and family support services
Specialised relationship services	Individual relationship therapists for ongoing support; sex therapists certified in sexual dysfunction treatment; affair recovery specialists for complex betrayal situations; domestic violence perpetrator programmes
Cultural and community resources	Religious leaders and pastoral counsellors; culturally specific therapists and consultants; LGBTQ+ affirming therapists and support services; culturally specific community organisations

Building Collaborative Professional Relationships

Initial connection involves introducing yourself and your practice, learning about their specialisation and approach, discussing potential collaboration opportunities, and establishing communication protocols.

Ongoing relationship building includes regular networking and professional development together, mutual referrals when appropriate, communication about referral outcomes (with client consent), and consultation relationships for complex cases.

Quality standards for referral sources: Ensure they have appropriate credentials and training, a good professional reputation, shared values about client care, responsive communication and collaboration, and ethical practice with professional boundaries.

Case Example: The Power of Good Referral Networks

I once received a call from David and Emma, both struggling with David's PTSD from military service affecting their relationship. While I could address some relationship impacts, David needed specialised trauma therapy before meaningful couple work was possible.

I referred them to a trauma specialist who treats veterans, maintaining contact with both therapist and couple. After six months of individual trauma work, David and Emma returned for Duo Coaching with a much stronger foundation. The trauma therapist and I coordinated approaches, creating comprehensive care neither could provide alone.

Outcome: David's PTSD symptoms significantly improved, their relationship transformed, and the collaborative care demonstrated to them the value of seeking appropriate specialised help. They now have a network of support for future challenges.

Making Effective Referrals

Preparation for Referral

When you recognise the need for referral, careful preparation ensures the transition serves the couple well.

Discuss with the couple clearly: Explain why referral is needed and what specialised support can offer. Emphasise that referral isn't rejection but ensuring appropriate care. Describe what to expect from the referred professional, and outline the timeline and process for accessing services.

Provide written information including the name, contact details, and location of the referral source, a brief description of their specialisation, what to say when contacting them, and your availability for questions or support.

Address concerns about referral: Discuss financial considerations and insurance coverage, fear about seeing another professional, disappointment about not continuing with you, and concerns about starting over with someone new.

Communication with Referred Professional

With client consent, provide a brief background about the couple and their needs, the specific reason for referral, relevant history affecting current presentation, and your availability for consultation or coordination.

Coordinate care when appropriate by clarifying timing of services (sequential or concurrent), communication protocols between professionals, shared treatment goals and approaches, and clear role definition preventing duplication or gaps.

Following Up on Referrals

Timeframe	*Actions*
Within one to two weeks	Check whether the couple accessed referred services; address any barriers or concerns; offer support for referral process; assess whether referral met their needs
Ongoing	Remain available for questions or concerns; coordinate with referred professional when appropriate; consider whether couple work can resume after specialised treatment; maintain relationship for future needs

Maintaining Professional Boundaries

The Foundation of Trust: Clear and Consistent Boundaries

Professional boundaries create the safety and structure that allows couples to engage in vulnerable relationship work. These boundaries must be clear, consistent, and maintained throughout the therapeutic process.

Essential Boundary Categories

Category	*Elements*
Time and session boundaries	Clear start and end times with respectful flexibility for natural completion; cancellation policies respecting both client and therapist needs; between-session contact availability and limitations; emergency contact protocols and appropriate use guidelines
Therapeutic timeline boundaries	Clear expectations about therapy duration and completion criteria; regular review of progress and remaining work; termination planning and transition to independence; follow-up availability and limitations after therapy completion
Physical and spatial boundaries	Appropriate office setup and professional environment; physical contact policies and cultural sensitivity; privacy and confidentiality protection in physical space; safety and comfort considerations for all participants
Professional presentation	Appropriate dress and professional appearance; personal disclosure limitations and professional focus; gift-giving policies and appropriate exchange guidelines; social media and online interaction boundaries
Emotional and relational boundaries	Professional caring vs. personal friendship distinction; emotional support provision within professional role; personal problem discussion limitations; therapeutic neutrality balanced with genuine care
Professional role clarity	Therapeutic vs. friendship relationship boundaries; professional advice vs. personal opinion distinctions; therapeutic goals vs. personal agenda; client welfare as primary consideration

Dual Relationships: Navigating Multiple Professional Connections

The co-therapy model creates unique boundary challenges: two therapists working together, each therapist relating to both partners, a complex web of professional and personal connections, and multiple relationships developing over time.

Common Dual Relationship Challenges

Type	*Examples*
Social or community overlap	Encountering clients in social settings; shared community or professional organisations; children in same schools or activities; common social networks
Professional overlap	Colleagues in professional organisations; workshop or training participants; supervision or consultation relationships; shared professional development activities

Managing Dual Relationship Complexity

Prevention strategies include clear policies about dual relationships from the start, informed consent about handling social encounters, boundaries around social media connections, and geographical distance when possible.

When overlap occurs, acknowledge publicly with discretion, keep interactions brief and professional in public, avoid any discussion of therapy content in social settings, and process implications in the next session if needed.

Case Example: Navigating Small Town Practice

Sarah and Michael practiced Duo Coaching in a town of 15,000 people where social and professional overlap was inevitable. They encountered former clients at school functions, grocery stores, and community events.

Their approach: A clear policy discussed during intake about handling public encounters; brief, friendly acknowledgment without therapy discussion; clients' choice about whether to acknowledge therapists publicly; and regular processing in supervision of boundary challenges.

Result: Clear boundaries enhanced rather than damaged therapeutic relationships. Clients appreciated transparency and respect for their privacy while allowing natural social interaction appropriate for small-town life.

Ethical Decision-Making Framework

Developing Clinical Judgement for Complex Referral Decisions

Many situations aren't clearly within or outside your scope of practice, requiring sophisticated clinical judgement about whether to refer, consult, or adapt your approach.

Assessment Questions for Borderline Cases

Domain	*Key Questions*
Competency assessment	Do I have adequate training and experience to work safely with this issue? What additional consultation or supervision would I need to work competently? Are there professionals better equipped to handle this couple's specific needs? Would adapting my approach serve this couple better than referring?
Safety evaluation	Can I ensure this couple's safety while working within my current competency? What risks exist if I work beyond my current skill level? What safeguards would need to be in place for me to work with this couple? Would a delay in referral create greater risk than working within my limitations?

(Continued)

Domain	*Key Questions*
Client welfare priority	What approach would best serve this couple's long-term welfare? How do my own professional interests or ego affect this decision? What would I recommend if this were my family member or close friend? Am I considering referral because it's easier or because it's better for the client?

Consultation and Supervision Process

Professional consultation involves regular supervision specifically addressing scope of practice decisions, peer consultation about challenging cases and referral decisions, expert consultation when working near edges of competency, and professional development planning to expand competency areas.

Documentation and accountability includes clear documentation of the decision-making process for complex cases, regular review of referral patterns and their effectiveness, professional development goals based on identified competency gaps, and accountability systems for staying within the appropriate scope of practice.

Conclusion: Professional Integrity through Wise Boundaries

The ability to make appropriate referrals and maintain professional boundaries isn't a limitation—it's a fundamental professional competency that protects both clients and practitioners while ensuring that couples receive the most appropriate care for their unique needs.

Developing this clinical wisdom requires ongoing self-assessment, professional development, and commitment to putting client welfare above personal or professional ego. The most effective Duo Coaching practitioners are those who know their strengths and limitations clearly and work collaboratively within a network of professionals to serve couples comprehensively.

Remember that referring couples to more appropriate services is often the most therapeutic intervention you can provide. Your role isn't to be all things to all couples, but to be the best practitioner you can be within your scope of competency while ensuring couples have access to whatever support they truly need.

The relationships you build with other professionals and the referral systems you develop will enhance rather than diminish your practice by demonstrating your commitment to comprehensive, ethical care. Couples will trust you more, not less, when they know you'll refer them to specialised services when needed.

This completes our exploration of working with complex cases and specialised populations. Your willingness to expand competency and adapt approaches to serve diverse populations contributes to making relationship healing more accessible and effective for couples who might otherwise struggle to find appropriate support.

> The privilege of a lifetime is being who you are.
>
> —Joseph Campbell

Integration and Self-reflection

Intermediate Level Skills Addressed in This Chapter

This chapter has addressed four key skills: **Referral Competency** (recognising when couples need specialised services beyond your scope), **Network Development** (building comprehensive professional relationships for collaborative care), **Boundary Management** (maintaining clear professional boundaries across all contexts), and **Ethical Decision-Making** (navigating complex situations with wisdom and integrity).

Reflection Questions

1 What situations in your current practice make you most uncertain about whether to refer?
2 Which professional relationships would be most valuable to develop in your referral network?
3 Where do you experience boundary challenges or uncertainty in your current practice?
4 How do you currently make decisions when your scope of practice feels unclear?

Self-assessment

Rate your referral and boundary competency development:

Trust your gut response. What number first comes to mind when you consider how ready you feel to take this further?

Score	*Interpretation*
1–2	Need significant development in recognising limitations and building networks
3–4	Growing awareness of when to refer, beginning network development
5–6	Solid referral competency, established network, clear boundaries
7+	Expert-level judgement, comprehensive network, boundary leadership

Action Planning

Timeframe	*Actions*
Within 30 days	Identify three priority referral sources to develop; review and clarify your boundary policies; schedule consultation for any current borderline cases
Within 90 days	Establish relationships with five to ten key referral sources; create written boundary and referral policies; conduct a thorough scope of practice self-assessment
Within 12 months	Comprehensive referral network across all major specialisations; clear, consistent boundary maintenance across all contexts; regular consultation for complex cases; additional training in identified competency gaps

The ability to make appropriate referrals and maintain professional boundaries isn't a limitation—it's a fundamental professional competency that protects both clients and practitioners while ensuring that couples receive the most appropriate care for their unique needs.

End of Part IV

Your clinical toolkit is now substantially complete. You can assess, plan, intervene, and navigate complexity. But sustainable practice requires more than clinical skill—it requires a viable professional life. Part V addresses what training rarely teaches: building a practice that supports both your clients and yourself.

Part V: Practice Building (Chapters 18–21)

Excellent clinical work means little if you can't sustain a viable practice. These chapters guide you through supervision, ethical considerations, research literacy, and the business realities of building a Duo Coaching practice. We address what training programmes rarely teach: How to thrive professionally while doing meaningful work.

Coming Next: Chapter 18—Supervision and Continuing Education

Professional boundaries protect practice integrity, but continued growth requires ongoing support. Chapter 18 addresses supervision needs for intensive relationship work, continuing education strategies, and professional development pathways that deepen mastery.

Discover supervision structures that support co-therapy partnerships, peer consultation models that provide collegial learning, specialised training that advances specific competencies, conference and workshop opportunities for skill development, and communities of practice that prevent professional isolation.

Chapter 18 recognises that implementing Duo Coaching is merely the beginning of your developmental journey. Expert practitioners remain perpetual learners, continually refining skills while supporting others' growth. Your professional development path unfolds from here.

Part V

Expert Level Development

Professional Leadership

Chapter 18

Supervision and Continuing Education

Developing Other Practitioners

> Relationships are perhaps the most powerful context for personal growth. They reveal us to ourselves in ways that solitary life cannot.
>
> —Neil Wilkie, *Relationship Inspirations*

Why Supervision Matters in Duo Coaching

After three years of practising Duo Coaching, Rachel approached me hesitantly: "I think I should be past needing supervision by now. Shouldn't I be able to handle couples independently?"

Her question reflects a common misconception: That supervision is only for beginners, a training requirement to be completed and left behind.

The reality is very different: The best practitioners are those who maintain supervision throughout their careers.

The Unique Demands of Duo Coaching

Duo Coaching creates supervision needs that differ from traditional therapy:

Demand	*Why Supervision Helps*
Intensive format challenges	Managing 2.5–3.5-hour sessions requires sustained focus and energy; extended time reveals dynamics that might remain hidden in 50-minute sessions; practitioners need help processing the intensity of this work
Co-therapy complexity	Partnership dynamics require ongoing attention and refinement; conflicts or misalignments need a skilled third-party perspective; co-therapists need support in maintaining healthy collaboration

(Continued)

DOI: 10.4324/9781003715627-24

Demand	*Why Supervision Helps*
Rapid transformation	Couples change quickly, creating unique clinical challenges; brief treatment timeline requires sophisticated clinical judgement; practitioners need help recognising when standard protocols should be adapted
High-stakes decision-making	Safety assessments and referral decisions carry significant weight; suitability determinations directly impact couple outcomes; clinical judgement develops through supervised experience

Supervision across Career Stages

Stage	*Focus*	*Supervision Frequency*
Foundation Level (Years 1–3)	Learning core competencies and framework application; building confidence with standard presentations; developing clinical judgement through guided experience	Weekly or biweekly (essential)
Intermediate Level (Years 3–7)	Working with increasingly complex cases; refining integration of multiple modalities; developing specialised expertise areas	Biweekly or monthly (maintaining quality)
Expert Level (Years 7+)	Managing most challenging presentations; contributing to field development and innovation; training and mentoring others	Monthly or quarterly peer consultation (sustaining excellence)

Finding Qualified Duo Supervision

Supervisor Pair Qualifications

Look for supervisor **pairs** who meet these essential requirements:

Requirement	*What to Look For*
Duo Coaching Certification	Both supervisors should be certified Duo Coaches who have completed accredited training through the Duo Coaching Academy
Working partnership	They should have an established supervision partnership, not just two individual supervisors meeting separately with you
Significant practice experience	Minimum 300+ hours each of supervised Duo Coaching practice

(Continued)

Requirement	*What to Look For*
Supervision training	Formal training in supervision methods, ideally as a co-supervision pair
Current practice	Both actively engaged in Duo Coaching work, not just supervision
Effective partnership	They demonstrate the co-therapy collaboration you're learning

Warning signs of inadequate supervision: Avoid supervisor pairs who haven't completed Duo Coaching Academy certification, don't actually work together (two separate individual supervisors), compete or undermine each other during sessions, primarily use supervision to promote their own approaches, become defensive when suggestions don't work, or don't model effective partnership dynamics.

Finding Your Supervisor Duo

Duo Coaching Academy Directory is the most reliable source for qualified supervisor pairs. Visit www.duocoachingacademy.com for current supervisor Duo listings; review supervisor pair profiles, specialisations, and experience levels; contact multiple potential supervisor pairs for initial consultations; and select based on fit, not just convenience or cost.

Initial consultation questions to ask potential supervisor pairs:

Area	*Questions*
Partnership experience	"How long have you been working together as a supervision Duo?" "What is your combined experience with Duo Coaching specifically?"
Working style	"How do you coordinate during supervision sessions?" "How do you handle situations where you disagree with each other?"
Expectations	"What are your expectations for supervision preparation?" "How do you provide feedback about partnership dynamics?"
Expertise	"What specialised areas of expertise does your Duo bring?" "How do you maintain your own supervision Duo partnership?"

Observe their partnership during the initial consultation. Notice whether they coordinate smoothly or compete for airtime, whether they can build on each other's observations, whether they demonstrate mutual respect, how they handle disagreement between them, and whether their partnership feels collaborative or hierarchical.

When Duo Supervision Isn't Available

If there are no certified Duo supervisor pairs in your area:

Option	*Description*
Virtual Duo Supervision	Many supervisor pairs offer video-based supervision—don't let geography limit access to the gold standard
Temporary Individual Supervision	Use individual supervision as a stepping stone while seeking to establish Duo supervision, building enough practitioners in your area to attract supervisor pairs, or working towards certification that might enable you to form a local supervisor Duo
Combination Approach	Primary individual supervisor for regular sessions, quarterly intensive sessions with Duo supervisor pair (travel or virtual), supplemented with peer consultation Duo

Don't settle for inadequate supervision simply because it's convenient. The couples you serve deserve practitioners who have received gold-standard Duo supervision.

Structuring Effective Supervision

Supervision Contract

Establish clear expectations through a written agreement:

Area	*Questions to Address*
Frequency and duration	How often will you meet? How long will each session last? What happens if you need to cancel or reschedule?
Focus and content	What types of cases will you present? How much preparation is expected? What recordings or documentation will be reviewed?
Feedback and evaluation	How will feedback be provided? Will there be formal competency assessments? What happens if significant concerns arise?
Confidentiality and boundaries	How will client confidentiality be protected? What are the boundaries of the supervisory relationship? How will conflicts or disagreements be handled?
Financial arrangements	What are the fees and payment terms? What expenses might arise (materials, travel, etc.)? What is the cancellation policy?

Preparing for Supervision

Before Each Session

1. **Select specific focus**—Don't try to cover everything. Choose one to two cases or issues that need attention.
2. **Prepare materials**—Brief written case summary, specific questions or concerns, relevant assessments or outcome data, and video clips if available (with consent).

3 **Identify learning goals**—What do you hope to gain from this supervision session?
4 **Reflect honestly**—Where did you struggle? What are you avoiding acknowledging?

Making Supervision Sessions Productive

Provide context efficiently: Brief couple background (two to three minutes), presenting concerns and treatment goals, your conceptualisation and approach, and where you're stuck or concerned.

Ask specific questions: Instead of "What should I do with this couple?" ask "I'm noticing they avoid conflict even in session. How do I create enough safety for productive disagreement without pushing them into premature confrontation?" Instead of "Am I doing this right?" ask "When Partner A shuts down like this, I usually [describe intervention]. But it's not working. What might I be missing?"

Be honest about limitations. The most valuable supervision happens when you acknowledge things like "I have no idea what to do next," "I'm avoiding something in this case and I don't know what," "I think I'm in over my head with this couple," or "My co-therapist and I are stuck in a pattern."

Receiving and Integrating Feedback

Good supervision sometimes means hearing things that feel uncomfortable: "I notice you consistently avoid addressing the sexual issues," "Your co-therapist seems to be doing most of the work," "I'm concerned you're missing safety concerns in this case," or "This couple might be beyond your current competency level."

How to receive challenging feedback: Breathe—don't immediately defend or explain. Listen fully to understand what's being communicated. Ask for clarification: "Can you help me understand what you're seeing?" Consider honestly whether there's truth here, even if it's uncomfortable. Develop an action plan: "What specific steps would help me address this?"

Disagreeing with supervision: It's appropriate to ask for rationale behind suggestions, express concerns about suggested approaches, request alternative perspectives, and try suggestions while maintaining reservations. It's concerning if you consistently dismiss supervisor input, feel you know better than experienced supervisors, avoid supervision when cases are challenging, or only present cases where you look competent.

Types of Supervision

Duo Supervision (Gold Standard)

Structure: Your co-therapy pair meeting with a pair of certified Duo Coach supervisors (four people total), with regular sessions (weekly/biweekly for Foundation, monthly for Intermediate), focusing on both clinical work and partnership dynamics.

Why this is the gold standard: Duo Coaching is fundamentally about partnership. Having supervision that mirrors the co-therapy model provides unique benefits:

Benefit	*How It Works*
Models the framework	Supervisors demonstrate effective co-therapy collaboration; you observe how experienced practitioners coordinate in real-time; the supervision process itself teaches partnership skills
Addresses partnership dynamics	Both supervisors can observe your co-therapy interaction; they can address partnership patterns and dynamics directly; provides balanced perspective on both practitioners' contributions
Reflects the Duo philosophy	Practises what we preach about the power of two perspectives; avoids the limitation of single-perspective supervision; creates richer, more nuanced feedback and learning
Provides comprehensive support	One supervisor might notice what the other misses; supervisors can model disagreement and collaborative resolution; offers multiple mentorship relationships simultaneously

Appropriate for: ALL practitioners who can access it (Foundation through Expert), especially critical when co-therapy partnership is new or strained. Required for full certification maintenance when available.

Individual Supervision (Alternative When Duo Unavailable)

Structure: One-on-one sessions with a single certified Duo Coach supervisor.

When this may be necessary: Geographic constraints (no Duo supervision pairs available locally), financial constraints (Duo supervision costs more), temporary arrangement while seeking Duo supervision, or specific personal issues requiring private exploration.

Important limitations: While individual supervision can be helpful, recognise that it doesn't model the co-therapy partnership you're being trained to provide, a single supervisor brings only one perspective, it may inadvertently reinforce individual rather than partnership thinking, and it doesn't address co-therapy dynamics as effectively.

If using individual supervision: Ensure your co-therapist also receives supervision, schedule joint sessions with your individual supervisor periodically, supplement with peer consultation or group supervision, and work towards transitioning to Duo supervision when possible.

Group Supervision

Structure: Multiple co-therapy pairs (three to four pairs, six to eight people total) meeting with Duo supervisor pair, in monthly or biweekly two- to three-hour sessions with rotating case presentations from different pairs.

Benefits: Learning from multiple co-therapy partnerships simultaneously, observing how different pairs handle similar challenges, cost-effective access to Duo supervision model, community building among practitioners, and normalised struggles and shared learning.

Appropriate for: Intermediate and Expert practitioners, those seeking cost-effective Duo supervision access, building professional community and peer learning, supplementing individual or Duo supervision.

Limitations: Less time for each co-therapy pair's specific issues, reduced privacy for sensitive partnership conflicts, and may not provide enough intensive support for Foundation practitioners.

Peer Consultation Duos

Structure: Two expert-level co-therapy pairs meeting together without hierarchical supervisors (four practitioners total), in monthly or quarterly meetings with rotating focus between the two pairs' cases.

Why in pairs: Maintains the Duo principle even in peer consultation—two partnerships supporting each other rather than isolated individual practitioners.

Benefits: Collegial exploration among equals, mutual support between two partnerships, learning from how another pair navigates challenges, and ongoing development without formal supervision costs.

Appropriate for: Expert-level practitioners only, ongoing professional development after certification, maintaining partnership health and preventing stagnation, and complex ethical dilemmas requiring multiple perspectives.

Important distinction: Peer consultation doesn't fulfil certification supervision requirements for Foundation or Intermediate practitioners. It's for ongoing development of established expert practitioners.

Working Effectively in Duo Supervision

Preparing as a Co-therapy Pair

When you attend Duo supervision (with your co-therapist and a pair of supervisors), preparation is essential:

Step	*What to Do*
Pre-meeting between co-therapists	Discuss what you want to bring to supervision; identify where you're aligned and where you differ; agree on which cases to present; name any partnership tensions that need attention
Prepare materials together	Joint case summary highlighting both perspectives; specific questions from each of you; video clips showing your partnership in action (with consent); assessment data or outcome measures
Set shared learning goals	What does each of you hope to learn? What partnership dynamics need attention? What clinical challenges need guidance?

Making Duo Supervision Sessions Productive

Presenting as a pair: Share airtime—both partners should contribute perspectives, even when you agree. Name disagreements—when you see things differently, say so explicitly, as supervisors can help you understand and integrate different perspectives.

Show your partnership: Demonstrate how you coordinate, support, and challenge each other—not just what you do with couples.

Be honest about partnership struggles: Don't hide difficulties. Say things like "We're not coordinating well in sessions lately," "We disagree about how to handle this couple's conflict," or "I feel like I'm doing more work than my co-therapist."

What Duo Supervisors Provide

What They Offer	*How It Helps*
Two perspectives on your work	One supervisor might focus on clinical content while the other notices partnership dynamics, or they might offer complementary frameworks for understanding challenges
Modelling effective partnership	Watch how your supervisors coordinate, disagree constructively, and integrate their different perspectives—this is learning by observation
Balanced feedback	With two supervisors, feedback is less likely to be one-sided or reflect only one person's bias
Partnership dynamics expertise	Duo supervisors understand co-therapy relationships intimately and can help you navigate partnership challenges

Continuing Professional Development

Beyond Supervision: Ongoing Learning

Supervision is essential but not sufficient. Effective practitioners commit to:

Area	*Activities*
Regular training	Duo Coaching Academy advanced training modules; specialised workshops in areas of interest; conferences and professional presentations; reading current research and literature
Peer learning	Study groups with colleague practitioners; case discussion groups; book clubs on relationship therapy topics; online communities and forums
Personal development	Your own therapy addressing personal relationship experiences; mindfulness or self-care practices preventing burnout; reflective journaling on clinical work; regular breaks and renewal activities

Maintaining Duo Coaching Certification

To maintain Duo Coaching certification, practitioners must complete continuing education requirements:

Level	*Requirements*
Foundation Level	20 hours annually of relationship therapy continuing education; quarterly supervision (minimum) with certified supervisor; annual outcome reporting to Academy; recertification every three years
Intermediate Level	25 hours annually of continuing education; monthly supervision or peer consultation; biannual outcome reporting; recertification every two years
Expert Level	30 hours annually of continuing education; regular peer supervision or consultation; annual professional contribution (teaching, writing, research); recertification every two years

For current requirements, visit: www.duocoachingacademy.com

Self-Care and Sustainable Practice

Recognising When You Need More Support

Warning signs: Pay attention when you experience dreading couple sessions, feeling overwhelmed consistently, making unusual clinical errors, difficulty maintaining boundaries, compassion fatigue or burnout symptoms, avoiding supervision or consultation, or increased personal relationship stress.

Appropriate Responses

Response	*When to Use*
Increase supervision frequency	Move from monthly to biweekly or weekly during difficult periods
Seek specialised consultation	Consult with experts when encountering new or complex presentations
Consider personal therapy	Address your own issues affecting clinical work
Reduce caseload temporarily	Create space for renewal and recovery
Take a break from practice	Sometimes stepping back is the most ethical choice

Building Sustainable Practice

Prevent problems before they start: Maintain regular supervision—don't wait until you're struggling to seek support. Balance your caseload by mixing straightforward and complex cases and avoiding all high-intensity work. Nurture your co-therapy relationship through regular check-ins, appreciation, and addressing tensions early. Engage in ongoing learning to stay curious and growing throughout your career. Maintain personal relationships—don't neglect your own relationship while helping others. Practise what you teach by using the Relationship Paradigm framework in your own life.

The Professional Development Journey

Learning Duo Coaching isn't a destination—it's a lifelong journey of growth, refinement, and ongoing discovery.

Career Stage	*Focus*
First three years	Master fundamentals; build confidence with standard cases; develop solid partnership with co-therapist; establish regular supervision rhythm
Years three to seven	Take on increasingly complex cases; develop specialised expertise areas; contribute to practitioner community; refine your personal integration of approaches
Years seven and beyond	Manage most challenging presentations; mentor developing practitioners; contribute to field through teaching or research; maintain ongoing learning through peer consultation
Throughout your career	Stay humble about what you don't know; remain curious about emerging research and approaches; prioritise your own well-being and relationships; remember why you entered this field

Conclusion: The Wisdom of Ongoing Learning

The best Duo Coaching practitioners are those who maintain supervision throughout their careers—not because they're inadequate, but because they're committed to excellence.

Supervision isn't a sign of weakness. It's a sign of wisdom, professionalism, and dedication to the couples who trust you with their relationships.

Every couple you see deserves you at your best. Supervision helps ensure that you consistently bring your most skilled, thoughtful, and effective self to this challenging and profoundly meaningful work.

Integration and Self-Reflection

Foundation Level Skills Addressed in This Chapter

This chapter has addressed four key skills: **Supervision Engagement** (actively seeking and utilising skilled supervision for professional growth), **Self-Assessment Capacity** (honest evaluation of competency limits and development needs), **Lifelong Learning Orientation** (commitment to ongoing education and skill advancement), and **Professional Network Development** (building collaborative relationships with experienced practitioners).

Reflection Questions

1 What has been your experience with supervision—positive or negative? How has it shaped your practice?
2 What makes it difficult for you to acknowledge limitations or ask for help? Where does this come from?
3 What specific areas of your Duo Coaching practice would benefit most from skilled supervision right now?
4 How do you maintain your own professional development and prevent stagnation?

Self-assessment

Rate your current engagement with supervision and professional development:

Trust your gut response. What number first comes to mind when you consider how ready you feel to take this further?

Score	*Interpretation*
1–2	Minimal supervision engagement; professional development inconsistent or lacking structure
3–4	Some supervision in place but not Duo-specific; professional development could be more intentional
5–6	Regular supervision established; clear continuing education plan; openness to feedback developing
7+	Strong supervision relationships; proactive professional development; committed to lifelong learning

Your Next Steps

Based on this chapter, commit to one specific action: schedule initial consultations with two to three potential Duo Coaching supervisors; increase frequency of current supervision during a challenging period; join or form a peer consultation group with colleague practitioners; attend Duo Coaching Academy advanced training in a specialised area; review and update your continuing education plan to maintain certification; or schedule a "state of the partnership" conversation with your co-therapist.

Next Chapter Preview

Supervision supports your development, but intensive relationship work raises ethical complexities that traditional practice guidelines inadequately address.

Chapter 19 provides comprehensive frameworks for navigating ethical dilemmas unique to extended sessions, co-therapy partnerships, and between-session contact.

Discover how to manage power dynamics in intensive formats where therapeutic influence intensifies, maintain appropriate boundaries when couples develop dependency through frequent contact, navigate dual relationships with co-therapists who may become friends, address confidentiality complexities when two therapists share client information, handle conflicts of interest in business partnerships, and respond to ethical violations you observe in colleagues' intensive work.

Chapter 19 doesn't provide simple rules—ethical practice requires nuanced judgement. You'll develop the moral reasoning capacity that protects couples, preserves professional integrity, and maintains the Duo Coaching reputation you're helping build. Your ethical sophistication deepens here.

Chapter 19

Ethical Considerations and Professional Standards

Maintaining Excellence and Professional Integrity

> Trust is not a single thing. It is woven from many threads. Practical trust, emotional trust, physical trust, and what we might call existential trust—the belief that your partner is fundamentally for you.
>
> —Neil Wilkie, *Relationship Inspirations*

The Ethical Foundation: Why Standards Matter

After 15 years of intensive couple work, I've learned this truth: Ethical practice isn't what protects you from complaints—it's what protects your clients from harm and your practice from compromising the values that drew you to this work.

I remember Sarah, a colleague who contacted me in distress. She'd been working with a couple for eight months when the female partner disclosed that her male partner had grabbed her arm forcefully during an argument between sessions. Sarah hadn't explicitly discussed domestic violence screening or safety protocols during intake. Now she faced a situation where continuing couple work might increase danger, but terminating felt like abandonment.

Her ethical dilemma wasn't about breaking rules—it was about making wise decisions in complex circumstances where competing values collided.

This chapter will guide you through developing ethical wisdom that goes beyond rule-following to thoughtful decision-making about the real dilemmas intensive relationship work presents.

Informed Consent: Beyond the Forms

The Complexity of Consent in Intensive Work

Traditional therapy informed consent typically covers basics: confidentiality limits, fee structure, appointment policies, therapist qualifications. Duo Coaching requires more comprehensive consent addressing unique aspects of the intensive format.

DOI: 10.4324/9781003715627-25

Essential Elements of Duo Coaching Informed Consent

Element	*What Couples Must Understand*
Session structure	Extended sessions (3.5 hours initial, 2.5 hours subsequent); physical and emotional demands of extended work; breaks included and how they're managed; between-session support availability and limits
Finite timeline	Typical six-session framework with flexibility; productive urgency vs. artificial pressure; what happens if more sessions are needed; completion criteria and transition planning
Co-therapy model	Two therapists working together simultaneously; how co-therapists coordinate and communicate; what happens if therapists disagree (rare but possible); continuity if one therapist becomes unavailable; both therapists having access to all case information
Confidentiality in co-therapy	Information shared with one therapist is shared with both; no secrets between co-therapists about the case; how this differs from individual therapy confidentiality; clear boundaries around what stays confidential to therapeutic team
Financial arrangements	Total investment for typical six-session programme; fee structure (per session or package pricing); payment policies and timing; cancellation and rescheduling policies; insurance coverage (or lack thereof); sliding scale availability if offered; financial hardship protocols
Between-session contact	24/7 availability for genuine crises vs. routine questions; what constitutes appropriate between-session contact; response time expectations; emergency protocols and backup coverage; limits to between-session support

Potential Risks and Benefits

Honest discussion of both potential benefits and risks is essential:

Potential Benefits	*Potential Risks*
Intensive format creating breakthrough opportunities	Emotional intensity of extended sessions
Extended time allowing deeper work	Relationship potentially worsening before improving
Two therapists providing a balanced perspective	Discovery of information that challenges relationship viability
Finite timeline maintaining focus and urgency	Financial investment without guaranteed outcomes
	Possibility that relationship cannot be saved

Outcome uncertainty requires reality-based expectations:

> While Duo Coaching has high success rates, we cannot guarantee outcomes. Some couples discover through this work that they're incompatible or that damage is irreparable. Our commitment is to help you understand your relationship clearly and develop the capacity for change if you both choose to continue the relationship.

The Ongoing Consent Process

Informed consent isn't a one-time form signing—it's an ongoing conversation throughout therapy.

Checkpoint	*What to Address*
Session 1 consent check	After comprehensive assessment: "Now that you understand more about what this work involves, do you want to proceed? Any questions or concerns?"
Mid-work consent check	Around Session 3: "We're halfway through. How is this process working for you? Anything about the format or approach we should adjust?"
Completion consent check	Session 6: "We've completed the initial six sessions. Based on outcomes, do you want to continue with additional sessions, transition to maintenance mode, or complete our work together?"

Case Example: When Consent Reveals Misalignment

Michael and Jennifer completed intake forms and began Session 1. Twenty minutes in, Jennifer said: "I want to make sure we're clear—I'm here to improve our communication so we can co-parent effectively after we divorce. Michael thinks we're here to save the marriage."

This fundamental misalignment in consent and goals required immediate address. We paused the session, clarified what each wanted, and helped them understand that Duo Coaching works best when both partners want to improve the relationship itself, not just manage its ending.

We referred them to a mediator specialising in collaborative divorce while Michael began individual therapy to process his grief about the relationship ending. The ethical response was recognising the mismatch and referring appropriately, not proceeding with work that couldn't serve both partners' actual goals.

Confidentiality: Navigating Complex Boundaries

The Co-therapy Confidentiality Challenge

Traditional therapy confidentiality is relatively straightforward: what clients tell therapist stays with therapist, except legally mandated exceptions. Co-therapy creates additional complexity.

The "No Secrets" Policy

Core principle: In Duo Coaching, both therapists have access to all case information. This means information shared with one therapist during individual consultations is shared with co-therapist, between-session contacts with either therapist are documented and shared, assessment information gathered by one therapist is available to both, and clinical observations and concerns are discussed between co-therapists.

Why This Policy Exists

Reason	*Explanation*
Clinical effectiveness	Both therapists need complete information to work effectively together, provide consistent responses, and make informed clinical decisions
Preventing triangulation	Secrets create alliances that undermine therapeutic neutrality and balanced perspective
Quality assurance	Both therapists reviewing case information provide safeguards against blind spots or concerning patterns
Ethical clarity	Explicit policy prevents confusion about confidentiality boundaries and inappropriate secret-keeping

Explaining to couples:

> Maria and I work as a team, which means we share all information about your case with each other. This ensures we're coordinated in our approach and can provide you with consistent support. If you tell something to one of us during a phone call or email, we'll share it with the other. We don't keep secrets from each other about your case, though everything stays confidential to our therapeutic team.

Individual Pre-session Consultations: The Disclosure Dilemma

During individual pre-session phone consultations (Chapter 14), partners sometimes disclose information they haven't shared with each other: affairs or betrayals, financial secrets or problems, sexual orientation or gender identity questions, mental health issues or diagnoses, or family secrets or past trauma.

The Ethical Framework

Immediate transparency:

> What you're sharing is important. I need you to know that I share all case information with my co-therapist Maria. Also, if this information significantly affects

> the relationship, we'll need to discuss how and when to share it with your partner. Secrets in relationships often create more problems than truth, even difficult truth.

Encouraging direct disclosure: "Would you be willing to share this with [partner] during our first session with our support? Or would you prefer to tell them privately before we begin?"

When disclosure is refused: If someone refuses to disclose significant information (like ongoing affairs):

> I understand this feels very difficult. However, I can't ethically work with you as a couple while you're maintaining this secret. It would compromise the therapeutic work and potentially cause harm. I can refer you to individual therapy to work through how to handle this disclosure, and then we can potentially work together as a couple afterward.

The rationale: Proceeding with couple work while maintaining significant secrets creates a false foundation for the work, places therapists in an impossible position, potentially increases harm when the truth eventually emerges, compromises therapeutic integrity, and may constitute an ethical violation.

Legal Limits to Confidentiality

Duo Coaching practitioners must break confidentiality when legally mandated:

Situation	*Requirement*
Child protection	Reasonable suspicion of child abuse or neglect requires reporting to social services (UK) or child protective services (US), regardless of client consent
Adult protection	In the UK, concerns about vulnerable adults require reporting; US requirements vary by jurisdiction
Imminent danger	Credible threats of serious harm to self or others require breach of confidentiality to protect safety
Court orders	Subpoenas or court orders may legally require disclosure of therapeutic records or testimony
Terrorism prevention	UK Prevent Duty requires reporting concerns about radicalisation or terrorism

Clear explanation during consent:

> Your confidentiality is extremely important to us and we protect it carefully. However, there are legal situations where we're required to break confidentiality: if we believe a child is being abused or neglected, if someone is at immediate risk of serious harm, or if we receive a court order. We'll always tell you if

we need to make a mandated report, except in rare circumstances where doing so would increase danger.

Case Example: The Secret Affair Dilemma

During her individual pre-session consultation, Emma disclosed she'd been having an emotional affair with a work colleague for six months. She insisted her husband David must never know, but wanted to work on the marriage.

My response:

> Emma, I understand you're in a very difficult situation. But I can't ethically work with you and David as a couple while you're maintaining this secret. The affair is affecting your marriage whether David knows or not, and working on your relationship without addressing it would be building on false foundation.
>
> We can have a 121 session to help you decide how to handle this situation—whether to end the affair and disclose to David, or to end the marriage. Once you've made those decisions and taken appropriate action, I'd be happy to work with you as a couple if you both still want that.

Emma was initially angry, but eventually acknowledged the wisdom. She ended the affair, disclosed to David, and they returned to Duo Coaching three months later after David's individual therapy helped him process the betrayal. The work was difficult but authentic, built on truth rather than deception.

Power Dynamics and Therapeutic Neutrality

Recognising Power Imbalances

Couple relationships always involve power dynamics. Effective therapy requires recognising these dynamics and avoiding inadvertently reinforcing problematic patterns.

Common Power Imbalance Patterns

Type	*Manifestations*
Financial control	One partner controls money and financial decisions; economic dependence creating vulnerability; financial abuse or manipulation; hidden resources or debts
Social and family power	One partner more socially connected or supported; cultural or family-of-origin status differences; immigration status affecting vulnerability; language barriers affecting access to support
Knowledge and education	Significant education or intelligence differences; one partner's expertise used to dominate decisions; intellectual intimidation or dismissal

(Continued)

Type	*Manifestations*
Physical intimidation	Size, strength, or aggression differences; history of violence creating fear; threats or menacing behaviour; physical space dominance
Emotional and psychological	One partner's mental health issues creating dependency; gaslighting or reality distortion; emotional manipulation or guilt; caretaker-dependent dynamics

Therapeutic Neutrality versus Power Awareness

The challenge: Maintaining therapeutic neutrality while recognising power imbalances creates tension. Pure neutrality can inadvertently support problematic dynamics, while taking sides undermines therapeutic alliance with both partners.

The Resolution

Approach	*How to Apply*
Name dynamics without blame	"I'm noticing a pattern where financial decisions consistently favour Tom's preferences. Can we explore how financial decisions get made in your relationship?"
Create structural balance	Equal speaking time, ensuring both perspectives heard, supporting less powerful partner's voice without dismissing more powerful partner
Address problematic patterns directly	When patterns approach abusive territory: "I'm concerned about [specific behaviour]. In healthy relationships, both partners have equal say in [specific domain]. Let's talk about how to create more balance."
Recognise when neutrality isn't appropriate	In cases of domestic violence or abuse, therapeutic neutrality is contraindicated. Safety takes priority over neutrality.

Case Example: Financial Control and Therapeutic Balance

James controlled all finances in his marriage to Sarah. She had to ask for money for groceries, had no access to bank accounts, and didn't know their financial situation. He presented this as "protecting her from stress" and insisted she was "bad with money."

This wasn't a neutral difference—it was financial control potentially constituting economic abuse.

Intervention: We named the pattern directly:

> James, I understand you see yourself as protecting Sarah. But what I'm observing is that Sarah has no financial autonomy or information, which creates unhealthy dependency. In balanced relationships, both partners have access to financial information and some independent resources.

We worked on creating financial transparency, separate accounts alongside joint accounts, and Sarah's financial literacy. James initially resisted but eventually recognised how control was damaging trust and Sarah's wellbeing.

This required moving beyond neutrality to name concerning patterns while maintaining a therapeutic alliance with both partners.

Cultural Sensitivity: Beyond Tokenism

The Complexity of Cultural Competency

True cultural sensitivity goes far beyond acknowledging differences or avoiding stereotypes. It requires ongoing learning, humility about what you don't know, and willingness to adapt approaches to serve diverse populations.

Dimensions of Cultural Diversity in Relationships

Dimension	*Considerations*
Race and ethnicity	Different cultural communication styles and conflict approaches; extended family involvement expectations; cultural identity and pride; experiences of racism affecting relationship stress; interracial relationship challenges
Religion and spirituality	Different religious values about relationships, sexuality, gender roles; interfaith relationship challenges; religious community support or judgement; spiritual practices affecting relationship dynamics; conflicts between religious teachings and personal values
Sexual orientation and gender identity	LGBTQ+ relationship dynamics and challenges; coming out processes and family acceptance; discrimination and minority stress; lack of legal protections or recognition; gender role flexibility vs. traditional expectations
Socioeconomic class	Different class backgrounds creating value conflicts; financial stress affecting relationship capacity; educational and opportunity differences; social mobility challenges; class-based communication and interaction styles
Immigration and language	Acculturation stress and identity negotiation; language barriers affecting expression; immigration status affecting vulnerability; cultural isolation and lack of support systems; transnational family obligations
Disability and health	Chronic illness or disability affecting partnership; caregiver-recipient dynamics; medical system navigation stress; accessibility and accommodation needs; mental health conditions and relationship impacts
Age and generation	Significant age differences in relationships; generational value differences; life stage mismatches; technology use generation gaps; different relationship models across generations

Moving Beyond Cultural Awareness to Cultural Humility

Level	*Definition*
Cultural awareness	Knowing about different cultures and their characteristics
Cultural competence	Having skills to work effectively across cultures
Cultural humility	Ongoing self-reflection and learning, recognising you'll never fully understand all cultures, maintaining learner stance

Principles of Culturally Humble Practice

Acknowledge what you don't know: "I don't have direct experience with [specific culture/identity]. I'd like to learn from you about how [cultural factor] affects your relationship. Please correct me if I make assumptions or mistakes."

Avoid stereotyping while recognising patterns: "Some couples from [culture] experience [pattern], but every couple is unique. How does this show up in your relationship, if at all?"

Adapt approaches to cultural context: Recognise that some interventions or assumptions may not translate across cultures—direct communication isn't universally valued, individual autonomy may conflict with collective family decisions, privacy and disclosure norms vary, meanings of commitment and fidelity differ, and cultural variations in gender role expectations exist.

Seek consultation when needed: When working outside your cultural expertise, consult with cultural specialists or refer to culturally matched practitioners when appropriate.

Address your own biases: Engage in ongoing reflection on how your cultural background, privilege, and biases affect your perceptions and interventions.

Case Example: Cultural Humility in Action

Priya and Amir, a British-Indian couple, came for Duo Coaching. As a white British practitioner, I recognised my limitations understanding their cultural context.

My approach:

> I want to acknowledge that I'm outside my own cultural experience working with you. I know some general things about Indian culture, but every family and individual is unique. I need you to teach me about how your specific cultural background affects your relationship—what values, expectations, family dynamics, and cultural factors matter to you. Please correct me if I make assumptions that don't fit your experience.

This invitation created safety for them to share cultural factors I wouldn't have known to ask about: extended family expectations about their living situation, different cultural expectations each had inherited, religious observances affecting time together, community gossip and reputation concerns, and different ideas about appropriate gender roles.

My cultural humility—acknowledging limits and learning from them—served better than pretending cultural expertise I didn't possess.

Financial Ethics and Accessibility

The Justice Principle: Fair Access to Effective Treatment

Duo Coaching's intensive format creates questions about accessibility and justice. If this approach achieves better outcomes than traditional therapy, doesn't economic justice require making it accessible across socioeconomic levels?

Pricing Ethics

Fair compensation for intensive work: Duo Coaching involves two therapists instead of one, extended sessions (3.5 hours) versus traditional (50 minutes), between-session availability and support, and extensive preparation and coordination.

The accessibility challenge: These rates make intensive work inaccessible to many couples who would benefit. How do we balance fair compensation for professionals with justice concerns about access?

Ethical Approaches to Accessibility

Approach	*Implementation*
Sliding scale based on income	Reserved slots at reduced rates for financial hardship; income verification for reduced rates; transparent criteria for sliding scale access; regular review ensuring financial accessibility
Package pricing with payment plans	Breaking total investment into monthly payments; reducing financial barrier of large upfront payment; clear payment agreements and policies; flexible timing when financial hardship occurs
Insurance and EAP coordination	While many insurance plans don't cover intensive formats, some do; Employee Assistance Programmes (EAPs) may cover sessions; providing documentation for insurance reimbursement; advocacy for insurance coverage of intensive formats
Pro bono work	Regular pro bono slots in practice (10–20% of capacity); selection criteria based on need and likelihood of benefit; clear boundaries and professional approach; preventing burnout through limited pro bono capacity

(*Continued*)

Approach	Implementation
Group programmes and workshops	More affordable group relationship education; workshops teaching core concepts and skills; relationship enrichment events; lower-cost alternatives for couples unable to afford intensive work
Training programmes with reduced fees	Couples working with supervised practitioners-in-training; reduced fees reflecting training status; appropriate informed consent about training; quality supervision ensuring effective service

The Ethical Questions We Must Ask

Question	Reflection
Am I charging what I need to sustain practice or what market will bear?	There's a difference between charging enough to sustain quality practice vs. maximising profit from those who can afford premium pricing
Am I serving diverse populations or only affluent clients?	If your entire practice consists of wealthy clients, you're not serving the full diversity of couples needing relationship support
How much financial sacrifice is reasonable for access to justice?	Practitioners deserve fair compensation for intensive work, but also bear some responsibility for ensuring access across economic levels
Am I transparent about costs and financial options?	Clear, honest communication about costs and payment options prevents couples from feeling misled or trapped

Case Example: Balancing Compensation and Access

My practice structure includes standard rate sessions (80% of slots) and pro bono work (20% of slots).

This balances fair compensation for quality work and pro bono for couples with no resources.

Result: Sustainable practice serving diverse populations while maintaining financial viability.

Professional Competency Boundaries

The Scope of Practice Question

One of the most important ethical responsibilities is knowing your competency limits and working within them.

Competency Self-assessment

Regular Reflection Questions

Domain	*Questions to Ask*
Issue competency	Am I competent to work with this specific issue (trauma, addiction, severe mental illness)?
Population competency	Am I competent to work with this particular population (LGBTQ+, specific cultural group, disability)?
Complexity competency	Am I competent to work with this level of complexity (high-conflict, domestic violence history, severe dysfunction)?
Co-occurring concerns	Am I competent to address these co-occurring concerns (mental health + relationship + trauma)?

When unsure: Seek consultation from experts, pursue additional training before proceeding, refer to more appropriate specialists, or work collaboratively with other professionals.

Continuing Professional Development Requirements

Area	*Minimum Standards*
Annual CEU requirements	Minimum 20–30 CEU (Continuing Education Unit) hours annually; specific hours in ethics; specific hours in cultural competency; diversity of learning (workshops, reading, conferences)
Regular supervision or consultation	Ongoing clinical consultation; peer supervision groups; individual supervision for complex cases; consultation with specialists for specific issues
Personal therapy	Ongoing personal growth work; processing countertransference issues; addressing personal limitations affecting practice; maintaining self-awareness and boundaries
Specialised training	Advanced training in modalities you use; cultural competency development; specialised population training; research and evidence-based practice updates

Case Example: Recognising Competency Limits

A couple contacted me where one partner had recently disclosed being transgender and wanted to transition. While I have general LGBTQ+ training and affirming practice, I recognised my limited expertise in trans-specific relationship dynamics.

My response:

> I'm honoured you'd consider working with me, and I'm absolutely affirming of your gender identity and transition. However, I want to be honest that I have

limited expertise in the specific challenges trans individuals and their partners face during transition. I'd like to refer you to a colleague who specialises in trans-affirming couple therapy, or if you prefer, I could work with you while consulting regularly with a trans-specialist supervisor.

They chose the specialist referral, and I then sought additional training to expand my competency for future trans couples. This illustrates ethical recognition of limits combined with commitment to ongoing competency development.

Ethical Dilemmas in Intensive Couple Work

Some ethical situations have clear answers. Others require wrestling with competing values and principles.

Dilemma 1: When One Partner Discloses Affair Mid-Treatment

The situation: Three sessions into Duo Coaching, one partner discloses (in between-session phone call) that they're having an ongoing affair they're not willing to end. Couple has been making progress on communication and connection.

Competing Values	*Arguments For Maintaining Secret*	*Arguments For Requiring Disclosure*
Therapeutic alliance and trust with disclosing partner	Respecting client confidentiality and autonomy	Cannot do authentic couple work on false foundation
Honesty and informed consent with non-knowing partner	Maintaining therapeutic alliance	Non-knowing partner has right to informed decision-making
Client autonomy and self-determination	Hoping disclosure will happen naturally	Maintaining secret potentially increases harm
Protection from harm (deceptive foundation)	Not wanting to force difficult decision	Professional integrity compromised by participating in deception
Professional integrity and ethical practice		

Resolution: Most ethics codes and clinical wisdom suggest: Cannot ethically continue couple work while partner maintains active affair. Must help disclosing partner either end affair and disclose, or end couple therapy.

I understand this is very difficult, but I cannot ethically continue working with you as a couple while you're maintaining this secret. The work we're doing is built on false foundation, and your partner doesn't have full information to make informed decisions about the relationship. I can provide individual therapy referral to help you decide what to do, and then potentially resume couple work if you both choose that after full disclosure.

Dilemma 2: When Couple Dynamics Suggest Possible Abuse

The situation: Working with a couple where one partner shows signs of being controlled—repeatedly looking to the partner before answering, minimising their own concerns, accepting blame for everything. No disclosure of violence, but the dynamics feel concerning.

Competing Values	*Arguments for not Intervening*	*Arguments for Intervention*
Respecting adult autonomy and choices	Haven't witnessed actual abuse	Safety concerns override other considerations
Protecting from harm (potential abuse)	May be misinterpreting cultural factors	Couple therapy can be dangerous with power imbalances
Avoiding false accusations or assumptions	Both adults capable of making their own choices	Professional responsibility to address concerning patterns
Maintaining therapeutic relationship with both	Could damage therapeutic alliance	Early intervention might prevent escalation
Professional responsibility for safety		

Resolution: Address concerns directly while remaining open to being wrong:

In session:

I want to check something. Sarah, I'm noticing you often look to John before responding and tend to accept responsibility for things that seem like mutual issues. John, I notice you make many of the decisions. This pattern concerns me because healthy relationships have more equal power. Can we talk about how decisions get made and whether you both feel equally heard?

Individual consultation with potentially vulnerable partner: "I want to check in privately about whether you feel safe in your relationship. Do you ever feel controlled, intimidated, or afraid?"

If safety concerns confirmed: Refer to domestic violence specialist, potentially discontinue couple work, provide safety resources.

Dilemma 3: When Practitioners Disagree About Treatment Approach

The situation: Co-therapists disagree about direction to take with couple. One believes intensive trauma work is needed; other believes couple isn't ready and should focus on stabilisation and skill-building first. Couple is waiting for your guidance.

Competing Values	*Arguments for Quick Resolution*	*Arguments for Careful Discussion*
Unified therapeutic approach Professional autonomy and judgement Client welfare as primary concern Co-therapist relationship and trust	Couples need clear direction Hesitation undermines confidence Delay could worsen situation	Wrong decision could harm couple Both perspectives may have validity Demonstrates healthy disagreement

Resolution

Brief pause for co-therapist consultation: "Give us just a moment to consult about the best approach for you."
Step outside briefly and discuss: "What are you seeing that suggests trauma work now? What concerns me is … Could we compromise by …?"
Return with unified approach: "We've consulted and here's what we're suggesting … We see some complexity here that we wanted to think through carefully together."
If cannot reach agreement: Seek external consultation before next session.

Quality Assurance and Professional Standards

Systematic Quality Monitoring

Ethical practice requires ongoing monitoring of outcomes and effectiveness, not just good intentions.

Individual Practice Quality Assurance

System	*Components*
Outcome measurement	Relationship Paradigm scores (pre, mid, post); client satisfaction surveys; completion rates vs. dropout rates; goal achievement assessment; follow-up outcomes (three to six months post)

(*Continued*)

System	*Components*
Regular review	Monthly review of outcome data; quarterly pattern analysis; annual comprehensive assessment; comparative analysis across cases; identification of concerning patterns
Intervention when outcomes substandard	Seeking consultation or supervision; additional training in areas of weakness; referral of cases outside competency; practice modifications based on data
Client feedback systems	Anonymous satisfaction surveys after each session (brief), at completion (comprehensive), and three to six months post-completion (follow-up)
Feedback questions	How helpful was this session/programme? Did you feel heard and understood? Did you learn useful skills? Has your relationship improved? What could have been more helpful? Would you recommend this service?
Review schedule	Weekly review of recent feedback; monthly pattern identification; annual comprehensive analysis; service improvements based on feedback

Peer Review and Consultation

Format	*Structure*
Monthly peer supervision groups	Four to eight practitioners meeting regularly; structured case presentations; honest feedback and suggestions; accountability for quality practice; continuing education integration
External consultation for complex cases	Consultation with subject matter experts; specialised supervision when needed; cultural consultants for diverse populations; legal or ethical consultation when needed

Professional Complaints and Accountability

Situation	*Response*
If client complaint received	Take seriously regardless of whether it seems justified; seek consultation about appropriate response; document thoroughly; respond professionally and non-defensively; learn from complaint regardless of validity; modify practice if appropriate
Professional accountability	Professional association complaint procedures; insurance company notification requirements; documentation and evidence preparation; professional consultation during complaint process; learning and improvement regardless of outcome

Creating an Ethical Practice Culture

The Ethical Climate of Your Practice

Individual practitioners don't practice in isolation—you create a practice culture that either supports or undermines ethical excellence.

Elements of Ethical Practice Culture

Element	*Implementation*
Monthly practice reviews	What ethical dilemmas arose this month? How did I handle them? What would I do differently? What consultation or training do I need? Are there patterns I should address?
Annual ethical audit	Review informed consent procedures, confidentiality protections, cultural sensitivity and inclusivity, financial practices and accessibility, competency boundaries, outcome data and effectiveness, professional development activities, and quality assurance systems
Consultation and supervision commitment	Monthly peer consultation groups; quarterly external supervision; immediate consultation for ethical dilemmas; specialist consultation for complex cases
Transparency with clients	Honest about limitations and uncertainties; open to feedback and complaints; willing to acknowledge and repair mistakes; clear communication about policies and boundaries
Transparency with colleagues	Honest about challenges and mistakes; seeking help when needed; contributing to collective learning; maintaining professional standards
Commitment to justice	Sliding scale availability; pro bono commitments; diverse client population; cultural sensitivity training; advocacy for systemic change

Conclusion: Ethical Wisdom as Foundation

Ethical practice isn't primarily about avoiding complaints or following rules—it's about consistently placing client welfare above personal convenience, maintaining professional integrity even when difficult, and developing wisdom to navigate grey areas where simple answers don't exist.

The intensive format of Duo Coaching, the co-therapy model, and the profound transformation possible create unique ethical responsibilities. Every couple who trusts you with their most intimate relationship deserves practitioners who take ethics seriously as foundation of practice, reflect regularly on ethical implications of decisions, seek consultation when facing dilemmas, maintain boundaries that create safety, practise cultural humility recognising limitations, measure outcomes ensuring effectiveness, commit to justice in access and service, and continue learning throughout careers.

The ethical frameworks provided in this chapter aren't meant to provide simple answers but to guide thoughtful decision-making when principles conflict and easy solutions don't exist. Developing ethical wisdom requires ongoing reflection, consultation, and commitment to placing client welfare above professional ego or convenience.

Your willingness to wrestle with ethical complexity, remain humble about limitations, and continuously work towards ethical excellence serves not only your direct clients but the broader profession. Every ethical decision you make reinforces or undermines the integrity of relationship therapy as a field.

> The time is always right to do what is right.
>
> —Martin Luther King Jr.

Integration and Self-reflection

Expert Level Skills Addressed in This Chapter

This chapter has addressed four key skills: **Ethical Leadership** (navigating complex ethical terrain with wisdom), **Professional Standards Development** (creating quality assurance systems), **Cultural Humility** (serving diverse populations respectfully), and **Accountability Systems** (monitoring outcomes and seeking improvement).

Reflection Questions

1 What ethical dilemmas have you encountered in relationship work? How did you navigate them?
2 How do you currently monitor outcomes and ensure quality in your practice?
3 What cultural competency areas need your ongoing development?
4 How accessible is your practice to diverse socioeconomic populations?

Self-assessment

Rate your ethical practice development:

Trust your gut response. What number first comes to mind when you consider how ready you feel to take this further?

Score	*Interpretation*
1–2	Need significant ethical framework development
3–4	Growing—ethical awareness developing
5–6	Solid foundation—navigating ethics competently
7+	Advanced—demonstrating ethical leadership

Coming Next: Chapter 20—Research and Innovation

Ethical practice protects current clients, but the field advances through research and innovation. Chapter 20 invites you beyond competent implementation into contributing to Duo Coaching's evidence base and continued evolution.

You'll discover practice-based research approaches accessible to clinicians (not just academics), outcome measurement frameworks that demonstrate intensive work effectiveness, case study methodologies that capture transformation narratives, data collection systems that inform your practice while building evidence, collaboration opportunities with academic researchers, and innovation processes for adapting Duo Coaching to emerging relationship challenges.

Chapter 20 recognises that you're not merely consuming therapeutic knowledge—you're creating it through daily practice. Your clinical observations, innovations, and outcomes contribute to collective understanding. The relationship therapy field needs your voice. Your contribution to the evidence base begins here.

Chapter 20

Research and Innovation

Contributing to the Evidence Base

> Research is to see what everybody else has seen, and to think what nobody else has thought.
>
> —Albert Szent-Györgyi

What Is Needed

Evidence-based practice represents the gold standard in therapeutic work—yet evidence doesn't materialise magically. It emerges from systematic investigation by practitioners willing to examine their work rigorously, measure outcomes honestly, and share findings openly.

During my doctoral research on the phenomenology of relationships, I was struck by the disappointing quality of evidence for relationship therapy's efficacy. The challenges are inherent to the work itself: relationship therapy is subjective and complex. We cannot conduct double-blind controlled trials. Confirmation bias is difficult to eliminate. And longitudinal studies examining long-term effectiveness are remarkably rare.

Yet this gap in the evidence base makes the work more urgent, not less important. Practitioners of any therapeutic approach should be able to demonstrate that their methods work—and we are uniquely positioned to do so.

The Practitioner's Unique Position

Academic researchers face significant constraints: controlled settings that don't reflect real-world practice, strict inclusion/exclusion criteria, and homogeneous samples. As practitioners, you work in the messy complexity of actual therapeutic relationships—precisely where evidence is most needed.

The Duo Coaching Academy provides infrastructure, support, and guidance for practitioner-researchers. Rather than conducting isolated projects, certified practitioners can participate in collaborative research that builds cumulative knowledge about what works, for whom, and under what conditions.

DOI: 10.4324/9781003715627-26

Your Role in Building the Evidence Base

Practitioners can contribute through:

- Systematic outcome tracking using validated measures
- Participating in Academy-coordinated research initiatives
- Documenting innovations and unexpected breakthroughs
- Sharing learnings through proper professional channels

This coordinated approach ensures quality, protects couples receiving services, and creates an evidence base that reflects real-world effectiveness. The goal is creating a community of practitioner-researchers who continuously improve the approach through collaborative investigation.

By contributing to this work, you're helping build the body of evidence that relationship therapy—and the Duo Coaching Framework specifically—urgently needs. Together, we can demonstrate not just that this work matters, but that it measurably transforms relationships.

Integration and Self-reflection

Reflection Questions

- How do you currently track outcomes in your couples work?
- What patterns or breakthroughs have you observed that deserve systematic documentation?
- What barriers—practical, emotional, or philosophical—do you experience around research participation?
- How might contributing to a collaborative evidence base enhance both your practice and the field?

Research is not separate from practice; it's practice made visible and sharable. Every couple you work with represents an opportunity to contribute to our collective understanding of what creates lasting relationship transformation. The question is not whether your work generates valuable data—it does. The question is whether that knowledge remains locked within your individual experience or becomes part of the growing body of evidence that strengthens the field.

Coming Next: Chapter 21—Completion and Mastery

Research and innovation advance the field, but individual mastery emerges through deliberate practice and reflective integration. Chapter 21 explores the journey from competent implementation to genuine expertise—the transformation that occurs when Duo Coaching shifts from techniques you use to embodied wisdom you inhabit.

Discover the developmental stages every intensive practitioner traverses, recognising where you currently stand and what comes next. You'll learn practices for deepening therapeutic presence, cultivating the intuition that guides moment-to-moment decisions, recognising your growing edges without harsh self-judgment, integrating inevitable failures into wisdom rather than shame, and knowing when you've achieved sufficient mastery to train others.

Chapter 21 honours that mastery is a journey, not destination. Even expert practitioners continue evolving, discovering new depths in familiar territory, finding fresh challenges that humble and teach. Your path towards mastery—and the humility that accompanies genuine expertise—unfolds here.

Chapter 21

Completion and Mastery

The Full Circle of Transformation

Image 15 Sailboat Approaching Tropical Island.

"Land in Sight: The Promise of Reaching Somewhere New Together"

> The work of healing is not to become someone new, but to become more fully who you already are—together.

What Completion Feels Like

After 21 chapters exploring the theory, practice, and mastery of Duo Coaching, we arrive at the question that matters most: **Does it work?**

Not "does it work in theory" or "does it work sometimes" but: When you do this work with full commitment, when you bring your whole self, when you navigate the challenges and stay present through the difficulty—what happens?

This chapter answers that question through the two stories you've been following: Susan and David Harper's transformation, and Maya Kapadia and James Crawford's journey to mastery.

But first, let's clarify what "completion" actually means in intensive relationship work.

DOI: 10.4324/9781003715627-27

Completion Is Not Perfection

Six sessions of Duo Coaching—even with the intensity, the advanced techniques, the co-therapy partnership—don't create perfect relationships. Perfect relationships don't exist.

What completion looks like:

- **Awareness replacing reactivity**: Couples recognise their patterns as they're happening, not days later
- **Tools replacing helplessness**: They have specific practices for reconnecting, repairing, navigating conflict
- **Agency replacing victimhood**: Both partners see their role in creating the dynamic, not just their partner's role
- **Hope replacing resignation**: They believe change is possible because they've experienced it
- **Connection replacing distance**: The space between them feels navigable rather than unbridgeable

The Shift from Therapist-Supported to Self-sustaining

The goal of intensive work isn't creating couples who need you forever. It's creating couples who have internalised the work—who've become their own best therapists.

You know completion is near when:

- Couples start solving problems *before* sessions, then report back
- They catch and repair ruptures quickly rather than letting them fester
- They reference the framework language naturally: "We need more Connection" or "My Trust is wobbling"
- They show genuine curiosity about each other rather than certainty about who's wrong
- Between-session contact decreases because they're managing well on their own

What Therapists Learn through First Completions

Your first successful completion teaches you things no training can:

That transformation is real: Not theoretical, not hoped-for, but actual visible change in how two people relate

That the work matters: The countless hours of training, the vulnerability of partnership formation, the challenges of learning new techniques—all of it serves something profound

That you're capable: Despite your doubts, your fears of not being good enough, your impostor syndrome—you can actually help people heal their most important relationship

That partnership is essential: You couldn't have done it alone; the complementarity of styles, the mutual support through difficulty, the modelling of healthy collaboration—these weren't luxuries, they were necessities

Now let's see what completion actually looks like.

INTERLUDE: SUSAN and DAVID *Session 6: Coming Home*

Six Weeks after Session 1

Maya

Susan and David walk into the practice room for Session 6, and Maya notices immediately: They're different. The space between them as they walk through the door—maybe 18 inches instead of the three feet of Session 1. David's hand briefly touches Susan's back as she moves towards her chair. Susan smiles at him before sitting.

Small things. Everything.

"So," James says, once they're settled, "this is our final session. How are you both feeling about that?"

Susan

Six weeks ago, the question "how do you feel?" would have unleashed a torrent of complaint. Today, she has to actually think about it.

"Sad, actually," she says. "Which is strange. I thought I'd be relieved. But I'm sad because ... because I think we're going to be okay. And I'll miss having you two as witnesses."

David reaches over—not quite holding her hand, but his fingers rest near hers on the chair arm. A year ago, even six weeks ago, this wouldn't have happened.

"I'm grateful," David says. "And terrified. Grateful for what we've learned, terrified we'll forget it all and slip back."

"That's honest," Maya says. "And very normal. Let's explore both of those—the progress you've made and the fear of losing it."

James

He's watching the couple with quiet satisfaction. In Session 1, they couldn't make eye contact. David checked his phone. Susan was already halfway out the door emotionally.

Now they're sitting closer, turned slightly towards each other, speaking without the defensive armour.

The work has worked.

"Before we go deeper," James says, "I'd like to invite you to do something. Remember Session 1, when you created pebbles constellations showing your relationship as it was?"

Both nod.

"I'd like you to do that again. Same instruction: Choose one pebble to represent yourself and place that where that needs to be. Then choose other pebbles to represent other important people or things in your life right now, and place those where those need to be."

"Oh God," Susan says. "I remember how painful that was."

"This time might be different," Maya says gently.

The Constellations Revisited

David (Session 1 Constellation—Recalled)

Six weeks ago:

- Large dark stone (himself) in the centre
- Rough grey stone (work) very close to him
- Smooth stone (Susan) at the far edge
- Jagged stone (guilt) between work and himself
- Light stone (his former self) in the corner, distant

David (Session 6 Constellation—New)

Now, he picks up stones with more confidence.

His "self" stone—he chooses a warmer tone this time, not the dark heavy one. Places it centre-left.

Work—still the rough grey stone, but he deliberately places it further back. Still present, but not dominating.

Susan—he picks up a smooth, rose-coloured stone. Places it much closer. Not merged, but near.

The guilt stone—he picks it up, holds it for a moment, then chooses a much smaller pebble to replace it. "It's still there," he says quietly. "But it doesn't control me anymore."

His former lighter self—he brings that stone much closer to centre. "He's coming back," David says, and his voice catches.

Then he adds a new stone he didn't have before. Blue-grey, calming. Places it in the centre space between himself and Susan.

"What's that one?" James asks.
"That's us," David says. "The relationship itself. It's not just me and her anymore. There's a third thing—the partnership—and it matters."

Susan (Session 1 Constellation—Recalled)

Six weeks ago:

- Large smooth stone (herself) in centre
- Similar stone right next to it (household management, barely distinguishable from herself)
- Polished stone (her former self as teacher) at far edge
- Sharp stone (anger) hidden between the centre stones
- Pale stone (hope) reaching tentatively outward

Susan (Session 6 Constellation—New)

She approaches the bowl slowly, thoughtfully.

Herself—she picks the same large smooth stone. But this time, places it with more confidence, more presence.

The household management stone—she creates a clear space between it and herself. "It's still part of my life," she explains, "but it's not ALL of me anymore."

Her teacher self—that polished stone comes much closer to centre. "I enrolled in the training course," she says, smiling at David. "Start next month."

David grins. "She's brilliant. They're lucky to have her."

The anger stone—Susan picks it up, studies it. Then places a smaller, smoother stone in its place. "The anger's still there sometimes. But it's not sharp anymore. It's more like ... sadness. And I can say it now instead of hiding it."

The hope stone—she moves it decisively closer and reorients it. Not just reaching towards where David's constellation is, but settled, grounded.

And she adds two new stones:

A warm amber stone near the centre: "This is pleasure. Joy. We're having fun again. I'd forgotten what that felt like."

And a small clear stone she places near David's "us" stone: "This is belief. I believe in us now. Not perfectly, not without fear. But I believe."

Maya and James (Observing)

They're sitting back, letting the couple work. Maya catches James's eye, and they share a look that says: *Look at what's possible.*

The spatial changes are dramatic:

- Susan and David have both moved closer to each other
- Work and household management have moved back
- Guilt and anger have shrunk
- Hope and lightness have come home
- New elements have emerged: "us," pleasure, belief

"Talk us through what you notice," Maya invites, "looking at both constellations together."

David

"We're both ..." he searches for words. "We're both more ourselves, but also more together? Like, Susan's teacher self is back, my lighter self is back, but we're also creating this thing between us."

"And the painful things," Susan adds, "guilt and anger—they're smaller. Not gone, but we're not ruled by them."

"What let them get smaller?" James asks.

Long pause. Then Susan: "Being seen. Actually being seen by you both, and by David. Having my loneliness named instead of denied."

"And for you, David?"

"Admitting the truth about Emma. Stopping the lies. And ..." he looks at Susan, "having Susan stay even after she knew. That changed something."

The Crucial Question (Again)

"In Session 1," Maya says, "after you created your ideal future constellations, we asked: What needs to happen to get from where you are to where you want to be? You both named things that needed to change."

"David," James continues, "you said you needed to choose home over work, be more present, forgive yourself. How have you done with that?"

David

He looks at his constellations—the before and after.

"I leave work by six now. Three days a week, at least. The world hasn't ended."

Susan laughs softly.

"I put my phone in a drawer during dinner. We have this rule—no screens from 7 to 9. We call it 'our time.'"

"And the guilt?"

"Still working on that. But ... I told Susan everything about the Emma situation. The full timeline, the texts, all of it. Transparency instead of hiding. And each day I keep that transparency, the guilt gets a little smaller."

"And being present?"

David smiles. "Last week, Susan was upset about something with her mum. And instead of offering solutions or checking my phone, I just ... sat with her. Held her hand. Let her cry. And she said afterward, 'That's what I needed.' I'm learning."

Maya

"Susan," Maya says gently, "you said you needed to reclaim your teacher self, let anger out safely, and risk hoping again. Tell us about that journey."

Susan

"The teaching course—that was huge. Actually doing it instead of talking about it. David's been so supportive, taking the kids on Saturday mornings so I can study."

"I want you to have your own life," David says. "I don't want to be married to the household manager. I want to be married to *you*."

Susan's eyes fill. "That. Right there. Hearing that."

"And the anger?" James prompts.

"I learned I can say it in the moment instead of storing it up. Last week, David forgot to tell me he'd be late, and instead of seething silently, I just said: 'That really frustrated me. I need you to text if plans change.' And he apologized and did better. No explosion, no resentment. Just ... communication."

"That's massive," Maya says.

"And hoping again?"

Susan looks at David. "I'm here, aren't I? Still married. Still trying. Six weeks ago, I was done. Now I'm ... I'm cautiously optimistic. We're not fixed, but we're facing the right direction."

The Integration: What They've Learned

James

"Let's talk about the Relationship Paradigm," James says. "Remember Session 1, you both rated each element? David, you rated Communication at 2, Connection at 1, Commitment at 4. Susan, you rated Communication at 2, Connection at 1, Commitment at 3."

He pulls out their Session 1 worksheets.

"Where would you rate them now?"

The New Ratings

Communication

David: "I'd say 6. We're actually talking. Not perfectly, but we're trying."
Susan: "I'd say 6 too. We have tools now. The 'I notice, I feel, I need' structure helps."

Connection

David: "Maybe 7? We're touching again. Having sex again. It feels wanted, not obligatory."
Susan: "7 for me too. I feel him actually seeing me. Asking about my day and meaning it."

Commitment

David: "8. I'm all in. Not just staying out of guilt, but actually wanting this."
Susan: "7. Still some fear, but I'm committed to the work."

Fun

David: "Maybe 5? We laughed last week. Like, really laughed. First time in years."
Susan: "5 or 6. We went to that comedy show. We held hands. It felt like dating."

Growth

David: "7. Susan's doing her course, I'm in individual therapy working on my anxiety."
Susan: "8. We're both growing. And supporting each other's growth."

Trust

David: "This is hardest to rate. Maybe 6? Susan's giving me the chance to rebuild it."
Susan: "5 or 6. It's fragile. But it's there. I'm watching for consistency."

Maya

"So," Maya says, "Communication went from 2 to 6. Connection from 1 to 7. That's transformation."

"It feels different," Susan says. "We're not where we want to be yet, but we're not where we were. There's movement."

"That's the key word," James says. "Movement. Relationships aren't static. The question isn't 'are we perfect?' but 'are we moving toward each other or away?'"

"Toward," David and Susan say, almost simultaneously, then smile at each other.

The Appreciation Exchange

Maya

"We're coming to the end of our time together," Maya says. "Before we close, we'd like to invite you to appreciate each other. Not everything, not a comprehensive list. Just ... what do you want the other person to know?"

David to Susan

He turns towards her, takes her hand fully this time.

"Thank you for not giving up. For suggesting this therapy when I would've just ... drifted apart. Thank you for telling the truth about how lonely you were, even though it hurt me to hear it. And thank you for staying after I admitted about Emma. I didn't deserve that, but you gave me the chance to earn it back."

Susan's crying now.

"And I love watching you come alive again. When you talk about your teaching course, your whole face lights up. You're so bloody good at it, and I'm sorry I ever made you feel like you had to be small."

Susan to David

She's crying but smiling too.

"Thank you for being brave enough to tell the truth about Emma, even though you knew it would hurt. That honesty—that's what I needed. And thank you for showing up. For actually changing, not just promising to. Coming home earlier, putting your phone away, asking about my day—those small things are everything."

She squeezes his hand.

"And thank you for wanting me back. Not the household manager version, but me. The messy, angry, scared me. You're seeing me again, and I'm seeing you again, and it's ... it's good."

Maya and James (Acknowledging)

"We want to appreciate you both too," Maya says. "Susan, your courage to say 'I'm lonely' when it would've been easier to just leave—that took so much strength. And you trusted us to hold that pain."

"David," James adds, "your willingness to be honest about Emma, to stop hiding, to admit you'd failed—that's the hardest work. And you didn't run from it."

"You both showed up," Maya continues. "Week after week, even when it was painful. You did the homework, you practiced the tools, you took risks. This transformation—you created this."

The Closing

Susan

"So what happens now?" Susan asks. "You've been our safety net. What if we fall?"

"You might stumble," James says. "Probably will. But falling isn't failing. You have tools now."

"When you notice distance growing," Maya adds, "you know how to reconnect. When conflict emerges, you know how to repair. You've practiced all of it."

"And," James continues, "you can always come back for a booster session. This isn't goodbye forever, just goodbye for now."

David

"Thank you," he says to both therapists. "I don't think I'd be married right now if not for this. And more than that—I wouldn't want to be. Now I actually want my marriage. Want my wife."

He looks at Susan. "Want *this*."

The Final Moment

They stand. Hugs all around—Maya hugs Susan, James shakes David's hand then pulls him into a brief hug.

Susan and David walk out together, his arm around her shoulders, her hand on his waist.

The door closes.

Maya and James (Alone)

They sit in silence for a long moment.

"We did it," Maya says softly.

"They did it," James corrects. "We just held the space."

"Don't diminish what we did," Maya says. "They couldn't have done it alone."

"Fair." James is smiling. "Our first completion. That feels significant."

"It really does."

They sit with it—the strange mix of joy and grief that comes with ending well. Joy at the transformation witnessed. Grief at the goodbye.

"Should we do the pebbles?" Maya asks.

"Our own?"

"Yeah. See what's shifted in us."

"Always learning," James says, reaching for the bowl.

What Therapists Learn from First Completions

Watching Susan and David walk out that door—transformed but not perfect, hopeful but not naive—taught Maya and James lessons that have nothing to do with technique:

The work is real: Transformation isn't theoretical. It's visible in how two people walk through a doorway, how they touch, how they speak to each other.

Six sessions is enough: Not for perfection, but for fundamental shifts in pattern, awareness, and agency.

The modelling matters: Susan explicitly said it—watching Maya and James navigate their own partnership taught as much as any intervention.

Both partners must change: David learning to be present, Susan reclaiming her identity—neither could transform the relationship alone.

Tools create sustainability: Susan and David leave with specific practices, not just insights. That's what prevents regression.

Completion is grief too: Saying goodbye to couples you've journeyed with—that loss is part of the work.

But the lesson that would echo for years to come, the one Maya and James would return to again and again: **This work changes the therapist as much as the couple.**

Four Years Later

Maya and James have now worked with fourty couples using the Duo Coaching Framework. Some have made it, some haven't. Some completions felt triumphant, others bittersweet. They've navigated their own partnership ruptures and repairs. They've grown as individuals and as a team.

Today, they're supervising a new partnership: Tom Chen and Alisha Patel, who met at the same Duo Coaching Academy training where Maya and James first connected.

Let's join them.

INTERLUDE: MAYA and JAMES *Four Years Later: Mature Partnership*

The Supervision Session

Maya

Tom and Alisha are sitting across from them, nervous energy crackling. They're three sessions into their first couple—a high-conflict pair teetering on divorce—and they're struggling.

"We're not coordinating well," Tom says. "I go left, she goes right. We're confusing the couple."

"And we had a fight after Session 2," Alisha admits. "About whether I was too confrontational with the wife."

Maya and James exchange a glance. They've been here.

"Tell us about the fight," James invites.

The Story Emerges

Alisha and Tom describe their rupture—eerily similar to Maya and James's own crisis four years ago. Alisha feeling controlled, Tom feeling anxious about the lack of structure, both activating each other's wounds.

"We don't know if we can keep working together," Tom says quietly.

Maya smiles. "We felt exactly that way. Three sessions into our first couple. Want to see something?"

She pulls out her phone, scrolls to a photo from four years ago. The pebbles constellation from their own supervision with Rachel.

Showing Their Own Journey

"This," Maya says, showing the photo, "was our constellation when we were stuck. See how my Protector was running the show? How James's Anxious One was gripping too tight?"

Tom and Alisha lean in, studying it.

"We had to do our own pebbles work," James explains. "Had to see our patterns, not just talk about them."

"You did constellation work? On yourselves?" Alisha asks.

"How else could we guide couples through it?" Maya says. "We can't ask them to do work we're not willing to do ourselves."

The Invitation

"Would you be willing," James asks, "to do constellation work on your partnership? Right here, right now?"

Tom looks at Alisha. She nods.

"We have to," she says. "If we're going to make this work."

Maya pulls out the wooden bowl of pebbles. The same bowl Susan and David used. The same stones that revealed Maya and James's own patterns.

"Same instruction we give couples," Maya says. "Choose one pebble to represent yourself in relationship to your co-therapist, and place that where that needs to be ..."

Tom's Constellation

He chooses stones carefully:

A solid, structured stone: "This is the Organised One. Holds the framework."

Dark stone very close: "The Controlling One. Afraid of mess, grips tight."

Lighter stone far away: "The Playful One. Wants to be spontaneous but can't let himself."

Small stone between them: "The Critic. Judges Alisha for being 'too much.'"

Alisha's Constellation

A vibrant, colourful stone: "The Intuitive One. Follows energy."

Red stone close: "The Rebel. Hates being told what to do."

Smooth stone far away: "The Collaborator. Wants partnership but is scared."

Sharp stone between: "The Defensive One. Ready to fight when criticized."

Maya (Seeing Herself Four Years Ago)

"Look at these," Maya says gently. "Tom, your Controlling One and Alisha's Rebel—they're in the same position, very close to you. They're running the show."

"And," James adds, "you both have partnership stones far away. The Playful One, the Collaborator. The parts that could actually work together are distant."

Tom and Alisha sit in silence, looking at their stones.

"This is us," Alisha says quietly. "This is exactly us."

The Question

"So," Maya says, "what do you need to have happen for the Playful One and the Collaborator to come closer? For the Controlling One and the Rebel to step back?"

And Tom and Alisha begin the work that Maya and James did four years ago. The work that all co-therapy partnerships must do.

After Tom and Alisha Leave

James

They're in the practice room, just the two of them. Four years of working together, and they've developed a comfortable silence that doesn't need filling.

"Watching them," James says finally, "was like watching us four years ago."

"I know." Maya's organising the pebbles back into the bowl. "The same patterns, the same fears."

"Do you remember how terrified we were?"

"Constantly." Maya laughs. "I thought we'd fail. Thought the partnership would collapse."

"Me too."

Silence.

"But we didn't," James says.

"No. We didn't."

Maya (Reflecting)

"You know what I'm grateful for?" Maya asks.

"Tell me."

"That we hit the rupture with Susan and David. That we had to do our own work early. Because we learned something crucial: the partnership needs maintenance. It's not 'one and done.' It's ongoing."

"Monthly supervision," James agrees. "Weekly check-ins. Doing our own constellation work whenever we get stuck."

"And admitting when we're stuck," Maya adds. "Not pretending we have it all figured out."

The Growth

"Remember when you used to grip so tight to structure?" Maya says, smiling.

"And you used to go completely rogue," James counters, grinning.

"We balance each other now."

"We do," James agrees. "I can let go more. Trust the emergence. And you..."

"I plan more," Maya finishes. "Share my intuitions before I act on them. It's not constraint anymore. It's collaboration."

James (The Deeper Truth)

"Can I tell you something?" James asks.

"Always."

"This partnership—working with you—it's healed something in me I didn't even know was broken."

Maya looks at him, surprised by the vulnerability.

"My dad leaving when I was twelve," James continues. "I told you that in our pebbles work. But what I didn't fully say: I stopped trusting that people would stay. So I controlled everything, held everything together, never let myself need anyone."

He pauses.

"But you stayed. Even when I was annoying with my structure, even when we fought, even when it was hard—you stayed. And that's taught me more than any therapy I've done. People can stay."

Maya (Her Truth)

"God, James." Maya's eyes are bright. "Can I tell you mine?"

"Please."

"My ex-husband made me feel like my intuition, my feeling-focus, was ... less than. Like I needed to be more cognitive, more structured to be valuable. I started doubting myself, second-guessing every instinct."

She looks at him.

"But you trust me. You let me follow the energy, even when it scares you. And you don't diminish my way of working—you celebrate it. That's given me back my confidence. My belief in myself."

Silence, thick with emotion.

"We healed each other," James says quietly.

"We did," Maya agrees. "Not just as therapists. As humans."

The Ripple Effect

James

"Do you ever think about Susan and David?" James asks. "Wonder how they're doing?"

"All the time." Maya smiles. "I got a text from Susan six months ago. They're doing well. Still together, still working on it."

"That's good."

"And you know what she said? She said they recommend us to all their friends now. Three couples have come to us because Susan and David told them about the work."

"The ripple effect," James says.

"Exactly." Maya's quiet for a moment. "We changed Susan and David's relationship. But they're changing their kids' understanding of what relationships can be. And those kids will grow up and create different relationships. And on and on."

"We're not just helping couples," James says slowly, realising it as he speaks. "We're changing relationship culture. One couple at a time."

Maya (The Biggest Lesson)

"You know what I've learned?" Maya asks.

"What?"

"The work never ends. We're always learning. Always growing. Even now, four years in, we're discovering new things about ourselves, about partnership, about this work."

"That used to scare me," James admits. "Never arriving, never being done. My Anxious One hated it."

"And now?"

"Now I find it comforting. We don't have to be perfect. We just have to keep showing up, keep being curious, keep doing our own work."

"That's mastery," Maya says. "Not perfection. Commitment to ongoing growth."

The Gratitude

James

"I need to say something," James says, and there's weight in his voice.

Maya looks at him.

"Thank you. For being my partner in this work. For trusting me enough to be vulnerable, to let me see your struggles, to do your own pebbles work even when it was painful."

He pauses.

"I couldn't have built this practice alone. I couldn't have helped forty couples alone. I couldn't have become the therapist I am without you."

Maya

She's crying now, not hiding it.

"Same, James. Thank you for staying when it was hard. Thank you for doing your own work. Thank you for modelling what healthy partnership looks like—with me, but also for our couples."

She reaches across, takes his hand.

"This partnership—it's the most important professional relationship of my life. Maybe the most important relationship of my life, period."

"Mine too."

They sit in the quiet of the practice room, holding that truth.

What They Know Now (That They Didn't Then)

Maya (Listing)

"What do we know now," Maya asks, "that we didn't know four years ago when Susan and David walked in?"

James thinks. "Co-therapy is harder than we imagined. And more rewarding."

"The techniques aren't enough," Maya adds. "The relationship between therapists is the container that holds everything."

"We'll keep activating each other's wounds. That doesn't stop. But we get faster at catching and repairing."

"Supervision isn't optional. It's essential."

"Doing our own constellation and parts work—that's not separate from clinical competence. It IS clinical competence."

"We can't give what we don't have. If we're not doing our own growth work, we can't hold space for couples' growth."

James (The Summary)

"You know what it all comes down to?" James asks.

"What?"

"The work is relational. Not just what we do with couples—the techniques, the framework, the interventions. But who we are with each other, and who we're becoming through this partnership."

"Susan said that in Session 6," Maya remembers. "That watching us work together taught them as much as anything we said."

"Exactly. We model it. We embody it. We live it."

"That's the real work," Maya says. "Not the doing. The being."

The Future

Maya

"What's next for us?" Maya asks. "We've got Tom and Alisha to supervise. We're training at the Academy twice a year. We've got our practice full of couples."

"Is this it?" James asks. "Is this the peak?"

"God, I hope not." Maya laughs. "I hope we're still growing at seventy."

"What would you want to do more of?"

Maya thinks. "Writing, maybe. Documenting what we've learned. Contributing to the literature."

"Research," James adds. "Outcome studies. Helping build the evidence base."

"Training more partnerships. Watching them discover what we discovered."

"Growing old in this work," James says. "Still learning. Still curious. Still doing our own pebbles work when we get stuck."

"That sounds perfect," Maya says.

The Closing Image

It's late afternoon. Golden light slants through the practice room window. Maya and James are sitting in companionable silence, the pebbles bowl between them on the table.

They've worked with 40 couples. Some have made it, some haven't. Some completions felt triumphant, others bittersweet. They've navigated their own partnership ruptures and repairs, done their own constellation work more times than they can count, supervised other partnerships through the same challenges.

And through it all, they've grown. Not just as therapists, but as humans. Not just professionally, but personally. The work has changed them as much as it's changed the couples they serve.

Maya looks at James. "Ready for tomorrow? We've got that new couple—married thirty years, first time seeking help."

"Ready," James says. "We've got this."

And they do. Because they've done the work. They've built a partnership that can hold complexity, navigate conflict, repair ruptures, and keep growing.

Because they've learned what Susan and David learned, what Tom and Alisha are learning, what every couple who walks through their door must learn:

Transformation is possible. But it requires showing up, staying present, doing your own work, and trusting the process.

And it's always, always relational.

What Mastery Feels Like

Maya and James, four years later, demonstrate what mature Duo Coaching practice embodies:

1 **Ongoing Personal Work**
Mastery isn't reaching a destination where you no longer need growth. It's commitment to continuous self-examination, supervision, and doing your own constellation work when patterns emerge.

2 **Partnership as Sacred Practice**
The co-therapy relationship isn't incidental to the work—it IS the work. How you relate to each other teaches couples more than what you say.

3 **Integration of Learning**
Early practitioners follow protocols. Mature practitioners have internalised the framework so deeply that it becomes second nature. The techniques emerge organically rather than mechanically.

4 **Comfortable with Not-Knowing**
James's Anxious One no longer needs to control everything. Maya's Protector no longer rebels against structure. They've learned to rest in uncertainty together.

5 **Supervision as Gift, Not Burden**
They don't see supervision as evidence of inadequacy. They see it as essential maintenance—like servicing a high-performance vehicle.

6 **Teaching What You're Still Learning**
They supervise Tom and Alisha not from a place of "we've mastered this" but "we're still learning it—let us show you what we've discovered so far."

7 **Gratitude for the Work**
After four years and forty couples, they haven't become jaded or burned out. They remain in wonder at transformation's possibility.

8 **Healing through the Work**
James's abandonment wounds healing through Maya's consistent presence. Maya's wounds around being diminished healing through James's respect. The work heals the worker.

The Interconnection of Both Transformations

Notice the parallel journeys:

Susan and David's Arc

- Session 1: Defended strangers → Session 6: Partners facing the right direction
- Constellation work revealed patterns → Changed patterns changed relationship
- Tools replaced helplessness → Agency replaced victimhood
- Distance became connection → Resignation became hope

Maya and James's Arc

- Day 1: Wary strangers → Four years later: Mature partners
- Their rupture and pebbles work → Changed patterns changed partnership

- Anxiety and protection softened → Trust and collaboration deepened
- Competition became complementarity → Doubt became confidence

The couple's transformation and the therapists' transformation are mirror images. Neither could happen without the other.

You cannot guide couples through work you haven't done yourself.

What This Means for Your Journey

You've followed Susan and David from the brink of divorce to a genuine partnership. You've watched Maya and James grow from uncertain beginners to skilled practitioners. Now you understand:

This is what Duo Coaching creates: Not perfect relationships, but transformed ones. Not couples without struggle, but couples with tools for navigating struggle. Not therapists who've mastered everything, but therapists committed to ongoing mastery.

The work is relational: Between partners, between co-therapists, between your past and present selves. Everything is connected.

Transformation is real: Not hoped-for, not theoretical, but visible in how people walk through doorways, touch each other, speak to one another.

It requires everything: Your vulnerability, your commitment to your own growth, your willingness to be changed by the work, your courage to stay when it's difficult.

And it's worth it: Every challenging moment, every rupture and repair, every hour of supervision, every constellation you create of your own patterns—all of it serves something profound.

Integration and Self-reflection

Foundation Level Skills Addressed in This Chapter

Integration of Learning: Synthesising knowledge across all framework elements

Advanced Practice Development: Moving from competence to mastery in Duo Coaching delivery

Professional Identity: Establishing yourself as confident, effective practitioner

Ongoing Evolution: Committing to continuous learning and refinement

Reflection Questions

1 How have you integrated the various elements of the Duo Coaching Framework into a coherent personal approach?
2 What areas of practice have evolved from initial learning to confident mastery? What still requires development?
3 How do you see yourself contributing to the broader field of relationship therapy?
4 What does your ongoing professional development pathway look like?

Self-Assessment

How fully have you developed Duo Coaching mastery?

Trust your gut response. What number first comes to mind when you consider how ready you feel to take this further?

Score	*Interpretation*
1–2	Still building foundational competencies
3–4	Solid practitioner with growing confidence and integration
5–6	Advanced practice with coherent personal framework
7+	Mastery level with capacity to train and supervise others

Next Steps: Continue deepening areas requiring development. Seek advanced training and supervision. Consider contributing through supervision, training, writing, or research as you develop expertise.

Bridge to Part VI: Building Sustainable Impact

You've now seen the complete arc:

- The theoretical foundation (Parts I–II)
- The practical implementation (Parts III–IV)
- The advanced competencies (Part V)
- The ongoing development (Part VI)
- **The transformation complete** (This chapter)

You understand not just how to do this work, but what it creates when done well. You've witnessed both couple transformation and therapist transformation. You've seen the beginning (Maya and James meeting), the middle (their rupture and repair), and the mastery (four years later).

Now comes the question: How do you build a sustainable practice that creates this transformation at scale?

Part VI explores:

- Exploring the Duo Coaching elements in your practice (Chapter 22)
- Relationship education and prevention (Chapter 23)
- The future of Duo Coaching and relationship therapy (Chapter 24)

But you enter that section differently now. Not as someone reading about possibility, but as someone who's witnessed transformation—who knows what's at stake, who understands the profound ripple effects of healing relationships.

Susan and David are changing their children's understanding of relationships.

Maya and James are training other partnerships who'll help more couples.

And you—you're about to join this lineage of transformation.

The work continues. The circle widens. The impact grows.

Let's explore how to build practices that sustain this sacred work.

End of Part V

You now have the foundations for both excellent clinical work and a sustainable practice. The practical questions have been addressed. In our final Part, we step back to consider the larger picture: prevention, research, and the future of relationship therapy itself. You're not just learning a method—you're becoming part of something larger.

Part VI: The Future (Chapters 22–24)

The final chapters look beyond individual practice to the broader field. We explore relationship education and prevention, emerging research, and where Duo Coaching—and relationship therapy itself—might be heading. You're not just learning a method; you're joining a movement.

Coming Next: Chapter 22 – Exploring the Duo Coaching Elements in Your Practice

Mastery develops through years of practice, but perhaps you're wondering whether you must adopt the complete Duo Coaching model or whether individual elements offer value. Chapter 22 explores how to integrate specific Duo Coaching components into your existing practice without wholesale transformation.

Discover how extending sessions from 50 minutes to 90 creates immediate impact, incorporating occasional co-therapy for complex cases even if not adopting full partnership models, implementing structured assessment without intensive formats, using the Relationship Paradigm as compass while maintaining weekly sessions, and adding between-session support selectively for couples needing additional stability.

Chapter 22 acknowledges that full Duo Coaching implementation isn't feasible for every practitioner. Agency constraints, geographic isolation, or personal preferences may limit adoption. This chapter shows how partial integration still elevates your practice while respecting your circumstances. Your customised implementation pathway emerges here.

Part VI

Expert Level Impact

Systemic Change and Community Leadership

Chapter 22

Exploring the Duo Coaching Elements in Your Practice

Testing New Approaches in Your Current Framework

A brand is no longer what we tell the consumer it is—it is what consumers tell each other it is.

—Scott Cook

Important: You cannot call yourself a Duo Coaching Practitioner or offer Duo Coaching services without completing the Duo Coaching Academy's training and accreditation programme. What you *can* do is explore whether elements of this framework enhance your existing work and determine if full training might be right for you.

What You Can Explore

As you read this book, certain elements may resonate with your practice philosophy and spark curiosity about implementation:

Session Structure Experiments

- Try extending one or two sessions from your standard 50–60 minutes to 90–120 minutes to experience how longer timeframes affect depth and breakthrough potential
- Notice what becomes possible when couples aren't watching the clock
- Observe how your own therapeutic rhythm changes with more time

Modality Integration

- Incorporate timeline therapy, parts negotiation, or hypnotherapy into your couples work if you're already trained in these approaches
- Experiment with the Relationship Paradigm framework as an assessment and intervention tool
- Test working with the unconscious dimensions of relationship patterns

DOI: 10.4324/9781003715627-29

Co-therapy Exploration

- If you have a trusted colleague, try co-facilitating a couples session to experience the dual-therapist dynamic
- Notice what you observe that you might have missed working solo
- Reflect on how the couple responds to having two therapeutic perspectives

The Critical Boundary

These explorations allow you to:

- Build your competence and confidence with new approaches
- Determine whether Duo Coaching aligns with your therapeutic values
- Experience firsthand whether intensive formats suit your working style
- Gather evidence about what resonates with your client population

These explorations do **not** allow you to:

- Market yourself as a Duo Coaching Practitioner
- Offer "Duo Coaching" as a service
- Claim Duo Coaching certification or accreditation
- Use Duo Coaching branding or materials

The full Duo Coaching Framework involves far more than extended sessions or co-therapy. It requires comprehensive training in the integrated methodology, supervised practice, quality assurance protocols, and adherence to specific practice standards. The accreditation programme ensures practitioner competence and protects both couples and the integrity of the approach.

Testing with Integrity

When exploring these elements in your practice:

Be transparent with clients: "I'm exploring a longer session format to see if it creates more space for deeper work" is honest and appropriate. "I'm offering Duo Coaching" when you're not accredited is misrepresentation.

Track your observations: What works? What feels challenging? What surprises you? This data informs whether pursuing full training makes sense for your practice.

Respect the methodology: Individual techniques can be borrowed; the complete framework requires proper training. There's a significant difference between using timeline therapy in couples work and implementing the full Duo Coaching approach.

Consider your motivations: Are you genuinely curious about whether this enhances your work, or are you looking for marketing differentiation without the training investment? The former is professional development; the latter is problematic.

The Path to Full Practice

If your explorations confirm that Duo Coaching aligns with your therapeutic approach and client needs, the Duo Coaching Academy accreditation programme provides:

- Comprehensive training in the complete methodology
- Supervised practice with feedback
- Quality assurance and ongoing professional development
- Authorisation to practice and market as a Duo Coaching Practitioner
- Community connection with other certified practitioners
- Access to proprietary materials and protocols

Integration and Reflection

Consider these questions as you explore:

- Which elements of Duo Coaching feel most aligned with your existing therapeutic strengths?
- What would need to shift in your practice structure to accommodate intensive sessions?
- How do your current clients respond when you extend session length or deepen unconscious work?
- What barriers—practical, financial, or philosophical—might influence your decision about pursuing full accreditation?
- How would offering Duo Coaching alongside or instead of your current modality serve your professional development and your clients' needs?

Exploration is how we grow as practitioners. Test what intrigues you, notice what emerges, and make informed decisions about whether the complete Duo Coaching Framework deserves a place in your professional repertoire. But remember: exploration is not the same as practice. Full implementation requires full training.

Coming Next: Chapter 23—Relationship Education and Prevention

Whether implementing complete Duo Coaching or integrating elements, you've been focusing on couples already experiencing distress. Chapter 23 expands beyond therapy into relationship education and prevention—applying intensive approaches before crisis emerges.

Discover how intensive workshops for healthy couples prevent future distress, premarital intensive formats that prepare couples for marriage far more effectively than traditional counselling, relationship enrichment retreats that strengthen already-good partnerships, psychoeducation programmes teaching relationship skills to communities, and preventive interventions for high-risk transitions like new parenthood, retirement, or empty nest.

Chapter 23 recognises that waiting until relationships collapse means missing opportunities to prevent suffering. Your expertise enables population-level impact beyond individual therapy. The couples you'll never see clinically—because they never develop severe distress—represent your greatest contribution. Your preventive work begins here.

Chapter 23

Relationship Education and Prevention

Moving Upstream—Beyond Therapy—Building Relationship Health

An ounce of prevention is worth a pound of cure—nowhere is this more true than in relationships.

—Benjamin Franklin (adapted)

Why Prevention Matters: The Big Picture

During a community talk on relationships, a young woman approached me afterward: "I wish I'd learned this before I got married. We're struggling now, and I keep thinking—if someone had taught us this stuff years ago, maybe we wouldn't be in this mess."

Her comment captures the prevention opportunity perfectly.

The Current Prevention Gap

The reality: Most schools offer zero relationship education. Religious organisations typically provide one to two brief premarital sessions. Community centres rarely include relationship programming. Healthcare systems don't screen for relationship health. Workplace wellness programmes ignore relationship factors.

The result: Couples learn relationship skills through trial and error—usually after patterns are established, resentments have built, and trust has been damaged. They enter therapy only when crisis strikes, often years after problems began.

The cost: Years of suffering that could have been prevented. Children growing up in distressed households. Divorce rates remaining stubbornly high. Mental and physical health consequences. Intergenerational transmission of unhealthy patterns.

The Prevention Vision

Imagine communities where every engaged couple receives comprehensive relationship education, schools teach relationship skills alongside maths and science, community centres offer ongoing relationship enrichment, workplaces support relationship health as wellness priority, healthcare systems routinely assess relationship health, and crisis intervention becomes the exception rather than the norm.

DOI: 10.4324/9781003715627-30

This isn't fantasy—it's possible. And practitioners like you hold knowledge that could make it reality.

Prevention versus Intervention: Understanding the Difference

Different Paradigms

Aspect	*Crisis Intervention (What You Know)*	*Prevention (Different Approach)*
When couples seek help	When distressed	Before struggling
Problem visibility	Problems are obvious and painful	Problems haven't developed yet
Motivation source	High (desperation)	Proactive (investment)
Focus	Fixing what's broken	Building what works
Format	Intensive, immediate work needed	Education and skill-building approach
Timeline	Clear before/after contrast	Gradual development over time
Success indicators	Relationship saved or ended well	Problems avoided (harder to see)

Why This Matters

You cannot simply "do therapy" with non-distressed couples. Prevention requires a different mindset (teaching vs. healing), different format (education vs. intensive intervention), different skills (group facilitation vs. couple therapy), different tone (hopeful vs. crisis-focused), and different outcomes (skill acquisition vs. transformation).

The good news: Your Duo Coaching expertise translates beautifully to prevention work. You know what healthy relationships require. You just need to teach it before couples need to repair it.

The Relationship Paradigm in Prevention

Remember the Relationship Paradigm framework you use in therapy: Communication, Connection, Commitment, Fun, Growth, and Trust.

Context	*How the Paradigm Is Used*
In Crisis Intervention	These elements are assessed to identify what's broken and needs repair
In Prevention	These same elements become the curriculum—teaching couples how to build and maintain each dimension proactively

Adapting Your Expertise

What You Know About Trust (from therapy)	*What You Teach in Prevention*
How trust breaks and how to rebuild it	How to build trust from the beginning
Warning signs of trust erosion	Practices that maintain trust daily
The devastating impact when trust fails	Early warning signs to address immediately
Proactive transparency and honesty	

The principle applies to all Paradigm elements. Your therapeutic knowledge of what goes wrong informs prevention teaching about how to do it right.

The Spectrum of Prevention Work

Prevention isn't one thing—it's a continuum of opportunities.

Level	*Focus*	*Examples*	*Your Role*
Universal Prevention (Everyone)	Broad population education	Relationship education in schools teaching adolescents and young adults relationship fundamentals before they couple; community workshops open to all on relationship health topics; public education through media, content creation, and community talks raising relationship literacy	Consider whether you want to contribute to broad community education through workshops, writing, or partnerships with schools and community organisations
Selective Prevention (At-Risk Populations)	Support during vulnerable transitions	Premarital education for engaged couples preparing for marriage; new parents receiving relationship support during the vulnerable transition to parenthood; major life transitions, including career changes, relocations, empty nest, retirement	Consider whether you want to develop specialised programmes for couples at predictable vulnerable moments
Indicated Prevention (Showing Early Signs)	Early intervention before crisis	Relationship enrichment programmes for couples noticing small concerns but not yet distressed;	Consider whether you want to create programmes

(Continued)

Level	*Focus*	*Examples*	*Your Role*
		skill-building groups for couples wanting to strengthen specific areas; marriage checkups providing periodic assessments helping couples address issues before crisis	for couples recognising they need support but not yet needing intensive intervention

Potential Prevention Roles

You don't have to do everything. Consider what might fit your interests and practice:

Role	*Focus*	*Activities*	*Best For*
The Educator	Teaching groups through workshops and courses	Evening relationship workshops; weekend enrichment programmes; premarital education courses; online relationship education	Practitioners who enjoy teaching groups, are comfortable with education format, and want to impact many couples simultaneously
The Community Partner	Collaborating with organisations to expand reach	Programmes through religious communities; workplace wellness relationship education; community centre partnerships; healthcare system integration	Practitioners skilled at building organisational relationships, adapting content for different contexts, and working collaboratively
The Content Creator	Reaching people through writing and media	Relationship blog or newsletter; books or workbooks for couples; podcast or video content; media interviews and articles	Practitioners who communicate well in writing, enjoy creating resources, and want to reach beyond geographic limits
The Programme Developer	Creating comprehensive prevention programmes	Curriculum development; training other facilitators; quality assurance systems; outcome measurement	Practitioners interested in building sustainable programmes, training others, and creating lasting infrastructure

(Continued)

Role	Focus	Activities	Best For
The Hybrid Practitioner	Blending therapy and prevention work	Traditional and intensive therapy as primary practice; prevention workshops supplementing practice; community contribution building reputation; helping some couples before crisis, others after	Most common approach—many practitioners maintain therapy practice while adding selective prevention work

Why You Might Choose Prevention Work

Professional Satisfaction

Prevention offers working with hopeful, motivated couples, teaching rather than healing, preventing suffering rather than treating it, seeing couples thrive not just survive, and building relationship health proactively.

Some practitioners find prevention more rewarding than crisis intervention. Others prefer the intensity and transformation of therapy. There's no right answer—just personal fit.

Expanded Impact: The Mathematics of Prevention

Model	Annual Reach	Nature of Contact	Direct Impact	Ripple Effect
Crisis intervention	40–50 couples per year	Each couple receives intensive, individual attention; profound transformation for those you serve	40–50 couples	Limited to immediate families
Prevention	200+ couples per year through workshops	Each couple receives education and skill-building; broader reach with less intensive contact	200+ couples	Their children, their communities

Different models create different kinds of impact. Neither is superior—they serve different purposes.

Community Contribution

Prevention work inherently serves broader community: It reduces relationship distress at population level, strengthens community fabric through healthy relationships, creates culture prioritising relationship health, prevents intergenerational transmission of unhealthy patterns, and builds relationship literacy in community.

This matters for social change, not just individual couples.

Professional Diversification

Adding prevention work provides alternative revenue streams, reduces burnout from only crisis work, builds reputation and referral sources, creates variety in professional life, and serves different populations.

Many practitioners maintain hybrid practice: intensive therapy with couples in crisis, prevention education with couples building foundations.

Starting to Think About Prevention

You don't need to make immediate decisions. Just consider:

Questions to Explore

Domain	*Questions*
Personal fit	Do you enjoy teaching groups or prefer intensive couple work? Does working with non-distressed couples appeal to you? Would prevention work energise or drain you? What professional satisfactions matter most?
Community need	What prevention services exist in your community? What populations are underserved? Where are the biggest gaps? What partnerships might be possible?
Professional goals	How might prevention work fit your practice vision? What impact do you want to create? What timeline makes sense for exploration? What support or training would you need?
Practical realities	Do you have time for prevention alongside clinical work? How would you fund programme development initially? What resources do you have available? What's your risk tolerance for new ventures?

No Pressure, Just Possibility

You don't have to do prevention work. Crisis intervention is valuable, needed, and may be exactly where you should focus.

But if prevention intrigues you, this chapter invites exploration. The Academy provides infrastructure, training, and support when you're ready.

The couples you could reach before they're struggling—before resentment builds, before trust is damaged, before they lose hope—are waiting for someone to teach them what healthy relationships require.

The Ripple Effect

After teaching a premarital education course, a young woman sent this email:

"I wanted to thank you for the course. My fiancé and I almost didn't come—we thought 'our relationship is great, why do we need classes?' But learning these skills has completely changed how we communicate. Last week we had our first real fight, and instead of shutting down or saying hurtful things, we actually used what you taught us. We worked through it in like an hour, and honestly felt closer afterward."

"Here's the thing though: my parents divorced when I was ten. They fought terribly for years before that. I grew up thinking that's just what marriage was—fighting and eventually breaking up. I was actually scared to get married because I thought we'd end up the same way."

"But now I realise—they never learned this stuff. Nobody taught them how to communicate, how to repair after conflicts, how to maintain connection. They were doing their best with what they knew, but what they knew wasn't enough."

"You've literally changed the trajectory of my life. And probably my future kids' lives too, because I'm not going to repeat the patterns I grew up with. That's pretty amazing."

This Is Why Prevention Matters

Conclusion: The Big Picture Vision

Relationship distress causes immense suffering—depression, anxiety, physical illness, diminished life satisfaction, damaged children, broken families, weakened communities.

Yet Most of This Suffering Is Preventable

We live in a culture that prepares people extensively for careers, minimally for parenting, and barely at all for relationships—despite relationships being central to human well-being.

Skilled Practitioners Can Change This

You have knowledge that could prevent countless couples from experiencing years of suffering. You understand what healthy relationships require and what makes them fail.

The Question Isn't Whether Prevention Matters—Research Proves It Does

The question is what role you'll play:

Path	*Description*
Crisis intervention focus	Focus exclusively on crisis intervention (valuable and needed)
Hybrid practice	Blend therapy with selective prevention work
Upstream focus	Shift primarily towards prevention education
Systemic impact	Develop programmes that others deliver

There's No Right Answer—Just Different Paths to Impact

The vision: Communities where relationship health is prioritised, couples receive education before crisis, children grow up seeing healthy relationship models, and crisis intervention becomes the exception rather than the norm.

Your contribution—whatever form it takes—moves us towards that vision.

Competency Self-reflection

Advanced Practice Skills Addressed in This Chapter

This chapter has addressed four key skills: Prevention Programme Design (creating educational content and workshops for relationship health), Community Engagement (building partnerships and delivering preventive interventions), Facilitation Mastery (leading groups and workshops effectively beyond therapy sessions), and Impact Assessment (evaluating prevention programme effectiveness and community reach).

Reflection Questions

1 Does prevention work appeal to you, or does crisis intervention feel like a better fit for your skills and interests?
2 What prevention services are missing in your community? Where are the biggest gaps?
3 If you were to experiment with prevention work, what would be your starting point? (One workshop? Premarital programme? Content creation?)
4 What would you need to learn or develop to feel confident offering prevention education?

Your Exploration

If prevention work intrigues you, consider: Offer one trial workshop in your community; partner with a local organisation for a pilot programme; create content (blog, videos) about relationship education; connect with other practitioners doing prevention work; research evidence on prevention programme effectiveness; assess community needs and partnership opportunities.

If prevention work doesn't appeal to you right now: That's perfectly fine—crisis intervention is valuable and needed. Stay informed about prevention approaches, refer couples to quality prevention programmes when appropriate, and keep the possibility open for future exploration.

Next Chapter Preview

Prevention expands your impact, but the relationship therapy field continues evolving. Chapter 24 explores emerging trends, technological innovations, and cultural shifts shaping Duo Coaching's future—preparing you for challenges and opportunities ahead.

You'll discover how virtual intensive sessions expand access while raising new clinical considerations, artificial intelligence applications that enhance rather than replace human connection, neuroscience research validating intensive work while revealing new intervention pathways, changing relationship structures requiring approach adaptation, and global expansion opportunities as intensive formats prove effective across cultures.

Chapter 24 envisions a future where intensive relationship work becomes standard rather than alternative, where couples access transformative support before crises develop, and where practitioners collaborate globally to advance collective wisdom. You're not just implementing existing methods—you're pioneering the therapy of tomorrow. The future you're helping create awaits.

Chapter 24

The Future of Duo Coaching and Relationship Therapy

Evolution and Your Role in What Comes Next

The best way to predict the future is to create it.

—Peter Drucker

Image 16 Lighthouse Silhouette.

"The Light That Stays On: A Fixed Point in Uncertain Waters"

DOI: 10.4324/9781003715627-31

Visualising Tomorrow

As we stand at the threshold of unprecedented technological advancement and growing recognition of relationship health's importance, the field of relationship therapy is poised for a remarkable transformation. The intensive formats, co-therapy partnerships, and integrated methodologies we've explored represent just the beginning of what's possible when we reimagine how to help couples thrive.

This final chapter explores emerging frontiers—from technological innovations revolutionising service delivery to global movements towards relationship literacy. More importantly, it positions you as a practitioner not just implementing existing approaches but contributing to the field's evolution.

The Evolution of Therapeutic Approaches

Every therapeutic approach faces a choice: evolve with changing times or become obsolete. Duo Coaching stands at an exciting threshold—grounded in solid principles yet poised for innovation.

The Lifecycle of Innovation

- **Phase 1: Innovation (Years 0–5)**—Charismatic founder develops new approach—Small group of early adopters—Enthusiasm and experimentation—Limited evidence but compelling case examples
- **Phase 2: Systematisation (Years 5–15)**—Approach becomes structured—Training programmes developed—Initial research evidence emerges—Broader adoption begins
- **Phase 3: Establishment (Years 15–30)**—Solid evidence base established—Widespread training and certification—Integration into graduate programmes—Mature practice community
- **Phase 4: Stagnation or Evolution (Years 30+)**

Two divergent paths emerge:

Path A: Stagnation—Rigid adherence to original model—Resistance to innovation—Declining relevance—Gradual obsolescence

Path B: Evolution—Core principles maintained—Adaptations for changing contexts—Integration with new discoveries—Ongoing vitality

Duo Coaching's Current Phase

Duo Coaching sits between systematisation and establishment—with core principles well-defined, training programmes emerging, initial evidence accumulating, and a growing practitioner community. The critical question: Will Duo Coaching evolve dynamically or calcify rigidly?

Principles for Healthy Evolution

Maintain Core Identity: Focus on relationship paradigm transformation—Intensive session format philosophy—Co-therapy when possible—Structured yet flexible approach—Commitment to both partners' growth

Embrace Thoughtful Innovation: Specific exercises and interventions—Technology integration—Cultural adaptations—Population-specific modifications—Format variations

Current Innovations Already Emerging

Innovation isn't future speculation—it's happening now.

Technology-Enhanced Duo Coaching

Virtual Intensive Sessions: Couples in separate rooms for individual work—Co-therapists coordinate via text/separate screen—Digital whiteboard for exercises—Effectiveness comparable to in-person

Between-Session Support Apps: Daily check-ins and exercise reminders—Progress tracking and secure messaging—Resource libraries—Data for outcome measurement

VR-Enhanced Exercises: Immersive environments for difficult conversations—Safe practice spaces for conflict resolution—Controlled exposure to challenging scenarios

Retreat-Based Intensives

Fully immersive experiences offering: -three to five days at retreat centres—All-day intensive sessions—Complete focus without distractions—Natural environment supporting healing—Time for deep processing

Anticipated Future Developments

Artificial Intelligence Integration

AI will enhance (not replace) Duo Coaching through:

Pattern Recognition Algorithms: Analyse communication samples for patterns—Identify cognitive distortions automatically—Predict likely challenges based on profiles—Suggest personalised intervention strategies

Real-Time Feedback Systems: Monitor communication during practice—Alert to Four Horsemen behaviours—Suggest repair strategies—Track progress over time

AI Practice Support: Between-session coaching chatbots—Automated progress monitoring—Training enhancement for practitioners

Critical Caveat: AI enhances but never replaces human wisdom, empathic attunement, therapeutic relationship, ethical reasoning, or cultural competence.

Neuroscience Integration

Brain science informing Duo Coaching refinement through:

Understanding Change Mechanisms: How relationship patterns are encoded neurologically—Optimal timing and sequencing for rewiring patterns—Why intensive formats may be more effective for lasting change

Neuroplasticity-Informed Interventions: Exercises designed to optimise neural rewiring—Techniques leveraging understanding of memory consolidation—Approaches that work with rather than against brain functioning

Global Expansion and Cultural Adaptation

Cross-Cultural Development: Culturally adapted versions for diverse populations—Materials available in multiple languages—International training programmes—Cross-cultural research collaborations

Specialised Applications for: Military and veteran couples—LGBTQ+ relationships—Intercultural and interfaith couples—Neurodivergent couples—Couples with chronic illness—Aging and eldercare challenges—Blended family complexities

Your Role in Shaping the Future

The future of Duo Coaching won't be written by experts in ivory towers. It will be created by practitioners like you—testing innovations in real-world practice, adapting principles for diverse populations, integrating emerging technologies thoughtfully, and sharing discoveries with the field.

The Practitioner-Innovator Mindset

Effective contributors maintain:

Humble Confidence: Confidence to try new approaches—Humility to acknowledge limitations—Openness to being wrong—Commitment to learning

Creative Rigour: Creativity in developing innovations—Rigor in testing effectiveness—Discipline in measurement—Honesty in reporting

Individual Voice, Collective Good: Unique perspective and contributions—Service to larger community—Balance of autonomy and collaboration—Building something bigger than yourself

How to Contribute

Through Clinical Practice: Document innovations systematically—Track outcomes rigorously—Share findings with the community—Contribute to case study database

Through Research: Conduct practice-based research—Collaborate with academic researchers—Publish findings in professional journals—Present at conferences

Through Training and Education: Develop training materials—Mentor new practitioners—Contribute to curriculum development—Lead workshops and supervision groups

Through Community Leadership: Develop prevention programmes—Build community partnerships—Advocate for relationship health—Create public education initiatives

A Vision for 2045: Twenty Years Forward

Imagine Duo Coaching two decades from now:

Mainstream Recognition: Recognised evidence-based practice—Standard offering in many therapy practices—Integrated into graduate training programmes—Covered by major insurance companies—Known by the general public

Prevention Infrastructure: Widely available premarital education—Relationship enrichment services—Early intervention programmes—Community-based prevention initiatives

Technology Integration: AI-enhanced assessment and matching—Virtual reality exercises seamlessly integrated—Between-session app support standard—Outcome tracking systems universal—Telehealth delivery perfected

Global Reach: Practitioners operating on six continents—Culturally adapted for dozens of cultures—Materials available in 30+ languages—International research collaborations

Your Immediate Next Steps

Commit to systematic outcome measurement in your practice, contributing to the evidence base while improving effectiveness.

Document and share your innovations, whether through case studies, professional presentations, or published articles.

Engage in collaborative relationships with other professionals, modelling the cooperation that strengthens the field.

Participate in community education, reaching couples before a crisis develops and building community support for relationship health.

Stay engaged with emerging developments, continuing your education and contributing to the field's evolution.

The Legacy You're Building

Every session you conduct with excellence, every professional relationship you build with integrity, every innovation you develop and share contribute to a legacy extending far beyond your individual career.

The couples who transform their relationships through your work will model healthy partnerships for their children. The professionals you influence will carry better practices to their communities. The community programmes you develop will reach hundreds of families. The research you contribute to will influence thousands of future practitioners.

Your commitment to excellence in relationship therapy is not just a professional choice—it's a contribution to building a more connected, healthier, and thriving world.

Master and Commander—Or Just Another Sailor?

There's a moment every experienced sailor knows.

You're at the helm, conditions are complex—wind gusting from multiple directions, current running contrary to your course, weather building on the horizon. Your crew partner calls out a concern from their position. You're processing a dozen variables simultaneously, making constant micro-adjustments, reading the water's surface for clues about what's coming.

And suddenly, you realise: You're not thinking about it anymore. You're just sailing.

The conscious effort has dissolved into something more fluid. You and your partner move in coordination without needing to discuss every decision. You read the conditions and respond before your mind has fully articulated what you're responding to. The vessel answers your touch because you've learned its language.

This is what mastery looks like.

Not the absence of challenge. Not sailing only in calm seas. But the capacity to navigate complexity with earned confidence—knowing you have the skills, the partnership, the tools, the awareness to handle whatever emerges.

You've reached the end of this guide, but not the end of your learning. If anything, you're just beginning.

The Paradox of Mastery

Here's what experienced sailors know that landlubbers don't: The sea is always teaching. Every voyage reveals something new—about conditions, about your vessel, about yourself, about partnership.

The moment you think you've mastered sailing is the moment you're most at risk. The sea humbles everyone eventually.

So mastery isn't reaching a point where you know everything. It's developing the capacity to keep learning—to stay curious rather than certain, to do your own constellation work when patterns emerge, to seek supervision when you're stuck, to remain humble before the complexity of human relationship.

Maya and James, four years into their partnership, are still doing their own pebbles work when they get activated. Still seeking supervision. Still discovering new layers in themselves and each other.

That's the model.

Not arriving at expertise that no longer requires growth. But committing to ongoing learning, ongoing navigation, ongoing partnership maintenance.

You're Not Sailing Alone

Remember: every sailor you admire was once terrified at the helm, unsure of their abilities, wondering if they'd made a catastrophic mistake choosing this path.

Susan Satir—yes, Virginia Satir's daughter—once wrote about watching her mother teach. She said Virginia would often admit to students: "I don't know if what I'm about to try will work. But let's find out together."

That vulnerability, that willingness to not-know, that invitation to discover together—that's what creates real transformation. Not the therapist as all-knowing expert, but the therapist as fellow traveller, skilled but still learning, confident but still humble.

You're joining a lineage of relationship navigators:

Virginia Satir, who pioneered family therapy and co-therapy partnership work

John Gottman, who mapped the patterns that sink or sustain relationships

Sue Johnson, who showed how attachment wounds can heal through partnership

The countless practitioners who've done this intensive work before you, each contributing their discoveries

And now you—with your unique gifts, your particular struggles, your specific partnership, your individual couples—you're adding to that lineage.

The Invitation

So here's what I want you to hear, as you close this book and prepare to begin:

You're ready. Not perfectly prepared—no one ever is—but ready enough to take the first voyage with a real couple in real distress needing real help.

You're not alone. Co-therapy means you'll have a partner at the helm with you. Supervision means experienced sailors will help you navigate challenges. The Academy community means you're part of something larger than yourself.

You'll make mistakes. Every sailor does. But mistakes are how you learn to read conditions you've never encountered before. The key isn't avoiding mistakes—it's learning to repair, adjust, and keep sailing.

The work will change you. Not just your couples—you. Maya and James's wounds healing through partnership. Your own patterns surfacing and transforming as you guide others through transformation. This is sacred work precisely because it changes everyone it touches.

And it's worth it. Every challenging moment, every hour of supervision, every constellation you create of your own stuck patterns, every rupture and repair with your co-therapist—all of it serves something profound.

Because on the other side of your efforts, couples who were resigned to quiet desperation finding their way back to each other. Children growing up in homes with healthier models. Relationships that don't just survive but thrive.

That's what this work creates when you do it with full commitment.

Final Words from a Fellow Sailor

I've been sailing these waters for 15 years now. I've navigated storms that terrified me. I've had partnerships that challenged me to grow in ways I didn't know I needed. I've witnessed transformations that still bring me to tears when I remember them.

And I'm still learning. Still doing my own constellation work. Still seeking supervision. Still discovering new layers in this endlessly complex, endlessly rewarding work.

If I can offer you anything as you set sail, it's this:

Trust the process. The Duo Coaching Framework works. The techniques access real transformation. The partnership model creates something neither therapist could achieve alone.

Trust yourself. You have skills, training, wisdom earned through your own journey. You're more capable than your impostor syndrome wants you to believe.

Trust your couples. They're the experts on their own relationship. Your job is holding space, providing tools, modelling possibility—not knowing better than they do what they need.

And trust the partnership. The co-therapist relationship will stretch you, activate your patterns, require vulnerability you didn't know you had. It will also heal you, teach you, and create the container that makes transformation possible.

Embarkation

The couples are out there, right now, struggling. Considering divorce. Feeling hopeless. Wondering if there's any point in trying one more thing.

They need what you're learning to offer.

So close this book. Do your own pebbles work. Find your co-therapy partner. Set up your practice room. Get supervision. Keep learning.

And set sail.

The sea is waiting. The couples are waiting. Your partnership is waiting to be discovered.

Virginia Satir was right: "A stream in which two people can be is very powerful."

Fair winds and following seas,

Dr. Neil Wilkie

Epilogue

A Letter to Future Practitioners

Dear Colleague,

If you're reading this, you've completed this comprehensive guide to Duo Coaching. You've invested significant time and energy in understanding this approach. Perhaps you're excited to begin, or maybe you're overwhelmed by everything there is to know.

Let me offer some perspective from years of practice:

You don't need to be perfect. Couples don't need perfect therapists—they need genuine, skilled, committed practitioners who care deeply about their well-being. You'll make mistakes. You'll miss important dynamics. You'll sometimes struggle to know what to do next. That's normal. What matters is your commitment to learning, your genuine care for couples, and your willingness to keep growing.

Start where you are. You don't need every skill mastered before beginning. Start with straightforward cases. Seek good supervision. Build competence gradually. Every expert was once a beginner. Give yourself permission to be on a learning curve.

Trust the process. The Duo Coaching framework works. When you follow the principles, maintain the structure, and honour the process, couples improve. Trust that even when you're uncertain, the framework supports the work.

Find your community. This work can be isolating. Find other practitioners. Build peer consultation groups. Attend conferences. Connect online. You need colleagues who understand this work, support your growth, and share your commitment.

Take care of yourself. You can't pour from an empty cup. This intense work demands much. Honour your limits. Maintain boundaries. Invest in your own well-being. Model the relationship health you're teaching.

Stay curious. The couples you see will teach you constantly. Stay curious about their experiences. Notice patterns across couples. Wonder about what works and why. Let curiosity guide your learning.

Contribute your voice. The field needs your perspective. Your innovations matter. Your research contributes. Your teaching impacts others. Share what you're learning. Build the community. Shape the future.

Remember why you're doing this. On difficult days, remember the couples you've helped. The relationships saved. The families preserved. The children who grew up in healthier homes because of your work. This matters. You matter.

DOI: 10.4324/9781003715627-32

Finally, know this: You're joining a community of practitioners who believe relationships can heal, couples can transform, and intensive work creates lasting change. We're honoured to welcome you to this community.

May your work be fulfilling, your learning continuous, and your impact profound.

Welcome to Duo Coaching.

A Final Word: Begin

You have the knowledge. You have the framework. You have the invitation.

Now begin.

One couple at a time.

One session at a time.

One intervention at a time.

One transformation at a time.

The work awaits.

Duo Coaching Academy

- Training programmes and certifications
- Supervision and consultation
- Research collaborations
- Practitioner community
- Visit: www.duocoachingacademy.com

Image 17 Sailboat on Open Sea, Seagulls.

"And So the Journey Begins: Welcome Aboard"

Connect With Us

- Email: info@duocoachingacademy.com
- Instagram: duocoachingrelationships
- Facebook: DuoCoachingUK
- LinkedIn: https://www.linkedin.com/in/neildwilkie
- Author: www.neilwilkie.com

Thank you for your commitment to helping couples heal, grow, and thrive. The journey continues. Welcome aboard.

Bibliography and Further Reading

Chapter 1: The Implementation Imperative

Statistical Data Sources

Office for National Statistics. (2023). *Marriage and civil partnership status in England and Wales: Census 2021*. Office for National Statistics.

Office for National Statistics. (2024). *Divorces in England and Wales: 2022*. Office for National Statistics.

Office for National Statistics. (2024). *Marriages in England and Wales: 2021 and 2022*. Office for National Statistics.

Relationship Research

Perelli-Harris, B., Hoherz, S., Lappegård, T., & Evans, A. (2019). Mind the "happiness" gap: The relationship between cohabitation, marriage, and subjective well-being in the United Kingdom, Australia, Germany, and Norway. *Demography, 56*(4), 1219–1246.

Wilcox, W. B., Dew, J., & ElHage, A. (2019). *Cohabitation doesn't compare: Marriage, cohabitation, and relationship quality*. Institute for Family Studies.

Chapter 2: The Limitations of Current Approaches

Co-therapy and Virginia Satir's Work

Starr, S. (1993). Heart and soul and communication: An interview with Virginia Satir-Part III. *Journal of Couples Therapy, 3*(1), 1–8.

Session Length and Therapeutic Format Research

Bierenbaum, H., Nichols, M.P., & Schwartz, A.J. (1976). Effects of varying session length and frequency in brief emotive psychotherapy. *Journal of Consulting and Clinical Psychology, 44*(5), 790–798.

Carey, T.A. (2011). As you like it: Adopting a patient-led approach to psychological treatments. *Journal of Public Mental Health, 10*(1), 6–16.

Carey, T.A. (2016). Boundaries: A pluralistic perspective and illustrative case study of the patient-led approach to appointment scheduling. In M. Cooper and W. Dryden (Eds.), *The handbook of pluralistic counselling and psychotherapy* (pp. 288–299). Sage.

Francis, K.C. (1975). Questions and answers: Two hours with Carl Rogers. Department of Education Services Brooklyn College. In C.P. Mountford (Ed.), *One size does not fit all. Counseling and Psychotherapy Journal*, 2005, *16*(5), 43–45.

Turner, P.R., Valtierra, M., Talken, T.R., Miller, V.I. & DeAnda, J.R. (1996). Effect of session length on treatment outcome for college students in brief therapy. *Journal of Counseling Psychology, 43*(2), 228–232.

Will, H. (2018). The concept of the 50-minute hour. Time forming a frame for the unconscious. *International Forum of Psychoanalysis, 27*(1), 1–10.

Chapter 3: The Duo Coaching Framework

Duo Coaching Framework Development

All framework elements, principles, and integration guidance in this chapter draw directly from:

Wilkie, N. (2019). *Reset: Finding a new course after drifting apart*. Academy for Relationships, Hampshire.

Wilkie, N. (2021). *Recover: Rebuilding trust after the shock of betrayal*. Academy for Relationships.

Wilkie, N. (2026). *Reinventing relationship therapy through the duo coaching framework*. Routledge. (See particularly Chapters 4–6 for framework foundations)

Wilkie, N. (2026). *A practitioner's guide to the duo coaching framework*. Routledge. (Book 2: This Volume)

Wilkie, N. (2026). *Demystifying relationship therapy – A view from the therapist's chair*. Routledge. (Book 3: Client perspectives)

Wilkie, N. (2026). *Reinventing relationship therapy through the duo coaching framework*. Routledge. (Book 1: Theory and Foundation)

Co-therapy and Collaborative Practice

Anderson, C.M., & Stewart, S. (1983). *Mastering resistance: A practical guide to family therapy*. Guilford Press.

Durana, C. (1998). The use of bonding and emotional expressiveness in the PAIRS training: A psychoeducational approach for couples. *Journal of Family Psychotherapy, 9*(2), 65–81.

Roller, B., & Nelson, V. (1991). *The art of co-therapy: How therapists work together*. Guilford Press.

Starr, S. (1993). Heart and soul and communication: An interview with Virginia Satir-Part III. *Journal of Couples Therapy, 3*(1), 1–8.

Extended Sessions and Intensive Formats

Bierenbaum, H., Nichols, M.P., & Schwartz, A.J. (1976). Effects of varying session length and frequency in brief emotive psychotherapy. *Journal of Consulting and Clinical Psychology, 44*(5), 790–798.

Carey, T.A. (2011). As you like it: Adopting a patient-led approach to psychological treatments. *Journal of Public Mental Health, 10*(1), 6–16.
Francis, K.C. (1975). *Questions and answers: Two hours with Carl Rogers*. Department of Education Services Brooklyn College.
Turner, P.R., Valtierra, M., Talken, T.R., Miller, V.I. & DeAnda, J.R. (1996). Effect of session length on treatment outcome for college students in brief therapy. *Journal of Counseling Psychology, 43*(2), 228–232.
Will, H. (2018). The concept of the 50-minute hour: Time forming a frame for the unconscious. *International Forum of Psychoanalysis, 27*(1), 1–10.

Integrative and Transdisciplinary Approaches

Gurman, A.S. (2008). *Clinical handbook of couple therapy* (4th ed.). Guilford Press.
Johnson, S.M. (2004). *The practice of emotionally focused couple therapy: Creating connection* (2nd ed.). Brunner-Routledge.
Lebow, J. (1997). The integrative revolution in couple and family therapy. *Family Process, 36*(1), 1–17.
Pinsof, W.M. (1995). *Integrative problem-centered therapy: A synthesis of family, individual, and biological therapies*. Basic Books.
Sprenkle, D.H., Davis, S.D., & Lebow, J.L. (2009). *Common factors in couple and family therapy: The overlooked foundation for effective practice*. Guilford Press.

Brief Therapy and Time-Limited Approaches

De Shazer, S. (1985). *Keys to solution in brief therapy*. W.W. Norton.
Hoyt, M.F. (2009). *Brief psychotherapies: Principles and practices*. Zeig, Tucker & Theisen.
Levenson, H. (2010). *Brief dynamic therapy*. American Psychological Association.
Seligman, M. (1995). The effectiveness of psychotherapy: The Consumer Reports study. *American Psychologist, 50*(12), 965–974.

Outcome Measurement and Evidence-Based Practice

Duncan, B.L., Miller, S.D., Wampold, B.E., & Hubble, M.A. (Eds.). (2010). *The heart and soul of change: Delivering what works in therapy* (2nd ed.). American Psychological Association.
Lambert, M.J. (2013). The efficacy and effectiveness of psychotherapy. In M. J. Lambert (Ed.), *Bergin and Garfield's handbook of psychotherapy and behavior change* (6th ed., pp. 169–218). Wiley.
Miller, S.D., Hubble, M.A., Chow, D.L., & Seidel, J.A. (2013). The outcome of psychotherapy: Yesterday, today, and tomorrow. *Psychotherapy, 50*(1), 88–97.
All references for this chapter are included in the comprehensive bibliography in:
Wilkie, N. (2026). *Reinventing relationship therapy through the duo coaching framework*. Routledge.

Chapter 4: Transdisciplinarity in Relationship Work

Bateson, G. (1972). *Steps to an ecology of mind: Collected essays in anthropology, psychiatry, evolution, and epistemology*. Chicago: University of Chicago Press.

Bateson, G. (1979). *Mind and nature: A necessary unity*. New York: E.P. Dutton.
Bateson, N. (2012). *Warm data: Contextual research and new forms of information*. International Bateson Institute. Retrieved from https://www.warmdatalab.org/
Bateson, N. (2016). *Small arcs of larger circles: Framing through other patterns*. Triarchy Press.
Bateson, N. (2016). *Symmathesy: A word in progress*. Retrieved from https://norabateson.wordpress.com
Bateson, N. (2018). *Warm data labs*. International Bateson Institute. Retrieved from https://www.warmdatalab.org/
Bateson, N. (2023). *Combining*. Triarchy Press.
Ingold, T. (2000). *The perception of the environment: Essays on livelihood, dwelling and skill*. Routledge.
Ingold, T. (2007). *Lines: A brief history*. Routledge.
Ingold, T. (2011). *Being alive: Essays on movement, knowledge and description*. Routledge.
Ingold, T. (2013). *Making: Anthropology, archaeology, art and architecture*. Routledge.
Ingold, T. (2015). *The life of lines*. Routledge.
Ingold, T. (2017). On human correspondence. *Journal of the Royal Anthropological Institute, 23*(1), 9–27. https://doi.org/10.1111/1467-9655.12541
Nicolescu, B. (1996). *La transdisciplinarité: Manifeste [Transdisciplinarity: Manifesto]* (K.-C. Voss, Trans.). State University of New York Press. (Original work published 1996)
Nicolescu, B. (2010). Methodology of transdisciplinarity: Levels of reality, logic of the included middle and complexity. *Transdisciplinary Journal of Engineering & Science, 1*(1), 19–38. https://doi.org/10.22545/2010/0009
Nicolescu, B. (2012). Transdisciplinarity: The hidden third, between the subject and the object. *Human & Social Studies, 1*(1), 13–28. https://doi.org/10.2478/v10317-012-0002-5
Nicolescu, B. (2014). Methodology of transdisciplinarity. *World Futures, 70*(3-4), 186–199. https://doi.org/10.1080/02604027.2014.934631
Nicolescu, B. (2016). *The hidden third*. Punctum Books.

Chapter 5: The Relationship Paradigm Framework

Relationship Paradigm Development: All Paradigm elements, assessment protocols, and intervention frameworks in this chapter draw directly from
Wilkie, N. (2019). *Reset: Finding a new course after drifting apart*. (Original introduction of the Relationship Paradigm framework)
Wilkie, N. (2026). *Reinventing relationship therapy through the duo coaching framework*. Routledge. (See particularly Chapter 9: The Relationship Paradigm)
Online Assessment Tool: The Relationship Paradigm questionnaire is available at: www.relationshipparadigm.com

Supporting Research

Gottman, J.M. (2008). Gottman method couple therapy. *Clinical Handbook of Couple Therapy, 4*(8), 138–164.
Gottman, J.M., & Silver, N. (2015). *The seven principles for making marriage work: A practical guide from the country's foremost relationship expert* (Revised ed.). Harmony Books.
Johnson, S.M. (2008). *Hold me tight: Seven conversations for a lifetime of love*. Little, Brown and Company.

Chapter 6: Finding and Working with a Co-therapist

Co-therapy Theory and Practice

Anderson, C.M., & Stewart, S. (1983). *Mastering resistance: A practical guide to family therapy*. Guilford Press.

Bobele, M., Gardner, G., & Biever, J. (1995). Supervision as social construction. *Journal of Systemic Therapies, 14*(2), 14–25.

Dunn, R.L., & Schwebel, A.I. (1995). Meta-analytic review of marital therapy outcome research. *Journal of Family Psychology, 9*(1), 58–68.

Gurman, A.S. (2008). *Clinical handbook of couple therapy* (4th ed.). Guilford Press.

Roller, B., & Nelson, V. (1991). *The art of co-therapy: How therapists work together*. Guilford Press.

Collaborative Professional Relationships

Bernard, J.M., & Goodyear, R.K. (2018). *Fundamentals of clinical supervision* (6th ed.). Pearson.

Egan, G. (2013). *The skilled helper: A problem-management and opportunity-development approach to helping* (10th ed.). Brooks/Cole.

Norcross, J.C., & Lambert, M.J. (2018). Psychotherapy relationships that work III. *Psychotherapy, 55*(4), 303–315.

Orlinsky, D.E., & Rønnestad, M.H. (2005). *How psychotherapists develop: A study of therapeutic work and professional growth.* American Psychological Association.

Non-verbal Communication and Coordination

Burgoon, J.K., Guerrero, L.K., & Floyd, K. (2016). *Nonverbal communication.* Routledge.

Ekman, P. (2009). *Telling lies: Clues to deceit in the marketplace, politics, and marriage* (3rd ed.). W.W. Norton.

Knapp, M.L., Hall, J.A., & Horgan, T.G. (2013). *Nonverbal communication in human interaction* (8th ed.). Wadsworth.

Mehrabian, A. (1972). *Nonverbal communication.* Aldine-Atherton.

Partnership Dynamics and Power

Bateson, G. (2000). *Steps to an ecology of mind.* University of Chicago Press.

Doherty, W.J., & Simmons, D.S. (1996). Clinical practice patterns of marriage and family therapists: A national survey of therapists and their clients. *Journal of Marital and Family Therapy, 22*(1), 9–25.

Duck, S., & Gilmour, R. (Eds.). (1981). *Personal relationships 2: Developing personal relationships*. Academic Press.

Karpman, S. (1968). Fairy tales and script drama analysis. *Transactional Analysis Bulletin, 7*(26), 39–43.

Conflict Resolution in Professional Relationships

Fisher, R., Ury, W., & Patton, B. (2011). *Getting to yes: Negotiating agreement without giving in* (3rd ed.). Penguin Books.

Patterson, K., Grenny, J., McMillan, R., & Switzler, A. (2011). *Crucial conversations: Tools for talking when stakes are high* (2nd ed.). McGraw-Hill.

Stone, D., Patton, B., & Heen, S. (2010). *Difficult conversations: How to discuss what matters most*. Penguin Books.

Ury, W. (2007). *The power of a positive no: Save the deal, save the relationship, and still say no*. Bantam.

Professional Boundaries and Ethics

Gutheil, T.G., & Gabbard, G.O. (1993). The concept of boundaries in clinical practice: Theoretical and risk-management dimensions. *American Journal of Psychiatry, 150*(2), 188–196.

Pope, K.S., & Keith-Spiegel, P. (2008). A practical approach to boundaries in psychotherapy: Making decisions, bypassing blunders, and mending fences. *Journal of Clinical Psychology, 64*(5), 638–652.

Welfel, E.R. (2015). *Ethics in counseling and psychotherapy: Standards, research, and emerging issues* (6th ed.). Cengage Learning.

Zur, O. (2007). *Boundaries in psychotherapy: Ethical and clinical explorations*. American Psychological Association.

Couple Therapy - Specific Considerations

Gottman, J.M., & Silver, N. (2015). *The seven principles for making marriage work*. Harmony Books.

Johnson, S.M. (2004). *The practice of emotionally focused couple therapy: Creating connection* (2nd ed.). Brunner-Routledge.

Lebow, J.L., Chambers, A.L., Christensen, A., & Johnson, S.M. (2012). Research on the treatment of couple distress. *Journal of Marital and Family Therapy, 38*(1), 145–168.

Shadish, W.R., & Baldwin, S.A. (2005). Effects of behavioral couple therapy: A meta-analysis of randomized controlled trials. *Journal of Consulting and Clinical Psychology, 73*(1), 6–14.

Professional Development and Growth

Castonguay, L. G., & Hill, C. E. (Eds.). (2017). *How and why are some therapists better than others? Understanding therapist effects*. American Psychological Association.

Rønnestad, M.H., & Skovholt, T.M. (2013). *The developing practitioner: Growth and stagnation of therapists and counselors*. Routledge.

Schön, D.A. (1983). *The reflective practitioner: How professionals think in action*. Basic Books.

Skovholt, T.M., & Rønnestad, M.H. (2003). Struggles of the novice counselor and therapist. *Journal of Career Development, 30*(1), 45–58.

Chapter 7: Session Structure and Process

Session Management and Extended Therapeutic Sessions

Bierenbaum, H., Nichols, M.P., & Schwartz, A.J. (1976). Effects of varying session length and frequency in brief emotive psychotherapy. *Journal of Consulting and Clinical Psychology, 44*(5), 790–798.

Carey, T.A. (2011). As you like it: Adopting a patient-led approach to psychological treatments. *Journal of Public Mental Health, 10*(1), 6–16.
Turner, P.R., Valtierra, M., Talken, T.R., Miller, V.I. & DeAnda, J.R. (1996). Effect of session length on treatment outcome for college students in brief therapy. *Journal of Counseling Psychology, 43*(2), 228–232.
Will, H. (2018). The concept of the 50-minute hour: Time forming a frame for the unconscious. *International Forum of Psychoanalysis, 27*(1), 1–10.

Constellation Work and Experiential Methods

Cohen, D.B. (2006). 'Family constellations': An innovative systemic phenomenological group process from Germany. *The Family Journal, 14*(3), 226–233.
Hellinger, B., Weber, G., & Beaumont, H. (1998). *Love's hidden symmetry: What makes love work in relationships*. Zeig, Tucker & Co.
Satir, V., Banmen, J., Gerber, J., & Gomori, M. (1991). *The Satir model: Family therapy and beyond*. Science and Behavior Books.
Sparrer, I., & Varga von Kibéd, M. (2008). *Ganz im Gegenteil: Tetralemmaarbeit und andere Grundformen Systemischer Strukturaufstellungen*. Carl-Auer Verlag.

Clean Language and Narrative Inquiry

Grove, D.J., & Panzer, B.I. (1989). *Resolving traumatic memories: Metaphors and symbols in psychotherapy*. Irvington Publishers.
Lawley, J., & Tompkins, P. (2000). *Metaphors in mind: Transformation through symbolic modelling*. The Developing Company Press.
Sullivan, W., & Rees, J. (2008). *Clean language: Revealing metaphors and opening minds*. Crown House Publishing.
Tompkins, P., & Lawley, J. (2002). *The magic of metaphor*. The Developing Company Press.

Co-therapy and Collaborative Practice

Anderson, C.M., & Stewart, S. (1983). *Mastering resistance: A practical guide to family therapy*. Guilford Press.
Durana, C. (1998). The use of bonding and emotional expressiveness in the PAIRS training: A psychoeducational approach for couples. *Journal of Family Psychotherapy, 9*(2), 65–81.
Roller, B., & Nelson, V. (1991). *The art of co-therapy: How therapists work together*. Guilford Press.
Starr, S. (1993). Heart and soul and communication: An interview with Virginia Satir-Part III. *Journal of Couples Therapy, 3*(1), 1–8.

Therapeutic Presence and Practitioner Well-being

Geller, S.M., & Greenberg, L.S. (2012). *Therapeutic presence: A mindful approach to effective therapy*. American Psychological Association.
Norcross, J.C., & Guy, J.D. (2007). *Leaving it at the office: A guide to psychotherapist self-care*. Guilford Press.

Rothschild, B. (2006). *Help for the helper: The psychophysiology of compassion fatigue and vicarious trauma*. W.W. Norton.

Skovholt, T.M., & Trotter-Mathison, M. (2016). *The resilient practitioner: Burnout and compassion fatigue prevention and self-care strategies for the helping professions* (3rd ed.). Routledge.

Crisis Management and Safety in Couples Therapy

Gottman, J.M., & Gottman, J.S. (2008). Gottman method couple therapy. In A. S. Gurman (Ed.), *Clinical handbook of couple therapy* (4th ed., pp. 138–164). Guilford Press.

Johnson, S.M., & Whiffen, V. E. (Eds.). (2003). *Attachment processes in couple and family therapy*. Guilford Press.

Simpson, L.E., Atkins, D.C., Gattis, K.S., & Christensen, A. (2008). Low-level relationship aggression and couple therapy outcomes. *Journal of Family Psychology, 22*(1), 102–111.

Stith, S.M., McCollum, E.E., & Rosen, K.H. (2011). *Couples therapy for domestic violence: Finding safe solutions*. American Psychological Association.

Documentation and Clinical Record Keeping

Cameron, S., & Turtle-Song, I. (2002). Learning to write case notes using the SOAP format. *Journal of Counseling & Development, 80*(3), 286–292.

Mitchell, R.W. (2007). *Documentation in counseling records: An overview of ethical, legal, and clinical issues* (3rd ed.). American Counseling Association.

Wiger, D.E., & Huntley, D.K. (2002). *Essentials of interviewing*. John Wiley & Sons.

Zuckerman, E.L. (2008). *The paper office: Forms, guidelines, and resources to make your practice work ethically, legally, and profitably* (4th ed.). Guilford Press.

Duo Coaching Framework and Practice

Wilkie, N. (2019). *Reset: Finding a new course after drifting apart*. (Foundational principles of intensive relationship work)

Wilkie, N. (2026). *Reinventing relationship therapy through the duo coaching framework*. Routledge. (See particularly Chapters 7-10 for session structure and process)

Chapter 8: Start Your Implementation Journey

Implementation Science

Miller, S.D., & Duncan, B.L. (2000). *The heroic client: Doing client-directed, outcome-informed therapy*. Jossey-Bass.

Norcross, J.C., & Wampold, B.E. (2018). A new therapy for each patient: Evidence-based relationships and responsiveness. *Journal of Clinical Psychology, 74*(11), 1889–1906.

Beginning Practice

Rønnestad, M.H., & Skovholt, T.M. (2013). *The developing practitioner: Growth and stagnation of therapists and counselors*. Routledge.

Skovholt, T.M., & Rønnestad, M.H. (2003). Struggles of the novice counselor and therapist. *Journal of Career Development, 30*(1), 45–58.

Chapter 9: Integrative Therapeutic Mastery

Psychodynamic Approaches

Dicks, H.V. (1967). *Marital tensions: Clinical studies towards a psychological theory of interaction*. Basic Books.
Framo, J.L. (1992). *Family-of-origin therapy: An intergenerational approach*. Brunner/Mazel.
Scharff, D.E., & Scharff, J.S. (1991). *Object relations couple therapy*. Jason Aronson.
Wile, D.B. (1981). *Couples therapy: A nontraditional approach*. Wiley.

Systemic and Family Systems Theory

Bowen, M. (1978). *Family therapy in clinical practice*. Jason Aronson.
Minuchin, S. (1974). *Families and family therapy*. Harvard University Press.
Selvini Palazzoli, M., Boscolo, L., Cecchin, G., & Prata, G. (1978). *Paradox and counter-paradox*. Jason Aronson.
Watzlawick, P., Weakland, J.H., & Fisch, R. (1974). *Change: Principles of problem formation and problem resolution*. W.W. Norton.

Attachment Theory and Emotionally Focused Therapy

Bowlby, J. (1988). *A secure base: Parent-child attachment and healthy human development*. Basic Books.
Greenberg, L.S., & Johnson, S.M. (1988). *Emotionally focused therapy for couples*. Guilford Press.
Johnson, S.M. (2004). *The practice of emotionally focused couple therapy: Creating connection* (2nd ed.). Brunner-Routledge.
Johnson, S.M. (2019). *Attachment theory in practice: Emotionally Focused Therapy (EFT) with individuals, couples, and families*. Guilford Press.
Tatkin, S. (2011). *Wired for love: How understanding your partner's brain and attachment style can help you defuse conflict and build a secure relationship*. New Harbinger Publications.

Cognitive-Behavioural Approaches

Baucom, D.H., Epstein, N.B., LaTaillade, J.J., & Kirby, J.S. (2008). Cognitive-behavioral couple therapy. In A. S. Gurman (Ed.), *Clinical handbook of couple therapy* (4th ed., pp. 31–72). Guilford Press.
Christensen, A., Doss, B.D., & Jacobson, N.S. (2020). *Reconcilable differences: Rebuild your relationship by rediscovering the partner you love—without losing yourself* (2nd ed.). Guilford Press.
Dattilio, F.M., & Padesky, C.A. (1990). *Cognitive therapy with couples*. Professional Resource Exchange.
Epstein, N.B., & Baucom, D.H. (2002). *Enhanced cognitive-behavioral therapy for couples: A contextual approach*. American Psychological Association.

Narrative Therapy

Freedman, J., & Combs, G. (1996). *Narrative therapy: The social construction of preferred realities*. W.W. Norton.

Morgan, A. (2000). *What is narrative therapy? An easy-to-read introduction*. Dulwich Centre Publications.

White, M., & Epston, D. (1990). *Narrative means to therapeutic ends*. W.W. Norton.

Zimmerman, J.L., & Dickerson, V.C. (1996). *If problems talked: Narrative therapy in action*. Guilford Press.

Solution-Focused Brief Therapy

Berg, I.K., & Miller, S.D. (1992). *Working with the problem drinker: A solution-focused approach*. W.W. Norton.

de Shazer, S. (1985). *Keys to solution in brief therapy*. W.W. Norton.

de Shazer, S., & Dolan, Y. (2007). *More than miracles: The state of the art of solution-focused brief therapy*. Haworth Press.

Nelson, T.S., & Thomas, F.N. (Eds.). (2007). *Handbook of solution-focused brief therapy: Clinical applications*. Haworth Press.

Somatic and Body-Centered Approaches

Aposhyan, S. (2004). *Body-mind psychotherapy: Principles, techniques, and practical applications*. W.W. Norton.

Levine, P.A. (2010). *In an unspoken voice: How the body releases trauma and restores goodness*. North Atlantic Books.

Ogden, P., Minton, K., & Pain, C. (2006). *Trauma and the body: A sensorimotor approach to psychotherapy*. W.W. Norton.

Porges, S.W. (2011). *The polyvagal theory: Neurophysiological foundations of emotions, attachment, communication, and self-regulation*. W.W. Norton.

van der Kolk, B.A. (2014). *The body keeps the score: Brain, mind, and body in the healing of trauma*. Viking.

Gottman Method

Gottman, J.M. (1999). *The marriage clinic: A scientifically-based marital therapy*. W.W. Norton.

Gottman, J.M., & DeClaire, J. (2001). *The relationship cure: A 5 step guide to strengthening your marriage, family, and friendships*. Harmony Books.

Gottman, J.M., & Gottman, J.S. (2017). The natural principles of love. *Journal of Family Theory & Review, 9*(1), 7–26.

Gottman, J.M., & Silver, N. (2015). *The seven principles for making marriage work* (2nd ed.). Harmony Books.

Gestalt Therapy

Joyce, P., & Sills, C. (2018). *Skills in Gestalt counselling & psychotherapy* (4th ed.). SAGE Publications.

Perls, F., Hefferline, R.F., & Goodman, P. (1951). *Gestalt therapy: Excitement and growth in the human personality*. Julian Press.
Wheeler, G., & Axelsson, L. (2015). *Gestalt therapy*. American Psychological Association.
Yontef, G.M. (1993). *Awareness, dialogue, and process: Essays on Gestalt therapy*. Gestalt Journal Press.

Internal Family Systems

Anderson, F.G., Sweezy, M., & Schwartz, R.C. (2017). *Internal family systems skills training manual: Trauma-informed treatment for anxiety, depression, PTSD & substance abuse*. PESI Publishing.
Herbine-Blank, T., Kerpelman, D., & Sweezy, M. (2016). *Intimacy from the inside out: Courage and compassion in couple therapy*. Routledge.
Schwartz, R.C. (1995). *Internal family systems therapy*. Guilford Press.
Schwartz, R.C., & Sweezy, M. (2020). *Internal family systems therapy* (2nd ed.). Guilford Press.

Imago Relationship Therapy

Hendrix, H. (1988). *Getting the love you want: A guide for couples*. Henry Holt.
Hendrix, H., & Hunt, H.L. (2004). *Receiving love: Transform your relationship by letting yourself be loved*. Atria Books.
Hendrix, H., & Hunt, H.L. (2019). *Getting the love you want: A guide for couples* (3rd ed.). St. Martin's Griffin.
Luquet, W. (1996). *Short-term couples therapy: The Imago model in action*. Brunner/Mazel.

Mindfulness-Based Approaches

Carson, J.W., Carson, K.M., Gil, K.M., & Baucom, D.H. (2004). Mindfulness-based relationship enhancement. *Behavior Therapy, 35*(3), 471–494.
Kabat-Zinn, J. (2013). *Full catastrophe living: Using the wisdom of your body and mind to face stress, pain, and illness* (revised ed.). Bantam Books.
Siegel, D.J. (2010). *The mindful therapist: A clinician's guide to mindsight and neural integration*. W.W. Norton.
Williams, M., & Penman, D. (2011). *Mindfulness: An eight-week plan for finding peace in a frantic world*. Rodale Books.

Clinical Hypnotherapy

Araoz, D.L. (1985). *The new hypnosis*. Brunner/Mazel.
Erickson, M.H., & Rossi, E.L. (1979). *Hypnotherapy: An exploratory casebook*. Irvington Publishers.
Hammond, D.C. (Ed.). (1990). *Handbook of hypnotic suggestions and metaphors*. W.W. Norton.
Yapko, M.D. (2012). *Trancework: An introduction to the practice of clinical hypnosis* (4th ed.). Routledge.

Neuro-linguistic Programming

Andreas, C., & Andreas, S. (1989). *Heart of the mind: Engaging your inner power to change with neuro-linguistic programming*. Real People Press.

Bandler, R., & Grinder, J. (1979). *Frogs into princes: Neuro linguistic programming*. Real People Press.

Dilts, R., Grinder, J., Bandler, R., & DeLozier, J. (1980). *Neuro-linguistic programming: Volume I - The study of the structure of subjective experience*. Meta Publications.

O'Connor, J., & Seymour, J. (2011). *Introducing NLP: Psychological skills for understanding and influencing people*. Conari Press.

Integration and Eclectic Approaches

Gurman, A.S., Lebow, J.L., & Snyder, D.K. (Eds.). (2015). *Clinical handbook of couple therapy* (5th ed.). Guilford Press.

Lebow, J.L. (2014). *Couple and family therapy: An integrative map of the territory*. American Psychological Association.

Norcross, J.C., & Goldfried, M.R. (Eds.). (2019). *Handbook of psychotherapy integration* (3rd ed.). Oxford University Press.

Prochaska, J.O., & Norcross, J.C. (2018). *Systems of psychotherapy: A transtheoretical analysis* (9th ed.). Oxford University Press.

Stricker, G., & Gold, J.R. (Eds.). (2013). *Comprehensive handbook of psychotherapy integration*. Springer.

Chapter 10: Working with What Comes Into the Room

Warm Data and Systems Thinking

Bateson, G. (2000). *Steps to an ecology of mind*. University of Chicago Press. (Original work published 1972)

Bateson, N. (2016). *Small arcs of larger circles: Framing through other patterns*. Triarchy Press.

Bateson, N. (2021). Warm data: Contextual information. *Systems Research and Behavioral Science, 38*(4), 500–507.

Capra, F., & Luisi, P.L. (2014). *The systems view of life: A unifying vision*. Cambridge University Press.

Family-of-Origin and Intergenerational Patterns

Boszormenyi-Nagy, I., & Spark, G.M. (1973). *Invisible loyalties: Reciprocity in intergenerational family therapy*. Harper & Row.

Bowen, M. (1978). *Family therapy in clinical practice*. Jason Aronson.

Framo, J.L. (1992). *Family-of-origin therapy: An intergenerational approach*. Brunner/Mazel.

McGoldrick, M., Gerson, R., & Petry, S. (2008). *Genograms: Assessment and intervention* (3rd ed.). W.W. Norton.

Williamson, D.S. (1991). *The intimacy paradox: Personal authority in the family system*. Guilford Press.

Intergenerational and Historical Trauma

Danieli, Y. (Ed.). (1998). *International handbook of multigenerational legacies of trauma.* Plenum Press.

DeGruy, J. (2017). *Post traumatic slave syndrome: America's legacy of enduring injury and healing.* Joy DeGruy Publications.

Kellermann, N.P.F. (2013). Epigenetic transmission of Holocaust trauma: Can nightmares be inherited? *Israel Journal of Psychiatry and Related Sciences, 50*(1), 33–39.

van der Kolk, B.A. (2014). *The body keeps the score: Brain, mind, and body in the healing of trauma.* Viking.

Yehuda, R., & Lehrner, A. (2018). Intergenerational transmission of trauma effects: Putative role of epigenetic mechanisms. *World Psychiatry, 17*(3), 243–257.

Attachment Theory and Adult Relationships

Bowlby, J. (1988). *A secure base: Parent-child attachment and healthy human development.* Basic Books.

Johnson, S.M. (2004). *The practice of emotionally focused couple therapy: Creating connection* (2nd ed.). Brunner-Routledge.

Levine, A., & Heller, R. (2010). *Attached: The new science of adult attachment and how it can help you find—and keep—love.* Tarcher/Penguin.

Mikulincer, M., & Shaver, P.R. (2007). *Attachment in adulthood: Structure, dynamics, and change.* Guilford Press.

Tatkin, S. (2011). *Wired for love: How understanding your partner's brain and attachment style can help you defuse conflict and build a secure relationship.* New Harbinger Publications.

Wallin, D.J. (2007). *Attachment in psychotherapy.* Guilford Press.

Unconscious Patterns and Psychological Defenses

Cramer, P., & Davidson, K. (Eds.). (1998). Defense mechanisms in contemporary personality research. *Journal of Personality, 66*(6): 879–1157. [Special Issue].

Dicks, H.V. (1967). *Marital tensions: Clinical studies towards a psychological theory of interaction.* Basic Books.

Fisher, J.V., & Crandell, L.E. (2001). *Patterns of relating: An adult attachment perspective.* Brunner-Routledge.

Scharff, D.E., & Scharff, J.S. (1991). *Object relations couple therapy.* Jason Aronson.

Wile, D.B. (1981). *Couples therapy: A nontraditional approach.* Wiley.

Corrective Emotional Experiences

Alexander, F., & French, T.M. (1946). *Psychoanalytic therapy: Principles and application.* Ronald Press.

Castonguay, L.G., & Hill, C.E. (Eds.). (2017). *How and why are some therapists better than others? Understanding therapist effects.* American Psychological Association.

Greenberg, L.S., & Goldman, R.N. (2008). *Emotion-focused couples therapy: The dynamics of emotion, love, and power.* American Psychological Association.

Johnson, S.M., & Greenberg, L.S. (1995). The emotionally focused approach to problems in adult attachment. In N. S. Jacobson & A. S. Gurman (Eds.), *Clinical handbook of couple therapy* (pp. 121–141). Guilford Press.

Somatic and Body-Centered Awareness

Dana, D. (2018). *The polyvagal theory in therapy: Engaging the rhythm of regulation*. W.W. Norton.

Levine, P.A. (2010). *In an unspoken voice: How the body releases trauma and restores goodness*. North Atlantic Books.

Ogden, P., Minton, K., & Pain, C. (2006). *Trauma and the body: A sensorimotor approach to psychotherapy*. W.W. Norton.

Porges, S.W. (2011). *The polyvagal theory: Neurophysiological foundations of emotions, attachment, communication, and self-regulation*. W.W. Norton.

Transformation and The Hero's Journey

Campbell, J. (2008). *The hero with a thousand faces* (3rd ed.). New World Library. (Original work published 1949)

Mezirow, J. (1991). *Transformative dimensions of adult learning*. Jossey-Bass.

Miller, W.R., & Rollnick, S. (2012). *Motivational interviewing: Helping people change* (3rd ed.). Guilford Press.

Prochaska, J.O., & DiClemente, C.C. (1983). Stages and processes of self-change of smoking: Toward an integrative model of change. *Journal of Consulting and Clinical Psychology, 51*(3), 390–395.

Cultural Context and Humility

Falicov, C.J. (2014). *Latino families in therapy* (2nd ed.). Guilford Press.

Hardy, K.V., & Laszloffy, T.A. (1995). The cultural genogram: Key to training culturally competent family therapists. *Journal of Marital and Family Therapy, 21*(3), 227–237.

McGoldrick, M., Giordano, J., & Garcia-Preto, N. (Eds.). (2005). *Ethnicity and family therapy* (3rd ed.). Guilford Press.

Sue, D.W., & Sue, D. (2015). *Counseling the culturally diverse: Theory and practice* (7th ed.). Wiley.

Tervalon, M., & Murray-García, J. (1998). Cultural humility versus cultural competence: A critical distinction in defining physician training outcomes in multicultural education. *Journal of Health Care for the Poor and Underserved, 9*(2), 117–125.

Complex Relationship Dynamics

Fisher, H. (2004). *Why we love: The nature and chemistry of romantic love*. Henry Holt.

Gottman, J.M. (1999). *The marriage clinic: A scientifically-based marital therapy*. W.W. Norton.

Perel, E. (2006). *Mating in captivity: Unlocking erotic intelligence*. Harper.

Schnarch, D. (1997). *Passionate marriage: Keeping love and intimacy alive in committed relationships*. W.W. Norton.

Systemic and Contextual Approaches

Haley, J. (1976). *Problem-solving therapy*. Jossey-Bass.

Imber-Black, E. (1993). *Secrets in families and family therapy*. W.W. Norton.

Minuchin, S. (1974). *Families and family therapy*. Harvard University Press.
Watzlawick, P., Weakland, J.H., & Fisch, R. (1974). *Change: Principles of problem formation and problem resolution*. W.W. Norton.

Chapter 11: Setting Up Your Practice

Business Development for Therapy Practices

Grodzki, L., & Allen, W. (2005). *The business and practice of coaching: Finding your Niche, making money, and attracting ideal clients*. W.W. Norton & Company.
Pope, K.S., & Vasquez, M.J.T. (2016). *Ethics in psychotherapy and counseling: A practical guide* (5th ed.). Wiley.
Zur, O. (2007). *Boundaries in psychotherapy: Ethical and clinical explorations*. American Psychological Association.

Physical Space and Environment

Devlin, A.S., & Nasar, J.L. (2012). Impressions of psychotherapists' offices: Do therapists and clients agree? *Professional Psychology: Research and Practice, 43*(2), 118–122.
Pearson, M., & Wilson, H. (2001). *Sandplay and symbol work: Emotional healing and personal development with children, adolescents and adults*. ACER Press.
Pressly, P.K., & Heesacker, M. (2001). The physical environment and counseling: A review of theory and research. *Journal of Counseling & Development, 79*(2), 148–160.

Virtual Therapy Delivery

Connolly, S.L., Miller, C.J., Lindsay, J.A., & Bauer, M.S. (2020). A systematic review of providers' attitudes toward telemental health via videoconferencing. *Clinical Psychology: Science and Practice, 27*(2), e12311.
Hertlein, K.M., Blumer, M.L.C., & Smith, J.M. (2014). Marriage and family therapists' use and comfort with online communication with clients. *Contemporary Family Therapy, 36*(1), 58–69.
Simpson, S., & Reid, C. (2014). Therapeutic alliance in videoconferencing psychotherapy: A review. *Australian Journal of Rural Health, 22*(6), 280–299.

Professional Insurance and Legal Considerations

Barnett, J.E., & Johnson, W.B. (2015). *Ethics desk reference for psychologists* (2nd ed.). American Psychological Association.
Bennett, B.E., Bricklin, P.M., Harris, E., Knapp, S., VandeCreek, L., & Younggren, J.N. (2006). *Assessing and managing risk in psychological practice: An individualized approach*. American Psychological Association Insurance Trust.
Margolin, G. (1982). Ethical and legal considerations in marital and family therapy. *American Psychologist, 37*(7), 788–801.

Financial Sustainability

Cameron, S., & Turtle-Song, I. (2002). Learning to write case notes using the SOAP format. *Journal of Counseling & Development, 80*(3), 286–292.

Walfish, S., & Barnett, J.E. (2009). *Financial success in mental health practice: essential tools and strategies for practitioners*. American Psychological Association.

Marketing for Therapy Practices

Halligan, B., & Shah, D. (2014). *Inbound marketing: Attract, engage, and delight customers online* (Revised ed.). Wiley.

Ryan, D. (2016). *Understanding digital marketing: Marketing strategies for engaging the digital generation* (4th ed.). Kogan Page.

Zur, O., Williams, M.H., Lehavot, K., & Knapp, S. (2009). Psychotherapist self-disclosure and transparency in the Internet age. *Professional Psychology: Research and Practice, 40*(1), 22–30.

Practice Management Systems

Falvey, J.E., Bray, T.E., & Hebert, D.J. (2005). *Managing clinical supervision: Ethical practice and legal risk management*. Brooks/Cole.

Falvey, J.E., & Cohen, C.R. (2003). The buck stops here: Documenting clinical supervision. *The Clinical Supervisor, 22*(2), 63–80.

Co-therapy Partnership Structures

Dick, B., Lessler, K., & Whiteside, J. (1980). A developmental framework for co-therapy. *International Journal of Group Psychotherapy, 30*(3), 273–285.

Roller, B., & Nelson, V. (1991). *The art of co-therapy: How therapists work together*. Guilford Press.

Accessibility and Ethical Pricing

Fisher, M.A. (2009). Replacing "Who is the client?" with a different ethical question. *Professional Psychology: Research and Practice, 40*(1), 1–7.

Smith, D. (2003). 10 ways psychologists can provide services for people who cannot afford them. *Monitor on Psychology, 34*(1), 60.

Data Protection and Confidentiality:

Fisher, M.A. (2008). Protecting confidentiality rights: The need for an ethical practice model. *American Psychologist, 63*(1), 1–13.

Smith-Bell, M., & Winslade, W.J. (1994). Privacy, confidentiality, and privilege in psychotherapeutic relationships. *American Journal of Orthopsychiatry, 64*(2), 180–193.

Professional Standards and Registration

American Psychological Association. (2017). *Ethical principles of psychologists and code of conduct.* APA.

British Association for Counselling and Psychotherapy. (2018). *Ethical framework for the counselling professions.* BACP.

United Kingdom Council for Psychotherapy. (2019). *Ethical principles and code of professional conduct*. UKCP.

Chapter 12: Advanced Techniques and Interventions

Constellation Work and Systemic Interventions

Cohen, D. (2006). Family constellations: An innovative systemic phenomenological group process from Germany. *The Family Journal, 14*(3), 226–233.
Franke-Gricksch, M. (2004). *You're one of us: Systemic insights and solutions for teachers, students and parents*. Carl-Auer-Systeme Verlag.
Hellinger, B. (2001). *Love's own truths: Bonding and balancing in close relationships*. Zeig, Tucker & Theisen.
Ulsamer, B. (2005). *The art and practice of family constellations: Leading family constellations as developed by Bert Hellinger*. Carl-Auer-Systeme Verlag.
Weber, G. (1999). *Zweierlei Glück: Die systemische Psychotherapie Bert Hellingers* [Two kinds of happiness: The systemic psychotherapy of Bert Hellinger]. Carl-Auer-Systeme Verlag.

Clean Language and Symbolic Modeling

Grove, D.J., & Panzer, B.I. (1989). *Resolving traumatic memories: Metaphors and symbols in psychotherapy*. Irvington.
Lawley, J., & Tompkins, P. (2000). *Metaphors in mind: Transformation through symbolic modelling*. The Developing Company Press.
Sullivan, W., & Rees, J. (2008). *Clean language: Revealing metaphors and opening minds*. Crown House Publishing.
Tompkins, P., & Lawley, J. (2002). *The magic of metaphor*. The Developing Company Press.
Way, M. (2013). *Clean approaches for coaches: How to create conditions for change using clean language and symbolic modelling*. Clean Publishing.

Neuro-Linguistic Programming (NLP)

Andreas, C., & Andreas, S. (1989). *Heart of the mind: Engaging your inner power to change with neuro-linguistic programming*. Real People Press.
Bandler, R., & Grinder, J. (1979). *Frogs into princes: Neuro linguistic programming*. Real People Press.
Bodenhamer, B.G., & Hall, L.M. (1999). *The user's manual for the brain: The complete manual for neuro-linguistic programming practitioner certification*. Crown House Publishing.
Dilts, R., Grinder, J., Bandler, R., & DeLozier, J. (1980). *Neuro-linguistic programming: Volume I - The study of the structure of subjective experience*. Meta Publications.
O'Connor, J., & Seymour, J. (2011). *Introducing NLP: Psychological skills for understanding and influencing people*. Conari Press.

Timeline Therapy

Bodenhamer, B.G., & Hall, L.M. (1997). *Time-lining: Patterns for adventuring in time*. Crown House Publishing.

James, T. (2007). *The secret of creating your future*. Advanced Neuro Dynamics.
James, T., & Woodsmall, W. (1988). *Time line therapy and the basis of personality*. Meta Publications.

Clinical Hypnotherapy

Alladin, A. (2008). *Cognitive hypnotherapy: An integrated approach to the treatment of emotional disorders*. Wiley.
Araoz, D.L. (1985). *The new hypnosis*. Brunner/Mazel.
Erickson, M.H., & Rossi, E.L. (1979). *Hypnotherapy: An exploratory casebook*. Irvington Publishers.
Hammond, D.C. (Ed.). (1990). *Handbook of hypnotic suggestions and metaphors*. W.W. Norton.
Yapko, M.D. (2012). *Trancework: An introduction to the practice of clinical hypnosis* (4th ed.). Routledge.

Parts Work and Internal Family Systems

Anderson, F.G., Sweezy, M., & Schwartz, R.C. (2017). *Internal family systems skills training manual: Trauma-informed treatment for anxiety, depression, PTSD & substance abuse*. PESI Publishing.
Herbine-Blank, T., Kerpelman, D., & Sweezy, M. (2016). *Intimacy from the inside out: Courage and compassion in couple therapy*. Routledge.
Schwartz, R.C. (1995). *Internal family systems therapy*. Guilford Press.
Schwartz, R.C., & Sweezy, M. (2020). *Internal family systems therapy* (2nd ed.). Guilford Press.
Stone, H., & Stone, S. (1989). *Embracing our selves: The voice dialogue manual*. New World Library.

Gestalt Therapy

Joyce, P., & Sills, C. (2018). *Skills in Gestalt counselling & psychotherapy* (4th ed.). SAGE Publications.
Perls, F., Hefferline, R.F., & Goodman, P. (1951). *Gestalt therapy: Excitement and growth in the human personality*. Julian Press.
Polster, E., & Polster, M. (1973). *Gestalt therapy integrated: Contours of theory and practice*. Brunner/Mazel.
Wheeler, G., & Axelsson, L. (2015). *Gestalt therapy*. American Psychological Association.
Yontef, G.M. (1993). *Awareness, dialogue, and process: Essays on Gestalt therapy*. Gestalt Journal Press.

Integration and Advanced Practice

Castonguay, L.G., & Hill, C.E. (Eds.). (2017). *How and why are some therapists better than others? Understanding therapist effects*. American Psychological Association.
Gurman, A.S., Lebow, J.L., & Snyder, D.K. (Eds.). (2015). *Clinical handbook of couple therapy* (5th ed.). Guilford Press.
Norcross, J.C., & Goldfried, M.R. (Eds.). (2019). *Handbook of psychotherapy integration* (3rd ed.). Oxford University Press.

Stricker, G., & Gold, J.R. (Eds.). (2013). *Comprehensive handbook of psychotherapy integration.* Springer.

Ethical Practice and Competence

American Psychological Association. (2017). *Ethical principles of psychologists and code of conduct.* Retrieved from https://www.apa.org/ethics/code

Barnett, J.E., & Johnson, W.B. (2015). *Ethics desk reference for counselors* (2nd ed.). American Counseling Association.

Pope, K.S., & Vasquez, M.J.T. (2016). *Ethics in psychotherapy and counseling: A practical guide* (5th ed.). Wiley.

Welfel, E.R. (2015). *Ethics in counseling and psychotherapy: Standards, research, and emerging issues* (6th ed.). Cengage Learning.

Chapter 13: Assessment and Intake Processes

Couple Assessment Fundamentals

Gottman, J.M., & Silver, N. (2015). *The seven principles for making marriage work* (Revised ed.). Harmony Books.

Halford, W.K. (2011). *Marriage and relationship education: What works and how to provide it.* Guilford Press.

Snyder, D.K., Heyman, R.E., & Haynes, S.N. (2005). Evidence-based approaches to assessing couple distress. *Psychological Assessment, 17*(3), 288–307.

Safety Assessment and Domestic Violence Screening

Dutton, D.G. (2006). *Rethinking domestic violence.* UBC Press.

Gondolf, E.W. (2012). *The future of batterer programmes: Reassessing evidence-based practice.* Northeastern University Press.

Herman, J.L. (2015). *Trauma and recovery: The aftermath of violence* (Updated ed.). Basic Books.

Stith, S.M., McCollum, E.E., & Rosen, K.H. (2011). *Couples therapy for domestic violence: Finding safe solutions.* American Psychological Association.

Attachment Assessment in Couples

Johnson, S.M. (2019). *Attachment theory in practice: Emotionally Focused Therapy (EFT) with individuals, couples, and families.* Guilford Press.

Mikulincer, M., & Shaver, P.R. (2016). *Attachment in adulthood: Structure, dynamics, and change* (2nd ed.). Guilford Press.

Tatkin, S. (2011). *Wired for love: How understanding your partner's brain and attachment style can help you defuse conflict.* New Harbinger Publications.

Clinical Judgment and Decision-Making

Gambrill, E. (2012). *Critical thinking in clinical practice: Improving the quality of judgments and decisions* (3rd ed.). Wiley.

Hunsley, J., & Mash, E.J. (2007). Evidence-based assessment. *Annual Review of Clinical Psychology, 3*, 29–51.

Spengler, P. M., White, M. J., Ægisdóttir, S., Maugherman, A. S., Anderson, L. A., Cook, R. S., ... & Rush, J. D. (2009). The meta-analysis of clinical judgment project. *The Counseling Psychologist, 37*(3), 350–399.

Structured Assessment Tools

Funk, J.L., & Rogge, R.D. (2007). Testing the ruler with item response theory: Increasing precision of measurement for relationship satisfaction with the Couples Satisfaction Index. *Journal of Family Psychology, 21*(4), 572–583.

Snyder, D.K., & Doss, B.D. (2005). Treating infidelity: Clinical and ethical directions. *Journal of Clinical Psychology, 61*(11), 1453–1465.

Spanier, G.B. (1976). Measuring dyadic adjustment: New scales for assessing the quality of marriage and similar dyads. *Journal of Marriage and the Family, 38*(1), 15–28.

Contraindications and Referral Decisions

Baucom, D.H., Whisman, M.A., & Paprocki, C. (2012). Couple-based interventions for psychopathology: A renewed direction for the field. *Family Process, 51*(3), 267–282.

Lebow, J.L., Chambers, A.L., Christensen, A., & Johnson, S.M. (2012). Research on the treatment of couple distress. *Journal of Marital and Family Therapy, 38*(1), 145–168.

Whisman, M.A., & Beach, S.R.H. (2012). Couple therapy for depression. *Journal of Clinical Psychology, 68*(5), 526–535.

Intake Processes and Informed Consent

Barnett, J.E., Wise, E.H., Johnson-Greene, D., & Bucky, S.F. (2007). Informed consent: Too much of a good thing or not enough? *Professional Psychology: Research and Practice, 38*(2), 179–186.

Beahrs, J.O., & Gutheil, T.G. (2001). Informed consent in psychotherapy. *American Journal of Psychiatry, 158*(1), 4–10.

Pope, K.S., & Vasquez, M.J.T. (2016). *Ethics in psychotherapy and counseling: A practical guide* (5th ed.). Wiley.

Multi-modal Assessment Approaches

Halford, W.K., & Markman, H.J. (Eds.). (2013). *Clinical handbook of couple therapy* (5th ed.). Guilford Press.

Hersen, M., & Rosqvist, J. (Eds.), *Handbook of psychological assessment, case conceptualization, and treatment* (pp. 420–450). Wiley.

Relationship Paradigm Assessment

Wilkie, N. (2026). *Reinventing relationship therapy through the duo coaching framework.* Routledge.

Pebbles Constellation and Spatial Techniques

Cohen, D.B. (2006). Family constellations: An innovative systemic phenomenological group process from Germany. *The Family Journal, 14*(3), 226–233.

Hellinger, B., Weber, G., & Beaumont, H. (1998). *Love's hidden symmetry: What makes love work in relationships*. Zeig Tucker & Theisen.

Chapter 14: Session Planning and Management

Time-Limited Therapy Frameworks

Bloom, B.L. (1997). *Planned short-term psychotherapy: A clinical handbook* (2nd ed.). Allyn & Bacon.

Budman, S.H., & Gurman, A.S. (1988). *Theory and practice of brief therapy*. Guilford Press.

Hoyt, M.F. (Ed.). (2009). *Brief psychotherapies: Principles and practices*. Zeig, Tucker & Theisen.

Session Planning and Structure

Duncan, B.L., Miller, S.D., Wampold, B.E., & Hubble, M.A. (Eds.). (2010). *The heart and soul of change: Delivering what works in therapy* (2nd ed.). American Psychological Association.

Lambert, M.J. (Ed.). (2013). *Bergin and Garfield's handbook of psychotherapy and behavior change* (6th ed.). Wiley.

Norcross, J.C., & Lambert, M.J. (2018). Psychotherapy relationships that work III. *Psychotherapy, 55*(4), 303–315.

Intensive Therapy Models

Christensen, A., Doss, B.D., & Jacobson, N.S. (2014). *Reconcilable differences: Rebuild your relationship by rediscovering the partner you love* (2nd ed.). Guilford Press.

Gottman, J.M., & Gottman, J.S. (2017). The natural principles of love. *Journal of Family Theory & Review, 9*(1), 7–26.

Johnson, S.M. (2019). *Attachment theory in practice: Emotionally Focused Therapy (EFT) with individuals, couples, and families*. Guilford Press.

Homework and Between-Session Work

Kazantzis, N., Whittington, C., & Dattilio, F. (2010). Meta-analysis of homework effects in cognitive and behavioral therapy: A replication and extension. *Clinical Psychology: Science and Practice, 17*(2), 144–156.

Scheel, M.J., Hanson, W.E., & Razzhavaikina, T.I. (2004). The process of recommending homework in psychotherapy: A review of therapist delivery methods, client acceptability, and factors that affect compliance. *Psychotherapy: Theory, Research, Practice, Training, 41*(1), 38–55.

Tompkins, M.A. (2004). *Using homework in psychotherapy: Strategies, guidelines, and forms*. Guilford Press.

Co-therapy Coordination

Dick, B., Lessler, K., & Whiteside, J. (1980). A developmental framework for co-therapy. *International Journal of Group Psychotherapy, 30*(3), 273–285.

Dugo, J.M., & Beck, A.P. (1997). Significance and complexity of early phases in the development of the co-therapy relationship. *Group Dynamics: Theory, Research, and Practice, 1*(4), 294–305.
Roller, B., & Nelson, V. (1991). *The art of co-therapy: How therapists work together*. Guilford Press.

Clinical Documentation

Cameron, S., & Turtle-Song, I. (2002). Learning to write case notes using the SOAP format. *Journal of Counseling & Development, 80*(3), 286–292.
Moline, M.E., Williams, G.T., & Austin, K.M. (1998). *Documenting psychotherapy: Essentials for mental health practitioners.* Sage Publications.
Zuckerman, E.L. (2008). *The paper office: Forms, guidelines, and resources to make your practice work ethically, legally, and profitably* (4th ed.). Guilford Press.

Outcome Monitoring and Tracking

Lambert, M.J., & Shimokawa, K. (2011). Collecting client feedback. *Psychotherapy, 48*(1), 72–79.
Miller, S.D., Duncan, B.L., Sorrell, R., & Brown, G.S. (2005). The partners for change outcome management system. *Journal of Clinical Psychology, 61*(2), 199–208.
Ogles, B.M., Lambert, M.J., & Fields, S.A. (2002). *Essentials of outcome assessment.* Wiley.

Responsive Adaptation in Therapy

Castonguay, L.G., & Beutler, L.E. (Eds.). (2006). *Principles of therapeutic change that work.* Oxford University Press.
Norcross, J.C., & Wampold, B.E. (2011). Evidence-based therapy relationships: Research conclusions and clinical practices. *Psychotherapy, 48*(1), 98–102.
Stiles, W.B., Honos-Webb, L., & Surko, M. (1998). Responsiveness in psychotherapy. *Clinical Psychology: Science and Practice, 5*(4), 439–458.

Chapter 15: Common Relationship Challenges

Communication Patterns and Dynamics

Gottman, J.M., & Silver, N. (2015). *The seven principles for making marriage work* (Revised ed.). Harmony Books.
Johnson, S.M. (2019). *Attachment theory in practice: Emotionally Focused Therapy (EFT) with individuals, couples, and families*. Guilford Press.
Markman, H.J., Stanley, S.M., & Blumberg, S.L. (2010). *Fighting for your marriage* (3rd ed.). Jossey-Bass.
Wile, D.B. (2013). *After the honeymoon: How conflict can improve your relationship* (Revised ed.). Collaborative Couple Therapy Books.

Infidelity and Betrayal Recovery

Glass, S.P., & Staeheli, J.C. (2003). *Not "Just Friends": Rebuilding trust and recovering your sanity after infidelity*. Free Press.
Perel, E. (2017). *The state of affairs: Rethinking infidelity*. Harper.
Snyder, D.K., Baucom, D.H., & Gordon, K.C. (2007). *Getting past the affair: A programme to help you cope, heal, and move on*. Guilford Press.
Spring, J.A. (2012). *After the affair: Healing the pain and rebuilding trust when a partner has been unfaithful* (Updated ed.). William Morrow.

Sexual and Intimacy Issues

McCarthy, B., & McCarthy, E. (2009). *Discovering your couple sexual style: Sharing desire, pleasure, and satisfaction*. Routledge.
Nagoski, E. (2015). *Come as you are: The surprising new science that will transform your sex life*. Simon & Schuster.
Perel, E. (2006). *Mating in captivity: Unlocking erotic intelligence*. Harper.
Schnarch, D. (2009). *Passionate marriage: Keeping love and intimacy alive in committed relationships*. W.W. Norton.

Values and Life Direction

Doherty, W.J. (2013). *Take back your marriage: Sticking together in a world that pulls us apart* (2nd ed.). Guilford Press.
Hayes, S.C., Strosahl, K.D., & Wilson, K.G. (2011). *Acceptance and commitment therapy: The process and practice of mindful change* (2nd ed.). Guilford Press.
Schwartz, S.H. (2012). An overview of the Schwartz theory of basic values. *Online Readings in Psychology and Culture, 2*(1), 1–20.

Parenting and Family Challenges

Cowan, C.P., & Cowan, P.A. (2000). *When partners become parents: The big life change for couples*. Erlbaum.
Gottman, J.M., & Gottman, J.S. (2007). *And baby makes three: The six-step plan for preserving marital intimacy and rekindling romance after baby arrives*. Crown.
Papernow, P.L. (2013). *Surviving and thriving in stepfamily relationships*. Routledge.

Technology Impact on Relationships

Hertlein, K.M., & Kathryn Stevenson, P. (2014). *Infidelity counseling: A practitioner-based approach to helping couples overcome betrayal and recover trust*. Routledge.
Newport, C. (2019). *Digital minimalism: Choosing a focused life in a noisy world*. Portfolio/Penguin.
Turkle, S. (2015). *Reclaiming conversation: The power of talk in a digital age*. Penguin Press.

Pattern Recognition and Assessment

Bowen, M. (1978). *Family therapy in clinical practice*. Jason Aronson.

Minuchin, S., & Fishman, H.C. (1981). *Family therapy techniques*. Harvard University Press.

Wachtel, E.F., & Wachtel, P.L. (1986). *Family dynamics in individual psychotherapy*. Guilford Press.

Integrative Couple Therapy:

Christensen, A., Doss, B.D., & Jacobson, N.S. (2014). *Reconcilable differences: Rebuild your relationship by rediscovering the partner you love* (2nd ed.). Guilford Press.

Gurman, A.S., Lebow, J.L., & Snyder, D.K. (Eds.). (2015). *Clinical handbook of couple therapy* (5th ed.). Guilford Press.

Halford, W.K., & Markman, H.J. (Eds.). (2013). *Clinical handbook of couple therapy* (5th ed.). Guilford Press.

Chapter 16: Complex Cases and Specialised Populations

Trauma-Informed Practice

Dana, D. (2018). *The polyvagal theory in therapy: Engaging the rhythm of regulation*. W.W. Norton.

Herman, J.L. (2015). *Trauma and recovery: The aftermath of violence—from domestic abuse to political terror* (3rd ed.). Basic Books.

Levine, P.A. (2010). *In an unspoken voice: How the body releases trauma and restores goodness*. North Atlantic Books.

Ogden, P., Minton, K., & Pain, C. (2006). *Trauma and the body: A sensorimotor approach to psychotherapy*. W.W. Norton.

Porges, S.W. (2011). *The polyvagal theory: Neurophysiological foundations of emotions, attachment, communication, and self-regulation*. W.W. Norton.

van der Kolk, B.A. (2014). *The body keeps the score: Brain, mind, and body in the healing of trauma*. Viking.

Addiction and Recovery

Dattilio, F.M., & Bevilacqua, L.J. (Eds.). (2000). *Comparative treatments for relationship dysfunction*. Springer.

Fals-Stewart, W., O'Farrell, T.J., & Birchler, G.R. (2004). Behavioral couples therapy for substance abuse: Rationale, methods, and findings. *Science & Practice Perspectives, 2*(2), 30–41.

Mate, G. (2010). *In the realm of hungry ghosts: Close encounters with addiction*. North Atlantic Books.

Miller, W.R., & Rollnick, S. (2012). *Motivational interviewing: Helping people change* (3rd ed.). Guilford Press.

O'Farrell, T.J., & Fals-Stewart, W. (2006). *Behavioral couples therapy for alcoholism and drug abuse*. Guilford Press.

Mental Health and Relationships

Baucom, D.H., Shoham, V., Mueser, K.T., Daiuto, A.D., & Stickle, T.R. (1998). Empirically supported couple and family interventions for marital distress and adult mental health problems. *Journal of Consulting and Clinical Psychology, 66*(1), 53–88.

Beach, S.R.H. (Ed.). (2001). *Marital and family processes in depression: A scientific foundation for clinical practice*. American Psychological Association.

Snyder, D.K., Castellani, A.M., & Whisman, M.A. (2006). Current status and future directions in couple therapy. *Annual Review of Psychology, 57*, 317–344.

LGBTQ+ Affirmative Practice

Bigner, J.J., & Wetchler, J.L. (Eds.). (2012). *Handbook of LGBT-affirmative couple and family therapy*. Routledge.

Greenan, D.E., & Tunnell, G. (2003). *Couple therapy with gay men.* Guilford Press.

Green, R.J., & Mitchell, V. (2008). Gay and lesbian couples in therapy: Minority stress, relational ambiguity, and families of choice. In A.S. Gurman (Ed.), *Clinical handbook of couple therapy* (4th ed., pp. 662–680). Guilford Press.

Lev, A.I. (2004). *Transgender emergence: Therapeutic guidelines for working with gender-variant people and their families*. Haworth Clinical Practice Press.

Pepping, C.A., Lyons, A., & Morris, E.M.J. (2018). Affirmative LGBT psychotherapy: Outcomes of a therapist training protocol. *Psychotherapy, 55*(1), 52–62.

Cultural Competency

Falicov, C.J. (2014). *Latino families in therapy* (2nd ed.). Guilford Press.

Hardy, K.V., & Laszloffy, T.A. (1995). The cultural genogram: Key to training culturally competent family therapists. *Journal of Marital and Family Therapy, 21*(3), 227–237.

Hook, J.N., Davis, D.E., Owen, J., Worthington Jr, E.L., & Utsey, S.O. (2013). Cultural humility: Measuring openness to culturally diverse clients. *Journal of Counseling Psychology, 60*(3), 353–366.

McGoldrick, M., Giordano, J., & Garcia-Preto, N. (Eds.). (2005). *Ethnicity and family therapy* (3rd ed.). Guilford Press.

Sue, D.W., & Sue, D. (2015). *Counseling the culturally diverse: Theory and practice* (7th ed.). Wiley.

Domestic Violence

Heyman, R.E., & Schlee, K.A. (1997). Toward a better estimate of the prevalence of partner abuse: Adjusting rates based on the sensitivity of the Conflict Tactics Scale. *Journal of Family Psychology, 11*(3), 332–338.

Holtzworth-Munroe, A., Meehan, J.C., Herron, K., Rehman, U., & Stuart, G.L. (2000). Testing the Holtzworth-Munroe and Stuart (1994) batterer typology. *Journal of Consulting and Clinical Psychology, 68*(6), 1000–1019.

Johnson, M.P. (2008). *A typology of domestic violence: Intimate terrorism, violent resistance, and situational couple violence*. Northeastern University Press.

Stith, S.M., Rosen, K.H., & McCollum, E.E. (2004). Treating intimate partner violence within intact couple relationships: Outcomes of multi-couple versus individual couple therapy. *Journal of Marital and Family Therapy, 30*(3), 305–318.

High-Conflict Couples

Fincham, F.D., & Beach, S.R.H. (1999). Conflict in marriage: Implications for working with couples. *Annual Review of Psychology, 50*, 47–77.

Gottman, J.M. (1999). *The marriage clinic: A scientifically-based marital therapy*. W.W. Norton.

Greenberg, L.S., & Johnson, S.M. (1988). *Emotionally focused therapy for couples*. Guilford Press.

Professional Ethics and Boundaries

American Psychological Association. (2017). Ethical principles of psychologists and code of conduct. Retrieved from https://www.apa.org/ethics/code

Pope, K.S., & Vasquez, M.J.T. (2016). *Ethics in psychotherapy and counseling: A practical guide* (5th ed.). Wiley.

Zur, O. (2007). *Boundaries in psychotherapy: Ethical and clinical explorations*. American Psychological Association.

Chapter 17: When to Refer and Professional Boundaries

Professional Boundaries and Ethics

Gutheil, T.G., & Gabbard, G.O. (1993). The concept of boundaries in clinical practice: Theoretical and risk-management dimensions. *American Journal of Psychiatry, 150*(2), 188–196.

Pope, K.S., & Keith-Spiegel, P. (2008). A practical approach to boundaries in psychotherapy: Making decisions, bypassing blunders, and mending fences. *Journal of Clinical Psychology, 64*(5), 638–652.

Welfel, E.R. (2015). *Ethics in counseling and psychotherapy: Standards, research, and emerging issues* (6th ed.). Cengage Learning.

Zur, O. (2007). *Boundaries in psychotherapy: Ethical and clinical explorations*. American Psychological Association.

Ethics in Couple and Family Therapy

Gottlieb, M.C., & Younggren, J.N. (2009). Is there a slippery slope? Considerations regarding multiple relationships and risk management. *Professional Psychology: Research and Practice, 40*(6), 564–571.

Margolin, G. (1982). Ethical and legal considerations in marital and family therapy. *American Psychologist, 37*(7), 788–801.

Pope, K.S., & Vasquez, M.J.T. (2016). *Ethics in psychotherapy and counseling: A practical guide* (5th ed.). Wiley.

Scope of Practice and Referral

American Psychological Association. (2017). *Ethical principles of psychologists and code of conduct.* APA.

British Association for Counselling and Psychotherapy. (2018). *Ethical framework for the counselling professions.* BACP.

Couple Therapy - Specific Considerations

Gottman, J.M., & Silver, N. (2015). *The seven principles for making marriage work.* Harmony Books.

Johnson, S.M. (2004). *The practice of emotionally focused couple therapy: Creating connection* (2nd ed.). Brunner-Routledge.

Lebow, J.L., Chambers, A.L., Christensen, A., & Johnson, S.M. (2012). Research on the treatment of couple distress. *Journal of Marital and Family Therapy, 38*(1), 145–168.

Shadish, W.R., & Baldwin, S.A. (2005). Effects of behavioral couple therapy: A meta-analysis of randomized controlled trials. *Journal of Consulting and Clinical Psychology, 73*(1), 6–14.

Professional Development and Growth

Schön, D.A. (1983). *The reflective practitioner: How professionals think in action.* Basic Books.

Skovholt, T.M., & Rønnestad, M.H. (2003). Struggles of the novice counselor and therapist. *Journal of Career Development, 30*(1), 45–58.

Rønnestad, M.H., & Skovholt, T.M. (2013). *The developing practitioner: Growth and stagnation of therapists and counselors.* Routledge.

Chapter 18: Supervision and Continuing Education

Supervision in Psychotherapy

Bernard, J.M., & Goodyear, R.K. (2019). *Fundamentals of clinical supervision* (6th ed.). Pearson.

Falender, C.A., & Shafranske, E.P. (2021). *Clinical supervision: A competency-based approach* (2nd ed.). American Psychological Association.

Hawkins, P., & Shohet, R. (2020). *Supervision in the helping professions* (5th ed.). Open University Press.

Professional Development

Rønnestad, M.H., & Skovholt, T.M. (2013). *The developing practitioner: Growth and stagnation of therapists and counselors.* Routledge.

Skovholt, T.M., & Rønnestad, M.H. (2003). Struggles of the novice counselor and therapist. *Journal of Career Development, 30*(1), 45–58.

Co-therapy Supervision

Roller, B., & Nelson, V. (1991). *The art of co-therapy: How therapists work together.* Guilford Press.

Reflective Practice

Schön, D.A. (1983). *The reflective practitioner: How professionals think in action*. Basic Books.

Continuing Professional Development

Rønnestad, M.H., & Skovholt, T.M. (2013). *The developing practitioner: Growth and stagnation of therapists and counselors*. Routledge.

Chapter 19: Ethical Considerations and Professional Standards

Ethics in Couple and Family Therapy

Gottlieb, M.C., & Younggren, J.N. (2009). Is there a slippery slope? Considerations regarding multiple relationships and risk management. *Professional Psychology: Research and Practice, 40*(6), 564–571.
Margolin, G. (1982). Ethical and legal considerations in marital and family therapy. *American Psychologist, 37*(7), 788–801.
Pope, K.S., & Vasquez, M.J.T. (2016). *Ethics in psychotherapy and counseling: A practical guide* (5th ed.). Wiley.

Informed Consent

Beahrs, J.O., & Gutheil, T.G. (2001). Informed consent in psychotherapy. *American Journal of Psychiatry, 158*(1), 4–10.
Fisher, C.B., & Oransky, M. (2008). Informed consent to psychotherapy: Protecting the dignity and respecting the autonomy of patients. *Journal of Clinical Psychology, 64*(5), 576–588.
Pope, K.S., & Vasquez, M.J.T. (2016). *Ethics in psychotherapy and counseling: A practical guide* (5th ed.). John Wiley & Sons.

Confidentiality

Fisher, M.A. (2008). Protecting confidentiality rights: The need for an ethical practice model. *American Psychologist, 63*(1), 1–13.
Smith-Bell, M., & Winslade, W.J. (1994). Privacy, confidentiality, and privilege in psychotherapeutic relationships. *American Journal of Orthopsychiatry, 64*(2), 180–193.

Professional Standards and Ethics References

Key ethical frameworks referenced in this book:

United Kingdom

British Association for Counselling and Psychotherapy. (2018). *Ethical framework for the counselling professions*. BACP.

British Psychological Society. (2021). *Code of ethics and conduct.* BPS.

UK Council for Psychotherapy. (2019). *UKCP code of ethics and professional practice.* UKCP.

United States

American Association for Marriage and Family Therapy. (2015). *Code of ethics.* AAMFT.

American Counseling Association. (2014). *ACA code of ethics.* ACA.

American Psychological Association. (2017). *Ethical principles of psychologists and code of conduct.* APA.

National Association of Social Workers. (2021). *Code of ethics.* NASW.

Cultural Competency

Hook, J.N., Davis, D.E., Owen, J., Worthington Jr, E.L., & Utsey, S.O. (2013). Cultural humility: Measuring openness to culturally diverse clients. *Journal of Counseling Psychology, 60*(3), 353–366.

McGoldrick, M., Giordano, J., & Garcia-Preto, N. (Eds.). (2005). *Ethnicity and family therapy* (3rd ed.). Guilford Press.

Sue, D.W., Arredondo, P., & McDavis, R.J. (1992). Multicultural counseling competencies and standards: A call to the profession. *Journal of Counseling & Development, 70*(4), 477–486.

Power Dynamics and Social Justice

Hardy, K.V., & Laszloffy, T.A. (2005). *Teens who hurt: Clinical interventions to break the cycle of adolescent violence.* Guilford Press.

Singh, A.A., & Moss, L. (2016). Using innovative methodologies to train multiculturally competent counselors. In E. Aldarondo (Ed.), *Promoting social justice through mental health practice* (pp. 279–297). Routledge.

Ethical Frameworks

American Psychological Association (2017). *Ethical principles of psychologists and code of conduct.*

British Association for Counselling and Psychotherapy (2018). *Ethical framework for the counselling professions.* BACP.

UK Council for Psychotherapy (2019). *UKCP code of ethics and professional practice.* UKCP.

Chapter 20: Research and Innovation

Practice-Based Research

Barkham, M., Hardy, G.E., & Mellor-Clark, J. (Eds.). (2010). *Developing and delivering practice-based evidence: A guide for the psychological therapies.* Wiley-Blackwell.

Castonguay, L.G., Barkham, M., Lutz, W., & McAleavey, A.A. (2013). Practice-oriented research: Approaches and applications. In M. J. Lambert (Ed.), *Bergin and Garfield's handbook of psychotherapy and behavior change* (6th ed., pp. 85–133). Wiley.

Lebow, J.L., Chambers, A.L., Christensen, A., & Johnson, S.M. (2012). Research on the treatment of couple distress. *Journal of Marital and Family Therapy, 38*(1), 145–168.

Shadish, W.R., & Baldwin, S.A. (2005). Effects of behavioral marital therapy: A meta-analysis of randomized controlled trials. *Journal of Consulting and Clinical Psychology, 73*(1), 6–14.

Outcome Measurement

Halford, W.K., & Markman, H.J. (Eds.). (2013). *Clinical handbook of couple therapy* (5th ed.). Guilford Press.

Lambert, M.J. (2013). Outcome in psychotherapy: The past and important advances. *Psychotherapy, 50*(1), 42–51.

Evidence-Based Practice

Sackett, D.L., Rosenberg, W.M., Gray, J.A., Haynes, R.B., & Richardson, W.S. (1996). Evidence based medicine: What it is and what it isn't. *BMJ, 312*(7023), 71–72.

Spring, B. (2007). Evidence-based practice in clinical psychology: What it is, why it matters; what you need to know. *Journal of Clinical Psychology, 63*(7), 611–631.

Intensive Couples Therapy Research

Bierenbaum, H., Nichols, M.P., & Schwartz, A.J. (1976). Effects of varying session length and frequency in psychotherapy. *Journal of Consulting and Clinical Psychology, 44*(5), 790–798.

Innovation in Therapy

Castonguay, L.G., & Hill, C.E. (Eds.). (2017). *How and why are some therapists better than others? Understanding therapist effects*. American Psychological Association.

Research Ethics

American Psychological Association. (2017). *Ethical principles of psychologists and code of conduct*. APA.

British Psychological Society (2014). *Code of human research ethics* (2nd ed.). BPS.

Chapter 21: Completion and Mastery

References for this chapter draw primarily from the comprehensive frameworks established in:

Wilkie, N. (2019). *Reset: Finding a new course after drifting apart.* Academy for Relationships, Hampshire.

Wilkie, N. (2026). *Reinventing relationship therapy through the duo coaching framework.* Routledge.

Additional Resources on Transformation and Mastery

Rønnestad, M.H., & Skovholt, T.M. (2013). *The developing practitioner: Growth and stagnation of therapists and counselors*. Routledge.

Chapter 22: Exploring the Duo Coaching Framework in Your Practice

Practice Development and Marketing

Barnett, J.E., & Cooper, N. (2009). Creating a culture of self-care. *Clinical Psychology: Science and Practice, 16*(1), 16–20.

Grodzki, L. (2000). *Building your ideal private practice: A guide for therapists and other healing professionals*. W.W. Norton.

Referral Networks

Norcross, J.C., & Lambert, M.J. (2019). Psychotherapy relationships that work III. *Psychotherapy, 56*(4), 537–547.

Community Engagement

Doherty, W.J. (2013). *Take back your marriage: Sticking together in a world that pulls us apart* (2nd ed.). Guilford Press.

Chapter 23: Relationship Education and Prevention

Prevention Effectiveness Research

Hawkins, A.J., Blanchard, V.L., Baldwin, S.A., & Fawcett, E.B. (2008). Does marriage and relationship education work? A meta-analytic study. *Journal of Consulting and Clinical Psychology, 76*(5), 723–734.

Stanley, S.M., Amato, P.R., Johnson, C.A., & Markman, H.J. (2006). Premarital education, marital quality, and marital stability: Findings from a large, random household survey. *Journal of Family Psychology, 20*(1), 117–126.

Relationship Education Programmes

Carroll, J.S., & Doherty, W.J. (2003). Evaluating the effectiveness of premarital prevention programs: A meta-analytic review of outcome research. *Family Relations, 52*(2), 105–118.

Halford, W.K., Markman, H.J., Kline, G.H., & Stanley, S.M. (2003). Best practice in couple relationship education. *Journal of Marital and Family Therapy, 29*(3), 385–406.

Markman, H.J., Stanley, S.M., & Blumberg, S.L. (2010). *Fighting for your marriage* (3rd ed.). Jossey-Bass.

Community-Based Prevention

Cowan, P.A., & Cowan, C.P. (2014). Controversies in couple relationship education (CRE): Overlooked evidence and implications for research and policy. *Psychology, Public Policy, and Law, 20*(4), 361–383.

Doherty, W.J., & Carroll, J.S. (2007). Health and the ethics of marital therapy and education. In J. L. Lebow (Ed.), *Twenty-first century psychotherapies: Contemporary approaches to theory and practice* (pp. 348–374). John Wiley & Sons.

Chapter 24: The Future of Duo Coaching and Relationship Therapy

Future Directions in Couples Therapy

Lebow, J.L., Chambers, A.L., Christensen, A., & Johnson, S.M. (2012). Research on the treatment of couple distress. *Journal of Marital and Family Therapy, 38*(1), 145–168.

Technology and Teletherapy

Hertlein, K.M., Blumer, M.L.C., & Mihaloliakos, J.H. (2015). Marriage and family counselors' perceived ethical issues related to online therapy. *The Family Journal, 23*(1), 5–12.

Innovation in Therapeutic Practice

Duncan, B.L., Miller, S.D., Wampold, B.E., & Hubble, M.A. (Eds.). (2010). *The heart and soul of change: Delivering what works in therapy* (2nd ed.). American Psychological Association.

The Duo Coaching Collection

Wilkie, N. (2019). *Reset: Finding a new course after drifting apart.* Academy for Relationships.

Wilkie, N. (2021) *Recover: Rebuilding trust after the shock of betrayal.* Academy for Relationships.

Wilkie, N. (2026). *A practitioner's guide to the duo coaching framework.* Routledge. [Book 2: This Volume]

Wilkie, N. (2026). *Demystifying relationship therapy – A view from the therapist's chair.* Routledge.

Wilkie, N. (2026). *Reinventing relationship therapy through the duo coaching framework.* Routledge. [Book 1: Theory and Foundation]

Online Resources and Training

Duo Coaching Academy: www.duocoachingacademy.com

Index

For Product Safety Concerns and Information please contact our EU representative GPSR@taylorandfrancis.com
Taylor & Francis Verlag GmbH, Kaufingerstraße 24, 80331 München, Germany

www.ingramcontent.com/pod-product-compliance
Ingram Content Group UK Ltd.
Pitfield, Milton Keynes, MK11 3LW, UK
UKHW020156200926
475702UK00016B/2732
* 9 7 8 1 0 4 1 2 0 1 8 5 4 *